I0605186

"Robert Letham's series on the doctrine of the divine persons of the Holy Trinity continues with this volume that treats the eternal Son. This new work in Christology exhibits what theology is supposed to be—historically sensitive and biblically grounded, theologically inquisitive, and confessionally responsible, engaging modern proposals with intellectual rigor and not afraid to enfold the insights of contemporary theologians within well-traveled lines of thought. Letham offers an erudite analysis of the doctrinal history surrounding the person of Christ, with an examination of the varied heresies that have forced the church to dogmatic clarity concerning the mystery of the incarnation. Our author handles these materials with integrity and sober assessment, as he takes up the mantle of the Reformation and its own diverse wrestlings with the mystery of Jesus Christ in the flesh. He also offers a chapter on the work of Christ. Given Letham's serious interactions with post-Enlightenment criticisms of Chalcedon, including older and new versions of kenosis doctrine, this volume proves itself to be most up-to-date. Letham's book drives us back to Scripture and to the great theologians of the past and present. Highly recommended!"

—**J. Mark Beach**, Professor of Doctrinal and Ministerial Studies, Mid-America Reformed Seminary

"The doctrine of the person of Christ is one of the church's greatest treasures. Thus, this subject is well worth careful theological reflection for the purpose of the sober reception and protection of biblical orthodoxy. Robert Letham has already established himself as a leading contemporary theologian on the doctrine of the Trinity. He once again proves to be an expert guide to the Christological views of a plenitude of theologians, including giants such as Athanasius, Cyril of Alexandria, Thomas Aquinas, Martin Luther, and John Calvin, as well as influential modern theologians—all the while offering his own trenchant analysis of this most precious topic. This is an outstanding book for anyone who wants to understand the view of Scripture and church history on the teaching of who Jesus Christ is."

—**Joel R. Beeke**, Chancellor and Professor of Systematic Theology and Homiletics, Puritan Reformed Theological Seminary; pastor, Heritage Reformed Congregation, Grand Rapids, Michigan

"In this concise, reliable, and comprehensive study of the doctrine of Christ, Robert Letham shows us how central our understanding of God's self-revelation in his Son is, and must be, for a robust Christian faith. From the earthly ministry of Jesus to the present day, our Lord's great question to

Peter, 'Who do you say that I am?' (Mark 8:29), has been the cornerstone of our belief and experience of salvation. This book is the perfect introduction to that vital subject, which remains as relevant today as it has always been."

—**Gerald L. Bray**, Research Professor of Divinity, Beeson Divinity School

"The fruit of a career-long research interest in Christology, Robert Letham's *The Eternal Son* ably navigates the history of the church's reflection on Scripture's witness to the person of Christ from the patristic period to the present day. Rightly challenging the conventional view that the Council of Chalcedon settled the Christological question, he engages contributions from across the Christian tradition—there is nothing parochial about this book! Pastors and seminary students will find here a reliable guide to these crucial, and indeed technical, debates. There is also a doxological thread running through this volume; all this is to the end that our understanding of salvation in Christ will be deepened and our worship of God encouraged."

—**William B. Evans**, Eunice Witherspoon Bell Younts and Willie Camp Younts Professor of Bible and Religion Emeritus, Erskine College

"It is rare to find works of Protestant systematic theology that show both a profound understanding of the history of the church's reflection and a deep appreciation for the Great Tradition. In particular, too many Protestant works on Christology regard that subject in merely formulaic terms (as though its whole significance lay in the formula 'two natures united into one person') and treat the Council of Chalcedon in 451 as the final word on the subject. Against the background of such reductive treatments, Robert Letham's work on Christology is one such rare find. He pushes us beyond a formulaic understanding to the Jesus Christ whom the historic church has found in the Scriptures: the eternal Son of God who has taken human nature into his own person so that he might live, die, and be raised as a man for us and for our salvation. The details of patristic Christology—especially of post-Chalcedonian Christology—are complex and daunting, but Letham is a reliable guide both to the importance of these details and to their interpretation. I recommend that modern systematic theologians drink deeply from Christological history under Letham's tutelage."

—**Donald Fairbairn**, Robert E. Cooley Professor of Early Christianity, Gordon-Conwell Theological Seminary; Professor of Historical and Systematic Theology, Union School of Theology

"After his award-winning volume on the Trinity and his more recent book on the Holy Spirit, Bob Letham has fittingly turned his attention to the eternal Son. This is a thorough and comprehensive volume, focusing on the second person of the Trinity. As with the volume on the Holy Spirit, Letham gives full attention both to the teaching of Scripture and to the historical development of the doctrine. He pays particular attention to the deliberations and conclusions of the early councils of the church. Unlike many English-language studies of Christology, Letham does not fall into the error of imagining that the Council of Chalcedon was the final word on the subject, giving full coverage to the post-Chalcedonian debates leading to the sixth ecumenical council in 680–81. Quite rightly, he gives due weight to the crucial teaching of Cyril of Alexandria, and his account of the teaching of the councils is thorough and accurate. Letham also examines some more recent expositions of Christology, from the Reformation to today, evaluating them judiciously in the light of the conciliar teaching. *The Eternal Son* is an excellent account of the doctrine that cannot be ignored by any with an interest in the topic. We look forward now to the volume on the Father!"

—**Tony Lane**, Professor of Historical Theology, London School of Theology

"Christology is not simply one among many points of doctrine. The triune God's saving work through Jesus Christ is the heart of the gospel. To the degree that we displace Christology in the system of doctrine, we disfigure, if not transfigure, the gospel itself. Letham's treatment of the eternal Son is full of biblical and historical insights into the person and work of Jesus Christ. Particularly noteworthy is the author's extended attention to medieval Christological developments, since many Protestants today are unaware that most of our Christological heritage is based in the medieval rather than the earlier church. Vitally, Letham contrasts classical Christology to modern tendencies to treat Christ as the adopted Son as well as the natural Son of God, which are growing in popularity in biblical studies. Anyone desiring deeper insight into who and what Jesus is as the foundation of how he saves will find an excellent introduction here."

—**Ryan M. McGraw**, Morton H. Smith Professor of Systematic Theology, Greenville Presbyterian Theological Seminary

"Robert Letham, in writing a volume on the second person of the undivided Holy Trinity, returns to something that has concerned him throughout his whole career: the Lord Jesus Christ, who became incarnate in the virgin's womb, was born, suffered, died, rose again, ascended on high, and is in session—all for us—and is properly said to be the same yesterday, today, and forever (Heb. 13:8). Though the Reformed may remain skittish about talk of deification/theosis (Letham gives that his best shot), our author brings to this whole subject that which the Reformed are, at least, not always as clear about: the integrity of the theanthropic person. Cyril of Alexandria and other fathers were crystal clear here, and Letham argues for Cyril's witness, as well as allied witnesses (Maximus the Confessor, John of Damascus, Thomas Aquinas, et al.), to the two natures of Christ in one person (the hypostatic union) that militates against all practical Nestorianism and upholds the real genius not only of the first four councils but of the additional two that followed to round out the church's great witness to God's revelation of the person of the eternal Son. Then the author proceeds to Reformational developments, especially the presence of Christ in the Eucharist and John Calvin's view of Christ as autotheos. Letham treats Christ's work, including the atonement, with surprising brevity, explaining that this book is about the Son himself, 'rather than a complete account of all his work.' Letham has also treated the subject of his work at length elsewhere, including a particularly fine treatment of definite atonement. All in all, a first-rate work on the great object of our faith, the Lord Jesus Christ."

—**Alan D. Strange**, President, Mid-America Reformed Seminary

"I do not know of any contemporary theologian more eminently qualified to write a trilogy on the Trinitarian persons than Robert Letham. In this second of a projected three-volume work, Letham tackles the challenging task of Christology proper, the doctrine of the person of the eternal Son, who 'for us and for our salvation, came down from heaven, and was incarnate' (Nicene Creed). No topic in theology is more important or difficult than that of the identity of the second person of the Holy Trinity. Drawing on his intimate acquaintance with the history of the church's engagement with Scripture's teaching on the eternal Son of God, who, in fulfillment of God's promises, assumed our human nature in its fullness, Letham painstakingly sets forth the truth concerning this 'great . . . mystery of godliness' (1 Tim. 3:16). In the course of his tour de force through the history of theological reflection on the doctrine of Christ's person as the incarnate Son of God, Letham's theological method views Christological doctrine as the fruit of a long conversation that belongs to the whole church—not only to its great creedal and conciliar documents but also to its best theologians, both Eastern and Western. Letham makes his own contribution to this conversation, but unlike many other contemporary theologians, he does so in a manner that eschews a biblicism that exhibits little appreciation for theological inheritances from the past. Old and new Christological errors are persuasively refuted, and the consensus teaching of the church is articulated in a magisterial fashion. Though some may find fault with some feature or another of his exposition, readers will nonetheless be challenged to maintain the great confession of the church about the eternal Son who assumed our flesh in order to accomplish the triune God's purposes in creation and redemption. Among contemporary books on the doctrine of Christ, Letham's should have a preeminent place."

—**Cornelis P. Venema**, Emeritus President and Professor of Doctrinal Studies, Mid-America Reformed Seminary

"An impressive book, indeed, that has freshness about it. Bob Letham is clear and helpful everywhere one looks. Whether discussing the Chalcedonian debates or recent kenotic Christologies, he is pertinent and wise. Letham does not just recycle respected sources. He exercises critical evaluation in a way that honors both Scripture and the confessions of the church. In so doing, he leads us to worship the one who alone could be Mediator because he is God and man."

—**Paul Wells**, Professor Emeritus, Faculté Jean Calvin, Aix-en-Provence, France

THE ETERNAL SON

Also by Robert Letham with P&R Publishing

The Holy Spirit
The Holy Trinity: In Scripture, History, Theology, and Worship
The Lord's Supper: Eternal Word in Broken Bread
The Westminster Assembly: Reading Its Theology in Historical Context
Union with Christ: In Scripture, History, and Theology

THE ETERNAL SON

ROBERT LETHAM

P&R PUBLISHING
P.O. BOX 817 • PHILLIPSBURG • NEW JERSEY 08865-0817

Unless otherwise indicated, all Scripture quotations are the author's own translation.

Italics within Scripture quotations indicate emphasis added.

ISBN: 978-1-62995-863-7 (pbk)
ISBN: 978-1-62995-864-4 (ePub)

Printed in the United States of America

Library of Congress Cataloging-in-Publication Data

Names: Letham, Robert author
Title: The eternal Son / Robert Letham.
Description: Phillipsburg, New Jersey : P&R Publishing Company, [2025] | Includes bibliographical references and index. | Summary: "Using an historical-theological approach supplemented by exegesis, Letham develops a biblically faithful Christology of the Son's deity, humanity, and incarnation, while examining major Christological heresies and creedal responses to them"-- Provided by publisher.
Identifiers: LCCN 2025021485 | ISBN 9781629958637 paperback | ISBN 9781629958644 epub
Subjects: LCSH: Jesus Christ--History of doctrines | Jesus Christ--Person and offices--Biblical teaching | Christian heresies--History
Classification: LCC BT198 .L4275 2025
LC record available at https://lccn.loc.gov/2025021485

We praise you, O God: we acknowledge you to be the Lord.
All the earth worships you: the Father everlasting.
To you all angels cry aloud: the heavens, and all the powers therein.
To you cherubim and seraphim continually do cry,
"Holy, holy, holy, Lord God of hosts;
heaven and earth are full of the majesty of your glory."

The glorious company of the apostles praise you.
The goodly fellowship of the prophets praise you.
The noble army of martyrs praise you.
The holy church throughout all the world acknowledges you,
the Father of an infinite majesty;
your honourable, true, and only Son;
also the Holy Ghost the comforter.

You are the king of glory, O Christ.
You are the everlasting Son of the Father.
When you took upon yourself to deliver man
you did not abhor the virgin's womb.
When you overcame the sharpness of death
you opened the kingdom of heaven to all believers.
You sit at the right hand of God in the glory of the Father.
We believe that you shall come to be our judge.

We therefore pray you, help your servants
whom you have redeemed with your precious blood.
Make them to be numbered with your saints in glory everlasting.
O Lord, save your people and bless your heritage.
Govern them and lift them up for ever.

Day by day we magnify you;
and we worship your name ever world without end.
Graciously grant, O Lord, to keep us this day without sin.
O Lord, have mercy upon us; have mercy upon us.
O Lord, let your mercy lighten upon us; as our trust is in you.
O Lord, in you have I trusted: let me never be confounded.[1]

1. Anon., *Te Deum laudamus* (4th cent.).

Contents

Foreword

Ever since I read Robert Letham's magnificent work *The Holy Trinity*, I have thought that his many writings exemplified the conviction of Martin Bucer (1491–1551), *Vera theologia non theoretica, sed practica est; Finis siquidem eius agere est hoc est vitam vivere deiformem* ("True theology is not theoretical, but practical. The end of it is living, that is, to live a godly life"). Letham writes in the grand tradition of catholic Reformed Christianity. He understands that theology that is truly Christian must never be recondite, far less abstract. The church fathers and the Reformers, John Calvin chief among them, became theologians in order to serve the church and nourish its members. Dr. Letham's writings breathe the same air as his theological heroes and richly serve the people of God as they pilgrim their way from this world to the world that is to come.

The Eternal Son is the second volume in a trilogy. The first volume focused on the person, mission, and ministry of the Holy Spirit (2023), and the third will expound the person, glory, and grace of God the Father. Robert Letham is a Trinitarian Christian, and his passion, both personal and theological, is to help and inspire his fellow Christians to prize the ineffable glory of the triune God revealed in the incarnation, life, death, resurrection, and ascension of Jesus Christ.

Letham understands that the grace and glory of the gospel of Christ rests on who he is. What gives the cross of Calvary its saving significance is the identity of the one who hung on that cross. In his great work *The Glory of Christ*, John Owen understood this fact and stood in theological solidarity with the early church fathers when he wrote about the hypostatic union that "this glory is the glory of our religion, the glory of the Church, the sole Rock whereon it is built, the only spring of present grace and future glory" (*Works*, 1:310).

One of the great attractions of Letham's work is that he is deeply immersed in the writings of both the Latin and Greek church fathers. When he quotes them, he understands the context of their writings and never plucks atomized statements from them to defend a particular theological proposition. Letham, however, engages with the present as well as the past, and is often at his most perceptive when he subjects the literature of the twentieth and twenty-first centuries to the teaching of the Bible, the theological conclusions and convictions of the church fathers, and the reflections of men such as Thomas Aquinas and John Calvin, alongside his own penetrating insights.

Another striking feature of *The Eternal Son* is Letham's willingness not only to faithfully reflect the teaching of theologians past and present, but to fairly critique them, always in the light of Holy Scripture and the accumulated wisdom of the church throughout the centuries.

The early church ecumenical councils are deeply significant for Letham. Of particular note is the lucidity with which he navigates the apparent, and sometimes real, differences between the Eastern and Western fathers. Much of the recent controversy over the Son's supposed eternal subordination to the Father could have been avoided if those who rushed to support or criticize this controversial question had digested the teachings of the fathers as deeply and reflectively as Robert Letham has done.

This is a book for theologians and pastors, but no less also for other serious-minded Christians who desire to "grow in the grace and knowledge of our Lord and Savior Jesus Christ. To him be the glory both now and to the day of eternity. Amen." (2 Peter 3:18). It is the greatest pleasure to commend this excellent treatment of the eternal Son, and I look forward with enormous anticipation to the final installment of the trilogy.

Ian Hamilton
Professor of Historical Theology
Westminster Seminary, UK

Acknowledgments

As is usual, I have been able to complete this book with a little help from my friends. I am very grateful to the noble army of readers who have scrutinized various chapters and sections. In particular, special thanks are due to Sherman Isbell for numerous suggestions from his vast fund of knowledge, together with incisive comments on the text of every chapter. Jonathan Humphreys has also read the entire script and pointed out many places where greater clarity was due. Additionally, I want to express my appreciation for the contributions of Tom Brand, Tim Brown, Lane Tipton, Ryan McGraw, Donald Fairbairn, and Ron Di Giacomo. Without the input I have received from them, this book would be much the poorer.

My work was helped by the facilities of Union School of Theology and Cambridge University Library. In particular, Donna Roof and Matt Knox, at the Montgomery Library, Westminster Theological Seminary, Philadelphia, were of great help in identifying and making available an article whose identity was not readily evident.

John Hughes of P&R has been unfailingly helpful and readily accessible with advice and encouragement, and Karen Magnuson excels at eagle-eyed copyediting. The entire team at P&R is worthy of high praise.

Once again, I am profoundly grateful to my wife, Joan, for her constant encouragement in every possible way. This has been the case throughout the forty-nine years of our marriage, and there can be no doubt that the lion's share of what I have achieved, such as it may be, is due to her.

Epiphany, 2025

Introduction

This book is the second in a projected trilogy on the Trinitarian persons, following the first of the collection on the Holy Spirit (2023). This series flows out of the second, revised, and enlarged edition of my book *The Holy Trinity* (2019). Initially, the publisher approached me with the suggestion that I write a book on the Spirit. Later, after I had begun work on that book, the suggestion expanded to include all three persons. Here we are; not surprisingly, this volume is thicker because there is more revealed of the Son.

It almost goes without saying that Christology is a vital subject. Virtually every error and heresy is at root a departure from the orthodox doctrine of Christ. A crucial and perennial need of the church is to believe and trust in Jesus Christ, our Savior and Lord. Right belief, under the direction of the Holy Spirit, is the root of right practice. The knowledge of the eternal Son, who, for us and our salvation, became man, is eternal life. It is true for the church as it is for the individual and family. Beyond that, it reaches out into the world and impacts the way that people live, whether for good or ill, as the influence of the truth waxes or wanes.

The need to maintain and enhance our knowledge of Christ is made ever more pressing by the neglect by leaders and thinkers of the full conciliar resolution of the Christological controversies of the early church. A widespread assumption has developed that the Council of Chalcedon in A.D. 451 was the effective terminus of such a process. This brought to a head the crisis over the teachings of Nestorius and, latterly, Eutyches. It affirmed that Jesus Christ is the eternal Son of God, one person in two natures, divine and human. In reality, as the Eastern church has known and as the most astute, if not the most vocal, scholars in the West are also aware, it was not the case that the conflict was over. The struggles over the person of Christ did not end at Chalcedon; they rumbled on and even intensified in the two hundred or so years that followed. Indeed, Chalcedon created at least as many problems as it solved. Those who think Chalcedon solved everything are doomed to repeat many of the problems that followed it. Very similar problems have reared their heads in the last decade or two in circles that might be supposed safe from such dangers. The real risk is that erroneous teaching on the person of Christ may gain ground again and ultimately threaten the gospel that is taught. For that reason, I have devoted a considerable amount of space in this book to a discussion of those ensuing matters. These chapters may seem at times abstruse, but they are vital, and the need to grasp their content is urgent.

From a slightly different angle, I have been surprised by comments made to me by some highly respected scholars that I should avoid referring to certain authors, either because they are Roman Catholic or because their theology is considered suspect at important points. I find this difficult to accept. When I was quite young, in my early twenties, my father gave me some wise advice. He indicated that my ministry would be richer and more effective if I were to interact with sources with which I might not always agree. In this, his recommendation was following in the wake of the practice of the Reformers and the Puritans. The divines at the Westminster Assembly were, by today's ministerial standards, extraordinarily learned. In debate they were able to cite the church fathers and the best of the medieval theologians with great frequency and authority. They treated the leading Roman Catholic theologian, Robert Bellarmine, with great respect. They were abreast of the heresies of the day, and of the teaching of the sects that were springing up with bewildering rapidity. No good comes from reading only material with which one is in full agreement. It is the road to stagnation.

Karl Barth was arguably the greatest theologian of the twentieth century and for that reason, among others, is cited here quite a lot. One does not have to agree with Barth, Jürgen Moltmann, or other prominent figures, but the very originality, the depth to which they are able to go, however reliably or not, can act as a catalyst for one's own thought. I recall Donald MacLeod's mentioning that while 90 percent of theological dross was to be found outside the circles of Reformed theology, 90 percent of gold was there too.

I was at a concert in Washington, D.C., many years ago at which the violinist Pinchas Zukerman, in a postconcert talk, expressed strong dissatisfaction with the impact of Arnold Schoenberg and his introduction of the twelve-tone scale, a view that I share myself. Like it or not, however, a history of music in the twentieth century that omitted reference to Schoenberg would not be a history of music in the twentieth century. Neither would a book on twentieth- and twenty-first-century theology be what it claimed to be if it did not refer to Barth. Books on theology that refer only to those with whom one is in basic agreement are usually sterile, just as ministers who rely only on the words of their friends will not grow and develop in their ministry, but rather lack depth.

Part of the book retreads familiar ground in the Trinitarian debates of the fourth century, although from a somewhat different direction. This element of repetition is necessary. It also reinforces those vital points I have mentioned. It is part of the re-creative process in which one retrieves and builds on what has gone before. I recall here how Gustav Mahler used music from his early song cycle *Des Knaben Wunderhorn* and simply dumped it into a number of his symphonies. Indeed, it is an interesting exercise to play the main subject of the final movement of Johannes Brahms's First Symphony followed by the opening subject of the Mahler Third —they are almost identical, as "any ass can hear."[1] Then listen to the Fantasia for Piano, Chorus, and Orchestra, op. 80 of Ludwig van Beethoven, and see how close it is, as the springboard, to the familiar theme in the finale of his Ninth Symphony, in which he sets to music Friedrich Schiller's poem "Ode to Joy."

A theme in the book *The Holy Spirit* (2023) underlies the present work. The past teaching of the church, epitomized in the ecumenical

1. Michael Steinberg, *The Symphony: A Listener's Guide* (Oxford University Press, 1995), 293.

creeds, was the result of its accumulated biblical exegesis. It is part of Christian wisdom to heed the voice of the church, the *consensus fidelium*. Scripture is our supreme authority; this does not mean that our own exegesis of Scripture is in that category. When the united voice of the church through the centuries—East and West, Protestant, Roman Catholic, and Orthodox—has affirmed certain truths, absolutely *overwhelming* evidence is required to depart from it. One of the most persistent attacks on the faith takes the form of either denigration or neglect of the classic creeds and confessions, often in the name of the Bible but in reality in support of deviant exegesis. We must always beware of those who claim that they have discovered something that has somehow eluded the glorious company of the apostles, the goodly fellowship of the prophets, and the noble army of martyrs who have gone before. It is more often than not the voice of heresy—potential, incipient, or overt.

In the first three chapters of what follows, we will explore the relations of the Son within the Trinity, follow biblical leads on God's decision that the eternal Son take human nature into personal union, and then consider the amazing wonders of the incarnation. This will draw us in chapters 4 through 8 to a detailed analysis of the development of the church's path to an understanding of the personal identity of Jesus in the wake of teachings that effectively undermined the gospel. In chapters 9 and 10, we will discuss issues that arose in the Reformation era, in the aftermath of the Enlightenment, and down to the present day. The final chapter will regard the whole process of salvation as centered from beginning to end in the Son.

This book is intended to reflect the altarpiece at Isenheim, where, on the far right-hand side, the figure of John the Baptist reaches out and points—points to the cross and the crucified Christ, the eternal Son, one of the Trinity, who suffered according to the flesh. "Behold, the Lamb of God who takes away the sin of the world," for "everyone who believes in him will have life eternal" (John 1:29; 3:15).

Abbreviations

ACO	Eduardus Schwarz, ed., *Acta conciliorum oecumenicorum* (Walter de Gruyter, 1914–40)
Ad Thalass.	Maximus the Confessor, *Ad Thalassium*
C	Niceno-Constantinopolitan Creed
CCSG	*Corpus Christianorum Series Graeca*
CCSL	*Corpus Christianorum Series Latina*
CD	Karl Barth, *Church Dogmatics*, ed. Thomas F. Torrance, trans. Geoffrey W. Bromiley, 14 vols. (T&T Clark, 1956–77)
CO	John Calvin, *Calvini Opera (Opera Quae Supersunt Omnia)*, ed. Guilelmus Baum, Eduardus Cunitz, and Eduardus Reuss, 59 vols., *Corpus Reformatorum* 29–87 (Brunswick, 1863–1900)
EQ	*Evangelical Quarterly*
HTR	*Harvard Theological Review*
IJST	*International Journal of Systematic Theology*
Institutes	John Calvin, *Institutes of the Christian Religion*, ed. John T. McNeill, trans. Ford Lewis Battles (Westminster Press, 1960)
JEH	*Journal of Ecclesiastical History*
JETS	*Journal of the Evangelical Theological Society*
JRT	*Journal of Reformed Theology*
JTS	*Journal of Theological Studies*
LN	Johannes P. Louw and Eugene A. Nida, eds., *Greek-English Lexicon of the New Testament Based on Semantic Domains* (United Bible Societies, 1988)

LS	*Louvain Studies*
LW	Jaroslav Pelikan, ed., *Luther's Works,* 55 vols. (Fortress Press, 1955–74)
MAJT	*Mid-America Journal of Theology*
NPNF[1]	Philip Schaff, ed., *Nicene and Post-Nicene Fathers of the Christian Church,* 1st ser. (repr., Eerdmans, 1978–79)
NPNF[2]	Philip Schaff, ed., *Nicene and Post-Nicene Fathers of the Christian Church,* 2nd ser. (repr., Eerdmans, 1979)
NTS	*New Testament Studies*
OS	Peter Barth and Wilhelm Niesel, eds., *Ioannis Calvini Opera Selecta,* 5 vols. (Kaiser, 1926–52)
PG	Jacques-Paul Migne et al., eds., *Patrologia Cursus Completus: Series Graeca,* 162 vols. (Paris, 1857–66)
PL	Jacques-Paul Migne et al., eds., *Patrologia Cursus Completus: Series Latina,* 217 vols. (Paris, 1844–64)
PO	R. Graffin and F. Nau, eds., *Patrologia Orientalis* (Paris, 1907–)
RD	Herman Bavinck, *Reformed Dogmatics,* 4 vols. (Baker Academic, 2003–8)
SBET	*Scottish Bulletin of Evangelical Theology*
SCG	Thomas Aquinas, *Summa contra Gentiles*
SJT	*Scottish Journal of Theology*
ST	Thomas Aquinas, *Summa theologiae*
StPatr	*Studia Patristica*
SVTQ	*St. Vladimir's Theological Quarterly*
Them	*Themelios*
WCF	Westminster Confession of Faith
WLC	Westminster Larger Catechism

1

The Son in the Divine Trinity

This book is part of a series on the Trinitarian persons, following the second edition of my book on the Trinity. Its focus is on the Son, and this chapter will consider the relations of the Son to the Father and the Holy Spirit within the Trinity, insofar as this has been revealed to us in Scripture and has formed the substance of the church's faith. This is a supremely glorious theme, and I hope that we will realize this in a new way as we proceed.

The book is not, therefore, an exposition of the doctrine of the Trinity as such, although the doctrine will clearly be integral to the argument. Nor is it precisely focused on the biblical record in the Gospels, although again we will refer to this in support; it is not a book simply about Jesus. Rather, it concerns the eternal Son, one of the Trinity both in himself and in his incarnation. Moreover, in this chapter I am not intending to spend time proving that Jesus of Nazareth is the Son of God, nor that God is triune, the Son being one with the Father from eternity. I am not attempting this from cumulative reference to the biblical teaching, still less from any process of logical analysis. For each of these, you may consult what I have written elsewhere and the literature as a whole, reaching back to the time of the church fathers.[1] We will assume the biblical teaching and the historic church doctrine.

1. Robert Letham, *Systematic Theology* (Crossway, 2019), 75–86; Robert Letham, *The Holy Trinity: In Scripture, History, Theology, and Worship*, rev. and expanded ed. (P&R Publishing, 2019).

As we consider the Son in the Trinity, we need to be clear right away about the names of the Trinitarian persons. The names, Father, Son, and Holy Spirit concern who God is in himself, not how he relates to his creation. The Father is Father eternally and is Father in relation to the Son. *Mutatis mutandis*, the Son is Son from eternity and is so in relation to the Father. Whatever relations God sustains to his creation, and even to his own believing people, these realities remain. Moreover, the names are neither dependent on nor related to anything in creation, or even the works that God does. Since he is sovereign, and chose freely to bring all other entities into existence, he is in himself entirely independent of what he has created. Moreover, God alone has the right to name himself, contrary to recent attempts to "reimagine" God.

Each of the Gospels has its own distinct starting point. Mark begins his narrative with the baptism of Jesus, his entry into public ministry. In doing so, he passes over all events in Jesus' life that preceded that point. Luke takes us back earlier, to the announcements by the angel of the impending conceptions of Jesus and John the Baptist, to the birth narratives, and to the immediately following events. He starts with the absolute beginning of the earthly life of Jesus. Matthew reaches still further into the past. For him, the birth announcement and the ensuing details are set within the history of Israel, in the covenant God made with David and Abraham. His genealogy in the first chapter is a royal genealogy, ensuring that his readers are aware that Jesus is in the line of David and so inherits the promises of the kingdom. Furthermore, as the seed of Abraham, Jesus is the one in whom all the families of the earth will be blessed, with Jesus' ultimate announcement that upon his resurrection, he is invested with plenipotentiary authority over the entire universe (Matt. 28:18–20).[2]

When we come to the fourth Gospel, John probes back before Jesus' public ministry, before his conception and birth, before David

2. W. D. Davies, *A Critical and Exegetical Commentary on the Gospel According to Saint Matthew* (T&T Clark, 1988), 1:149–60, 185–86; R. T. France, *The Gospel According to Matthew: An Introduction and Commentary* (Inter-Varsity Press, 1985), 71–75; David Hill, *The Gospel of Matthew* (Marshall, Morgan & Scott, 1972), 74–75; Roger Amos, *Matthew: A Commentary* (Paul Thomas, 2023), 3–4.

and Abraham, even before Adam, back before history, before the creation of the world, into the transcendent mists of eternity. "In the beginning was the Logos [Word], and the Word was with God and the Word was God," he writes (John 1:1). Moreover, the Logos is the Creator of all things, and is life itself (vv. 2–4). The identity of the Logos is made known in verse 14, where John continues, "The Word became flesh and lived among us." Jesus Christ, Jesus of Nazareth, was and is the Logos. He is *sui generis*, beyond comparison to anything or anyone else, to all created entities. In reference to John 1:1, Karl Barth comments that "the Word as such is before and above all created realities. It stands completely outside the series of created things."[3] Here "πρός must be understood quite plainly and simply to mean this: that he could be 'in the beginning' who was with God, who is beyond all created reality, because he belongs to God, because his being is as the being of God himself. . . . The sentence tells us, then, that the Word was itself God."[4]

While this is a realm beyond our experience and far above our practical knowledge, we need to begin there ourselves in order to place in its ultimate context the biblical teaching and historical reflection on all that the Son did and does in this world, the one in which we live. It should go without saying that we need help in this. Our help comes from the Word of God, all that God has revealed, from the illumination of the Holy Spirit, and from those who have investigated these things before us. In this chapter, we will see, in broad outline, what the church has understood on the matter. In the second chapter, we will attempt to grapple with the biblical revelation itself.

From the New Testament to Constantinople I (A.D. 381)

As time went by, after the last of the apostles had died, among the various pressures that the church encountered were teachings that appeared to contravene the gospel it believed and preached.

3. Karl Barth, *CD*, II/2:95.

4. Barth, *CD*, II/2:96; Letham, *Holy Trinity*, 25–45; Letham, *Systematic Theology*, 75–86; Robert Letham, *The Message of the Person of Christ: The Word Made Flesh* (Inter-Varsity Press, 2013), 41–63, 111–30.

Ultimately, these novel ideas were attempts to explain, insofar as it was possible, how the Son is related to God. But the result was a loosened grasp of his personal identity and status. These were no merely academic questions, for if Jesus was not God, one with the Father from eternity, there would be no gospel to proclaim, for he could not have saved us, he could not have said to Philip, "He who has seen me has seen the Father" (John 14:9), and he could not have truly made God known. In short, we would not have a true knowledge of God if these erroneous claims were received and accepted.

Two Main Heresies[5]

Until the early fourth century, two deviant tendencies were affecting the church's grasp of the Trinity. While in time the ensuing controversies were resolved, these ideas linger and reappear in different forms down through the succeeding centuries to the present day.

On the one side, *modalism* blurred the distinctions of the three persons. In the third century, Sabellius held that God revealed himself like an actor taking on different roles: as Father in the Old Testament, as Son in the New Testament, and now, after Pentecost, as Holy Spirit. God as such was solitary and unipersonal. Consequently, Christ the Son was merely an appearance of the one God but did not have any distinct identity of his own.[6] With such a view, God's revelation in history did not reveal who he is eternally. The Son would be simply a theophany, a temporary appearance; as such, he could not give us true knowledge of God, nor could he save us. This undercut the gospel. Tertullian countered modalism in his book *Aduersus Praxean*. The church recognized that the Bible, in maintaining the oneness of God, simultaneously points to the reality and irreducible distinctions between the Father, the Son, and the Holy Spirit.

5. The rest of this chapter is a condensed version of Letham, *Holy Trinity*, 87–206.

6. Bertrand de Margerie, *The Christian Trinity in History*, trans. Edmund J. Fortman, Studies in Historical Theology 1 (St. Bede's Publications, 1982), 85–87; Boris Bobrinskoy, *The Mystery of the Trinity: Trinitarian Experience and Vision in the Biblical and Patristic Tradition*, trans. Anthony P. Gythiel (St. Vladimir's Seminary Press, 1999), 217–20.

On the other side of the spectrum was *subordinationism*. This recognized the distinctions of the three but accorded a lower status to the Son and the Spirit. It held that God was a hierarchical being, and sought to maintain the unity of God by holding that the Father imparted a lesser deity to the Son and the Spirit. Once again, since Scripture ranks the Son and the Spirit with the Father (cf., *inter multa alia*, Matt. 28:19–20), if the Son and the Spirit were not held to be fully God, we would not have true knowledge of God and there could be no viable proclamation of the gospel. Put bluntly, if Christ were not unimpaired God, if the Son were not of the identical being with the Father eternally, he could not save us.

Both modalism and subordinationism were attempts to make the Trinity intelligible to human reason. We would be left with either the one God, with the Son and the Holy Spirit temporary appearances, or a graded deity, with Son and Spirit semidivine. This latter mix was like a time bomb, destined sooner or later to explode. The chief problem was how to reconcile the unity of the one God with the status of Christ. While modalism was suppressed at the Synod of Antioch in 268, the subordinationist issue was unresolved.

The Fourth-Century Crisis

Suddenly, bursting on the scene in around 318 came a popular, charismatic Alexandrian presbyter called Arius. He maintained that the Son was not coeternal with the Father but had come into existence out of nothing, and was in fact a creature. The dangers for the church were great.[7] For Arius and those who agreed with him, God was not Father eternally any more than a man is a father before he begets his son. The Son had an origin, *ex nihilo*, so it was claimed; at some point he did not exist, and now he exists by the will of God. God used the Son as an intermediary to create other entities; God is effectively at arm's length from the creation. Hence, the Son is a different *ousia* (being) from the Father, for the Father is his God. He is called Word and Son by grace only.[8] Jesus' statement

7. In many ways, Arius was a precursor of the modern Jehovah's Witnesses.
8. Athanasius, *Of Synods*, 16, for Arius's Profession of Faith.

"I and the Father are one" (John 10:30) was taken to mean a harmonious agreement of their two wills, not identity of being. The Son was an assistant to the Father, operating under orders. Thus Arius considered that the monarchy of God was preserved, since the Son was and is not true God.[9] Effectively, Arius's claims severed the Son's connection with God. His views were outlawed as heretical by the Council of Nicaea in 325. The council affirmed that the Son is *homoousios* ("of the identical being") with the Father.

The controversy erupted again in the 350s. Political intrigue and terminological confusion abounded. The words eventually used to resolve the crisis—*ousia, hypostasis*—had been used in a variety of ways in Greek thought, as well as by figures in the church. People spoke past one another. A coherent and agreed language was lacking.[10] The details of the debate are confusing and bewildering. As R. P. C. Hanson remarks, "The theologians of the Christian Church were slowly driven to a realization that the deepest questions which face Christianity cannot be answered in purely biblical language, because the questions are about the meaning of biblical language itself."[11]

The most prominent figure in the later "Arian" movement, Eunomius, was a bishop and more able than Arius, but his ideas were similar. He and his followers were rationalists, confident in the capabilities of human logic. They assumed a direct correspondence between the mind of God and of humans such that meaning is identical for both. Because of this, the Son's generation from the Father is to be understood in terms of human generation and thus

9. Robert C. Gregg, *Early Arianism—a Way of Salvation* (Fortress Press, 1981), 1–129.

10. R. P. C. Hanson, *The Search for the Christian Doctrine of God: The Arian Controversy 318–381* (T&T Clark, 1988), 99–675; Lewis Ayres, *Nicaea and Its Legacy: An Approach to Fourth-Century Trinitarian Theology* (Oxford University Press, 2004).

11. Hanson, *Search*, xxi. On the conflict, see also the works below; de Margerie, *Christian Trinity*, 87–91; J. N. D. Kelly, *Early Christian Doctrines* (Adam & Charles Black, 1968), 226–31; Bobrinskoy, *Mystery of the Trinity*, 220–21; Basil Studer, *Trinity and Incarnation: The Faith of the Early Church*, ed. Andrew Louth, trans. Matthias Westerhoff (Liturgical Press, 1993), 103–5; Gregg, *Early Arianism*, 1–129; Charles Kannengiesser, *Arius and Athanasius: Two Alexandrian Theologians* (Variorum, 1991); Rowan Williams, *Arius: Heresy and Tradition* (Darton, Longman, and Todd, 1987).

must have had a beginning. Although he is the instrument by which God created the world, he himself is the first to be created, and so there was a point at which he did not exist.

For the Arian tradition, the line between God and creation came between the Father and the Son, with the Son on the side of the creature. Conversely, the supporters of Nicaea placed it between the triad (the Father, the Son, and the Holy Spirit) and all other beings.[12] But Eunomius did not think the Son was a creature identical to all others, for he created all others.[13] His triad was a hierarchy, the one God who became the Father, plus two different, subordinate, and noneternal entities.

Eunomius was opposed by Athanasius and later the Cappadocians —Basil the Great, his brother Gregory of Nyssa, and Gregory of Nazianzus—who argued that the Son and the Holy Spirit were one being with the Father from eternity. In reply to the Eunomian concept of generation and relying on a welter of biblical exegesis, they asserted that the names Father and Son denote identity of nature and that it is fallacious to argue from human experience back to God.[14]

The Crisis Resolved

Some held that the Son is *homoiousios* ("of like being") with the Father. Athanasius had the breadth of mind to recognize that differences of terminology should not prevent agreement if the intention behind those different terms was the same.[15] This was a major breakthrough, paving the way for resolution of the crisis at the Council of Constantinople in A.D. 381, spearheaded by the three Cappadocians. Among other things the council decided, Eunomianism was rejected as heresy.[16]

12. Richard Paul Vaggione, *Eunomius of Cyzicus and the Nicene Revolution* (Oxford University Press, 2000), 23–24.

13. Vaggione, *Eunomius of Cyzicus*, 124–26.

14. Letham, *Holy Trinity*, 153–77.

15. Athanasius, *To the Antiochenes*, 5–8; *PG*, 26:799–806; Hanson, *Search*, 644–45.

16. On the controversies on the Holy Spirit before the council and its response, see Robert Letham, *The Holy Spirit* (P&R Publishing, 2023), 3–34; Athanasius, *Letters to Serapion on the Holy Spirit*; Didymus the Blind, *On the Holy Spirit*; Basil of Caesarea, *On the Holy Spirit*; Gregory of Nazianzus, *Oration 31*. Later, Cyril wrote: "It is

A number of factors lay behind this resolution. First, the discussion was simplified by the Cappadocians' using terms in a nontechnical way, avoiding the morass of philosophical misunderstandings that had dogged discussion earlier. This overcame the confusion. Second, biblical exegesis was dominant, including, prominently, Old Testament exegesis. These men were bishops, pastors, preachers, used to mingling with their congregations, which were mostly composed of farmers. They were not ivory-tower philosophers, although some might consider Gregory of Nyssa to come close to that. Both these factors helped promote clarity. Third, Basil proposed to reserve *ousia* for the way in which God is one and *hypostasis* for the way in which he is three. This helped communication. Fourth, appeal was made to "the sense of Scripture" rather than to precise proof texts, so as to clarify meaning by providing a wider context than bare words and phrases alone.

As a result, it was recognized that the Son is one identical being with the Father and that this was integral to the gospel itself. So the Council of Constantinople (A.D. 381) unequivocally rejected the claim that the Son and the Spirit are simply intermediaries between God and humanity. Such an idea would have destroyed the gospel. We would have been baptized into the name of God and two creatures, which would be not only nonsense but blasphemy.[17] Jesus Christ would not have given us true knowledge of God because he would not have been one with God from eternity. Thus, he could not have saved us.[18] He would have been merely a man, a prophet who spoke in the name of the Lord, rather than being the Lord himself.

The Niceno-Constantinopolitan Creed (C)

The Niceno-Constantinopolitan Creed, probably dating from the Council of Constantinople (A.D. 381), reads as follows:

---

inconceivable that created being should have the power to deify. This is something that can be attributed only to God." Cyril of Alexandria, *Dialogue on the Most Holy Trinity*, 7.644d, in Norman Russell, *The Doctrine of Deification in the Greek Patristic Tradition* (Oxford University Press, 2004), 195.

17. It would have put the Creator on the level of the creature if that had been true.

18. See Letham, *Holy Trinity*, 179–207.

We believe in one God
the Father Almighty,
maker of heaven and earth
and of all things visible and invisible;

And in one Lord Jesus Christ
the Son of God, the Only-begotten,
begotten by his Father before all ages,
Light from Light,
true God from true God,
begotten, not made,
consubstantial with the Father,
through whom all things came into existence,
who for us men and for our salvation
came down from the heavens
and became incarnate by the Holy Spirit and the Virgin Mary
and became a man,
and was crucified for us under Pontius Pilate
and suffered and was buried
and rose again on the third day in accordance with the Scriptures
and ascended into the heavens
and is seated at the right hand of the Father
and will come again with glory
to judge the living and the dead,
and there will be no end to his kingdom;

And in the Holy Spirit,
the Lord and life-giver,
who proceeds from the Father,
who is worshipped and glorified together with the Father and the Son,
who spoke by the prophets;
And in one holy, catholic and apostolic Church;
We confess one baptism for the forgiveness of sins;
We wait for the resurrection of the dead and the life of the coming age. Amen.[19]

19. Translation by R. P. C. Hanson from the Greek text printed by G. L. Dosetti, *Il Simbolo di Nicaea e di Costantinople*, 1967, in Hanson, *Search*, 816.

An official letter from the Synod of Rome the following year said that "we believe that there is one substance (*ousia*) of the Father and of the Son and of the Holy Spirit in three most perfect *hypostases* or three perfect Persons (*prosopois*)."[20] The Father is the maker of all things, the Lord Jesus Christ is the one through whom all things came into existence, and the Holy Spirit is the Lord and giver of life. Creation is a work of the whole Trinity.

J. N. D. Kelly sums up the profound achievements of the fourth century, culminating in C:

> What is not always noticed, however, is the profound intellectual revolution which the triumph of the new orthodoxy at the two great councils implied. To make my point as clearly and as simply as I can, prior to Nicaea the accepted Christian doctrine of God was an Origenistic one of a holy Triad, of an ineffable Godhead with two subordinate and, in the last resort, disparate hypostases; but after Nicaea the pressure group which pushed through the introduction of the *homoousion* dragged, if you will forgive the crude metaphor, these two inferior hypostases within the divine essence. During the four or five decades following Nicaea the predominant view in the church continued to be Origenistic, pluralistic. . . . But once the creed of Constantinople both reaffirmed and supplemented the Nicene creed proper, there could be no future for such pluralism. The Son and the Spirit were "one in being" (as we now translate *homoousion*) with the Father, and the Godhead was an indivisible unity expressing itself in three eternal modes [not to be understood in terms of modalism] differing only in their relations. The Nicene creed, in its original form N and its more mature development C, symbolised this far-reaching revolution.[21]

Later, this theology was further elaborated in systematic form by Augustine, in his *De trinitate*, in his *Tractates on John*, and in some of his letters. All this should be seen against the background described by

20. De Margerie, *Christian Trinity*, 107, quoting J. Alberigo, *Conciliorum oecumenicorum decreta* (Herder, 1962), 24. See Studer, *Trinity and Incarnation*, 158.

21. J. N. D. Kelly, "The Nicene Creed: A Turning Point," *SJT* 36, no. 1 (1983): 38–39.

Georges Florovsky, that "*the classical world did not know the mystery of personal being*."[22] In short, bearing in mind the then absence of linguistic resources relating to personality, the bringing of the whole notion of personhood to the surface was a radical—even revolutionary—new development.

We will now consider the underlying foundations of the Niceno-Constantinopolitan settlement insofar as they provided the rationale for the status and relations of the three Trinitarian persons, and the Son in particular.

Indivisibility

Since the Son is one being with the Father and the Spirit from eternity, it follows that God is one and indivisible. The three persons, or *hypostases*, are subsistences in the one God. They are identical with the one divine essence or being, yet the distinctions between them are real. Hence, the Son cannot be abstracted from the Trinity. None of the three are ever alone. Where the Son is—which is everywhere—so is the Father and the Spirit, for there is one God, eternal, immense, infinite.

A generation or so after Constantinople I, Augustine was to reflect on this in his book *De trinitate*. The personal distinctions were not distinctions of substance, and therefore not referring to three "things" with separate identities. If that were so, there would be a quarternity, the divine essence and the three persons. Nor were these distinctions only formal, mere manners of human speech. If that were the case, there would not be a Trinity but rather a relapse into modalism. At root, God would be one and solitary, the three being simply metaphors. Rather, Augustine reasoned, the distinctions are relational, real distinctions in the one being of God.[23]

Hence, each *hypostasis* is identical with the one being of God. Each is comprehensively and exhaustively God. There can be no internal division. All three are present and active together in all the

22. Georges Florovsky, "Eastern Fathers of the Fourth Century," in *The Collected Works of Father Georges Florovsky*, ed. Richard S. Haugh, vol. 7 (Büchervertriebsanstalt, 1987), 32 (italics original).

23. *PL*, 42:912–14; Augustine, *De trinitate*, 5.4–6.

works and ways of God. All three are equal in power and glory. In our present concern, the Son is one, equal with and indivisible from the Father, one with him and the Spirit from eternity.

One Being, Three Persons (*Hypostases*)

That God is one indivisible being (essence, from *esse*, "to be") is, from the biblical background, axiomatic. That the one being of God consists eternally of three distinct persons is a matter that the church fathers saw as essential to salvation, for if it were not so, the truth and reliability of God's revelation would be destroyed. Creation and salvation are presented in the Bible as works of God. Since the Son and the Holy Spirit are, together with the Father, direct and distinct personal actors in both realms, it follows that all three have the status of deity. Since all three persons are the one God, from one side God is one being, three persons, while from another angle he is three persons, one being.[24]

Similarly, the one God is simple, not divisible. It is impossible to cut off and detach part of God, as can be done with any created being. That is why each of the Father, the Son, and the Holy Spirit constitute all of God both severally and together. It follows that none of the three are less than all three together. This is so because there is but one divine essence or being. Nor is the divine being a fourth entity; God *is* the Father, the Son, and the Holy Spirit. So God is not divisible into parts less than the whole of who he is. Augustine maintains that "some things are even said about the persons singly by name; however they must not be understood in the sense of excluding the other persons, because this same three is also one, and there is one substance and godhead of the Father and Son and Holy Spirit."[25] Again, when we think of the Son, we must think of him not in detachment, but together with the Father and the Holy Spirit. When we contemplate the one God, we are to understand that

24. See Thomas F. Torrance, *The Christian Doctrine of God: One Being, Three Persons* (T&T Clark, 1996), 112–67, for a developed exposition of this point.

25. Augustine, *De trinitate*, 1.9.19; *The Works of Saint Augustine: A Translation for the 21st Century: The Trinity*, ed. John E. Rotelle, trans. Edmund Hill (New City Press, 1991), 79. See also Augustine, *On the Gospel of John*, 77.2; *NPNF*[1], 1:339.

he is always and wholly the Father, the Son, and the Spirit. While Augustine has been particularly noted for his defense of divine simplicity, he was following in the footsteps of the Cappadocians.[26]

Homoousios

It follows that all three persons are of one substance (*consubstantial*), of the one identical being (*homoousios*). Further, each person is God in himself. Nothing in the creed (C) suggests that the Son—or the Spirit—derives his deity from the Father. While at times Gregory of Nyssa appeared to suggest a chain of causal dependency, Gregory Nazianzus corrected him, and both stressed that the relations of origin (begetting and procession) refer to the relations between the persons in eternity. The theme present in Athanasius, taken up by the two Gregorys, that the Son is all that the Father is except for being the Father, entails the full status of deity *a se* ("of himself"). Gregory of Nazianzus could not have been more emphatic on the point.[27] Even statements in the Niceno-Constantinopolitan Creed ("light of light," "true God of true God") taken by some to refer to remnants of subordination[28] are understood by contemporaries and the tradition to refer to the *homoousion*.[29] It follows that all the divine attributes are possessed comprehensively by all three persons. The Son is fully, comprehensively, exhaustively God.

Hypostatic Distinctions

Stephen Holmes remarks that "the three divine *hypostases* are distinguished by eternal relations of origin—begetting and

26. Gregory of Nyssa, *Against Eunomius*, 1.19; *NPNF*², 5:57; Gregory of Nyssa, *On the Holy Spirit Against the Macedonians*, 6; *NPNF*², 5:317; Gregory of Nazianzus, *Oration 29*, 17; *NPNF*², 7:307; *Oration 31*, 14; *NPNF*², 7:322; *St. Gregory of Nazianzus: On God and Christ: The Five Theological Orations and Two Letters to Cledonius*, trans. Frederick Williams and Lionel Wickham (St. Vladimir's Seminary Press, 2002), 84–85, 127–28; Lewis Ayres, *Augustine and the Trinity* (Cambridge University Press, 2010), 208–16.

27. Gregory Nazianzus, *Oration 30*, 20; *PG*, 36:128–32; *Oration 31*, 14, 16; *PG*, 36:148–52; *Oration on Holy Baptism 40*, 43; *PG*, 36:420–21.

28. B. B. Warfield, "The Biblical Doctrine of the Trinity," in *Biblical and Theological Studies* (Presbyterian and Reformed, 1952), 51–59.

29. Gregory of Nyssa, *Against Eunomius*, 3.4; Photius, *On the Mystagogy of the Holy Spirit* (Studion, 1983).

proceeding—and not otherwise."[30] That is to say, all that we are given to know of the personal distinctions is that the Father begets the Son, the Son is begotten of the Father, and the Spirit proceeds from the Father and the Son (or from the Father, in the eyes of the Eastern church). That is all. All we know of the Son's relations is that he is begotten of the Father and shares with the Father in the spiration of the Spirit.

In reference to the immanent Trinity, this is correct, but as an absolute statement it needs some nuancing. The missions in human history disclose significant distinctions between the three that reflect back on the immanent relations. There is a difference between the Son's becoming permanently incarnate and the Spirit's appearing temporarily as a dove.[31] The Son took human nature into personal, hypostatic union, whereas the Spirit indwells the church. The Father neither is sent nor proceeds. These clear differences indicate eternal distinctions. God acts in all things in ways compatible with his nature, suggesting that the distinct ways in which the Son works in creation compared with the way that the Spirit operates reflect distinct features in their internal relations. Yet since all three persons act together in all of God's works, these distinctions are not divisions. They point to harmony and indivisibility together; they are distinctions of congruity. Brian Davies refers to Thomas Aquinas's conviction that since God is simple, and the relations between the persons are real, as are the distinctions, not existing merely in our minds, it follows that they are coextensive with God's essence, with who God is.[32] We will consider later whether any of the three could have become incarnate. The argument here (not mine alone, of course) suggests that it would not have been appropriate for the Father to have been sent, or the Spirit to have taken permanent bodily form.

30. S. R. Holmes, *The Holy Trinity: Understanding God's Life* (Paternoster, 2012), 200. "Personae enim divinae, quum in essentia conveniant, non possunt distingui nisi per relationem originis." Thomas Aquinas, *SCG*, 4.26.

31. See Augustine, *De trinitate*, 2.6.11; Hill, *Augustine: The Trinity*, 104–5.

32. Thomas Aquinas, *ST*, 1a.28.1–3; cf. 1a.28–32; Brian Davies, *Thomas Aquinas's* Summa theologiae*: A Guide and Commentary* (Oxford University Press, 2014), 100–101. Also Aquinas, *SCG*, 4.2–26; Brian Davies, *Thomas Aquinas's* Summa contra Gentiles*: A Guide and a Commentary* (Oxford University Press, 2016), 300–304.

Order—the ταξις (*Taxis*)[33]

In terms of the *relations* between the three, a clear order occurs throughout the Bible: *from the Father through the Son by the Holy Spirit*. These relations cannot be reversed—the Son does not beget the Father any more than the Spirit begets the Son. In this sense only, the Father is the first, the Son the second, and the Holy Spirit the third.

T. F. Torrance argued that Gregory of Nazianzus regarded the monarchy (the one eternal source of the persons) to be that of the whole Trinity.[34] But the evidence must be qualified. Some passages seem to support the case, but others do not. T. A. Noble highlights a distinction that Gregory makes that explains his own apparent ambiguity. On the one hand, the monarchy resides in the whole Trinity—being indivisible—but the Father is the *principium* in terms of the hypostatic relations.[35] These two perspectives are not contradictory, since they refer to distinct aspects. Indeed, Torrance's own support for the claim was on the grounds that all three persons are coequally God, while retaining the distinctive relations for the persons in a similar way to Gregory, who also held to the monarchy of the Father.[36]

Though the three persons are identical with the divine essence, they are not identical to one another. Modalism confused the persons, conflated or identified them; this confusion continues to surface whenever the personal distinctions are in any way blurred or confined

33. The word ταξις has a range of meanings. It was often used in military contexts and had the idea of rank, entailing a hierarchy of some kind. This fitted in well with the Arian view of a gradation between the Father and the Son, with the latter of a lower and subordinate status. But it was also used of role, office, class, orderliness and regularity of the stars, order in the church or monastery, or an ordered constitution. It is in the sense of order, not rank, closer to what is fitting and suitable rather than any hierarchy, that the Orthodox use the term. See G. W. H. Lampe, ed., *A Patristic Greek Lexicon* (Clarendon Press, 1961), 1372–73.

34. Torrance, *Christian Doctrine of God*, 180–85.

35. T. A. Noble, "Paradox in Gregory Nazianzen's Doctrine of the Trinity," *StPatr* 27 (1993): 94–99. See also John Calvin, *Institutes*, 1.13.18–20; Gregory of Nazianzus, *Oration 29*, 2, 15; *PG*, 36:76, 93; *Oration 31*, 13f.; *PG*, 36:148f.

36. Torrance, *Christian Doctrine of God*, 180–85; Christopher A. Beeley, *Gregory of Nazianzus on the Trinity and the Knowledge of God: In Your Light Shall We See Light* (Oxford University Press, 2008), 206–10.

to human history. Thus, in orthodox Trinitarian doctrine, the Son is identical to the divine essence and so is one with the Father in the indivisible Trinity. He is not the Father, however, and the Father is not the Son. Moreover, the *relations* that the three sustain to one another are inseparable from their identity and so are eternal and unchangeable. Thus, the Father is the Father of the Son, and the Son is the Son of the Father and is so for eternity. The Father begets the Son; the Son is begotten by the Father. This relation is neither interchangeable nor reversible—it is eternal and unchangeable.[37] The Father neither is begotten nor proceeds, the Son neither begets nor proceeds, while the Spirit neither begets nor spirates. These relations exist together with the mutual indwelling of the three (*perichoresis*). Indeed, the Spirit is the Spirit of the Son, and so by the same token the Father is the Father of the Son, while the three persons mutually indwell one another, and thus the relations of the Father and the Son are in the Holy Spirit.[38] There is a distinction—not a division—between the three as they distinctly and together constitute the one undivided being of God and the three in their eternal and distinct personal relations. Since there is only one being of God consisting of the three persons, generation concerns the relations of the Father and the Son. Since the Father's being is the one being of God, however, the monarchy can also be said to be that of the whole Trinity. John Calvin sums this up when he says of the Son that he is God of himself (*ex seipso esse*), whereas in terms of his personal subsistence he is from the Father (*ex Patre*).[39]

Thus, the Father allows the Son to bring in the kingdom, while the Son leads us to the Father and the Spirit does not speak of himself

37. *Mutatis mutandis*, the Spirit proceeds from the Father (the West adds "and the Son"), while the Father (and the Son, according to the West) spirates the Spirit. This is never reversed.

38. All the intra-Trinitarian relations entail the mutual indwelling of all three.

39. Calvin, *Institutes*, 1.13.25; cf. 1.13.17–19. For an extensive and, to my mind, definitive assessment of Calvin's assertion that the Son is *autotheos* (God of himself), together with comprehensive discussion of secondary literature, see Richard A. Muller, "Trinity and the Son's Aseity: Formulation and Debate in Calvin and Reformed Orthodoxy," in *Understanding the Divine in Early Modern Reformed Theology* (Reformation Heritage Books, 2024), 71–131. Especially important is the distinction drawn in Reformed orthodoxy, which Muller highlights, between generation and communication of essence.

but testifies of the Son.[40] This was originally articulated by Gregory of Nyssa when he wrote that in their mutual indwelling, the three seek the glory of the others. There is, he says, "a revolving circle of glory from like to like. The Son is glorified by the Spirit; the Father is glorified by the Son; again the Son has his glory from the Father; and the Only-begotten thus becomes the glory of the Spirit. . . . In like manner . . . faith completes the circle, and glorifies the Son by means of the Spirit, and the Father by means of the Son."[41]

Eternal Generation

Since Irenaeus in the second century, the church has held that the Father begat the Son in eternity. This comes to expression in C and is repeated in later confessions.[42] This doctrine has come under fire on both biblical and theological grounds. Since the nineteenth century, many New Testament scholars have held that this teaching does not find biblical support, since the word *monogenēs* (translated "only-begotten" in older New Testament translations) means "only" or "one and only." It is also held that the passage in Psalm 2:7, "You are my Son; this day I have begotten you," is quoted in the New Testament with reference to Jesus' resurrection (Acts 13:33) and so does not refer to the relation between the Father and the Son in eternity. From the theological angle, it is argued that the eternal generation of the Son implies a subordinate status for the Son, and that its roots are neo-Platonic. Similar arguments have been advanced on the eternal procession of the Holy Spirit.

I have discussed this question in some detail elsewhere.[43] In recent years, there has been a movement back to the traditional doctrine.[44] The second Council of Constantinople in 553 anathematized

40. Wolfhart Pannenberg, *Systematic Theology*, trans. Geoffrey W. Bromiley (Eerdmans, 1991), 1:315–17.

41. Gregory of Nyssa, *On the Holy Spirit Against the Macedonians*, 24; *NPNF*², 5:324.

42. WCF 2.3; WLC 10.

43. Letham, *Holy Trinity*, 193–201.

44. Fred Sanders and Scott R. Swain, eds., *Retrieving Eternal Generation* (Zondervan, 2017).

those who disputed it.[45] As Herman Bavinck wrote, creation would not have been possible if the Father did not beget the Son.[46] Eternal generation signifies that God is infinitely brimful of life, for he is life itself. The Father's generation of the Son in eternity is the ground for his free and sovereign decision to create other entities and grant them contingent life, and his determination to offer everlasting life in Christ to his chosen people. Without it there would be no gospel to proclaim; to reject it is heresy.[47]

Let us look first at the biblical criticisms, although the doctrine neither was developed on those grounds nor is hostage to the meaning of any one word or to biblical exegesis alone. It is a theological predicate grounded in the eternal relations of the Son and the Father in the one being of God.

The idea emerged in the last century that *monogenēs* in the New Testament meant simply "one and only." Yet as I have pointed out elsewhere, its occurrence in soteriological passages in John is invariably in conjunction with the (re)generation of believers. The verb *gennaō* ("to beget" or "to give birth") is used in each such context (John 1:14, 18; 3:16, 18; 1 John 4:9; 5:18).[48] Arguments that the reference to Psalm 2:7 ("You are my Son; today I have begotten you") in Acts 13:33 is to the resurrection of Christ beg the question. While that is the immediate application in Acts, it does not require limitation to that alone. Support has been recently reinforced by the outstanding contributions of Lee Irons, D. A. Carson, and Kevin Giles.[49]

45. Richard Price, trans., *The Acts of the Council of Constantinople of 553* (Liverpool University Press, 2009), 2:120.

46. Herman Bavinck, *RD*, 2:308–10.

47. Robert Letham, "The Trinity: The Doctrine of God and the Pulpit," in *Theology for Ministry: How Doctrine Affects Pastoral Life and Practice*, ed. William R. Edwards, John C. A. Ferguson, and Chad Van Dixhoorn (P&R Publishing, 2022), 25–35; Price, *Constantinople 553*, 2:120.

48. Letham, *Systematic Theology*, 115–17; Letham, *Holy Trinity*, 194–98.

49. D. A. Carson, "John 5:26: *Crux Interpretum* for Eternal Generation," in *Retrieving Eternal Generation*, ed. Fred Sanders and Scott R. Swain (Zondervan, 2017), 79–97; Charles Lee Irons, "A Lexical Defense of the Johannine 'Only-Begotten,'" in *Retrieving Eternal Generation*, ed. Fred Sanders and Scott R. Swain (Zondervan, 2017), 98–116; Kevin Giles, *The Eternal Generation of the Son: Maintaining Orthodoxy in Trinitarian Theology* (IVP Academic, 2012).

Additionally, criticisms have been made of eternal generation on theological grounds. It is claimed that the teaching posits a lesser status for the Son, as an emanation from the Father in neo-Platonic guise. But this is not how the framers of C understood the matter,[50] for they consistently urge that all ideas of human generation be removed from the picture. Human begetting entails sexual passion and a beginning of existence, for human fathers exist before their sons are begotten. This is not the case here. The Father is always the Father, the Son is always the Son, and their relation is self-evidently devoid of passion.[51] The consistent stress is that generation entails distinction of person but identity of nature, for the Son is the same nature, or being, as the Father.

Entailments

As Bavinck states, "God's fecundity is a beautiful theme." He argues that the doctrine of the generation of the Son displays God as "no abstract, fixed, monadic, solitary substance, but a plenitude of life. It is his nature to be generative and fruitful."[52] Indeed, "without generation, creation would not be possible. If, in an absolute sense, God could not communicate himself to the Son, he would be even less able, in a relative sense, to communicate himself to his creature."[53] In this, Bavinck reflects the classic Trinitarian doctrine that the persons are oriented to the other. This relationality underlies God's free determination to create—an act of his will, exercised in harmony with his nature.[54]

50. Cf. Gregory of Nyssa, *Against Eunomius*, 3.4.

51. Peter Widdicombe, *The Fatherhood of God from Origen to Athanasius* (Clarendon Press, 1994), 85–86. On the eternal generation of the Son and its application to the relations of the persons, not the divine essence, see Francis Turretin, *Institutes of Elenctic Theology*, ed. James T. Dennison (P&R Publishing, 1992), 1:278–302, esp. 292–302.

52. Bavinck, *RD*, 2:308.

53. Bavinck, *RD*, 2:420.

54. This connection between the generation of the Son and creation has also been considered by Aquinas, *ST*, 1a.14.8, 19.1–4; Hans Urs von Balthasar, *Theo-Drama: Theological Dramatic Theory*, trans. Graham Harrison (Ignatius Press, 1994), 4:323–31. See Eugene R. Schlesinger, "Trinity, Incarnation and Time: A Restatement of the Doctrine of God in Conversation with Robert Jenson," *SJT* 69, no. 2 (May 2016): 189–213, esp. 200.

Generation is ineffable and incomparable. It reflects the incomprehensibility of God and is a transcendent mystery, beyond the grasp of our minds. This was uniformly recognized by the church fathers. The idea that they were given to speculation is not borne out by the sources.

Generation is contrasted to creation. "Begotten, not created," as the hymn runs.[55] This was the basic issue in the Trinitarian crisis, the one foremost for Athanasius. Eternal generation obviates any notion of the Son as a creature.

With identity of nature, generation asserts personal distinction. So as Aquinas says, the Father is other than the Son but not something else, while they are one thing but not one person.[56] The Father is the principle (*principium*), citing Augustine,[57] "that whence another proceeds." Aquinas argues against calling the Father the cause of the Son, since it implies diversity of substance, but *principle* entails simply an order between them, a procession and no inferiority. The word does not signify priority but origin.[58]

Generation thus highlights an irreversible hypostatic order. While the New Testament refers to the three persons in differing orders (Matt. 28:19–20; 1 Cor. 12:4–6; 2 Cor. 13:14; Eph. 4:4–6; Rev. 1:4–5), yet a general pattern is evident throughout the economy of creation, providence, and grace: from the Father through the Son by the Spirit (Matt. 28:19). In turn, our response to God's grace is enabled by the Spirit, offered through the Son, and resting on the Father (Eph. 2:18). God's revelation in human history reflects eternal antecedent realities in himself. The missions concern the sendings of both the Son and the Spirit in an economic, historical sense and reflect the eternal processions.

Eternal generation is indispensable to the doctrine of the Trinity. As Bavinck puts it, "rejection of the eternal generation of the Son involves not only a failure to do justice to the deity of the Son, but also

55. Attributed to John Francis Wade, "O Come, All Ye Faithful" (1751), trans. Frederick Oakeley (1841).

56. Aquinas, *ST*, 1.31.2.

57. Augustine, *De trinitate*, 4.20.

58. Aquinas, *ST*, 1.33.1.; Calvin, *Institutes*, 1.13.18.

to that of the Father," and "It is not something that was completed and finished at some point in eternity, but an eternal unchanging act of God, at once always complete and eternally ongoing. . . . The Father is not and never was ungenerative; he begets everlastingly."[59]

Perichoresis

This idea was developed, and the term introduced, by John of Damascus in the eighth century.[60] Although this precise word, referring to the mutual indwelling of the three in the one indivisible essence, is not used in Trinitarian discourse until then, the truth it signifies was already in vogue. It is already entailed in the pervasive reference to the three persons as indivisible, their union unbreakable. Athanasius and the Cappadocians had brought to the forefront the idea of the full mutual indwelling of the three persons in the one being of God. It is entailed by all that C expresses. It follows from the *homoousial* identity of the three and the indivisible divine being. Since all three persons are fully God and the whole God is in each of the three, the three mutually contain one another. As Gerald Bray puts it, all three occupy the same infinite divine space.[61] Here divine and human persons differ, as the *Leiden Synopsis* explains. Human persons do not exist in one another.[62] As human beings, we are not only distinct but apart. We act differently, we go our separate ways, and some are healthy and live a long time, while others die young. Moreover, there are a huge number of different human beings, and the sum total increases or diminishes as time goes by. But the divine persons are three, no more and no less, and are so eternally without change.

This is in contrast to some modern uses of *perichoresis*, in support of social Trinitarianism, in which the three hypostases are likened to human persons dancing around one another. Here the Trinitarian hypostases are understood in terms of human realities, the same

59. Bavinck, *RD*, 2:310.

60. Charles C. Twombly, *Perichoresis and Personhood: God, Christ, and Salvation in John of Damascus* (Pickwick Publications, 2015).

61. Gerald Bray, *The Doctrine of God* (Inter-Varsity Press, 1993), 158.

62. Johannes Polyander, *Synopsis Purioris Theologiae, Disputationibus Quinquaginta Duabus Comprehensa* (Leiden: Ex Officina Elzeverianus, 1625), 77.

process as the Arians adopted. In this case, the result is a loose view of divine unity that can border on tritheism.[63]

Inseparable Works

This theme is a constant leitmotif in the fourth- and fifth-century pro-Nicenes of both Greek and Latin churches.[64] From it comes the phrase *opera trinitatis ad extra indivisa sunt* ("the external works of the Trinity are indivisible"). Since God is one indivisible being, in all his works all three persons operate inseparably.

Creation was a work of the whole Trinity. Genesis 1:1–5 hints at that—"in the beginning, God created. . . . The Spirit of God was hovering over the waters. . . . And God said." There is God, the Spirit, and the Word of God. The same idea surfaces in Psalm 33:6–9, reinforced by the New Testament teaching on Christ and the Spirit (John 1:1–3; Col. 1:15–17; Heb. 1:1–3). It is true too with providence. The incarnation involved the Father's sending the Son (John 3:16–17; 5:23–24, 37–39) and the Son's taking human nature into union, conceived by the Holy Spirit (Luke 1:34–35). At Jesus' baptism, the Father speaks, declaring him to be his Son, while the Spirit descends as a dove and rests upon him (Matt. 3:13–17). On the cross, the Son offered himself through the eternal Spirit to the Father (Heb. 9:14), and was raised from the dead by the Spirit of the Father (Rom. 8:10–11). This is underlined by Paul as he surveys the whole field of redemption (Gal. 4:4–6; Eph. 1:3–14). Thus we have access to God the Trinity, by the Spirit through Christ to the Father (Eph. 2:18).

Inseparable Operations and Distinct Appropriations

The inseparability of the Trinitarian actions was a major theme of Augustine, but it was also held by the Cappadocians.[65] Augustine

63. Catherine Mowry La Cugna, *God for Us: The Trinity and Christian Life* (Harper, 1991); Jürgen Moltmann, *The Trinity and the Kingdom: The Doctrine of God* (SCM, 1991).

64. Athanasius, *Letters to Serapion*, 1.17–18, 28, 30–31; Didymus the Blind, *On the Holy Spirit*, 75–80; Gregory of Nazianzus, *Oration 31*; Gregory of Nyssa, *On "Not Three Gods"*; Augustine, *De trinitate*, 1–2, 6.

65. Augustine, *On the Gospel of John*, 20.3, 8; *NPNF*[1], 7:132, 134; *Letter 169 to Evodius*, 2.5–7; *NPNF*[1], 1:540–41.

strenuously affirms that "just as Father and Son and Holy Spirit are inseparable, so do they work inseparably."[66] Yet as the three are eternally distinct, each work is specifically attributed (or *appropriated*) to one of them. The Son was sent by the Father, conceived by the Spirit, but only he became flesh. Only the Spirit was sent at Pentecost, while sent by the Father and the Son. In Augustine's words, "although in all things the Divine Persons act perfectly in common, and without possibility of separation, nevertheless their operations behoved to be exhibited in such a way as to be distinguished from each other."[67] We might say that they work in harmony rather than in unison.

Congruity Between the Processions and the Missions

The sending by the Father of the Son in human history (the missions) is distinguishable from the missions' eternal antecedent relations (the processions). The eternal relations are necessary; they cannot have been otherwise. That is the way that God is in himself. The missions are not necessary; God could have decreed not to create and, having created, not to redeem by sending the Son and the Spirit. Yet at the same time, the missions reflect the processions, since God always acts in keeping with who he is.[68] Gilles Emery writes of "a profound correspondence between . . . the eternal property of the Son and the Holy Spirit and . . . their visible missions."[69]

This brings us to the relationship between the Son in eternity and in human history, between his relation to the Father in the indivisible Trinity and his mission here for us and our salvation. Emery comments: "The patristic and medieval tradition will be especially attentive to the correspondence between the sending of the Son into the world and his eternal origin: in the same way that the Son is sent by the Father, he has his existence from the Father. In other words, when Trinitarian doctrine speaks of the divine person in terms of

66. Augustine, *De trinitate*, 1.4.7; Hill, *Augustine: The Trinity*, 70.

67. Augustine, *Letter 11 to Nebridius*, 4; *NPNF*[1], 1:230.

68. See Aquinas, *ST*, 1a.43.2.

69. Gilles Emery, *The Trinity: An Introduction to Catholic Doctrine on the Triune God* (Catholic University of America Press, 2011), 183.

'relation of origin,' it is not a speculation detached from the economy of salvation, but rather it proposes a doctrine grounded on the teaching of the Gospels about Jesus, whose existence is always relative to his Father. The *mystery* of the Father and the Son is present and revealed in the *economy*."[70] So Emery adds: "This teaching makes manifest a profound correspondence between, on the one hand, the eternal property of the Son and the Holy Spirit and, on the other hand, their 'visible mission.' The Son is begotten from all eternity by the Father. As Son, he receives from the Father his being the principle of the Holy Spirit, along with the Father: with the Father, the Son spirates the Holy Spirit. It therefore pertains to the Son, in his very quality as Son, to be sent by the Father as *Author of sanctification*—that is to say, as *Giver of the Holy Spirit*. This is a dimension of the 'fittingness' of the Son's incarnation that we discover here."[71]

Aquinas comments that sending does not imply inferiority but rather procession of origin, which is according to equality.[72] Since mission is according to procession of origin, and the Father is the principle of the Trinity and is not from another, "in no way is it fitting for him to be sent."[73] Thus also the missions of the Son and the Holy Spirit are distinct, as generation is distinguished from procession.[74]

This highlights the connection between the immanent Trinity (what God is in himself) and the economic Trinity (how he acts in this world), which are simply concepts for our own benefit, since there is only one Trinity. If the economic Trinity, the Trinity as revealed in history, did not reveal the immanent Trinity, we would have no true knowledge of God and could not be saved. There can be no possibility of God's being other than what he has revealed himself to be.

The Monarchy

The Eastern church has typically been seen as basing its Trinitarian doctrine on the Father as the source of the personal subsistence of

70. Emery, *Trinity*, 27.
71. Emery, *Trinity*, 183–84 (italics original).
72. Aquinas, *ST*, 1.43.1.
73. Aquinas, *ST*, 1.34.4.
74. Aquinas, *ST*, 1.43.5.

the Son and the Spirit, in contrast to the Western stress on the unity of the one divine essence. This characterization is overdone; both hold to the indivisibility of the Trinity, and both regard the Father as the *arche* (East) or *principium* (West).[75]

Among the Cappadocians, for Gregory of Nazianzus this was the fundamental element of his theological system.[76] In Christopher Beeley's words, "the unity or oneness of the Trinity . . . is constituted by the Father's begetting of the Son and sending forth of the Spirit." Reflecting on the confusion among some modern historians and theologians, who think that the monarchy of the Father, the generation of the Son, and the procession of the Spirit conflict *a priori* with their unity and equality in being,[77] Beeley argues: "To put it more sharply, Gregory is firmly rejecting the notion that the monarchy of the Father in any way conflicts with the equality of the three persons—on the grounds that it is precisely what brings about that equality!"[78]

> Of the Father's love begotten, ere the worlds began to be,
> he is Alpha and Omega, he the Source, the Ending he,
> of the things that are, that have been, and that future years shall see,
> *evermore and evermore!*
>
> O that birth forever blessed, when the Virgin, full of grace,
> by the Holy Ghost conceiving, bore the Savior of our race;
> and the babe, the world's Redeemer, first revealed his sacred face,
> *evermore and evermore!*
>
> This is he whom heav'n-taught singers sang of old with one accord,
> whom the Scriptures of the prophets promised in their faithful
> word;
> now he shines, the long-expected; let creation praise its Lord,
> *evermore and evermore!*

75. On Augustine and the Trinitarian ταξις and the Father as *principium*, see Ayres, *Augustine and the Trinity*, 178–83, 263–65.

76. Gregory of Nazianzus, *Oration* 25, 15–18; Beeley, *Gregory of Nazianzus*, 206.

77. Beeley, *Gregory of Nazianzus*, 209.

78. Beeley, *Gregory of Nazianzus*, 210.

O ye heights of heav'n, adore him; angel hosts, his praises sing;
all dominions, bow before him and extol our God and King;
let no tongue on earth be silent, ev'ry voice in concert ring,
evermore and evermore!

Christ, to thee, with God the Father, and, O Holy Ghost, to thee,
hymn, and chant, and high thanksgiving, and unwearied praises be,
honor, glory, and dominion, and eternal victory,
evermore and evermore![79]

79. Aurelius Clemens Prudentius (348–413), "Of the Father's Love Begotten," trans. John Mason Neale (1854); trans. Henry W. Baker (1859); tune: DIVINUM MYSTERIUM (plainsong, 12th cent.).

2

Before the Beginning

This is the great and hidden mystery. This is the blessed end for which all things were brought into existence. This is the divine purpose conceived before the beginning of beings, . . . the preconceived goal for the sake of which everything exists, but which itself exists on account of nothing, . . . a super-infinite plan infinitely pre-existing the ages.
(Maximus the Confessor, Ad Thalassium 60.3[1]*)*

External Works

We are now thinking of the external works of God, those decisions and actions he has made that relate to creation, to his relationships with all other entities, all of which he had freely brought into existence. In this, he is entirely independent of those entities, all his actions being constrained by nothing other than his sovereign will. Here the Son acts in indivisible union with the Father and the Holy Spirit; the external works of the Trinity are inseparable. The Son does not act by himself, apart from the Father and the Spirit.

As we discussed in chapter 1, all three persons operate in one harmonious and inseparable manner. This is evident in creation, providence, and grace. All three were integrally involved in creation (Gen. 1:1–3). In the beginning God created (v. 1), while the Spirit of God was hovering over the waters (v. 2) and the Word of God initiated

1. Maximos Constas, trans., *St. Maximos the Confessor: On Difficulties in Sacred Scripture: The Responses to Thalassios* (Catholic University of America Press, 2018), 428–29.

light (v. 3). The plural "let us make man" in verses 26–27 indicates the same for the creation of humans, male and female. The establishment of the cosmos is ascribed to the entire Trinity (Ps. 33:6–9).

In terms of grace, Paul unfolds the entire panorama of redemption as Trinitarian action (Eph. 1:3–14). The incarnation of the Son was in accordance with the Father's sending him and the Spirit's effecting his conception (Matt. 1:18–25; Luke 1:34–35; John 5:24–30; 6:37–40). At his crucifixion, the Son offered himself through the eternal Spirit to the Father (Heb. 9:14). The Father raised the Son from the dead by the Spirit (Rom. 8:10–11). The risen Son ascended to the Father, there to pour out the Spirit on his people (Luke 24:50–51; Acts 1:6–8; 2:33–36). These are merely sample passages; we could add many more. I have discussed this in some detail elsewhere.[2]

Trinitarian action comes to particular expression in predestination and election. In Ephesians 1:3–4, Paul writes that the Father chose us in Christ before the foundation of the world, granting us in Christ every spiritual blessing in the heavenly places. This latter phrase, in accordance with Paul's characteristic usage,[3] refers to the blessings granted by the Spirit; acute questions arise here of the relation between time and eternity.

Time and Eternity

There are a range of conceptual conundrums that we need to work out as far as we are able. One immediately obvious problem for us is the relationship between eternity, the realm of God, and time, which applies to the whole creation and all entities in it. Connected to this is the vast gulf between God's knowledge, which encompasses everything in instantaneous cognition, and our own time-bound and limited minds. Needless to say, much as we would like to do so, we cannot solve all these issues now![4] As Augustine wrote:

2. Robert Letham, *The Holy Trinity: In Scripture, History, Theology, and Worship*, rev. and expanded ed. (P&R Publishing, 2019), 25–84.

3. Paul does not write in terms of a material versus spiritual contrast, nor does he deal in an ill-defined "spirituality." When he uses πνεῦμα or its derivatives, he almost invariably refers to the Holy Spirit or to the Spirit's work.

4. I am tempted to say, jocularly, "give us time!" In reality, this is a matter inseparable from our created nature; we cannot transcend it.

> It is not as if the knowledge of God were of various kinds, knowing in different ways things which as yet are not, things which are, and things which have been. For not in our fashion does he look forward to that which is future, nor at what is present, nor back upon what is past; but in a manner quite different and far and profoundly remote from our way of thinking. For he does not pass from this to that by transition or thought, but beholds all things with absolute unchangeableness; so that of those things which emerge in time, the future, indeed, are not yet, and the present are now, and the past no longer are; but all of these are by him comprehended in his stable and eternal presence. Nor does he see in one fashion by the eye, in another by the mind, for he is not composed of mind and body; nor does his present knowledge differ from that which it ever was or shall be, for those variations of time, past, present, and future, though they alter our knowledge, do not affect his, "with whom is no variableness, neither shadow of turning."[5]

So this, from our limited perspective, poses problems. The Christian tradition has overwhelmingly considered that God is eternal, without time or temporal sequence. This is exceedingly difficult, well-nigh impossible, to get our heads around.

Paul Helm remarks: "It makes no sense to suppose that one can ask what happened before the universe existed, and hope to get an answer which specifies some other event or events. There comes a point when such questions are logically odd, inappropriate because although the question can be framed there could not be an answer to it. Such logical inappropriateness in this case signals the limit, or one of the limits, of the universe."[6] Recognizing these limits, Helm continues: "The concept of foreknowledge applies not to a timeless knower's knowledge of certain events or actions, but to a temporal agent's recognition of timeless knowledge under certain temporal circumstances. What is it that the timeless knowledge is before? It cannot be before anything for the timeless knower, for for him

5. Augustine, *City of God*, 11.21; *NPNF*[1], 2:216.

6. Paul Helm, *Eternal God: A Study of God Without Time* (Clarendon Press, 1988), 68–69.

there is no temporal before or after, since he occupies no position in time."[7] Further, "in a similar way . . . it will not do to claim that for a timeless knower every event is simultaneous with every other event. For simultaneity is a temporal relation, or can be."[8] Helm suggests that "it makes sense to speak of a timeless knower's foreknowledge of events where the notion of foreknowledge expresses a temporal knower's belief or recognition that certain events were known timelessly before this time" and that "if it is proper to speak of God's knowledge in this timeless way, then from the point in time of the temporal agent God knows beforehand."[9] If your head is spinning, don't worry; so is mine!

Indeed, Helm continues, "the extent to which divine timelessness can be articulated and defended against objections is both evidence for its intelligibility and also provides a refutation of [Immanuel] Kant's claim that intellectual attempts to transcend time and space generate antinomies. . . . The difficulty is real enough, but it need be no more intellectually embarrassing than is talk of unobservable electrons."[10] Finally, he concludes that "a more theocentric point of view than most of us habitually adopt in thinking about God would allow us to think of God accommodating himself to human time-bound and space-bound modes of thought."[11]

In short, thought on matters such as this requires of us a rigorous mental self-discipline in which, as T. F. Torrance frequently argued, we proceed from a center in God and his revelation. For the Christian tradition, the work of Augustine is foundational. Since he was, in some sense, building on similar lines to Irenaeus, Basil, and Gregory of Nyssa, as the leading representative of the Latin church he is in harmony with the Greek fathers here.

7. Helm, *Eternal God*, 98.

8. Helm, *Eternal God*, 100.

9. Helm, *Eternal God*, 101.

10. Helm, *Eternal God*, 107. As physicist Jonathan Humphreys observes in commenting on this quotation, electrons are observable through such things as the double-slit experiment, electron diffraction, and so on. We don't need to see them to know that they are there. I suggest that Helm's point is nonetheless valid despite the details.

11. Helm, *Eternal God*, 108.

Richard Sorabji notes the foundational point for Augustine that God is the sole Creator and everything continues to depend on him thereafter. He writes: "When a builder puts up a house and departs, his work remains in spite of the fact that he is no longer there. But the universe will pass away in the twinkling of an eye if God withdraws his ruling hand."[12] In a similar move to his famous psychological analogies for the Trinity in *De trinitate,* Augustine roots the question of time and eternity, of God and creation, in the human mind. In the eleventh chapter of the *Confessions,* he writes of the past, present, and future in terms of the triad memory-attention-expectation, treating time as three mental states that "can all be available at once as a *distentio* in the mind[, which] has the paradoxical effect of making time more like eternity. Time is frozen for inspection, and available all together." Notwithstanding, he actually intends to contrast God's eternity with our time. "Nor again does Augustine want to say that time is unreal."[13]

Sorabji comments that many of the church fathers "do not always have a very firm grasp of the idea of timelessness" and think more of God's existing through time without beginning or end—a literal reading of anthropomorphic expressions in the Bible, perhaps, one suggests. He adds that Augustine and Origen often speak in this way of foreknowledge, not of timeless knowledge. Nevertheless, Origen can say, "Wisdom is . . . believed to be begotten beyond the limits of any beginning that we can speak of or

12. Augustine, *De Genesi ad litteram,* 4.12.22; John Hammond Taylor, trans., *St. Augustine: The Literal Meaning of Genesis,* vol. 1, *Books 1–6* (Paulist Press, 1982), 117; Richard Sorabji, *Time, Creation, and the Continuum: Theories in Antiquity and the Early Middle Ages* (Cornell University Press, 1983), 303–4.

13. Augustine, *Confessions,* 11.20, 26; Sorabji, *Time,* 29–30. In *City of God,* 12.16, Augustine introduces the theory of angelic time, dependent on the mental movements of angels. This had surfaced earlier, expressed in *De Genesi ad littera liber imperfectus,* 3.8, and in *De Genesi ad litteram,* 5.5.12, in connection with the six days of creation. In his exposition of the chapter, angels alternate between seeing things as they are in themselves and as they exist in the wisdom of God. See Augustine, *De Genesi ad littera liber imperfectus,* 3.8; Roland J. Teske, *Saint Augustine on Genesis Against the Manichees, and On the Literal Interpretation of Genesis: An Unfinished Book,* Fathers of the Church 84 (Catholic University of America Press, 1991), 149–51; Augustine, *De Genesi,* 5.5.12; Sorabji, *Time,* 31.

understand."[14] Moreover, Sorabji points out that in the *Confessions*, Augustine made eternity exclude duration, as Gregory of Nyssa had done. In eternity, everything is present *totum praesens* (11.11). God's years stand all together (*anni tui omnes simul stant*) (11.13). There can be no succession in God's Word, but all is spoken together (*simul*) (11.7).[15] Hence, there was no time before creation (11.13, 30). God created time when he created movement (12.8–12, 19), since it makes no sense to speak of time when there is no movement.[16] Sorabji considers that this "is the best of the solutions offered by Jews and Christians." Others, such as Origen, held that God had created a world of patterns, outside time, grasped only by the mind. Irenaeus simply confessed that these are things that we cannot know.[17]

The idea that time began with the cosmos goes back to Plato and was mediated via Philo. Ambrose took it up,[18] but earlier Athanasius,[19] Basil,[20] and Gregory of Nyssa[21] held to it. Gregory wrote, in Sorabji's précis, "God is prior to all time, and where there is no time questions of earlier and later make no sense." It is doubtful whether Augustine had access to Gregory, however, and besides, the work from which the quotation arose had not yet been translated into Latin.[22]

Thomas Aquinas has an interesting discussion in both his *Summa theologiae* and his *Summa contra Gentiles*. He did not think that it could be logically established that the universe had a beginning, although he himself believed that it did. Nevertheless, he concluded that nothing stands in the way of holding that the world has not always existed, which he acknowledges the Roman church affirms is the case.[23]

14. Origen, *On First Principles*, 1.2.2; John Behr, ed. and trans., *Origen: On First Principles: A Reader's Edition* (Oxford University Press, 2019), 21–22; Sorabji, *Time*, 123.

15. Sorabji, *Time*, 124.

16. Sorabji, *Time*, 233.

17. Irenaeus, *Against Heresies*, 2.28.3; Sorabji, *Time*, 234.

18. Ambrose, *De fide*, 1.2; *NPNF*², 10:203.

19. Athanasius, *Orations Against the Arians*, 1.12–13; *NPNF*², 4:333–43.

20. Basil of Caesarea, *The Hexaemeron*, 1.6; *NPNF*², 8:54–55.

21. Gregory of Nyssa, *Against Eunomius*, 1.8; *NPNF*², 5:35–100.

22. Gregory of Nyssa, *Against Eunomius*, 9.2; *NPNF*², 5:214; *PG*, 45:809b–c; Sorabji, *Time*, 235.

23. Thomas Aquinas, *SCG*, 2.32–38; Brian Davies, *Thomas Aquinas's* Summa contra Gentiles*: A Guide and a Commentary* (Oxford University Press, 2016), 154–60, 166–68; Aquinas, *ST*, 1.46.a1.

Sorabji quotes Anthony Kenny, who in commenting on Nelson Pike's book *God's Timelessness* (London 1970) wrote, "I agree with the general conclusion of Pike's book which is that the doctrine of the timelessness of God is theologically unimportant and inessential to the tradition of western theism."[24] This, to my mind, is highly questionable. Given that temporality entails change, the doctrine of God's timelessness is built on the premise of the immutability and also the simplicity of God, both of which, individually and together, are foundational to Christian doctrine.

Sorabji concludes: "It only needs to be spelled out a little more explicitly that talk of a beginning of time or of motion does not imply some earlier *time* at which they were absent. At most it implies the *absence* of any earlier time at which they were present. Augustine actually discusses the absurd suggestion that there was a time when there was no time. But he points out that this absurdity does not follow from the suggestion that time began, but only from the different, and absurd, suggestion that time has not existed for all time." In the same place, Sorabji refers to Richard Swinburne's remarking to him that there is no clear way to express time's beginning. Can any sense be attached to such an idea? Sorabji states that it depends on other factors—whether we are convinced that time must be accompanied by change or whether we are convinced by the sense of talking of a first change.[25] Earlier he reflected: "It turns out to be very hard to define time without making some reference to change. But we must be very careful to consider whether the reference implies that time requires actual change or only the possibility of change."[26]

It seems to me that change is inherent to time: there is movement from one day to the next, from one rotation of the earth to another. The basic considerations here are, first, that God is immutable, for any change would entail at least one state of imperfection, movement either to or from a condition less than the other. Immutability is also

24. Anthony Kenny, *The God of the Philosophers* (Clarendon Press, 1979), 40, quoted in Sorabji, *Time*, 253.

25. Sorabji, *Time*, 280.

26. Sorabji, *Time*, 80–81.

demanded by the faithfulness of God. The second foundational axiom is that change is inherent to the cosmos, for it is dependent on God at every moment. Since creation entails contingency and change, time follows. This makes reflection on God's eternity and what has been revealed as occurring in that realm more than difficult to grasp.

James Cassidy argues that for Karl Barth, reconciliation of the problem of time and eternity "is found, of course, in Jesus Christ, who fulfills *both ends* of the covenant—as the eternal electing God and the temporal elected man."[27] Cassidy also states an important point—although it is not clear whether it is his comment, or his reflection on Barth, or a quoted remark by Eunsoo Kim—to the effect that "time is not an entity that has an independent existence with and alongside of God. God is the Lord of our time and thus surrounds it."[28] Could not one say that the same could be applied to eternity? Eternity is not some abstract entity that has existence alongside God to which he in some sense conforms. There is God—the Father, the Son, and the Holy Spirit—and the whole creation, which he brought into existence, including its movement and time. God self-evidently transcends the creation and time while being Lord of it all and pervading it, while granting it its own distinct existence, its space and time. This conundrum is no problem to him.[29]

I have every confidence that many would agree with H. R. Mackintosh, who commented that "we need have no hesitation in confessing that the preexistence of Christ outstrips our faculty of conception. . . . Christ cannot after all be pre-existent in any sense except that in which God himself is so relatively to the incarnation."[30] I'd suggest that the water is muddied considerably by expressions often heard in popular circles such as "eternity past" and "eternity future," which are little more than meaningless nonsense.

27. James J. Cassidy, *God's Time for Us: Barth's Reconciliation of Eternity and Time in Jesus Christ* (Lexham Press, 2016), 20 (italics original).

28. Cassidy, *God's Time for Us*, 22.

29. Steven J. Duby, *Jesus and the God of Classical Theism: Biblical Christology in the Light of the Doctrine of God* (Baker Academic, 2022), 130–38, provides an excellent treatment of the question.

30. H. R. Mackintosh, *The Doctrine of the Person of Jesus Christ* (T&T Clark, 1912), 457.

Nevertheless, to the extent that we are capable, God has accommodated himself to our sphere and modes of thought and made known realities that transcend them. Among these are his eternal decrees, his sovereign authority over the whole creation from beginning to end, and in particular his decisions, which have epistemological, conceptual, theological, logical, and realistic priority over all with which we are familiar in this mode of existence. In the words of Torrance, in writing of the humanity of Christ as essential for revelation, "God has actually come among mankind to reveal himself and to reconcile men and women to himself."[31] The incarnation is also "the guarantee that God's revelation is revelation to creaturely humanity, in the language and life of man, man who is involved within the limitations of time and space, and who cannot escape from them, who can know only within them, within time and history. Because the eternal has become temporal, men and women can know the eternal truth in time."[32]

Again, the Word *became* flesh: "the eternal God, without ceasing to be eternal, has taken *temporal form*, as well as creaturely existence. God has assumed our time into union with himself without abrogating it. He the eternal has become temporal for us in the form of our own temporal and historical existence, not simply by embracing our time and historical existence and ruling it, but by permitting time and our historical existence to be the form of his eternal deity. Thus he is not only accessible to us in time and history, but we in time and history are free to approach the eternal and to live with him."[33] It is a relation—between God and humanity—that has no parallel anywhere in creation.[34]

Therefore, the expression "before the foundation of the world" is speaking "improperly"—not meaning that it is wrong but rather that the language open to us to use cannot encapsulate the reality that it is designed to disclose. It is an extended use of language,

31. Thomas F. Torrance, *Incarnation: The Person and Life of Christ* (Paternoster, 2008), 184.

32. Torrance, *Incarnation*, 186.

33. Torrance, *Incarnation*, 66.

34. Torrance, *Incarnation*, 66.

expressing in terms that we can grasp a reality that is over and above and beyond what we can comprehend.

The Primal Decision

We will now consider some of these staggering realities as they have been disclosed to us in Holy Scripture.

Ephesians 1:3–4

> Blessed be the God and Father of our Lord Jesus Christ, who has blessed us in Christ with every spiritual blessing in the heavenly places, even as he chose us in him before the foundation of the world [καθὼς ἐξελέξατο ἡμᾶς ἐν αὐτῷ πρὸ καταβολῆς κόσμου], that we should be holy and blameless before him. (ESV)

Paul here writes of the foundation of our salvation residing in God's eternal choice, in election. Three elements are present, signifying a threefold aspect to election. There is the election by God (principally the Father) in Christ of a people, the church, whom he was to take into covenantal and existential union. Within this is the election of the particular members of the church. There is yet a third element, the foundation of the whole, the election of Christ. We will come to this last aspect after discussing the first two.

Election of the Church

Paul is writing to the church at Ephesus, although the evidence suggests that Ephesians was a circular letter distributed to a range of congregations in the region, of which Ephesus was one.[35] The letter addresses the church inclusive of all who could be said to belong to it, including children and slaves. This corporate element is frequently overlooked in the Western world because of the pervasive growth of individualism. In Ephesians in particular, Paul's reference to the church goes far beyond the specific congregation or

35. In the earliest manuscripts, ἐν Ἐφέσῳ ("in Ephesus") in Ephesians 1:1 does not appear, the absence of reference to any particular church indicating that it was probably a circular letter, with a space for the courier to fill in before delivery.

congregations who received his letter. He includes the whole church of Jew and Gentile, the one body of Christ (Eph. 2:11–22). This is found throughout the world and from one generation to another through the corridors of time. Its foundation in Christ ensures that any one instance of the church is an organic part of the whole, as a limb is a member of the body.

In this concern, the church—the entire church, and each constituent part of the church—has been elected in Christ. In chapter 5, Paul compares it to a bride in relation to her husband, and in chapter 4 to a body, with the working of its various organs and ligaments, connected to its head. In short, God the Father, in Christ the Son, and with the Holy Spirit in one concerted and indivisible decision determined to bring the church into existence by the power of the Spirit as a bride for the Son. Its existence as the church was in union with Christ. We will consider what this may mean shortly.

Election of the Particular Members of the Church

We are familiar with the question of the election of particular members of the body of Christ. On the popular level, this has been the most frequently discussed aspect of election. Each such individual is part of the church, which is the body of Christ, and as such has been chosen by the Trinity in eternity. All of these are part of the church, for which Christ gave himself (Eph. 5:25–27). That this election as such is *in Christ* is clear from the references Paul makes to it here and elsewhere (we will refer to 2 Timothy 1:9 below), from the comments of Jesus himself in his Upper Room Discourse in John 15–17, and from the overall biblical teaching on union with Christ.[36]

What does election *in Christ* mean?[37] Many of the attempts by biblical scholars to articulate their understanding of this phrase are less than satisfactory. This is at least in part due to their general lack of attention to theological debate, past and present, flowing from the remorseless development of specialisms over the past centuries.

36. See Robert Letham, *Union with Christ: In Scripture, History, and Theology* (P&R Publishing, 2011).

37. From a slightly different angle, see Duby, *Jesus and the God of Classical Theism*, 97–105.

Something similar could be said of the other specialisms. It also stems from a built-in dualism in the Enlightenment worldview in which the material and spiritual are viewed apart, God and creation held at arm's length. As a result, attention has been fixed, laserlike, on what occurs in verifiable human history.[38]

Some talk in purely representational terms. Andrew Lincoln argues that in Ephesians 1:3, "believers experience the blessings of the heavenly realms not only through Christ's agency but also because they are incorporated into the risen Christ as their representative, who is himself in the heavenly realms."[39] Again, "the notion of being chosen in Christ here in Ephesians is likely then to include the idea of incorporation into Christ as the representative on whom God's gracious decision was focused."[40] He concludes, correctly, that "if God's election of believers took place before the foundation of the world *in Christ*, this could well presuppose the existence of Christ before the foundation of the world," and that the church does not preexist the foundation of the world, but it is "the choice of the church which precedes the foundation of the world."[41] To restrict this relationship to the purely representational, however, is to confine it to something extrinsic. It overlooks the reality of the incarnation, the sending and indwelling of the Spirit (cf. vv. 13–14), and its dynamic consequences (vv. 15–23), each of which goes beyond the legal and forensic.

Others comment that it refers to a "sphere" in which those united to Christ are to be located.[42]

Harold Hoehner rightly judges an instrumental sense inadequate —such as "the place in whom salvation consists," still less if it is said to be based on our own faith, as John Chrysostom thought. Hoehner considers that the choice boils down to two alternatives:

38. See the important chapter "Theological Questions for Biblical Scholars," in *Reality and Evangelical Theology: The 1981 Payton Lectures*, by Thomas F. Torrance (Westminster Press, 1982), 52–83.

39. Andrew T. Lincoln, *Ephesians*, Word Biblical Commentary 42 (Word Books, 1990), 22.

40. Lincoln, *Ephesians*, 23.

41. Lincoln, *Ephesians*, 24.

42. Harold W. Hoehner, *Ephesians: An Exegetical Commentary* (Baker Academic, 2002), 170–77.

either a relational connection on the basis of Christ's foreordained work, or a dative of sphere, we being chosen in Christ as the head and representative of the spiritual community as Adam was of the natural community.[43] He adopts the former. While none of these proposals is inherently wrong, for each highlights an aspect of the whole, the result is imprecise. Perhaps this is unavoidable to an extent, since we are dealing with matters that are ultimately beyond us. Yet Hoehner dismisses Gadolf Deissmann's suggestion that ἐν Χριστῷ signifies a local and mystical sense, intimate fellowship with the living spiritual Christ, perhaps too readily.[44] The context is much wider than the grammatical, syntactical, and linguistic. Election is bound up with the whole succeeding process of redemption, which embraces dynamic resurrection and transformation, individual, corporate, cosmic. We will consider this in chapter 11.

Still others consider it mainly in terms of relationships, socially, as in "one another."[45] S. M. Baugh does not reflect at length on the phrase.[46] John Calvin simply refers to the "freedom of election. For if we are chosen in Christ, it is outside ourselves . . . because our heavenly Father has engrafted us . . . into the body of Christ (*Nam si in Christo sumus electi, ergo extra nos . . . sed quoniam caelestis Pater nos insuerit in Christo corpus*)."[47] He makes no comment on the meaning of the phrase in his Ephesians commentary.

Charles Hodge is more thorough. The phrase, he writes, is "variously explained." He rejects proposals that God chose us in himself, since this is contrary to both text and context—or because we are

43. Hoehner, *Ephesians*, 177.

44. Hoehner, *Ephesians*, 170.

45. Clive Bowsher, *Life in the Son: Exploring Participation and Union with Christ in John's Gospel and Letters* (Apollos, 2023). Bowsher does not comment to any extent on Paul. Originally a PhD dissertation, his work isolates John from Paul and the history of discussion, a method common and often necessary in dissertations, but this is itself indicative of the problem that Torrance highlighted above.

46. S. M. Baugh, *Ephesians* (Lexham Academic, 2016).

47. John Calvin, *Commentarii in Pauli Epistolas ad Galatas, ad Ephesios, ad Philippenses, ad Colossenses*, ed. Helmut Feld, Ioannis Calvini Opera Omnia (Librairie Droz, 1992), 158; John Calvin, *Calvin's Commentaries: The Epistles of Paul to the Galatians, Ephesians, Philippians and Colossians*, ed. Thomas F. Torrance and David W. Torrance, trans. T. H. L. Parker (Eerdmans, 1965), 125.

(already?) in him, since that is based on God's foreseeing our faith. In contrast, we were elected in order to have faith; the text stresses the good pleasure of God. Nor are we said to be chosen to be in him at some later point, as Theodore Beza argued, for this is more than the words contain.[48] Rather, "the purpose of election is very comprehensive[:] . . . to bring his people to holiness, sonship, and eternal glory . . . through a redeemer . . . in Christ as their head and representative . . . , in virtue of what he was to do on their behalf. There is a federal union with Christ which is antecedent to all actual union, and is the source of it. God gave a people to his Son in the covenant of redemption." This, again, is a representational interpretation. In short, "their federal union is the ground of their voluntary union." "It is, therefore, in Christ, i.e., as united to him in the covenant of redemption, that the people of God are elected to eternal life and to all the blessings therewith connected. Much in the same sense the Israelites are said to have been chosen in Abraham."[49] This restricts election to a decision about a reality that is distinct from it and follows it by a distance. By omitting a connection with dynamic transformation by the Spirit, it places it on the same level as the situation of the Israelites. Moreover, it overlooks other elements of Ephesians that demand such an inclusion.

While not necessarily wrong in themselves, each such proposal ignores the assumption of human nature by the Son, one of the Trinity, and tends to downplay the indwelling of the Holy Spirit, who unites us to Christ. Yet Ephesians is full of reflection on these themes, and it seems somewhat arbitrary to restrict ἐν αὐτῷ / ἐν Χριστῷ to representation, when the rest of the overall context of the letter, to say nothing of the wider theological ramifications, suggests otherwise.[50]

48. Charles Hodge, *A Commentary on the Epistle to the Ephesians* (Banner of Truth, 1964), 30.

49. Hodge, *Ephesians*, 30–31.

50. Someone might point to the strictures of James Barr over totality transfer, importing more meaning into the text than the context will allow. That is an important warning. Yet the context is eternity and its relation to the whole of time and, within that, the great sweep of redemptive history. That argues for a wider reference than normal, certainly than the immediately syntactical and lexical, important though those are. See James Barr, *The Semantics of Biblical Language* (repr., SCM, 1983).

We need to consider the nature of the risen Christ in his humanity, body and soul, mentioned by Paul in passages such as 1 Corinthians 15:45, for there are both representational and dynamic aspects to it.

Election of Christ

Prior to all this, foundational to the rest, to everything else, epistemologically and in reality, is God's election to be God in Christ, to take human nature into permanent union. As revealed, this is God's primal decision, with priority over all other elements. The election in Christ of the church, together with the election in Christ of the members of the church, entails the prior election of Christ, into whom the church in its various ramifications is united. It also entails as a consequence his decision to create the universe, to fill and populate it and to unite humanity to himself in the person of his Son. The hypostatic union is the foundation, for Calvin the pledge of our salvation, for "our common nature with Christ is the pledge of our fellowship with the Son of God."[51]

- First in order, logically (but not, of course, temporally, since the realm is supratemporal), was God's foundational decision that the Son would assume human nature into everlasting union. This follows from election being *in Christ*, the same Christ who is the subject of the rest of the paragraph, in whose blood we have redemption, in whom we are raised to new life and with whom we are seated in the heavenly realms. It entails God's decision that human nature be taken into union with himself

51. John Calvin, *Institutes*, 2.12.3. On the debate between infralapsarianism and supralapsarianism, see J. V. Fesko, *Diversity Within the Reformed Tradition: Supra- and Infralapsarianism in Calvin, Dort, and Westminster* (Reformed Academic Press, 2001); Robert Letham, *Systematic Theology* (Crossway, 2019), 422–27; Karl Barth, *CD*, II/2:127–45. While this argument relates clearly to this debate and can most readily be understood from a supralapsarian perspective, it is even more foundational. Whereas that discussion concerned the relationship between God's decree of election and his decree concerning the fall of man, both relating to the creaturely, human realm, our argument here concerns God's decision that the Son would take human nature into personal union in himself so that he would forever have a whole human nature while remaining who he was, is, and ever shall be.

forever in the person of the Son, that God now has a human body and soul, that in Christ man with God is on the throne. It is reasonable to suppose that God's eternal decision related first to his own actions and, as Ephesians 1 suggests, his own glory, a glory that is not that of a self-centered megalomaniac but of a loving Father who wishes his creature to participate in it. While it would be a huge fallacy to divide up and separate elements of God's eternal plan and pit one against another, it seems reasonable to suppose that "[God's] own glory" has some precedence to "man's salvation, faith and life,"[52] even though the latter is inseparably dependent on, and intertwined with, the former, while the former comes to full expression in the latter. First in priority is what relates to God, in this case particularly to the Son but, as we have repeatedly stressed, an indivisible and harmonious engagement of all three persons. Moreover, this was a free and sovereign decision. It was not a matter of necessity, as though God were incomplete in himself. Of course, it was fully compatible with his nature, with who he is, since it was by his own will. But in willing this, he was under no obligation; it was not an outflow of his being.[53]

- Consequent to this in terms of order and priority was God's determination to form the church and to bring it into union with the Son by the Holy Spirit, for eternity.
- Consequent to that in order of priority, but inseparably together with the other elements, was the election of individuals, an innumerable gathering from all nations, as members of the church in union with Christ.
- From that, entailed in all the preceding elements, was God's decision to create the universe, with its nature, structure, constitution, and population, including preeminently the human race, and to effect all the events that were to occur in creation throughout its existence, including and focusing on the historical outworking of his primal plan, as outlined above. Legitimate questions can

52. WCF 1.6.

53. See Duby, *Jesus and the God of Classical Theism*, 108–09.

> be, and have been, asked about the relative positions of these last three elements, and on this it is unwise to be dogmatic. As a fundamental principle, that historical outworking must have its own place, its own integrity, since for us the history of redemption is crucially and existentially relevant. From that angle, it is vital to stress the centrality of the death, resurrection, and ascension of Christ for our redemption. In the broadest picture, however, this history is to be seen as fitting into this wider, kaleidoscopic, cosmic plan.[54]

None of the consequent aspects can be considered, in this particular context, in a temporal way, for all are elements of an eternal decision. Moreover, the according of priority is for our own benefit, to convey a modicum of intelligibility to what, being eternal and timeless, is beyond our capacities.

This was a determination by God that he would not be alone but would unite to himself humanity, that he would forever, in his Son, have a human nature—body as well as soul—while remaining unchanged and unchangeable in himself.[55] It is, for us, the assurance that our salvation was and is secure. It is the cast-iron, eternal guarantee of the indestructible future of the human race.

This is foundational to all that follows—humans created in the image of God, salvation and all its ramifications. It is the primal

54. Elsewhere I have written, in relation to the Westminster Assembly: "This question of perspective is, of course, important in the interpretation of any text, ancient or modern. In north-west Scotland, there is a remarkable mountain, Suilven, an abrupt and bulbous protrusion when viewed from the south-west, an elongated ridge from the south, a jagged, nightmarish apparition out of Tolkien from the east. The contours are the same but the appearance differs radically. The documents of the Westminster Assembly share with Suilven—and any object in relation to which a human agent can be placed—a prospect shaped by the location of the observer." Robert Letham, *The Westminster Assembly: Reading Its Theology in Historical Context* (P&R Publishing, 2009), 47–48. See chapter 11 for a summation of these ideas.

55. *Contra The Children's Catechism* answer, "God is a spirit and does not have a body like us." It is true that God as such does not have a body, but because of the incarnation he does have a *human* body (and soul), a body like ours! Moreover, he is Spirit, not *a* spirit, signifying one among many others of a class. I know of no worse catechetical answer.

decree insofar as it has been revealed to us. It rules out other incarnations, an endless sequence of possible incarnations, pantheism, deism, and panentheism. It means that the incarnation was neither an emergency measure nor a response to an event, as though God were taken by surprise and had to turn to plan B.

As we will consider later in this chapter, Barth, Torrance, and others have taken a similar line with the consequence, despite their protestations, of a perspective that appears universalist.

A Free and Sovereign Decision

God was not bound to make this decision. It was made freely. Consequently, he cannot be viewed in terms of his creation or named after any element within it. The practice of *naming* God Creator, Redeemer, Sanctifier involves naming him in relation to creation, entailing that he is dependent on what he made and on what he did. Moreover, this is to accord different works to particular Trinitarian *hypostases*, eroding the point that in all his works, all three work together inseparably. Furthermore, only God has the right to name himself. His revealed names tell us who he is in himself, in his internal relations. He *is* the Father, the Son, and the Holy Spirit even if he had never decided to create the universe. At least it can be said that these erroneous attempts to name God build on genuine aspects of his work; the "reimagining" that has been going on in various radical circles in recent decades does not even get that far.

No, God was under no obligation whatsoever to create any entity, let alone the vast universe that there is, nor to make humanity in his own image and to plan the incarnation of the Son.[56] He is self-sufficient in his immense vitality. Nothing that he has made adds, or can add, anything to him. His choice that the Son be incarnate, that human nature be taken into union forever, was and is a free and sovereign decision, entirely of grace.

This by no means erodes human freedom. Since God is free and sovereign, and has made humanity in his own image, freedom is inherent to human flourishing and enhancement. The incarnation

56. See Barth, *CD*, I/2:134–35.

itself establishes the point; who, par excellence, is free beyond all others but Jesus Christ, the incarnate Son? As the Westminster Confession of Faith stresses, God's sovereign rule over creation preserves the liberty of secondary causes (WCF 5.2).

Back prior to everything, to creation, time, and space, to when God alone was and is, God's primal decision was to become incarnate in the person of the Son. It was made by the whole Trinity, the Father, the Son, and the Holy Spirit in indivisible union.

In this sense, Barth, following Calvin and Augustine before him, was right that Christ is both electing God and elect man. He writes that since, on the basis of John 1:1–2, Jesus Christ is in the beginning with God and is God, therefore he is God who elects. Moreover, since God determines to be God in this man, Jesus, in that decree Jesus Christ is also elect man; "primarily, then, electing is the divine determination of the existence of Jesus Christ, and election (being elected) the human."[57] While the Son elects together with the Father and the Holy Spirit, he is both elector and elected. He is more than the *means* of reconciliation between God and man, the instrument of such reconciliation, for he is *himself* the reconciliation.[58] In his person, God and man are one: one in indivisible union, one in the integrity of both natures. In effect, the election encompasses creation, covenant, incarnation, and atonement (reconciliation), for it is an election by and of Jesus Christ.

- Creation, since the Son takes a created (conceived) human nature into union.
- Covenant, since God is our God in Christ, and we are God's people in Christ.
- Incarnation, since God and man are one person in Christ.
- Reconciliation, since the personal union is the evidence and seal of the union of God and estranged man, for Christ *himself* is our peace (Eph. 2:14).[59]

57. Barth, *CD*, II/2:101.

58. Barth, *CD*, II/2:105.

59. We can speak of humanity's being saved, but this does not entail that all particular humans will be saved. We know from Scripture that, sadly, this is not so.

Athanasius had written, on the phrase "before the foundation of the world": "How has he chosen us before we came into existence? . . . In him we were represented beforehand." How were we adopted, "but that the Lord himself was 'founded before the world' taking on that economy which was for our sake?" Thus, "in Christ was stored the grace that should reach us." Referring to Matthew 25:34, he commented that "'before the world' there had been prepared for us the hope of life and salvation." Consequently, "nor in any other way was it fitting that our life should be founded, but in the Lord who is before the ages, and through whom the ages were brought to be; that, since it was in him, we too might be able to inherit everlasting life." He provided an analogy of "a wise architect, proposing to build a house, [who] consults also about repairing it, should it at any time become dilapidated after building and . . . makes preparation and gives to the workmen materials for repair; and thus the means of the repair are provided before the house; in the same way prior to us is the repair of our salvation founded in Christ, that in him we might even be new created."[60]

In turn, Augustine concluded that "the most illustrious light of predestination and grace is the Saviour himself,—the Mediator between God and men." That Christ exhibits grace is evident, since the human nature assumed into union by the Son in the incarnation had no prior existence to its conception and assumption and so could not have attained any merit that earned for it that status.[61] Augustine asks: "By what preceding merits of his own, whether of works or faith, did the human nature which is in him procure for itself that it should be this? . . . To be assumed by the Word co-eternal with the Father into unity of person, and be the only-begotten Son of God? . . . What did he do before?" "Therefore in him who is our head let there appear to be the very fountain of grace, whence . . .

Only through faith in the incarnate Son, Jesus Christ, can we be saved, with the sole exceptions of elect infants who die in infancy and other elect persons incapable of understanding and believing the gospel (WCF 10.3).

60. Athanasius, *Against the Arians*, 2.22 (76–77); *NPNF*², 4:389–90.

61. Of course, as we will discuss in chapters 4 and 6, the human nature taken into union by the person of Christ has no independence or autonomy apart from that union.

he diffuses himself through all his members. It is by that grace that every man from the beginning of his faith becomes a Christian, by which grace that one man from his beginning became Christ. Of the same Spirit also the former is born again of which the latter was born." Thus, the predestination of the saints shines in the Saint of saints. Therefore, Jesus was predestined so that he would be the Son of God. As he was predestined to become our head, so we, being many, are predestined to be his members.[62]

Calvin stressed that the Son, with the Father and the Spirit, is the electing God, author of election. He wrote that Christ "claims for himself, in common with the Father, the right to choose" and thus "makes himself the author of election."[63] He is also "the pre-eminent example of the Father's mercy and kindly heart . . . on whom alone God's Spirit rests" so that "those whom God has adopted as his sons are said to have been chosen not in themselves but in his Christ [Eph. 1:4]; for unless he could love them in him, he could not honor them with the inheritance of his kingdom."[64]

2 Timothy 1:9–10

Paul reinforces his comments in Ephesians in this, his final extant letter. He writes:

> God . . . who saved us and called us to a holy calling, not because of our works but because of his own purpose and grace, which he gave to us in Christ Jesus before eternal ages [κατὰ ἰδίαν πρόθεσιν καὶ χάριν τὴν δοθεῖσαν ἡμῖν ἐν Χριστῷ Ἰησοῦ πρὸ χρόνων αἰωνίων], and which now has been manifested through the appearing of our Savior Christ Jesus, who rendered death inoperative and brought life and immortality to light through the gospel.

Here the structure of thought is much the same as in Ephesians, moving from eternity into time and thereafter following the temporal order.

62. Augustine, *De praedestinatione sanctorum*, 30–31; *NPNF*[1], 5:512–13.
63. Calvin, *Institutes*, 3.22.7.
64. Calvin, *Institutes*, 3.24.5.

Before Eternal Ages

Taken as it stands, and as it appears to us, this makes little sense. How can something occur before, and thus in a temporal sequence, what is eternal and timeless? The solution is most likely to be that Paul precludes any created entity or event from any possibility of involvement. God's purpose and grace was given us (by the Father) in Christ Jesus without reference to anything other than his own sovereign will. The intervention, actual or potential, of any created being or force is ruled out entirely. This was a decision made by God in eternity.[65] As in Ephesians, it consists of granting us grace, favor, and life—since it contemplates a temporal state in which life and immortality is brought into effect in place of death—and it does so "in Christ Jesus." The prior, implied and entailed, datum is Christ Jesus. Grace is found in the Christ, who is Jesus of Nazareth; it is given in eternity, before the ages; he, the Christ, is in eternity, the decree to assume human nature already in effect. *Christ himself* is given to us; the grace and life are not independent and autonomous entities but what flows from Christ.

Now

This grace has been made known through the appearing of our Savior, Jesus Christ, who abolished—having the sense of rendering inoperative—death and made evident life and immortality through the gospel. "Now" in this sense is in relation to the eternal determination before the ages, and expresses the integrity of history; it is also "now" in relation to the times in the era that preceded the epiphany of Jesus Christ, the time of expectation; it is "now" in terms of the manifestation of Christ on earth; and "now" in relation to the time of fulfillment that follows it in which Paul and we find ourselves.

This is evident in Romans, where Paul contrasts past times with the "now time" (Rom. 3:21, 25–26). In each case, the demarcation is the resurrection of Jesus, the bringing to light of life and immortality.

65. A knowledgeable reader remarks that I haven't conclusively resolved the relationship between time and eternity evidenced here. I agree. I cannot do so. As Charles Wesley famously penned in "And Can It Be That I Should Gain" (1738), "'Tis myst'ry all!"

This was Paul's theme in his speech at Athens, contrasting "the times of ignorance" with the "now" effected by the resurrection (Acts 17:30–31).

You (plural)

"God called us with a holy calling, not because of our works" again speaks of the consequence of the appearing of Christ. Since the letter is addressed to Timothy personally, the plural may well indicate that Paul is quoting a familiar hymn or creedal statement. Again, there is a similar pattern to the passage in Ephesians 1, where the flow of argument runs from before the foundation of the world (vv. 3–5) to redemption through Christ's blood (v. 7), being sealed with the Holy Spirit (vv. 13–14), with exhortations following (vv. 15–18).

Again, here in 2 Timothy, the epiphany of Christ in his incarnation, together with all that flows from it, including our own incorporation into him, is an outflow of God's decision (that of the Father, the Son, and the Holy Spirit in one indivisible act) to unite humanity to himself in his Son.

Comments here are thin. William Mounce remarks that this happened "before time began" and says not much more.[66] J. N. D. Kelly writes that both here and Ephesians 1:4 "presuppose the idea of Christ's pre-existence, and also imply that he is the unique mediator through union with whom men have the grace of God imparted to them."[67] For I. Howard Marshall, "the divine gift was thus contained in the pre-existent Christ before the world was created, and it was given to us in that it was given to Christ,"[68] and "the statement implies some kind of pre-existence for Christ Jesus."[69] All Calvin can say is that "this grace was laid up for us in him before the foundation of the world."[70]

66. William B. Mounce, *Pastoral Epistles*, Word Biblical Commentary 46 (Thomas Nelson, 2000), 483.

67. J. N. D. Kelly, *A Commentary on the Pastoral Epistles* (Adam & Charles Black, 1963), 163.

68. I. Howard Marshall, *A Critical and Exegetical Commentary on the Pastoral Epistles* (T&T Clark, 1999), 706.

69. Marshall, *Pastoral Epistles*, 707.

70. John Calvin, *Calvin's Commentaries: The Second Epistle of Paul to the Corinthians*

Interestingly, there is more expansive reflection on Christ and the eternal origins of salvation among the church fathers and the Greeks. Maximus the Confessor, in *Ad Thalassium* 60.2, wrote of the mystery of Christ in terms of "the ineffable and incomprehensible union according to hypostasis of divinity and humanity."[71] In 60.7, he considered that "it was his incarnation for humanity's sake in the economy of salvation that was foreknown."[72] Moreover, in 60.4, he added that "it is for the sake of Christ that all the ages and beings received their beginning and end in Christ."[73]

Earlier, Irenaeus argued that Adam was created in the image of Christ, who is the image of God.[74] He explained something of what this means when he wrote, "For in long times past, it was said that man was created in the image of God, but it was not [actually] shown: for the Word was as yet invisible, after whose image man was created." When the Word became flesh, "he both showed forth the image truly, since he became himself what was his image: and he re-established the similitude after a sure manner, by assimilating men to the invisible Father through the means of the visible Word."[75] Bogdan Bucur argues that for Irenaeus, "Adam enjoys a special ontological condition, due to the fact that he is made in God's image: not God's image, however, but rather *in* the image of God, i.e., structured in relation to—*through, in,* and *unto* the divine Logos, the true image of God."[76] He remarks that "since Irenaeus was using and passing on such Christian traditions[,] . . . one may assume that speculations on Genesis 1:26 and Christ as the prototype of Adam must have been widespread, perhaps even part of catechetical instruction, in the second and third centuries."

---

and the Epistles to Timothy, Titus, and Philemon, ed. David W. Torrance and Thomas F. Torrance, trans. T. A. Smail (Eerdmans, 1964), 297.

71. Constas, *Ad Thalass.*, 427.

72. Constas, *Ad Thalass.*, 431.

73. Constas, *Ad Thalass.*, 429.

74. Irenaeus, *Against Heresies,* 3.23.1, 4.33.4.

75. Irenaeus, *Against Heresies,* 5.16.2.

76. Bogdan G. Bucur, "Foreordained from Eternity: The Mystery of the Incarnation According to Some Early Christian and Byzantine Writers," *Dumbarton Oaks Papers* 62 (2008): 211.

He concludes by stating that it should be clear that "christomorphic anthropology can boast of venerable roots in Christian tradition."[77] We will discuss this further in chapter 11.

In the fourteenth century, Nicholas Cabasilas summed it up: "it is therefore the hypostatic union, by which the distance between Godhead and humanity is overcome, that corresponds to the end that God had in mind when he fashioned Adam."[78] This becomes apparent when we examine Genesis 1.

Genesis 1:1–2:3

There are clear pre-echoes of the Trinity in this section of Genesis. In the beginning God created, the Spirit of God was hovering over the waters, the Word of God was uttered, and light emerged (Gen. 1:1–5). Throughout the section, God creates in a threefold form: by direct fiat, by making things, and by co-opting the ministerial capacities of those entities he had brought into existence. Above all, there is the self-deliberation concerning the creation of humanity as male and female: "Let us make man in our image" (vv. 26–27).

This unique self-deliberation indicates that the weight of the section is on the last portion. The creation of humanity is presented in poetic parallelism, standing out from the rest of the section. It is as though Moses had taken a highlighter to draw obvious attention to the crucial significance of this particular statement. The announcement of the first five days lacks the definite article in both the Hebrew text and the Septuagint. The seventh day is represented as unending, with no refrain, and three times within the account of events that took place there is the statement "the seventh day," whereas such a statement is lacking for all the preceding days.

Bearing in mind the direction in which Genesis 1:1–2:3 heads, to the creation of humanity in the image of God, the creation as it was originally formed was entirely inhospitable. It had no shape, it was empty, it was utterly dark, and it was wet. It was unfit for humans to inhabit, indeed for any kind of dwelling (Gen. 1:1–3). Chapter 1

77. Bucur, "Foreordained from Eternity," 214.

78. Nicholas Cabasilas, *Life in Christ*, trans. Margaret I. Lisney (Janus, 1995), 3:5, quoted in Bucur, "Foreordained from Eternity," 208.

shows that God progressively changed it into a place fit for us to live. He brought forth light, and he separated the waters, thus forming the sea and the clouds, so that it was pervasively wet no longer. He brought to existence and shaped the dry land. He began to populate it by creating vegetation, and put birds and fish into place in the sea and the sky. Then he created land animals of various kinds. Finally, as the apex of his creation, he brought the human race into being as the goal of this great work.

But God's purpose went beyond even this. When he created *adam* as male and female, he created them *in* the image and likeness of God. What was, and is, the image of God? We have to await the New Testament to discover the answer. Paul tells us that the image of the invisible God is Jesus Christ, the firstborn of all creation (Col. 1:15), the image of God himself (2 Cor. 4:4). The author of Hebrews states that the incarnate Son is "the brightness of the Father's glory and the express image of his being" (Heb. 1:3), while John states that "no one has ever seen God; the only-begotten God, who is in the heart of the Father, has made him known" (John 1:18). Creation is the backcloth in each of these contexts. Thus, Jesus could say to Philip that "he who has seen me has seen the Father" (John 14:9).

The creation of Adam was with a view to the incarnation of the second Adam. The decision for the Son to become incarnate had precedence over the decision to create Adam in his image. Consequently, the first Adam's creation in the image of God was creation *in* Christ, in his case in a provisional sense, a proleptic manner, looking for and anticipating the full reality that was to come. Everything in the chapter is a preparation for Adam and humans to live, with a view to the incarnation of the Son. The incarnation is the goal. As such, while it is later in execution it is evidently first in intention.

We are all reminded, I am sure, of the prayer in the *Festal Menaion*: "Thou, O Christ, with invisible hands hast fashioned man in thine image and hast now displayed the original beauty in this same human body formed by thee."[79]

79. Mother Mary and Kallistos Ware, *The Festal Menaion* (St. Tikhon's Seminary Press, 1998), 486.

Attempts to Understand This Mystery[80]

Here we are pointing to the genuine fact that we are thinking of matters that occurred in the mind of God. While revealed, they still remain elusive to us. Insofar as we can consider them, we should confess and recognize our limitations.

Covenant of Redemption

Historical Emergence

The idea of the *pactum salutis* ("covenant of redemption") emerged in Reformed theology in the first half of the seventeenth century. The plan of salvation had been seen as covenantal in the covenant of grace, first voiced in the 1520s by Huldrych Zwingli and then, in a dedicated treatise, by Heinrich Bullinger.[81] Later, from 1585, the prefall situation began to be understood as a covenant of works or life.[82] From this, some began to construe the eternal counsels of God in covenantal terms. Caspar Olevian wrote of an eternal *pactum* as early as 1585,[83] but the idea of a pretemporal covenant between the Father and the Son emerged more clearly in the 1630s. Richard Muller has identified the idea as broached by Jacob Arminius in 1603, taken up by Paul Bayne in 1618, by Edward Reynolds in 1632, by David Dickson from 1635, on the continent by Johannes Cloppenburg in 1643, in England again by John Owen in 1647, and famously and idiosyncratically by Johannes Cocceius the following year.[84] Unlike the prefall covenant, it has not attained confessional status, and so, while commonly expounded and defended, it is still more of a theological opinion.

80. Some bright spark is likely to chime in by saying that the New Testament use of "mystery" is of something hidden that has now been revealed, and so to write of mystery here in the conventional and general use of the word is invalid. Yes, of course that is the way the word is used in the New Testament, but we are not duty bound to use a word at all times in one way and in no other.

81. Heinrich Bullinger, *De Testamento seu Foedere Dei Unico & Aeterno Brevis Expositio* (Zürich, 1534).

82. Dudley Fenner, *Sacra Theologia, sive Veritas Quae Secundum Pietatem* (Geneva, 1585).

83. Caspar Olevian, *De Substantia Foederis Gratuiti Inter Deum et Electos* (Geneva, 1585).

84. Richard A. Muller, "Toward the Pactum Salutis: Locating the Origins of a Concept," *MAJT* 18 (2007): 11–65.

Various Constructions

This putative covenant has taken more than one form. Most typically, it is described as a covenant between the Father and the Son. The Father promises the Son a people from every nation, on condition that the Son become incarnate, suffer, die an atoning death, and be raised from the dead. It is an attempt to articulate the Trinitarian basis of redemption. It provides a ground for the atonement.

In some constructions, it assumes a mercantile form. *The Sum of Saving Knowledge* (1647) explains it as "a bargain" between the Father and the Son.[85] It is hard to see how, by construing the relations of the Trinitarian *hypostases* in this way, they are other than autonomous agents, with the obvious risk of tritheism. Other proposals carry some of the additional weaknesses of this document. There is no mention of the Holy Spirit. A. A. Hodge makes this mistake.[86] Thus, it appears as a binitarian agreement. In both instances, the internal relations of the Trinity are patterned on contemporary seventeenth-century commercial practices. The anachronism is very plain. Some have attempted to avoid these problems. John Owen, Herman Bavinck, Iain D. Campbell, and J. V. Fesko are four who come to mind.[87]

A second type of formulation seeks to escape these Trinitarian problems by construing the covenant as between God the Trinity and Christ as second Adam.[88] In this presentation, the Trinitarian issue is

85. "But by virtue of the aforesaid bargain, made before the world began, he is in all ages, since the fall of Adam, still upon the work of applying actually the professed benefits unto the elect. . . . By the sacraments, God will have the covenant sealed for confirming the bargain on the foresaid condition." "The Sum of Saving Knowledge: or, A Brief Sum of Christian Doctrine," in *The Confession of Faith, the Larger and Shorter Catechisms with the Scripture Proofs at Large, Together with The Sum of Saving Knowledge* (Publications Committee of the Free Presbyterian Church of Scotland, 1970), 321–26, here 324–25.

86. A. A. Hodge, *Outlines of Theology* (Eerdmans, 1972), 372.

87. Herman Bavinck, *RD*, 2:214; John Owen, *The Works of John Owen*, ed. William H. Goold, 16 vols. (Banner of Truth, 1965–68), 10:163, 168, 178–79; Iain D. Campbell, "Re-Visiting the Covenant of Redemption," in *The People's Theologian: Writings in Honour of Donald MacLeod*, ed. Iain D. Campbell and Malcolm Maclean (Mentor, 2011), 173–94; J. V. Fesko, *The Covenant of Redemption: Origins, Development, and Reception* (Vandenhoeck & Ruprecht, 2016).

88. Patrick Gillespie, *The Ark of the Covenant Opened: Or, A Treatise of the Covenant of Redemption Between God and Christ, as the Fountain of the Covenant of Grace* (London,

avoided. But the problems are shifted from Trinitarianism to Christology; the Son as God ("Christ-God"), with the Father and the Spirit, makes a covenant with the Son as incarnate ("Christ God-Man"). This divides the person of the Son and so entails Nestorianism.[89]

It is important for us, in order to grasp some of the issues at stake, to see that a number of distinct layers exemplify the relative degrees of authority to be attached to dogmatic proposals of this, or any other, kind.[90]

The primary layer is the reality that happens within the Trinity in eternity. Some have labeled this archetypal theology, borrowed awkwardly from Aristotle's construction of archetype and ectype. We have no access to this, other than what God may have revealed. This is the reality that these proposals are attempting to attest. Since this occurs in the being of God, we can begin to think adequately only on the basis of the second layer below.

The second layer is the revelation of that eternal reality within the internal relations of the Trinity that is given us in Holy Scripture. God's revelation is, by its very nature, accommodated to our capacity; otherwise, we could not understand it and it would not be revelation at all. It is related to the first layer analogically rather than identically. There are some elements that we can, with the Spirit's help, begin to appreciate, while the full reality eludes us. There is enough to make clear that in all of God's works, all three persons are integrally involved, while each work is particularly attributable to one Trinitarian *hypostasis*. In this, we can conclude that the whole of creation, providence, and grace was and is a work of the whole Trinity, the Son included. Salvation rests on a decision made by the Trinity, a plan hatched in eternity, in which we had no input whatsoever.

1677), esp. 73–78, 118, 188–89. Note that Westminster Larger Catechism 31 has a similar construction to Gillespie but considers it as "the second covenant," which is the covenant of grace.

89. See my discussion in Letham, *Holy Trinity*, 315–24.

90. What follows is built on the paradigm proposed by Oliver D. Crisp, *God Incarnate: Explorations in Christology* (T&T Clark, 2009), 17, as mentioned in my *Systematic Theology*, 34–35.

A third level consists of the articulation of that revelation, insofar as the church has been enabled to grasp it, in the ecumenical confessions of the entire church. These are the ecumenical councils, one of which (Constantinople I in 381) produced what we call the Nicene Creed. Article 8 of the Thirty-Nine Articles expresses why these creeds "ought thoroughly to be received and believed: for they may be proved by most certain warrants of holy Scripture." These confessions contain no significant reflection on the matter before us, other than ascribing all of God's works to the indivisible Trinity, all three persons working together. Our question is not something on which the whole church has yet agreed in any formal sense.

A fourth level embraces the confessions of particular branches of the church. In this case, the Reformed church is in view, since here there has been more prolonged reflection on the covenant and on God's eternal decrees than has been the case elsewhere. Yet while covenant theology, in terms of the covenant of works or life, and the covenant of grace, has been expressed confessionally in the documents of the Westminster Assembly, which are foundational to Presbyterianism and also highly regarded in other Reformed churches, the proposed covenant of redemption, while widely believed, has not itself secured such confessional status.[91]

The fifth level comprises the expressions of individual theologians. These are of greater or lesser significance, depending on the degree of respect accorded by the church to the particular author. One expects and hopes John Calvin to be given greater honor than Bob Letham! These proposals are what the Greeks term *theologoumena,* "theological opinions." Some articulations are more and others less viable. Critical examination is required; as the Berean believers even scrutinized the teaching of the apostle Paul on the basis of Scripture (Acts 17:11),[92] so ought any human author to be held accountable. Appropriate humility is needed or we will elevate individual opinions to quasi-confessional status without proper process. It is on this level that discussion and criticism is currently to be undertaken.

91. Only the *Savoy Declaration* (1659), of the Independents, has adopted it.

92. Presumably with Paul's own approval, since he was on the scene, and Luke, the author of Acts, was frequently in his traveling entourage.

We should assert that the eternal decision of God is a plan of the whole indivisible Trinity—the Father, the Son, and the Holy Spirit. Equally, it cannot be a contract between the Trinitarian persons, a bargain suggesting quasi-autonomous agents with separate wills. Nor is it an imposition by one Trinitarian person on another. Moreover, there is a grave danger of thinking of it in terms of commercial or legal transactions. Even more, a covenant requires more than one party; the Trinity is indivisible. It would be far preferable to talk of the Trinitarian counsel of redemption, which avoids any notion of binitarianism and autonomous agents.

Karl Barth

Barth had a different approach to the question. He was strongly opposed to an absolute decree by God in himself concerning man in himself, and a concentration on the election and rejection of individuals as such. He comments that "insofar as these works are done in time, they rest upon the eternal decision of God by which time is founded and governed."[93] Again,

> in the beginning, before time and space as we know them, before creation, before there was any reality distinct from God which could be the object of the love of God or the setting for his acts of freedom, God anticipated and determined within himself . . . that the goal and meaning of all his dealings with the as yet nonexistent universe should be the fact that in his Son he would be gracious towards man, uniting himself with him. In the beginning it was the choice of the Father himself to establish this covenant with man by giving up his Son for him, that he himself might become man in the fulfillment of his grace. In the beginning it was the choice of the Son to be obedient to grace, and therefore to offer up himself and to become man in order that this covenant might be made a reality. In the beginning it was the resolve of the Holy Spirit that the unity of God, of Father and Son should not be disturbed or rent by this covenant with man.[94]

93. Barth, *CD*, II/2:99.
94. Barth, *CD*, II/2:101.

Further, "as the subject and object of this choice, Jesus Christ was at the beginning. He was not at the beginning of God, for God has indeed no beginning. But he was at the beginning of all things, at the beginning of God's dealings with the reality which is distinct from himself. Jesus Christ was the choice or election of God in respect of this reality. He was the election of God's grace as directed towards man. He was the election of God's covenant with man."[95] We should ascribe to him as the electing God the active determination of electing, while, as he is man, the passive determination of election is proper to him.[96] Indeed, "There is no such thing as a will of God apart from the will of Jesus Christ." Not only is he the manifestation and mirror of our election, but "he reveals to us our election as an election which, like his and with his, is made by him, by his will which is also the will of God. He tells us that he himself is the one who elects us."[97] Furthermore, he is elected man, for he stands before God and on behalf of others as no mere creature, for he is the Creator. "In one and the same person he must be both elected man and the electing God."[98] Predestination is always only by the free grace of God, and as Augustine wrote,[99] the clearest light of predestination and grace is the Savior himself, the Mediator between God and man, Jesus Christ.[100]

The weakness of Barth's proposal is its cramming everything into the eternal decree, with its universalizing entailments, from which Barth tried with limited success to extricate himself. The point is that he considered this covenant to be made with man as such, indiscriminately. There are no other elect but those who are "in him," in Christ's person, in his own choice, for this is more than his being the executor of salvation, and it is more than merely being with him, in his company.[101] Barth states that Christ's election

95. Barth, *CD*, II/2:102.
96. Barth, *CD*, II/2:103.
97. Barth, *CD*, II/2:115.
98. Barth, *CD*, II/2:116.
99. Augustine, *De praedestinatione sanctorum*, 15.
100. Barth, *CD*, II/2:118.
101. Barth, *CD*, II/2:116–17.

carries with it the election of the rest.[102] Election has priority over all else, for it includes within it all else. Christ is electing God, elect man. He also took on rejection, reprobation, in being judged in our place.[103] So "man cannot evade his responsibility by complaining that God required too much of him, for what God required of himself on man's behalf is infinitely greater than what he required of man. In the last analysis what God required of man consists only in the demand that he should live as the one on whose behalf God required the very uttermost of himself."[104] This has a noticeably universalistic flavor to it, although Barth denied universalism.[105] Oliver Crisp has argued that Barth is incoherent. With covenant, incarnation, and atonement all located in Christ, it is hard to see how the incorporation of humanity in Christ can, given the efficacy of Christ's death, fail to issue in universal salvation. Barth's denial of this conclusion is a triumph for his recognition of biblical teaching; it also renders his overall argument self-contradictory.[106] Barth's construction was adopted in all salient details by T. F. Torrance. I have written about this elsewhere, my conclusions agreeing with Crisp's discussion of Barth.[107]

Jesus' Statements About His Eternal Relations with the Father

Despite the paucity of our capacity, God has revealed something of the internal relations of the Trinity, sufficient for us and our salvation. Jesus' prayer in John 17 is crucial in this regard.

102. Barth, *CD*, II/2:117.

103. Barth, *CD*, IV/1:211–83.

104. Barth, *CD*, II/2:166.

105. Barth, *CD*, II/1:264, 553; Geoffrey W. Bromiley, *An Introduction to the Theology of Karl Barth* (Eerdmans, 1979), 97–98.

106. Oliver D. Crisp, "On Barth's Denial of Universalism," *Them* 29, no. 1 (September 2003): 18–29.

107. Robert Letham, "The Triune God, Incarnation, and Definite Atonement," in *From Heaven He Came and Sought Her: Definite Atonement in Historical, Biblical, Theological, and Pastoral Perspective*, ed. David Gibson and Jonathan Gibson (Crossway, 2013), 447–59. Controversy has been raised around the argument of Bruce McCormack that Barth considered that God chose in election to be triune. See Letham, *Holy Trinity*, 348–52; Letham, *Systematic Theology*, 429–30.

First, *Jesus speaks of the glory he had with the Father before the world was*. At once, this demonstrates the personal identity of Jesus of Nazareth with the eternal Son. He was, and is, one of the Trinity, who has become man. These statements also indicate his distinction from the Father, together with his equality and identity with him. Additionally, he refers to his sharing the glory that was his with the Father:

> Glorify me, Father, with the glory I had with/beside you before the world was. (John 17:5)

In that identity and equality, there was the glory of God in which both the Father and the Son belonged. At the same time, there is an order, for the Father is the one to whom the Son prays and it is the Father who is able to glorify the Son in his incarnate state. In turn, the Son has glorified the Father in fulfilling the mission on which he had been sent (John 17:4). In John 17:22, Jesus presents another nuance, for the glory possessed by the Son and to be possessed by him is conferred by the Father, and in this immediate case, in response to the Son's own request. It is glory that will now encompass the humanity of the Son.[108] In doing so, there would be nothing new insofar as the glory to be conveyed would be the same glory as the Son had, together with the Father, in eternity. What this indicates is the hypostatic order in the Trinity, with the Father as the *principium*.

There is mutual indwelling. Later in the prayer, Jesus refers to the fact that he, the Son, and the Father dwell in each other (John 17:21, 23). He prays that those whom the Father had given him "may see my glory which you gave me" (v. 24). Again, there is an order between the Father and the Son, the Father's giving glory to the Son. It is seen in the context of their equality, identical essence, and mutual indwelling, "as you, Father, are in me and I in you" (v. 21).

Moreover, this union is pervaded by love. Love is something that only persons can have and exercise. The Son and the Father were one

108. I am grateful to Sherman Isbell for this observation.

in love. Jesus prays that the world might come to understand the love that the Father has for the Son, "because you loved me before the foundation of the world" (John 17:24). Then, in turn, people would begin to see how the Father loves them, on the grounds that first he loves the Son (v. 23). This mutual intra-Trinitarian love is the basis and ground for the love that the Father—and thus the Son and the Spirit—has for the disciples. The expression "before the foundation of the world" is identical to the one Paul uses in Ephesians 1:4 and refers to the timeless eternity, God's eternity, in which he is love and from which, in his free and sovereign decision, he chose to create a people made in his image to love too.

Second, *Jesus prays in connection with the gifts that the Father had given him,* which he mentions twelve times in the prayer, gifts of a people to be united to him (John 17:2, 6–7, 9, 24), gifts of authority over the creation (vv. 2, 7), and all that was necessary in his incarnate life, his life as man in our world for the accomplishment of his great task, including the words that the Father gave him (vv. 4, 7–8). The Father also gave him his name (vv. 11–12). This expresses an order —irreversible—between the Father and the Son in the unity of the indivisible Trinity. Not only is it specifically to the Father that the prayer is made, bearing in mind the indivisibility of the Trinity, but it is the Father who is the one who gives gifts to the Son.

Third, *Jesus refers to the Father as having sent him into the world for the task he undertook.* Again, we note the hypostatic order, *from* the Father, which in terms of the missions is seen in the *sending* by the Father. Seven times in the course of this prayer, Jesus mentions—in praying to the Father—that he has been sent by the Father:

- "Jesus Christ, whom you have sent" (v. 3)
- "I have come from you" (v. 8)
- "you sent me" (v. 8)
- "you sent me into the world" (v. 18)
- "that the world might believe that you sent me" (v. 21)
- "that the world might believe that you sent me" (v. 23)
- "they know that you sent me" (v. 25)

Both "sent" and "given" are present pervasively, throughout the prayer, on nineteen occasions.

These statements, among others, bring before us the complete ontological identity and equality between the Father and the Son, which consists also in hypostatic distinctions and an irreversible hypostatic order. *Mutatis mutandis*, it follows that the same pattern of equality and identity, on the one hand, and of hypostatic order applies to the Spirit also.

The Debate on the Relationship Between the Trinity and Election

I have written elsewhere on the debate initiated by Bruce McCormack on the relationship between the Trinity and election.[109] The traditional view is that Trinity precedes election. This is the idea that God is eternally triune, and is so necessarily. There is no possibility that he could be otherwise. Election, on the other hand, is a free decision dependent on his will. He was under no obligation to elect, for he was free not to elect. This is the position that Paul Molnar and George Hunsinger adopt in this debate and the one I advocate. On the other hand, McCormack, basing his claims on his interpretation of Barth, argued that God chooses to be Trinity. Not only is election prior to Trinity, but God's being Trinity follows from his free choice to be so. Matthias Gockel writes that for Barth, election is "a constitutive or necessary aspect of God's being."[110] Debate has been held at the level of Barth studies as well as in terms of theology proper.

109. See the original proposal, Bruce L. McCormack, "Grace and Being: The Role of God's Gracious Election in Karl Barth's Theological Ontology," in *The Cambridge Companion to Karl Barth*, ed. John Webster (Cambridge University Press, 2000), 92–110; Bruce L. McCormack, *The Humility of the Eternal Son: Reformed Kenoticism and the Repair of Chalcedon* (Cambridge University Press, 2021). Opposed to McCormack are the following: Paul D. Molnar, *Faith, Freedom, and the Spirit: The Economic Trinity in Barth, Torrance, and Contemporary Theology* (InterVarsity Press, 2015), 129–86; George Hunsinger, "Election and the Trinity: Twenty-Five Theses on the Theology of Karl Barth," *Modern Theology* 24, no. 2 (2008): 179–98; Alex Irving, "A Critical Assessment of Bruce L. McCormack's Christological Proposal," *SJT* 77, no. 2 (2024): 149–62. See Letham, *Holy Trinity*, 348–52; Letham, *Systematic Theology*, 148–52.

110. Matthias Gockel, "How to Read Karl Barth with Charity: A Critical Reply to George Hunsinger," *Modern Theology* 32, no. 2 (April 2016): 260, quoted in Shao Kai

It might conceivably be argued that if God is Trinity necessarily, this is a restriction of his freedom, that any possibility of his being otherwise is thereby ruled out. It seems to me that this argument cannot be sustained. Rather, if God is Trinity—better, since he is Trinity—that includes the fact that he is free to be who he is. On the other side of the debate, it could equally be argued that if God chose to be Trinity, if being Trinity was the consequence of his electing choice, then there was a possibility that he was not so. Moreover, it would follow that prior to making that choice he was not Trinity; rather, he became Trinity upon making that choice. This would seem to posit arbitrariness in God and entails abandonment of the doctrine of divine immutability. It represents a voluntaristic view of God, to which, incidentally, Barth was strongly opposed.[111]

I myself would argue that God is eternally the Father, the Son, and the Holy Spirit, and is so of necessity, not any necessity arising from outside himself, of which there could be none, but by necessity of nature, because that is who he eternally is. If that sounds tautologous, it seems unavoidable in this case. Furthermore, since God is immutable, there is no possibility of his being anything other than who he is. That does not rule out the point that he chooses to be triune, for it is equally self-evident that he delights to be who he is.[112]

Tseng, *Trinity and Election: The Christocentric Reorientation of Karl Barth's Speculative Theology, 1936–1942* (T&T Clark, 2024), 183.

111. Tseng, *Trinity and Election*, 183.

112. See also the following references supplied by Sherman Isbell, which affirm that there could not be from within God a volition or actuation that carried him to what would be a development in God: Owen, *Works*, 12:70–72, 114–15 ("Vindiciae Evangelicae"); Ursinus, *Opera theologica*, 1.476 ("Loci theologici"). Charnock, *Works*, 1:392–94 ("Discourse upon the Immutability of God") (quotation from 393–94): "Mutability is absolutely inconsistent with simplicity, whether the change come from an internal or external principle. . . . Now God being infinitely simple, hath nothing in himself which is not himself, and therefore cannot will any change in himself, he being his own essence and existence." Zanchi, *Operum*, 2:80 ("De Natura Dei," II.iv, q. 2.i); L. Trelcatius Jr., *Scholastica, et Methodica, Locorum Communium Institutio*, 21–22; Polanus, *Syntagma Theologiae Christianae*, 1.967 (II.xiii); Franciscus Junius (1545–1602), *Opera Theologica*, 2 vols. (vol. 1, Geneva: Samuel Crispinus, 1613; vol. 2, Geneva: Petrus and Jacobus Chouet, 1613), 2:1850 ("Summa aliquot locorum communium ss. Theologiae," II.xi); Maccovius, *Loci Communes Theologici*, 137 (XVI); Ridgley, *Body of Divinity*, 1:62 (Q. VII.vi); De Moor, *Commentarius Perpetuus in Marckii Compendium*,

The *Consilium Salutis*

God, from eternity, before the foundation of the world, determined the plan of salvation for the human race and the renewal and consummation of the cosmos. The Father, in his wise and inscrutable counsel, chose that Christ the Son become incarnate as man, and that he be the head of his church, make atonement for sin, rise from the dead, and ascend and reign with him and the Holy Spirit in the indivisible unity of the Trinity forever. Since the Trinity is indivisible, the Father's choice was inseparably the Son's and the Spirit's too, for they have one will. The Son's determination to take human nature was indivisibly that of the Father and the Holy Spirit. In this indivisible determination, the Holy Trinity chose in Christ for salvation, out of pure, free, and sovereign grace, a vast number from every nation of the world, out of the fallen human race, as integral to his purpose of renewing and consummating in Christ his entire creation, leaving the rest to the consequences of their sinful rebellion, to the praise of his glorious justice. *Mutatis mutandis,* the undivided Trinity also determined that the Holy Spirit would bring into effect this plan in inseparable working with the Father and the Son, by upholding the incarnate Son in his earthly life and ministry, raising him from the dead, granting faith to those elected to salvation, sustaining them in the course of their lives, and energizing the renewal of the cosmos. In this great plan, entailing the establishment of the covenant of grace with his chosen people, the will and purpose of God was one, the three acting together in distinct ways in all its aspects.

From all this, creation, providence, and redemption flow, but not as some logical consequence that we construct. They are an integral part of the primal decision. The election of the incarnate Son and of a people, the church, and its members rests on and is accompanied and sustained by God's determination to create the universe for that very purpose. In terms of the Son, incarnation, atonement, ascension, and glorification are all comprised within the grand overall

---

1:619 (IV.xxvi.β.c). Bavinck, *RD*, 2:155: "Common to all pantheistic criticism is that the idea of becoming is transferred to God, thus totally obliterating the boundary line between the Creator and the creature."

design. It assumes and requires that the incarnate Christ be a single subject with the eternal Son, that there be personal identity, such that Jesus can say to Philip, "He who has seen me has seen the Father" (John 14:9). Union with Christ follows from this, in his death, burial, resurrection, ascension, and glorification.

This eternal counsel does not ride roughshod over the freedom of humans, for their freedom consists in their faithful relationship to Christ, of being united to Christ and transformed by the Spirit from one degree of glory to another into the liberty of the children of God in unbroken and unfettered love.

The following comments of Myk Habets are close to what I have been arguing:

> I have shown that the Dominical man is to be identified directly with the eternal Son and his procession or generation from the Father, but not in such a way that would conflate the *Logos asarkos* with the *Logos ensarkos* in anything other than their personal identification—both are the eternal Son but not *simpliciter*. Likewise, the *Logos incarnandus* is the *Logos incarnatus*, but in a very specific way (*secundum quid*). The triune God covenants to become human in the Son in order to achieve the participation of created human persons in the Divine life in the incarnate Son and by the Holy Spirit. The doctrine of the primacy of Christ is the one way in which a christologically conditioned doctrine of election makes sense of both Scripture and the tradition. In the Dominical Man —Jesus Christ—humanity is made to participate in the Divine life and love.[113]

Upon that sovereign and free determination the creation of the universe and the plan of salvation was conceived. In union with the person of the incarnate Son, the church was to be formed in which God's glory would ultimately be made known. The incarnation, life, and ministry of the incarnate Son and his death, burial, resurrection,

113. Myk Habets, "A Supralapsarian Christological Interpretation of the Logos Asarkos" (n.d., but post-2011), 14–15, https://www.academia.edu/3615450/A_Supralapsarian_Christological_Interpretation_of_the_Logos_Asarkos.

and ascension are each essential parts of this one integral movement of God's unfathomable grace. Incarnation leads to atonement; atonement is for the purpose of *theosis* or glorification. Even above that, God's decree entails his decision to assume human nature into permanent and everlasting union in the Son. "Man with God is on the throne"[114]—man is united to God, while being forever distinct. This is not the absorption of humanity in God but rather its full enhancement as created and destined to be in union with God. We will discuss this further in chapter 11.

114. Christopher Wordsworth, "See, the Conqueror Mounts in Triumph," in *The English Hymnal*, ed. Ralph Vaughan Williams (Oxford University Press, 1933), no. 145.

3

The Word Became Flesh

For it was fitting for the creator of the universe, who by the economy of his incarnation became what by nature he was not, to preserve without change both what he himself was by nature and what he became in his incarnation. (Maximus the Confessor, Ad Thalassium 60[1]*)*

At the center of the gospel is the incarnation—"the Word became flesh and lived among us" (John 1:14). As Paul describes it, "God was in Christ" reconciling the world to himself (2 Cor. 5:19). Without it, we could not be saved. It was the incarnate Christ who died on the cross, rose from the dead, and ascended into heaven, now at God's right hand, making intercession for us. In the words of Christopher Wordsworth, "Thou hast raised our human nature in the clouds to God's right hand."[2] Thomas Aquinas wrote, "Nothing more marvelous can be thought of than this divine work: that the true God, the Son of God, should become true man."[3]

1. Paul M. Blowers and Robert Louis Wilken, trans., *On the Cosmic Mystery of Jesus Christ: Selected Writings from St. Maximus the Confessor* (St. Vladimir's Seminary Press, 2003), 124–25.

2. Christopher Wordsworth, "See, the Conqueror Mounts in Triumph," in *The English Hymnal*, ed. Ralph Vaughan Williams (Oxford University Press, 1933), no. 145.

3. "Nihil enim mirabilius excogitari potest divinitus factum quam quod verus Deus Dei Filius fieret homo verus." Thomas Aquinas, *SCG*, 4.27.1.

Underlying this mystery is the astonishing point that God alone could not save us. This is not due to any lack or deficiency on his part; he has the power to do as he pleases. But since he declares himself to be just, salvation by fiat would have been inconsistent with his character. The prime question in our deliverance from sin and death was the satisfaction of God's own justice (Rom. 3:21–26). God's freedom is to act in harmony with who he is. He is not constrained by anything external. Atonement for sin accords with divine justice. The sin of Adam could be atoned for only by a second Adam who did not bear the guilt and corruption inherited from the first. The Savior needed to be man, perfect and righteous man. This is eloquently expressed by the Heidelberg Catechism (1563), QQ. 15–17:

15. Q. What kind of mediator and deliverer should we look for then?
    A. He must be truly human and truly righteous, yet more powerful than all creatures, that is, he must also be true God.
16. Q. Why must he be truly human and truly righteous?
    A. God's justice demands it: man has sinned, man must pay for his sin, but a sinner can not pay for others.
17. Q. Why must he also be true God?
    A. So that, by the power of his deity, he might bear the wrath of God in his humanity and earn for us and restore to us righteousness and life.

Discussion has surrounded whether any of the Trinitarian persons could have become incarnate.[4] On the one hand, God is able to do whatever he likes, in accordance with his nature, and is not limited or constrained by anything he has made. In *De incarnatione Verbi*, however, Anselm argued that it was supremely fitting, or appropriate, for the Son—rather than the Father or the Holy Spirit—to become incarnate. First, Anselm establishes *that* only the Son became incarnate. Later, he argues that *if* either the Father or the Holy Spirit had become flesh, there would have been two Sons. If

4. Anselm, *De fide trinitatis et de incarnatione Verbi*, 3.27–29; *PL*, 158:276–77.

the Father were incarnate, the Son would be the virgin's grandson, and the Father would be the grandson of the virgin's parents. This would be inappropriate for God, and "there cannot be any least inappropriate thing in God."[5] Second, we might add, is the congruity between the immanent and economic Trinity. God is as he reveals himself to be. The fact that the Son—and neither the Father nor the Spirit—became incarnate indicates that there is something in the Trinity to which this corresponds. Beyond this, it would be at least anomalous for the Father to be sent by the Son, while the name "the Holy Spirit"—by definition—is associated with a realm different from our own embodied condition.

We recall the context. The human race was plunged into sin, guilty before God and under his wrath. There was no way for it to be delivered other than by the incarnation, life, atoning death, and ascension of the incarnate Son.

Maximus the Confessor summarizes the received teaching of the church:

> The only-begotten Son, one of the holy and consubstantial Trinity, who is perfect God by nature, has become a perfect human being in accordance with his will, by truly assuming flesh that is consubstantial with us and endowed with a rational soul and mind from the holy Theotokos. . . . He united it properly and inseparably to himself in accordance with the hypostasis. . . . Remaining God and consubstantial with the Father, when he became flesh, he became double, so that being double by nature, he had kinship by nature with both extremes, and preserved the natural difference of his own parts each from the other.[6]

5. "Quoniam ergo quamlibet parvum inconveniens in Deo est impossibile, non debuit alia Dei persona incarnari quam filius." Anselm, "On the Incarnation of the Word," in *Anselm of Canterbury: The Major Works*, ed. Brian Davies and G. R. Evans (Oxford University Press, 1998), 250–51; *PL*, 158:276.

6. Maximus, *Opusculum 7*; *PG*, 91:73B–C, quoted in Christopher A. Beeley, *The Unity of Christ: Continuity and Conflict in Patristic Tradition* (Yale University Press, 2012), 297.

The Eternal Son and the Incarnation

It Is Appropriate That the Son Became Incarnate Rather than the Father or the Holy Spirit

Anselm argued this point against Roscelin, who argued that either the three are three separate things or, if they are not, then the Father and the Spirit became incarnate with the Son.[7] Anselm saw this latter charge as Sabellian; while it affirms that God is one "thing" (quiddity), it gives no grounds for any personal distinctions.[8] In contrast, he argued that it was fitting that the Son should be incarnate and was unsuitable for the Father to be so.[9] Again in opposition to Roscelin, Anselm insisted that the fact that it is fitting that the Son alone became incarnate does not mean that the three persons are three things. Nor does it imply that if the three persons are one thing, all three became incarnate.[10]

Anselm proceeded to discuss the reasons why it was the Son who became incarnate. No other divine person could have become incarnate, since there is nothing inappropriate in God.[11] This follows from Anselm's conviction that God is perfect and always does what is best. Since the Son was incarnate, no other course of action was viable. Furthermore, since the Incarnate One was to intercede for humanity, it is more intelligible *for us* that that person be the Son pleading with his Father.[12] Further, Anselm cited Philippians 2:7,

7. Anselm states that "we are accustomed to apply the term 'thing' to whatever we in any way assert to be something." Anselm, "On the Incarnation of the Word," 239. He agrees that the Father and the Son can be termed "things" if we do not mean that they are distinct or separate substances (quiddities) but rather speak purely in terms of relations. Yet Roscelin appeared to say that they would either be separate "things" or else be effectively indistinguishable.

8. Anselm, *De fide trinitatis et de incarnatione Verbi*, 3; Davies and Evans, *Anselm: Major Works*, 241–43.

9. Anselm, *De fide trinitatis et de incarnatione Verbi*, 2; Davies and Evans, *Anselm: Major Works*, 238–41.

10. Anselm, *De fide trinitatis et de incarnatione Verbi*, 6; Davies and Evans, *Anselm: Major Works*, 245–47.

11. "Quoniam ergo quamlibet parvum inconveniens in Deo est impossibile, non debuit alia Dei persona incarnari quum Filius." Anselm, *De fide trinitatis et de incarnatione Verbi*, 10; Davies and Evans, *Anselm: Major Works*, 250–52; *PL*, 158:276.

12. "Est et aliud, cur magis conveniat Filio incarnatio quam alii." Anselm, *De fide trinitatis et de incarnatione Verbi*, 10; Davies and Evans, *Anselm: Major Works*, 251; *PL*, 158:277.

stating that none of the three more appropriately emptied himself than the Son.[13] In this, Anselm was saying what Augustine had said centuries earlier in reply to a question from Nebridius.[14]

The Incarnation Establishes the Compatibility of God and Humanity

As Anselm argued against Roscelin, in Christ there is no division. There is not one who is God and one who is a human being. Instead, the very same one who is the human being is God.[15] The Son assumed into union *a human nature*, not a human person; the Son and the assumed human nature are *the same person*. While the Creator is infinite and the creature finite—the Creator-creature distinction remains inviolable—God has established a compatibility between himself and humanity, such that the humanity of Christ is the humanity of the eternal Son.

This is crucial. If the Creator-creature distinction applied absolutely, an infinite chasm would preclude that unbreakable union between God and humanity in Christ.

Despite being the author of a range of controversial speculative ideas, Sergei Bulgakov had important things to say. He argued that the creation of humanity underlies the incarnation; there is some inalienable characteristic in humanity by which the possibility of the incarnation is comprehensible.[16] This is found in the person of Christ. In the same place, following the Christological controversy, "we must infer that, since the person of the Word found it possible to live in human nature as well as in its own, therefore it is itself in some sense a human person too." By this Bulgakov did not propose some mixture of divine and human, nor an autonomous human person somehow attached to the Word. Rather, in order to serve as person

13. "Nulla igitur trium personarum Dei congruentius semetipsum exinanivit formam servi accipiens . . . quam Filii." Anselm, *De fide trinitatis et de incarnatione Verbi*, 10; Davies and Evans, *Anselm: Major Works*, 252; *PL*, 158:277.

14. Augustine, *Letter 11 to Nebridius*, 2; *NPNF*[1], 1:229.

15. Anselm, *De fide trinitatis et de incarnatione Verbi*, 11; *PL*, 158:279.

16. Sergius Bulgakov, *The Wisdom of God: A Brief Summary of Sophiology* (Williams and Norgate, 1937), 126.

to humanity, the divine person of the Word must itself be human "or, more exactly, co-human." Man, on his side and for his part, must be capable of receiving and making room for a divine person in place of the human. Bulgakov continued, "The incarnation thus appears to postulate, on its hypostatic side at least, some original analogy between divine and human personality, which yet does not overthrow all the essential difference between them." He pointed to the account in Genesis 2:7, where the personal spirit of man has its divine, uncreated origin from "the spirit of God." It is a spark of the divine. Man is made a partaker of the divine nature and capable of divinization. "Thus it is possible for the person of the heavenly God-man, the Word, to become the person of a created human nature." So, Bulgakov concluded, it was natural for the Word to take the place of the human personality of the human nature of Christ.[17]

There Is Personal Identity Between the Eternal and the Incarnate Son

Following the Christological controversies in the early centuries of the church, the ecumenical councils affirmed that the eternal Son had taken into union a human nature, body and soul, conceived by the Holy Spirit in the womb of the virgin Mary. This is not two separate natures coming together but rather the assumption by the person of the Son of a human nature into unbroken union. We will discuss these vital debates in chapters 4 through 7.

The most significant architect of this settlement was Cyril of Alexandria. He wrote of an ontological union that involved no change in the Son himself, for "the Word who is God came down out of heaven and entered our likeness . . . while ever remaining what he was."[18] The result is an "inseparable union" (*henōsin adiaspaston*),[19]

17. Bulgakov, *Wisdom*, 129–31.

18. John A. McGuckin, *St. Cyril of Alexandria and the Christological Controversy: Its History, Theology, and Texts* (St. Vladimir's Seminary Press, 2004), 61; *PG*, 75:1269. See Thomas G. Weinandy, "Cyril and the Mystery of the Incarnation," in *The Theology of St. Cyril of Alexandria: A Critical Appreciation*, ed. Thomas G. Weinandy and Daniel A. Keating (T&T Clark, 2003), 27–28.

19. McGuckin, *Cyril*, 75; *PG*, 75:1289.

an "indissoluble union" (*henōsin adiatmēton*).[20] Referring to Cyril's writings before ever the Nestorian crisis arose, Thomas Weinandy states that for Cyril, "Jesus is one ontological entity, and the one ontological entity that Jesus is is the one person of the Son of God existing as a complete and authentic man."[21] So "the incarnational act does not bring about a union of natures, but rather it is an act by which the humanity is united substantially to the person of the Word."[22] Jesus is the same Son who existed eternally with the Father who came to exist as man.[23] Hence, in terms of his personal identity —*who* he is—he is the eternal Son, one of the Trinity according to the flesh, and his humanity—both body and soul—is that of the Son.

Virginal Conception

But when we think of the incarnation, we are immediately confronted by a singularity—Jesus' unique conception. This appears to set him apart from the rest of us. It has also faced critical attacks on the assumption that the records are mythological and reflect similar stories in other religions. We need to ask what exactly is entailed.

Here the main contributions are a classic defense against the skeptical attacks of his day from J. Gresham Machen,[24] a professedly objective assessment by the Roman Catholic scholar Raymond Brown, which relies on autonomous reasoning,[25] and a superb exposition of its biblical and theological basis and significance by T. F. Torrance.[26]

Jesus' birth was a normal human delivery following a normal gestation. The conception was unique, without the involvement of a human father. The term *virginal conception* better describes the reality.

Karl Barth provides a positive demonstration of its importance. The New Testament, like the church councils, takes an interest in

20. McGuckin, *Cyril*, 77; *PG*, 75:1289.
21. Weinandy, "Cyril," 30.
22. Weinandy, "Cyril," 41.
23. Weinandy, "Cyril," 43. See McGuckin, *Cyril*, 107–16.
24. J. Gresham Machen, *The Virgin Birth of Christ* (repr., Baker, 1965).
25. Raymond E. Brown, *The Virginal Conception and Bodily Resurrection of Jesus* (Paulist Press, 1973).
26. Thomas F. Torrance, *Incarnation: The Person and Life of Christ* (Paternoster, 2008), 88–104.

Mary in a purely Christological sense; "she is simply man to whom the miracle of revelation happens."[27] Mariology as such "is an arbitrary innovation in the face of Scripture and the early church, . . . a falsification of Christian truth."[28] From that, Barth considers "the miracle of Christmas," which leads to his defense of the virginal conception.[29] It was the birth of a real son of a real mother, "an event in this world of ours, yet such that it is not grounded upon the continuity of events in this world nor is it to be understood in terms of it," for it is a sign set up by God.[30]

The clause in the creed, "conceived by the Holy Spirit," indicates the ground and content of the sign.[31] It states from God's side what "born of the Virgin Mary" states from man's side.[32] It rules out all attempts to understand it as a natural possibility.[33] The possibility of man's being adopted into unity with the Son of God is the Holy Ghost.[34] It points to the mystery of God himself.[35] It does not mean that he is begotten by the Holy Spirit—there was no marriage between the Holy Spirit and the virgin Mary.[36] The Holy Spirit is God himself—it is withdrawn from any kind of human analogy except the analogy of faith.[37] In short, to call Mary "the mother of God" is a test of the proper understanding of the incarnation of the Word.[38]

The Gospel Narratives

Matthew 1:18–25

This account is from Joseph's perspective. Joseph is considered Jesus' father, since he accepted legal responsibility as his earthly father. The narratives make clear that he was not Jesus' biological

27. Karl Barth, *CD*, II/1:139–40.
28. Barth, *CD*, I/2:143.
29. Barth, *CD*, I/2:185–202.
30. Barth, *CD*, I/2:187.
31. Barth, *CD*, I/2:196.
32. Barth, *CD*, I/2:197.
33. Barth, *CD*, I/2:198.
34. Barth, *CD*, I/2:199.
35. Barth, *CD*, I/2:199.
36. Barth, *CD*, I/2:200.
37. Barth, *CD*, I/2:201.
38. Barth, *CD*, II/1:138.

father. In the genealogy in Luke 3:23, Joseph is entered as the supposed father of Jesus. Since betrothal was legally binding, Joseph had a right to divorce Mary when he discovered that she was pregnant. Because he was a good man, he determined to do this privately rather than shaming Mary in public. Only after the information provided by the angel did he relent.[39]

Luke 1:26–29

The Lukan material presents the events from Mary's perspective and in a fuller way. No wonder she was shocked and perturbed! Suddenly she had an unexpected visitor from another dimension. "The angel Gabriel was sent *from God to a city of Galilee named Nazareth*." His departure point was God; his destination was an obscure village in northern Israel. This was a conjunction of the spiritual and the material, heaven and earth. This great spirit appeared in bodily form. He left the presence of God; he spoke to Mary in Hebrew. These factors together sent Mary into extreme agitation. Furthermore, she was young—"a virgin betrothed to a man whose name was Joseph"—legally married to Joseph, for that is what betrothal entailed, although the customary period before the marriage was consummated had not yet passed.

Twice in Luke 1:27, Luke records that Mary was a *parthenos*, a virgin.[40] As John Nolland remarks, this is a clear barrier to the promised

39. R. T. France, *The Gospel According to Matthew: An Introduction and Commentary* (Inter-Varsity Press, 1985), 77–80; W. D. Davies, *A Critical and Exegetical Commentary on the Gospel According to Saint Matthew* (T&T Clark, 1988), 196–223.

40. The word could mean "a young woman of marriageable age" (*LN*, 1:109), but as we will see in a moment or two, the passage points unmistakably to virginity. As Morris points out, "the evidence of the Gospel as we have it is plain." Leon Morris, *Luke: An Introduction and Commentary* (Inter-Varsity Press, 1997), 79. Fitzmyer calls "the normal understanding" of *parthenos* to be "virgin." Joseph A. Fitzmyer, *The Gospel According to Luke (I–IX)*, Anchor Bible (Doubleday, 1970), 343. See also Joel B. Green, *The Gospel of Luke* (Eerdmans, 1997), 85–86. The context—see Luke 1:34—establishes this beyond question. For a detailed discussion of competing interpretations, see I. Howard Marshall, *The Gospel of Luke: A Commentary on the Greek Text*, New International Greek Testament Commentary (Paternoster Press, 1978), 68–70. Besides, a young woman of marriageable age would be assumed to be a virgin in first-century Israel.

child, just as Elizabeth's barrenness was to the birth of John the Baptist.[41] Both events are the results of the sovereign power of God. On the other hand, Joseph—who features here only tangentially—is described as being "of the house of David." Consequently, the family is in David's line, and the inheritance of the promises given to David in 2 Samuel 7 is of immediate relevance and about to be fulfilled.

Gabriel's first words—words evidently *from God*—are words of greeting: "Hail, highly favored one, the Lord be / is with you" (Luke 1:28–29). Mary is the passive receiver of God's grace. She has been favored by Yahweh. Yahweh is with her. She is in a relation to God, receiving and continuing to receive God's favor. There is not the slightest hint that Mary herself is a conduit of grace to others, still less a dispenser of the favor of God.[42] The participle is passive—if Mary represents anything, it is the faithful who *receive* the bountiful goodness of God. Gabriel's statement is intended to reassure her in the face of the agitation and perplexity that gripped her. It is a declaration that her status with God is secure.

Nevertheless, Mary is terrified and needs something further to convince her that there is no reason to fear (Luke 1:29–30). There are good reasons for Mary not to fear but to rejoice (vv. 30–33; cf. vv. 46–55). The angel repeats that she has found favor with God; the nature of this favor becomes clear in what follows. She will conceive a son. He is to be called Jesus, meaning "Yahweh saves."[43] Here is an explicit declaration that *this* is the child who will be the Savior.

Mary's child will excel everything. He will be great. John was to be "great in the sight of the Lord" (Luke 1:15), but Jesus' greatness will surpass every potential rival. "He will be called the Son of the Most High" (v. 32)—the lack of definite articles in Greek indicates the quality of the terms, demonstrating his uniqueness. The phrase "the Most High" is often used in the Old Testament to refer to God.

41. John Nolland, *Luke 1–9:20*, Word Biblical Commentary 35A (Word Books, 1989), 49.

42. The Jesuit scholar Fitzmyer acknowledges that the later scholastic tradition went beyond the Lucan perfect participle. Fitzmyer, *Luke (I–IX)*, 345–46. See Marshall, *Luke*, 65.

43. On the meaning, see Fitzmyer, *Luke (I–IX)*, 347.

In the background, perhaps, is Isaiah 9:6–7, where the child born to deliver the covenant people of God is called "the mighty God."

Additionally, "the Lord God will give to him the throne of his father David" (Luke 1:32). He will be the inheritor of the promises of the Davidic covenant (2 Sam. 7:12–16; Ps. 89:26–29). Contrary to the Davidic kings, Jesus "will reign over the house of Jacob forever, and of his kingdom there will be no end" (Luke 1:33). The Son of Man in Daniel 7, who is given a universal and unending kingdom, may also be in view. Luke's point in 1:27 about Joseph becomes clear; Jesus will be in the line of David, since in Israel legal paternity decided the matter. Jesus' opponents never questioned his Davidic claim; his relatives boasted of it. In the trial of his brothers' grandsons under the Emperor Domitian, it was brought against them by the authorities. For Paul, it would be a crucial element of his view of Christ: "born of the seed of David according to the flesh" (Rom. 1:3–4).

But this was beyond comprehension to Mary, for she was still a virgin (Luke 1:34).[44] People in first-century Israel were no more gullible or credulous than people today. One of the three main religious groups at the time, the Sadducees, were anti-supernaturalists, rationalists who opposed the idea of the resurrection and angels. For them, the very idea that the angel Gabriel had visited Nazareth was in the realm of fairy tales, to say nothing about the details of his message. Mary was not taken in; she questioned the angel, not out of skepticism—her faith is evident in verse 38—but as one who believes but needs to understand.[45]

So Gabriel explains. His comment is poetic, presented in parallelism:

> The Holy Spirit will come upon you,
> and the power of the Most High will overshadow you. (Luke 1:35)

The poetic explanation indicates something deeply mysterious, which cannot be captured in prose. The imminent pregnancy will

44. Green, *Luke*, 89.
45. Green, *Luke*, 89; Nolland, *Luke 1–9:20*, 55; Fitzmyer, *Luke (I–IX)*, 348.

be due to the Holy Spirit, resulting from the action of God. The language is reminiscent of the creation narrative in Genesis, which says that "the Spirit of God was hovering over the face of the waters" of creation like a mother bird (Gen. 1:2). The implication is that the Spirit, in overshadowing Mary, has initiated a new creation, a new creative act on God's part, the start of a new humanity of which the child is the head, a new creation that will stand and flourish for eternity.[46] This is the decisive point in the history of redemption, in world history as a whole. As with all the other direct acts of God, such as the creation and the resurrection, no one is there to observe it, to analyze its mechanics, at the instant the work is done. It remains a mystery, known only by revelation (Job 38:1f.). To underline this, in our day we know that *parthenogenesis* can produce only a female, since, without the participation of a male, the Y chromosome is missing. This effectively requires a supervening action of God to create what would otherwise be absent. This, in itself, precludes speculations of a biological or genetic nature. We assume that Mary provided her DNA and that the action of the Spirit produced the rest, but as Torrance remarks, "the virgin birth cannot be understood *biologically*. If you ask biological questions of the virgin birth you will only get biological answers."[47]

The consequence of the Spirit's creative action is that the child to whom Mary gives birth will be called the holy Son of God. The stress falls on the last words—*hiuos theou* ("Son of God"). In his humanity, Jesus will be the Son of God. Israel had been called God's son (Ex. 4:22; Hos. 11:1). The Davidic king was the embodment of sonship (Ps. 2:7), and Israel was anticipating this to be developed by great David's greater son. Having already described Jesus as "the son of the Most High" (Luke 1:32), and against the backcloth of

46. Most commentators draw attention to a kindred phrase in Acts 1:8, to manifestations of the glory of God in the exodus and wilderness period, or to the transfiguration, but miss this point. Joel Green is right, however, in that "these parallel affirmations do not suggest sexual activity, but do connote divine agency." Green, *Luke*, 90. Yet what element of divine agency is more compelling in this case than creation? Barth expresses it well when he describes the virgin birth as "a creative act of divine omnipotence." Barth, *CD*, IV/1:207.

47. Torrance, *Incarnation*, 95.

Isaiah 9:6–7, where the son born is "the mighty God," Luke gives a clear attribution of deity to the child. This the church has recognized through the ages in calling Mary *theotokos* ("God-bearer").[48]

But other descriptions of the child Jesus are present here too. He is a child and has a mother; so he is human. He is holy (*hagios*), set apart for God, his call, and his purposes. Entailed in this is separation from sin.[49] In Matthew's account of the birth announcement—the one given to Joseph—Jesus is to "save his people from their sins" (Matt. 1:21). In order to do this, he must be free from the corruption that sin has brought into the world.

The angel points to the invincible power of the word of God (Luke 1:37). No word from God is powerless; he always accomplishes what he says he will do. With the Spirit of God hovering over the waters, God said, "Let there be light," and there was light (Gen. 1:1–5). He spoke; it was done. He created. He brought into existence what previously had no existence. He calls the things that are not as though they are. For Mary, what in human terms was impossible—to conceive a male child without the participation of a male—could be effected by the word of God in an instant. Luke points to the Spirit and the word of God working together, inseparably, powerfully, effectively, effortlessly.

For Mary, there were to be potentially difficult social consequences. Joseph had originally intended to divorce her for marital infidelity (Matt. 1:20–21). The penalty for sexual immorality by a betrothed woman was death by stoning (Deut. 22:23–24). The comments and the gossip would be bound to arise—how many would believe the story of an intervention by an angel or an entirely secret action of the Holy Spirit? Later, some of Jesus' opponents would make barbed comments (John 8:41). Yet Mary's immediate reply is one of pure faith—"be it to me according to your word" (Luke 1:38)—echoing David's similar response to a surprising revelation (2 Sam. 7:25). Mary believes God's word, submits to it, and follows it.

48. We will discuss this in chapter 4.

49. As we will discuss later, this does not obviate the reality that the incarnate Son endured the consequences of sin as it has affected the world and the human race. He was "a man of sorrows and acquainted with grief" (Isa. 53:3).

Her own circumstances are secondary. Faith is a matter of denying oneself, taking up one's cross, and following Jesus. Mary, far from being a co-redemptrix, is a pattern for the church of saving faith. The whole scenario, as Barth stressed, portrays the relationship between the regenerating work of the Spirit and the consequent response of faith.[50] Additionally, the virgin womb stands at the start of the Gospels as the empty tomb at the end, like bookends framing the whole, pointing to the mighty acts of God constituting and establishing the entire drama of salvation.[51]

Allusions to the Virginal Conception in the Rest of the New Testament[52]

Outside the accounts in Matthew and Luke, there are other references or allusions to the virginal conception in the New Testament. Mark describes Jesus as "the son of Mary" (Mark 6:3); in Jewish society, a man was normally seen in relation to his father. Paul uses *gennaō* for human begetting of sons three times in Galatians 4, but when in the same context (Gal. 4:4) he refers to the birth of Jesus, he uses *ginomai;*[53] it seems that he knows that something unusual surrounded it—hardly a surprise, since Luke was a regular traveling companion. He also uses *ginomai* to indicate Christ's birth of the seed of David in Romans 1:3. In common with the church fathers of the first five centuries, Tertullian, writing around A.D. 200,[54] insists on a reading of John 1:13 from early Latin manuscripts in the singular *qui non* ("*who was* born not of bloods"), referring to the birth of Jesus, and castigates the Valentinian gnostics for corrupting the text by intruding the plural *hoi ouk* ("*who were* born") in reference to believers. Tertullian's preferred reading suggests that the Word who became flesh was not conceived in the normal way, by the action

50. Barth, *CD*, I/2:138–41.

51. The finest exposition of the doctrine of the virgin birth is Torrance, *Incarnation*, 94–104.

52. For an extended exposition of these instances, see Torrance, *Incarnation*, 88–94, to whom I am indebted in this section.

53. Meaning "to become."

54. Tertullian, *On the Flesh of Christ*, 19, 24, in *The Ante-Nicene Fathers*, ed. A. Roberts and J. Donaldson, rev. A. C. Coxe (repr., Eerdmans, 1993), 3:537–38, 541–42.

of a human male. We should also note John 8:19, 41, where Jesus' opponents appear to mock him, asking, "Where is your father?"

The Significance of the Virginal Conception

(1) There are two sides to this—Jesus was born of the virgin Mary, conceived by the Holy Spirit. There is a normal gestation and birth, but also a dimension beyond our knowledge, an act of God as Creator.

(2) The virginal conception comes in the context of the incarnation, and is to be seen in connection with the resurrection. Again, both events are like bookends enclosing the events recorded in the Gospels, individually and together pointing to the sovereign creative power of God. Christ's birth is not something under human power. It is the union of God and man achieved entirely on the part of God.

(3) It displays the true humanity of Christ—he was born of a human mother after the normal period of gestation. The Docetists, in the process of opposing the full humanity of Christ, denied the virgin birth.

(4) It indicates that human capacity is disqualified and that salvation is from the Lord. The initiative is God's. Mary is believingly receptive (Luke 1:38). She is a picture and pattern of God's grace in regeneration and faith.

(5) It is a new creation—a renovation of the old (Luke 1:34–35). As in the original creation and the resurrection, we understand by the Holy Spirit in faith, not by a process of human logic and argumentation, even though it can be logically defended.

John of Damascus, the great synthesizer of the orthodox fathers, understood three things to have occurred simultaneously. First was the assumption of human nature by the Logos; second, its coming into being; and third, its being made divine by the Word.[55] By the last category we should understand the sanctification or deification of the assumed humanity,[56] with the endowment of the Holy Spirit. Oliver Crisp argues along similar lines:

55. John of Damascus, *On the Orthodox Faith*, 3.12; *NPNF*², 9:2:56–57.

56. On deification, see Robert Letham, *Union with Christ: In Scripture, History, and Theology* (P&R Publishing, 2011), 91–128; Robert Letham, *Systematic Theology* (Crossway, 2019), 768–89.

> The Virginal Conception teaches us that, at a certain moment in time, the Word becomes incarnate. So the human nature he assumes at the Virginal Conception, he assumes "into" his person. . . . And, of course, all of this happens at one-and-the-same-time, according to most orthodox accounts of the Incarnation. . . . There is no time lapse between the generation of the human body in the womb of the Virgin by the Holy Spirit, the creation and "attachment" / integration of the soul to the body, and the assumption and "personalization" of this complete human nature (the body + soul composite) by the Word of God. All these events take place simultaneously at the Virginal Conception. If there were any delay between these different "moments" of the Virginal Conception and Incarnation, the result, I suggest, would be something other than an orthodox account of the Incarnation.[57]

John of Damascus also refers to Christ's two begettings.[58] Here the virginal conception corresponds not so much to the resurrection as to the eternal generation by the Father. In eternity the Son is generated by the Father without a mother, while in time he is generated through the mother without a father. Charles Twombly refers to John's discussion of whether someone can be human while lacking a human father. His answer points to Adam and Eve, who are regarded as truly human.[59]

John Calvin supports the idea that it is not the virgin birth as such that guarantees Christ's holiness but rather the work of the Spirit. "For we make Christ free of all stain not just because he was begotten of his mother without copulation with a man, but because he was sanctified by the Spirit that the generation might be pure and undefiled as would have been true before Adam's fall."[60]

57. Oliver D. Crisp, *God Incarnate: Explorations in Christology* (T&T Clark, 2009), 86. See also Oliver D. Crisp, *Divinity and Humanity: The Incarnation Reconsidered*, Current Issues in Theology (Cambridge University Press, 2007), 62.

58. John of Damascus, *On the Orthodox Faith*, 3.7; *NPNF*², 9:2:51.

59. Charles C. Twombly, *Perichoresis and Personhood: God, Christ, and Salvation in John of Damascus* (Pickwick Publications, 2015), 68.

60. John Calvin, *Institutes*, 2.13.4.

The Enfleshment of the Son

This is the heart of the Christian faith—"the Word became flesh" (John 1:14). Eternity and time intersect, Creator and creature are conjoined, God and man united. As we saw from Luke 1:34–35, the incarnation is a new creation. Athanasius summed this up in these immortal words:

> It is, then, proper for us to begin the treatment of this subject by speaking of the creation of the universe, and of God its artificer, that so it may be duly perceived that the renewal of creation has been the work of the self-same Word that made it at the beginning. For it will appear not inconsonant for the Father to have wrought its salvation in Him by whose means he made it.[61]

The verb "became" (*ginomai*) denotes the Word's entering into something new. The Word himself remained the same, but the environment into which he went was different. In John 1:1–4, John consistently uses the imperfect of *eimi* in referring to the Word, indicating continuance. He reserves *ginomai* for the creation (John 1:3); all things *became* through him. He uses this verb for John the Baptist (v. 6), who was a man, in contrast to the Word, who always was and is. Yet here in verse 14, the Word is also said *to become*, existing in the same manner as all other things created by him. He appeared in history, as John the Baptist did. It is, as Rudolf Schnackenburg stresses, a unique event.[62]

This was not, however, something that was imposed on the Word, something that happened as the result of an outside agency, as it did in the case of the Baptist; he chose it. He was not humbled; he humbled himself. The subject of the clause is *ho logos*; the Word is the active agent. The subject of the following clauses is still the Word.[63] The Word who always was and is, who is with God and

61. Athanasius, *On the Incarnation*, 1.

62. Rudolf Schnackenburg, *The Gospel According to St. John*, vol. 1, *Introduction and Commentary on Chapters 1–4*, trans. Kevin Smyth (Burns & Oates, 1968), 266.

63. The subject of a clause or sentence is the person or entity that performs the actions indicated by the main verb. In the sentence "Letham writes a book," the verb is "writes" and "Letham" is the subject. In John 1:14 and following, the Logos / Word

who is God, who is the Creator of all things, and who is life itself, having become flesh, continues to be who he always is.

Superficially, it might appear that the Word changed into something else, in a metamorphosis akin to a caterpillar's changing into a butterfly, the Word's becoming flesh and so ceasing to be the Word that he always was. In such a case, the Word would have changed into a human and ceased to be the Word. That this is not the case is clear from the Word's being the active agent, in control of what happened, and his continuing to be the subject of all that follows.

Again, it might be supposed that the Word mingled with flesh and so formed a third substance, as ingredients in a recipe merge and become something other than what they were before they were mixed together. If this were so, the Word and flesh would have combined to form an entity composed of both yet different from either. Once more, we must point to the fact that John states that not only did the Word become flesh but he lived among us; the Word, not some composite entity, lived and was seen.

If John means that the Word remained what he always was and is, what does John mean by his becoming *flesh*? The physicality of humanity is obviously involved, but he intends something more than simply the flesh and blood of a human body. The flesh that the Word became is humanity in its weakness and dependence, creaturely existence in its vulnerability and smallness, its fragility and trajectory of decay.[64] The Jews considered humans to be psychosomatic unities, body and soul together. This Jesus was without dilution. He grew tired and hungry after a long journey (John 4:1ff.). He was distressed at the death of a friend (11:33–35). He interacted with others (1 John 1:1). The Word assumed, adopted, and incorporated human nature, body and soul, into union with himself so that it was his own. He remains the Word. What is there, and who is there, after the *egeneto* (the "becoming") is the same as what was

---

is the subject who acts. At the same time, in other than a strict grammatical sense, the Word is the center of attention here, the one who is the focus—the subject—of John's writing.

64. Barnabas Lindars, *The Gospel of John*, New Century Bible Commentary (Eerdmans, 1972), 93–94; Schnackenburg, *St. John*, 1:267–68.

there and who was there before. The difference is that there is now an addition. The Word now has flesh, a full human nature.[65] In the words of Paul, he who was—and eternally is—in the form of God has now added the form of a servant (Phil. 2:6–8). He has not ceased to be in the form of God. There is no subtraction, only addition. Not that the addition augments his divine being, for that is perfect, and nothing can be added to it. The addition, for want of a better word, is that of the humanity, the "form of a servant" that he takes into union. And it is the Word who is the subject of the whole event.

So if we are to ask *who* is Jesus of Nazareth, what is his personal identity, he is the eternal Word of the Father, the Son of God, one of the Trinity, one with the Father and the Holy Spirit from eternity. But if we are to ask of *what* he consists, what is the manner of his existence, he is the Son of God incarnate in human nature.[66] Again, the Word is still the personal subject; *the Word* became flesh. It is flesh that *is added—permanently—*"not for the years of time alone, but for eternity." The Word is the agent of the first and the new creation. He is the eternal Son, now enfleshed, "so truly man in the midst of mankind that it was not easy to recognize him as other than man or to distinguish him from other men."[67]

He Lived in a Tent Among Us

In the Old Testament, Yahweh dwelt in the tabernacle, eventually inserted into the innermost part of the temple, where Yahweh and Israel met, the center point of the covenant relationship. Now the Word has his permanent tent-dwelling among his people; Jesus Christ is the place where God and they meet, the center and focus of covenant worship, "the tabernacle of God among men and women."[68] True worship is in the Spirit and in the truth, the incarnate Christ

65. The idea of flesh (*sarx*) as corrupt and sinful, a theme prominent in Paul and evident in 1 John 2:16, is not in view here; see Schnackenburg, *St. John*, 1:267–68.

66. One of the best descriptions of the Christology of John that I have read is Thomas Weinandy's description of the Christology of Cyril of Alexandria, in "Cyril," 23–54.

67. Torrance, *Incarnation*, 61.

68. Torrance, *Incarnation*, 60.

(John 4:21–24).[69] God takes the initiative; it is his work from start to finish. The Word is in the driver's seat throughout. Thus, Jesus displays the grace and truth of God, pointing to his loyalty to his covenant and its promises.[70]

Barth comments that "if we have let ourselves be led to Jesus Christ along the only sensible, legitimate path for the church, i.e., by the prophetic and apostolic witness to revelation, then the statement, 'Jesus Christ is very God and very man,' is the assumption upon which all further reflection must proceed."[71] John 1:14 must guide us in our discussion of this dogmatic statement.[72] In the statement "the Word became flesh," the Word is the subject, and he acts. His becoming a creature is a new creation, a sovereign divine act distinct from creation.[73] It does not rest on any necessity in the divine nature.[74] The Word is still the free, sovereign Word of God.[75] Apart from the Word, the flesh would have no being at all.[76] Consequently, there can be no "Jesus-worship" in which the human Jesus is the object. As Cyril commented, we do not worship the flesh; rather, we worship the Son with his flesh. Or, as Barth again states: "This man was thus never a reality by himself, and therefore, since the Son of God became this man, he is not another or second being in Jesus Christ alongside the Son of God. . . . It means that Jesus Christ, the Son of God and thus himself true God, is also a true man. But this man exists inasmuch as the Son of God is this man."[77]

The Witnesses: John 14b–18

The Apostles: John 1:14b

"We have seen his glory." The Law required two or three witnesses to establish a matter as true; here there is a superabundance.

69. Note Basil's striking turn of phrase, referring to the Spirit as the place of the saints, mentioning expressly John 4:21–24. Basil of Caesarea, *On the Holy Spirit*, 26.62.
70. Lindars, *John*, 95.
71. Barth, CD, I/2:131.
72. Barth, CD, I/2:132.
73. Barth, CD, I/2:134.
74. Barth, CD, I/2:135.
75. Barth, CD, I/2:136.
76. Barth, CD, I/2:136.
77. Barth, CD, I/2:150.

First are the apostles, including John himself, referring to the transfiguration, where he, Peter, and James saw Jesus appear dazzling white, a preview of his glorification.[78] Yahweh's presence in the tabernacle, the glory that he had revealed in part to Israel, was now fully embodied in Jesus Christ. Human beings could not look directly on the glory of Yahweh and live, but in Jesus this was reality.

Jesus' glory, however, was radically different from what human expectations might have suggested. He came as a servant, washing his disciples' feet, the action of a Gentile slave (John 13:1–20). His glorification was at the cross, where he hung as a condemned criminal (12:20–33), in a state of dereliction so that we might become the children of God (20:31).

The Incarnation Is the Ultimate Revelation of God: John 1:18

We cannot know God as God. No one has seen God as he is in himself. He is invisible (Ex. 33:20; 1 Tim. 1:17; 6:16). When he revealed himself, it was as man, on our level, in our nature. Jesus Christ has made God known. The expression "only begotten God" (*ho monogenēs theos*) has greater textual support than the variant "only begotten Son."[79] The reference is to the unique and only Son, begotten of the Father before all ages.[80] He is in an intimate and indivisible relation to the Father. There is a fellowship and union of love within the Trinity from eternity.[81] From this, the Son has interpreted[82] the mystery of God to us, making known the indivisible love in the Trinity in self-sacrificial love to us.

78. C. K. Barrett, *The Gospel According to St John: An Introduction with Commentary and Notes on the Greek Text*, 2nd ed. (SPCK, 1978), 166; A. M. Ramsey, *The Glory of God and the Transfiguration of Christ* (Longmans, 1949), passim.

79. It is supported by the Nestlé-Aland 28th and the United Bible Societies 4th editions, although not by the Tyndale House, Cambridge edition, which presents the earliest attested text.

80. Barrett, *St John*, 169; Lindars, *John*, 98; Leon Morris, *The Gospel According to John: The English Text with Introduction, Exposition and Notes* (Marshall, Morgan & Scott, 1971), 113–14; Schnackenburg, *St. John*, 1:269–71.

81. Barrett, *St John*, 169–70; D. A. Carson, *The Gospel According to St John* (Inter-Varsity Press, 1991), 135.

82. Barrett, *St John*, 170; Lindars, *John*, 99.

Torrance points to the breathtaking reality. He writes:

> This means that in the *egeneto sarx* (becoming flesh) we have something unique, a relation between God and man, the creator and the creature, which has no parallel anywhere in creation. We must speak of a personal presence of God in all created being, and in a certain sense therefore of a unity of all created being with God, but as such created being has an existence different from and parallel to God's existence, though absolutely dependent upon him and derived from him. But here, in the Word *become* flesh in the unity of God and man in Jesus Christ, Jesus Christ *is* God. Jesus Christ has no existence apart from or different from or parallel to God's existence. He has his existence only in this divine act of condescension in which God gathers man into coexistence with himself. That means that here in the Word made flesh God and man are so related in Jesus Christ, that *Jesus exists as man only so far as he exists as God*, and yet as God he also has an existence as flesh or *sarx*. There would have been no Jesus apart from the incarnation, so that the existence of Jesus even as man is an existence only in the Word become flesh, but in that the Word became flesh, there now exists a man Jesus who is true man and exists as historical human beings exist.[83]

> O wisest love! that flesh and blood
> Which did in Adam fail,
> Should strive afresh against their foe,
> Should strive and should prevail;
>
> And that a higher gift than grace
> Should flesh and blood refine,
> God's presence and his very Self,
> And Essence all-divine.[84]

83. Torrance, *Incarnation*, 67.
84. John Henry Newman, "Praise to the Holiest in the Height" (1865).

The Son as Man

Biblical Evidence for Christ's Humanity

In the early church, the heresy of Docetism was at times a threat. This held that the humanity of Jesus was only apparent, not real.[85] It most likely stemmed from the false supposition that matter was inferior to the spiritual realm and that, consequently, it would have been demeaning for God to be mixed up with the bodily aspects of life. There are hints in 1 John of the threat of this pernicious idea, where John asserts that the test for the genuineness of Christian profession is whether a person confesses that Jesus Christ has come in the flesh (1 John 4:1–6). Whoever denies the reality of his humanity is not of God. It has been widely thought that John may have been dealing with the ideas of Cerinthus or his followers, who held that the Christ descended on Jesus at his baptism and left him before his crucifixion. If that claim were true, there could have been no incarnation, only a temporary inspiration of a man, like one of the prophets. The Son would not have taken human nature for his own. In that case, we could not be saved.

In contrast, the New Testament is full of evidence for the reality of the Son's humanity. Indeed, in the modern world it is a fact hardly, if ever, disputed. The trend in the theology of the last hundred years or so has been to insist that we begin our thinking about Christ with the historical record and with the reality of his being a man in first-century Israel.

He is portrayed as undergoing normal human growth; experiencing weariness, hunger, and thirst; being filled with normal human emotions; being horrified at the prospect of death; being engaged in regular relationships with family and friends; aging; trusting and obeying God; undergoing temptation and suffering; and dying and being buried. He eats and drinks, grows from infancy to maturity, and progresses in wisdom and stature, in favor with God and man (Luke 2:42, 52). While a child, he is subject to his parents (v. 51), later entering the family business as a carpenter.

85. This was named after the Greek verb δοκεω, "to seem" or "appear."

The Gospels present a full picture of Jesus as a real man. Beginning with his conception, Luke in particular describes Jesus' development from embryo to birth to infancy, childhood, and maturity. As the doctor that he was, Luke chronicles the announcement of Jesus' conception, the progress of Mary's pregnancy, and the birth, infancy, childhood, and later developments (Luke 1–2). John refers to Jesus' experiencing weariness, hunger, and thirst (John 4:1–7; 19:28). He knew the full range of human emotions. He wept in grief at bereavement as he faced the horrors of a friend's death (11:32–38). Faced with the impending reality of his own death on the cross, he entered a time of intense sorrow (Matt. 26:38 and parallels). He provided for the care of his mother after his departure (John 19:25–27). He had a normal circle of friends—Peter, James, and John among the apostles, Mary, Martha, and Lazarus beyond.

He trusted Yahweh, his Father, and obeyed him (Heb. 5:8; 10:1–10). He faced the most powerful temptations and searing sufferings (Matt. 4:1–10 and parallels; Heb. 2:18; 4:14–5:10). He died (Matt. 27:50–56 and parallels). He was buried (Matt. 27:57–66 and parallels; 1 Cor. 15:3–4). His resurrection is, of course, resurrection *from the dead*. Consequently, he can sympathize with us in our own predicaments (Heb. 4:14–16), interceding for us at the right hand of the Father (7:25).[86] In short, as a result of having a common nature with us, he shares a common faith, common temptations, common sufferings, and a common death (2:10–18).

The Son of the Father

Jesus Christ is one integral person, God living as man in reality, not pretense. As Paul wrote, "God was in Christ" (2 Cor. 5:19). Throughout the Gospel of John, Jesus describes himself as the Son and God as his Father. This was at the very least highly unusual in first-century Israel, and arguably unprecedented for an individual. Since, in John 1, the Word is the subject of the incarnation, he remains the subject in all that follows, in all of Jesus' actions. This includes his

86. As for what exactly a human nature is and in what sense it applies to Christ, see Crisp, *Divinity and Humanity*, 34–71.

sufferings, death, and burial. Hebrews reinforces this in chapter 2, where the author stresses that the Son, who created and sustains the world, who made atonement for sin, also shares our faith, our temptations, our sufferings, and our death (Heb. 2:10–18). Paul refers to the one who was in the form of God and identical to God as taking the form of a servant (Phil. 2:6–7).

The Son dies. Since he is life, he cannot die himself (John 10:15–18); he died "according to the flesh," as Cyril was to put it. He experienced *human* suffering, *human* death, *human* burial. In short, he experienced to the full what it means to be human. It was not a case of a weak God's being overcome by outside forces. Instead, it was one of the Trinity's freely giving himself to the life and experiences of the creature, of humanity.[87] From this, Jesus rose from the dead and ascended to the right hand of the Father in our flesh, in our nature, exalting it to the very presence of the Father.

Jesus' Life and Ministry Is an Outflow of Who He Is

His work is an outflow of who he is, his person. "For us and our salvation" the everlasting Son of the Father came down from heaven, was born of the virgin Mary, lived among us, and offered himself to the Father as a lamb without blemish or spot. The efficacy of his work flows from the dignity of his person and the obedience he lived out in our nature.

Thus, his words were truth, words of a prophet but of greater than a prophet, for he spoke in his own name, "truly, truly, I say unto you." His actions were those of a priest, a high priest offering sacrifice, but in his case he offered *himself* to the Father, infinitely transcending the limitations of the Aaronic sacrifices. He was exalted as king, not over a limited territory with a transient and passing reign, but to rule the universe forever at the right hand of the Father.

Each of these elements of his work reflected the threefold office in Old Testament Israel of prophet, priest, and king. His whole

87. See Thomas G. Weinandy, *Does God Suffer?* (University of Notre Dame Press, 2000).

ministry, seen in these ways, was an outflow of who he was and is. Paul, in Romans 1:1–7, wrote that the gospel of God, for which he was set apart, is to be understood as "concerning [God's] Son, Jesus Christ our Lord." While the good news covers a wide area—the whole counsel of God, creation, providence, and grace—and is the fruit of the history of redemption, while it embraces a range of words ending in *-tion*, it is focused unequivocally on God's Son, Jesus Christ our Lord. All relates to him as the rim of a bicycle wheel is connected to the hub through the spokes. The very incarnation itself is the gospel, insofar as it is the assumption of man into permanent and eternal union with God, without diminishing or degrading the identity of either but rather raising our human nature to its zenith of fulfillment and freedom.

Jesus and the Holy Spirit

The early chapters of Luke bring together an unusual number of connections between the Holy Spirit and the events surrounding the conception, birth, infancy, and growth of Jesus. With this frequent concatenation Luke invites us to consider that this is an ongoing reality throughout Jesus' life and ministry.

Jesus is conceived by the Holy Spirit. An angel of the Lord tells Joseph that the shocking news of Mary's pregnancy is a result of the work of the Spirit (Matt. 1:20). More expansively, Gabriel informs Mary that "the Holy Spirit will come upon you, and the power of the Most High will overshadow you; therefore the child to be born will be called holy—the Son of God" (Luke 1:35 ESV). The angel compares the Spirit's role in Jesus' conception with his work in creation, when he brooded over the primeval waters (Gen. 1:2). Jesus was to be the author of a new creation, begun as the first through the overshadowing action of the Spirit of God. In turn, the holiness of the child is the result of his conception by the Holy Spirit.

In Luke's account, the Holy Spirit surrounds the events at the nativity. Boris Bobrinskoy writes of "an exceptional convergence between the outpouring of the Spirit and the birth of Christ," so much so that he describes the Holy Spirit as "the Spirit of the incarnation, the One in whom and through whom the Word of God breaks into history."[88] When Mary visits her cousin, Elizabeth is filled with the Holy Spirit, and her baby leaps for joy in her womb (Luke 1:41–44). Elizabeth's husband, Zechariah, is also filled with the Holy Spirit when he prophesies concerning his son, John the Baptist (vv. 67ff.). After Jesus' birth, when his parents take him to the temple for the ritual of purification, Simeon receives them, the Holy Spirit upon him. Simeon had been informed in advance by the Spirit that he would see the Christ in person, and on that day, he entered the temple "in the Spirit" (2:25–28).

Later, at the outset of Jesus' public ministry, the Holy Spirit pervades all that happens. John the Baptist's ministry includes, *inter alia*, announcing that the one who was to come would baptize "with the Holy Spirit and with fire" (Luke 3:16). At Jesus' baptism, the Spirit descends on him in the form of a dove (Luke 3:22 and parallels; John 1:32–33). Bobrinskoy calls this "a revelation of the eternal movement of the Spirit of the Father who remains in the Son from all eternity," the Savior's entire being defined "in a constant, existential relation with the Father in the Spirit."[89] It manifests the eternal resting of the Spirit on the Son.[90] Jesus returns from the Jordan "full of the Holy Spirit," and in turn he is led by the Spirit into the wilderness to be tempted by the devil (Luke 4:1). After this great ordeal, which nevertheless was self-evidently under the direction of the Spirit of God, Jesus returns to the public sphere, to Galilee, "in the power of the Spirit" (v. 14). There in the synagogue, he reads from the prophet Isaiah, where he refers to the Spirit of the Lord resting on the Messiah for his work (vv. 17ff.), declaring that this is now fulfilled in himself. And so on and so forth—in all this, Luke is telling his readers that Jesus himself was governed and directed by the Holy Spirit in all that he did. His ministry as the Christ, the Anointed One, was empowered by the Spirit. Behind that, Jesus from his earliest days was in all his human development (cf. 2:40–52) under the immediate leading of the Spirit.

88. Boris Bobrinskoy, *The Mystery of the Trinity: Trinitarian Experience and Vision in the Biblical and Patristic Tradition*, trans. Anthony P. Gythiel (St. Vladimir's Seminary Press, 1999), 87.

89. Bobrinskoy, *Mystery of the Trinity*, 88, 91.

90. Bobrinskoy, *Mystery of the Trinity*, 94, 99.

It is therefore no surprise when Scripture regards the Spirit as active in later experiences of Jesus. At the cross, he offers himself to the Father through the eternal Spirit, and one of his final comments is to commit his Spirit to the Father, a statement usually thought to refer to his own spirit, soul, or self but, it can be argued, is better seen as returning the Spirit (*his* Spirit) who had descended on him at his baptism. Additionally, it is the Spirit of the Father who raised Jesus from the dead and who will do the same to us in the future (Rom. 8:10–11), the Spirit who is not given to the church until Jesus is glorified following his ascension to the Father (John 7:37–39).

From this, consideration of how exactly the Son's incarnate life and ministry is dependent on the Spirit naturally follows. Anthony Thiselton refers to J. A. T. Robinson's suggestion that since Jesus was fully human and every human depends on the Holy Spirit for communion with God, therefore Jesus lived in dependence on the Holy Spirit.[91] Moreover, as the church fathers acknowledged, wherever the Father and the Son are active, the Holy Spirit is present as well.[92] The author of Hebrews writes that Jesus learned obedience. He did so in conjunction with the things he suffered (Heb. 5:8). Evidently, his human learning was enabled by the Spirit.

This claim is not new. John Owen argued for it. Edward Irving, at a later date, also advocated the idea. Bruce McCormack has written that this is typical of Reformed theology in contrast to the church fathers.[93] The fathers generally considered that Jesus was sustained in his humanity and preserved from sin by the indissoluble hypostatic union, his humanity being suffused by divine qualities flowing from his divine person. Owen, on the other hand, seeking to do justice to the reality of the incarnation, considered that humans depend on the Holy Spirit for their relationship with God. Since the eternal Son took into union a human nature and lived as man, so in his incarnate

91. Anthony C. Thiselton, *The Holy Spirit—In Biblical Teaching, Through the Centuries, and Today* (SPCK, 2013), 42.

92. See chapters 1–4 passim.

93. Bruce L. McCormack, *For Us and Our Salvation: Incarnation and Atonement in the Reformed Tradition*, Studies in Reformed Theology and History (Princeton Theological Seminary, 1993), 17–22.

state he too lived in dependence on the Spirit. This was necessary in order to restore the image of God in man that was lost at the fall; first it had to be renewed in the incarnate Christ. What the Holy Spirit does in the mystical body of Christ, the church, he did first in his natural body.[94] I have written of this elsewhere.[95]

Owen refers to the Son's human nature as being not only created but sanctified by the Holy Spirit, "positively endowed with all grace. . . . And this work of sanctification, or the original infusion of all grace into the human nature of Christ, was the immediate work of the Holy Spirit."[96] This work continued, since Christ's "divine nature was not unto him in the place of a soul, nor did immediately operate the things which he performed, as some of old vainly imagined; but being a perfect man, his rational soul was in him the immediate principle of all his moral operations, even as ours are in us."[97] It seems here that Owen is veering toward treating the human nature as an active agent. This idea is strengthened when he goes on to write that "the human nature of Christ was capable of having *new objects* proposed to its mind and understanding, whereof before it had a *simple nescience*."[98] In this, Owen is dangerously close to flirting with a Nestorian dualism that treats the natures as active subjects, which would be contrary to what we will see is the unitive Christology affirmed by the ecumenical councils. Further, Owen continues, the Spirit anointed Christ with all the extraordinary powers and gifts necessary for the discharge of his office. Owen cited in support Isaiah 61:1 and other kindred passages.[99] As a result, Christ was "full of the Holy Ghost."[100]

This claim has the advantage that it provides a paradigm for our own experience and finds biblical support in the portrayal of

94. John Owen, *A Discourse Concerning the Holy Spirit* (1674), in *The Works of John Owen*, ed. William H. Goold, 16 vols. (Banner of Truth, 1965–68), 3:168–88. This is the section on "Work of the Holy Spirit in and on the human nature of Christ."

95. Robert Letham, *The Work of Christ* (Inter-Varsity Press, 1993), 114–15.

96. Owen, *Works*, 3:168.

97. Owen, *Works*, 3:169.

98. Owen, *Works*, 3:170.

99. Owen, *Works*, 3:171.

100. Owen, *Works*, 3:172.

Christ's humanity in Hebrews (Heb. 2:10–11; 5:7–9). It also allows for development, particularly for the endowment with the Spirit at his baptism and entry into public ministry.[101] It demonstrates that, the Spirit being active in these ways, all Trinitarian persons act together inseparably.

Yet it is not a case of two opposed realities. The very fact that the humanity assumed into union in the incarnation is the human nature of the eternal Son of the Father should be enough to establish that these things took place within the indivisible person of the incarnate Son. Since his human nature has no existence apart from its having been assumed into union by the Son as his own human nature, having been conceived by the Spirit, the Spirit's direction cannot be seen apart from that union.[102] To distinguish the work of the Spirit from the Father and from the indivisible union into which the human nature was assumed is a false dichotomy. The assumed human nature has no independent existence of its own; it is the human nature of the eternal Son, who is indivisibly one with the Father and the Spirit. Cyril, the principal architect of the church's approved Christology, repeatedly stressed that the Spirit is Christ's own Spirit.

The Two States

It is clear in the New Testament that Jesus lived as one of us, in lowliness and in a world that bore the marks of the fall and its consequences. While free from sin, he faced the physical defects common to the race, as Aquinas argued.[103] In an important statement in Romans 1:3–4, Paul refers to him as having "become according to the seed of David." Isaiah had foretold of him that he would be a man of sorrows and acquainted with grief (Isa. 53:1–6). In contrast, from the resurrection he was transformed, passing through closed doors, disappearing, ascending to the presence of the Father, appearing again in such a way that Saul, as he then was, and John were both overwhelmed (Acts 9:3–9; Rev. 1:9–20). He was raised with power according to the Holy Spirit and himself, as man, became "life-giving

101. Owen, *Works*, 3:172–75.

102. Letham, *Systematic Theology*, 500–503.

103. Thomas Aquinas, *ST*, 3a.14.1–3.

spirit" (1 Cor. 15:45). These two states, the state of humiliation and the state of exaltation, are clearly distinguished. Paul terms them as "the form of a servant/slave" and being "highly exalted" (Phil. 2:6–11).

Barth preferred to speak of these two states as in some way simultaneous. He wrote that "we have not spoken of two states that succeed one another, but of two sides or directions or forms of that which took place in Jesus Christ for the reconciliation of man with God." His focus was on the action, the work, of Christ rather than historical sequence. This took the form of the Lord who became servant and the servant who became Lord, describing the twofold action of Jesus Christ, the actuality of his work.[104] Indeed, Barth continued, there is no doctrine of the two natures that is not related to the divine action that has taken place in Christ, nor can there be any autonomous doctrine of the humiliation and exaltation that took place in him.[105] Rather, "the humiliation . . . is the humiliation of God, the exaltation the exaltation of man."[106] This highlights the depth of condescension that the Lord underwent in becoming flesh, from birth to the cross, outcast, despised, rejected, suffering, together with the amazing heights to which humanity was and is elevated by being taken into union with the Son, raised to the highest heavens. Nevertheless, this should always be held in tandem with the reality of the historical sequence. It appears that in this instance, Barth adopted a dehistoricizing perspective that was too close to Docetism for comfort, short of going the whole way.

The Goal of the Incarnation

"He makes his own overmastering impression and subdues us to himself."[107] "There never has been a Christianity in the world which did not worship Christ the Lord as personally identical to Jesus of Nazareth."[108] With these words, H. R. Mackintosh reflected on the

104. Barth, *CD*, IV/1:133.
105. Barth, *CD*, IV/1:133.
106. Barth, *CD*, IV/1:134.
107. H. R. Mackintosh, *The Doctrine of the Person of Jesus Christ* (T&T Clark, 1912), 312.
108. Mackintosh, *Jesus Christ*, 318.

reality that incarnation and atonement are inseparably linked. He wrote that "the believer . . . has 'an interest' in Christ's death because he has an interest in Christ himself."[109] Mackintosh warned against pitting one against the other, remarking that "it is indeed an error alike in method and interpretation when the atonement and the incarnation are viewed as rival or competing interests, either of which gains at the other's cost."[110] They "have concrete and intelligible reality only as they constitute and define each other in the unity of a single experience . . . ; in Jesus Christ supremely being and doing are one."[111]

The humanity of Christ is essential for revelation, Torrance asserts. It "means that God has actually come among mankind to reveal himself and to reconcile men and women to himself."[112] It is also "the guarantee that God's revelation is revelation to creaturely humanity, in the language and life of man, man who is involved within the limitations of time and space, and who cannot escape from them, who can know only within them, within time and history. Because the eternal has become temporal, men and women can know the eternal truth in time."[113]

Torrance comments: "The hypostatic union is also known as 'personal union,' but personal union here means union in the one *person*. That is a personal union unlike any personal union we know even at its most intimate in marriage, which is union in one flesh, but union of two persons in one flesh. But this is such a union of natures and acts that they are united in one and only one person."[114] Torrance adds that the deity and humanity have no revelatory or saving significance apart from this union—in fact, the humanity of Christ has no existence apart from this union. "It is only because Christ himself is personally God that his human speech and actions, and his human forms of thought are also divine revelation."[115]

109. Mackintosh, *Jesus Christ*, 336.
110. Mackintosh, *Jesus Christ*, 342.
111. Mackintosh, *Jesus Christ*, 343.
112. Torrance, *Incarnation*, 184.
113. Torrance, *Incarnation*, 186.
114. Torrance, *Incarnation*, 191.
115. Torrance, *Incarnation*, 193.

To sum up, the proximate, immediate, end of the incarnation was the atonement (Rom. 8:3; Heb. 2:14–18). There is no incarnation without atonement. Equally, there is no atonement without incarnation, for since man had sinned, man must atone, a perfect, sinless man. Moreover, both incarnation and atonement are directed to the grand consummation of all things, when the church will be betrothed to Christ at the marriage supper of the Lamb and the vast universe brought under the consummate sovereign lordship of Christ. In this, Christ's church will be integrally involved, for the ultimate end is the glorification of humanity in Christ, *theosis* (Eph. 1:3–11; 5:25–27; Rev. 22:1f.).

To quote from later in this book, in discussing Maximus the Confessor, Paul Blowers and Robert Louis Wilken refer to "Maximus's integrative cosmic vision in which the economies of creation-deification, on the one hand, and (postlapsarian) intervention-redemption, on the other, merge as one dramatic plot whose 'thickness' and internal connections can only truly be discerned from the standpoint of the mystery which *is* Jesus Christ 'the mystery hidden throughout the ages' (Col. 1:26)."[116] They also point out that in Maximus's writings, "'Christ' and 'the mystery of Christ' are one and the same thing, in the sense that the whole universal mystery of salvation and deification is recapitulated deep within the composite hypostasis of the incarnate Logos."[117] In this, Maximus means that the incarnation in itself is revelatory of the entire redemption, not only of humanity but also of the whole cosmos.[118] Supremely, the absolute end is the glory of God in his assuming humanity into union and transforming those whom he unites to Christ into a glorious church, renewing the creation to display his glory. Andrew Louth describes this as taking the form of two arcs, creation and renewal enveloping creation-fall-redemption.[119]

116. Blowers and Wilken, *Cosmic Mystery*, 26. Blowers and Wilken also refer in a note to *Ad Thalass. 60*.

117. Blowers and Wilken, *Cosmic Mystery*, 26n41.

118. On this great theme, see Andrew Louth, "The Place of *Theosis* in Orthodox Theology," in *Selected Essays*, vol. 2, *Studies in Theology*, ed. Lewis Ayres and John Behr (Oxford University Press, 2023), 178–90.

119. Andrew Louth, "The Place of *Theosis* in Orthodox Theology," in *Partakers of the Divine Nature: The History and Development of Deification in the Christian*

God the Son Suffers as Man

Barth refers to John the apostle, "who leaves no possible doubt about the deity of Christ," yet "no less plainly . . . represents him as the one who is sent, who has a commission and who has to execute it as such, as the Son who lives to do his Father's will, to speak his words, to accomplish his work and to seek his glory."[120] He adds that "we have to do with a divine commission and its divine execution, with a divine order and divine obedience,"[121] and that it is "a difficult and elusive thing to speak of obedience which takes place in God himself."[122]

Two major problems arise. One is subordinationism. The subordinationists found it impossible to reconcile this with the assertion of Christ's true deity, and so they sacrificed the deity of Christ. How can anyone be justified by a creature, Barth wonders.[123] A second response was modalism in some form or other, whose advocates regarded it as speaking only of "a forecourt of the divine being," something purely economic. The problem, then, is this: "If his economy of revelation and salvation is distinguished from his proper being as worldly, does it bring us into touch with God himself or not?"[124] Clearly, in such a case, God has not made himself worldly for the world's sake. It is an act—how can reconciliation be achieved on this basis? Barth proceeds to ask who the acting subject of reconciliation is. It is Jesus Christ, whose deity is to be taken seriously.[125] We have to do with God. The one true God is identical with the lowly, humiliated, and obedient man, Jesus of Nazareth.[126] "Granted that we do see and understand this, we cannot refuse to accept the humiliation and lowliness and supremely the obedience of Christ

---

Traditions, ed. Michael J. Christensen and Jeffery A. Wittung (Fairleigh Dickinson University Press, 2007), 32–44, esp. 35–36. Thanks to Karen Magnuson for tracking down this reference.

120. Barth, *CD*, IV/1:194.
121. Barth, *CD*, IV/1:195.
122. Barth, *CD*, IV/1:195.
123. Barth, *CD*, IV/1:196.
124. Barth, *CD*, IV/1:196.
125. Barth, *CD*, IV/1:197.
126. Barth, *CD*, IV/1:199.

as the dominating moment in our conception of God. Therefore we must determine to seek and find the key to the whole difficult and heavily freighted concept of the 'divine nature' at the point it appears to be quite impossible—except for those whose thinking is orientated on him in this matter—the fact that Jesus Christ was obedient unto death, even the death of the cross. It is from this point, and this point alone, that the concept is legitimately possible."[127] Both subordinationists and modalists evade the cross of Christ. They do this by thinking of Christ as distinct from God or, on the other hand, as a mere mode of appearance of God.[128] We must avoid any idea of a gradation of deity, Barth insists,[129] for Christ is "the one who rules and commands in majesty but also in his own divine person, although in a different mode of being, the one who is obedient in humility."[130]

The incarnation is asymmetrical in this sense, since

> the participation of his divine in his human essence is not the same as that of his human in his divine. As his divine essence is that which is originally proper to him, and his human body is only adopted and assumed to it, it is clear that we must see their mutual determination in the distinction in which we have described it. The determination of his divine essence is *to* his human, and the determination of his human essence *from* his divine. He gives the human essence a part in his divine, and the human essence receives this part in the divine from him. This means that the word mutual cannot be understood in the sense of interchangeable. The relationship between the two is not reversible. . . . It takes place from above to below first, and only then from below to above. It is the self-humiliated Son of God who is also exalted man.[131]

127. Barth, *CD*, IV/1:199.
128. Barth, *CD*, IV/1:200.
129. Barth, *CD*, IV/1:202.
130. Barth, *CD*, IV/1:204.
131. Barth, *CD*, IV/2:70–71.

In this light, that the Son is *under* the Father in his incarnate lowliness according to the flesh is compatible with his being *from* the Father eternally in the unity of the indivisible Trinity. Nowhere is this expressed more vividly than by Paul in Philippians 2:5–8. "Have this mind in you which was also in Christ," he says. The incarnate Christ followed a path of obedience and humiliation, leading to the cruel and, especially for those in Philippi (a Roman colony), shameful death of the cross. He looked not to his own interests but to those of others. This loving self-sacrificial obedience is the fruit of his decision in eternity not to exploit his status "in the form of God" for his own advantage.[132] "Being in the form of God he did not use his status of equality with God for his own advantage[133] but emptied himself, taking the form of a slave." His self-emptying involved an addition—not an addition to his deity, of which there could be none, but an assumption into union by his person of a human nature. He emptied himself by becoming man, and following a path of obedience that led to the death of the cross. He added the form of a slave to the form of God. His choice to do this, however, was prior to his doing it. His determination not to exploit his true and real status for his own advantage was made in eternity. His self-emptying on earth flowed from his refusal to pursue self-interest in eternity. His human obedience reflects his divine self-effacement.[134] The latter no

132. On the phrase *en morphē theou*, see, *inter alia*, Ralph P. Martin, *Carmen Christi: Philippians ii.5–11 in Recent Interpretation and in the Setting of Early Christian Worship* (Eerdmans, 1983).

133. The word *harpagmos* has been the subject of intense debate through the years. See Roy W. Hoover, "The Harpagmos Enigma: A Philological Solution," *HTR* 64, no. 1 (1971): 95–119; Ralph P. Martin, *Philippians*, New Century Bible (Eerdmans, 1980), 96–97; N. T. Wright, "*Harpagmos* and the Meaning of Philippians ii.5–11," *JTS* 37, no. 2 (1986): 321–52.

134. Lossky comments that there is a twofold *kenōsis* ("self-emptying"). In the first place, the Son submitted his will to the will of the Father. This is actually the will of the whole Trinity, for the Father's will is the source of will, the will of the Son is expressed in obedience, and the will of the Spirit is expressed in accomplishment. The Son's submission led to his incarnation. Second, there is also the *kenōsis* of the deified humanity of Christ, by which he submitted to the fallen condition of humanity, which entailed suffering and death. The first *kenōsis* is the basis of the second. Vladimir Lossky, *The Mystical Theology of the Eastern Church* (James Clarke & Co., 1957), 144–46.

more detracts from his full deity than his postresurrection exaltation diminishes his full humanity. Since his obedience on earth did not curtail his deity, neither does his self-effacement in eternity.

This is what the eternal Son is like. We are to follow suit, for this is what God is like. When he seeks his glory, he is not pursuing self-interest like a celestial bully. The Trinity is an indivisible union, a union of love, each person seeking the interests of the others.

Hebrews 5:1–10 runs along similar lines, referring to Christ's refusal to claim the office of High Priest for himself but rather accepting his appointment by the Father. While his office as High Priest began on earth, this statement cannot be restricted in scope to his incarnate life, since the appointment preceded the work.

The incarnation demonstrates the magnitude of the grace of God. The Son, who with the Father and the Holy Spirit in indivisible union lived in the glory he had with the Father in eternity, nevertheless committed himself to come and live in this mess of a world. The world populated by fallen humanity is a moral cesspool, a world of frustrated hopes, of unimaginable suffering, of cruelty, abuse, violence, threats, wars, breakdowns of communication, suspicion, and jealousy. It is populated by people who are in indescribable pain, have vile diseases, are in economic distress, and are victimized, dominated, heading for inevitable pain, decay, and often agonizing deaths. Yet the Son from eternity chose to enter this world as one of us, to become a man of sorrows, to weep, to be rejected and despised, to die the death of the lowest of the low, expiring in excruciating agony after one of the worst tortures ever devised by a perverted race of renegades. Above all, he the eternally righteous Son came to bear the sins of those who traduced him. God commends his love toward us in that while we were sinners, Christ died for us.

This, of course, was not the end of the matter, for "God highly exalted him" (Phil. 2:9), having raised him from the dead. This is the decisive event in the history of the creation, the breaking in of the new creation that will ultimately lead to its entire renovation. Upon his resurrection, the incarnate Son, Jesus of Nazareth, is given plenipotenitary authority over heaven and earth (Matt. 28:19–20), made head of all things for the church (Eph. 1:21–23), and crowned with glory and honor in our nature (Heb. 2:5–9). He rose from the dead and ascended to the right hand of the Father in our own flesh and blood, such that "man with God is on the throne."[135] We will reflect more on this in chapter 11.

135. Wordsworth, "See, the Conqueror Mounts in Triumph."

4

The Incarnate Son

"Torniamo all'antico: sarà un progresso"
(Let us turn to antiquity: it will be a step forward).[1]

Returning to antiquity, we will note the problems the church had with erroneous teaching and how it was able to refine its understanding so as to present a portrayal of Christ attuned to the reality of who he is.

Apollinaris of Laodicea

Apollinaris (c. 315–before 392), a strong supporter of the Council of Nicaea, in his thinking and teaching on Christ had focused on the Johannine statement "the Word became flesh" (John 1:14). This he took to mean that the Son had taken human flesh, a body, into union with himself but that he, the Logos, provided the soul. Consequently, Jesus Christ did not have a human soul.[2] Understandably, this raised intense opposition. It threatened the gospel; "what is

1. Giuseppe Verdi to Francesco Florimo, January 5, 1871, in *Autobiografia Dalle Lettere*, ed. Carlo Graziani (Verona, 1941), quoted in Michael Steinberg, "Notes on the Quartets," in *The Beethoven Quartet Companion*, ed. Robert Winter and Robert Martin (University of California Press, 1994), 269.

2. Aloys Grillmeier, *Christ in Christian Tradition*, vol. 1, *From the Apostolic Age to Chalcedon (451)*, ed. John Bowden, 2nd rev. ed. (John Knox Press, 1975), 330–40; Charles E. Raven, *Apollinarianism: An Essay in the Christology of the Early Church* (Cambridge University Press, 1923).

not assumed cannot be healed," wrote Gregory of Nazianzus in his *Letter to Cledonius*.[3]

The obvious point was that a human body without a human soul is not properly human. If the Son did not take into union a full humanity, including a soul, there was no incarnation. We could not then be saved, since Christ would have been less than human. Since Adam, a man, had sinned, man—a perfect man, a second Adam—must make atonement. As John of Damascus later wrote, "He in his fullness took upon himself me in my fullness, and was united whole to whole that he might in his grace bestow salvation on the whole man."[4] Apollinaris was condemned for heresy by the same Council of Constantinople (381) that had resolved the Trinitarian crisis.

Nestorius

Following the concerns over Apollinaris, and largely in reaction to him, in the early fifth century another major crisis erupted over the identity of Jesus Christ. Since he was and is the eternal Son of God, how are his deity and humanity related? How does this affect our reading of the Gospels? What is its significance for salvation? These questions were thrust onto center stage in 428 by Nestorius, Patriarch of Constantinople.[5] He attacked the term *theotokos* ("God-bearer"), a popular liturgical title for Mary. In opposing with vehemence the Apollinarian denial of the human soul in Christ, he had veered to the other extreme in adopting what Georges Florovsky termed "anthropological maximalism," so stressing the humanity of Christ as to jeopardize the personal union.[6] The immediately presenting issue

3. Gregory of Nazianzus, *Letter 101 to Cledonius*, in *St. Gregory of Nazianzus: On God and Christ: The Five Theological Orations and Two Letters to Cledonius*, trans. Frederick Williams and Lionel Wickham (St. Vladimir's Seminary Press, 2002), 158.

4. John of Damascus, *On the Orthodox Faith*, 3.6; *NPNF*^{2}, 9:2:50. In relation to recent monistic approaches to anthropology, based on developments in neuroscience, and a resultant new warmth to Apollinarian interests by such people as J. P. Moreland and William Lane Craig, see Mark Harris, "When Jesus Lost His Soul: Fourth-Century Christology and Modern," *SJT* 70, no. 1 (2017): 74–92.

5. On Nestorius, see G. L. Prestige, *Fathers and Heretics* (SPCK, 1940), 120–49; J. N. D. Kelly, *Early Christian Doctrines* (Adam & Charles Black, 1968), 310–17.

6. Quoted in John Meyendorff, *Christ in Eastern Christian Thought* (St. Vladimir's Seminary Press, 1975), 17.

was that he considered that *theotokos* undermined the humanity of Christ. His preference was for *christotokos* ("Christ-bearer") or even *anthropotokos* ("man-bearer").

The main primary source for Nestorius is his book *The Bazaar of Heracleides*, written in exile. Unfortunately, it is extraordinarily difficult to decode what exactly he means because the language is so abstruse. This is not made any easier by the translation of G. R. Driver and Leonard Hodgson, which in turn is from a Syriac translation of a lost Greek original. In their introduction, the translators recognize the problem; their aim was to preserve the sense of the Syriac rather than paraphrase into a third language.[7] Indeed, we learn at least as much of Nestorius's ideas from his chief opponent, Cyril of Alexandria, and his own replies to Cyril's attacks.

In his concentration on the full humanity of Christ, Nestorius drew a sharp distinction between Christ's deity and his humanity.[8] He held that Mary could be called mother only of *the man* Jesus. She could be termed *christotokos* ("Christ-bearer") with no qualms, since in this there was no danger of confusing deity and humanity. Talk of Mary as *theotokos* conjured up in his mind the specter of Arianism, a blurring of the Creator-creature distinction, a mixture of deity and humanity. He wanted to maintain the integrity of the human nature.

Nestorius was correct in affirming against Apollinarianism the complete wholeness of Christ's human nature. His problem was that while he had a firm grasp of the distinctiveness of Christ's divinity and humanity, he was less sure of the unity of his person. So he spoke of a "conjunction" of the divinity and humanity rather than a "union." This conjunction resulted in a *prosopon* of union, a single object of appearance, which was identical with neither of the two natures. The *prosopon* of union, not the Logos or Word, was the subject of the incarnate Christ. This laid Nestorius open to the charge of positing a *tertium quid*, a third entity. Moreover, it implied that the Logos had taken into union a man, a man who preexisted

7. Nestorius, *The Bazaar of Heracleides*, ed. G. R. Driver and Leonard Hodgson (Clarendon Press, 1925), xvi.

8. See D. S. Wallace-Hadrill, *Christian Antioch: A Study of Early Christian Thought in the East* (Cambridge University Press, 1982).

the union and remained distinct from the eternal Son. The result was that Jesus was the son of Mary, distinct from the Son of God. This would entail that Jesus of Nazareth was a man precisely like other men, and that, given that there was merely a conjunction between deity and humanity, he was on a similar level to the prophets. If that were the case, we could not be saved.

Nestorius denied that he himself taught that there were two Sons.[9] His unbreakable commitment to a chasm between Creator and creature, however, underpinned his dominant stress on two natures without confusion and thereby to his denial of *theotokos*. He writes:

> And we ought to say unto thee, Acacius, that I have confessed in one Christ in two natures without confusion. By one nature, on the one hand, that is [by that] of the divinity, he was born of God the Father; by the other, on the other hand, that is, [by that] of the humanity, [he was born] of the holy virgin. How then canst thou name her "Mother of God," when thou hast confessed that he was not born of her? . . . If thou, even thou, confessest that he was not born [of her] in the divinity, in that thou confessest that he was not born, how dost thou confess her Mother of God?[10]

Nestorius's opposition to the *theotokos* was a symptom of a deep commitment to the separation of the two natures on the basis of the Creator-creature distinction. In contrast to Cyril, who said that God the Word and the flesh are united, and called it incomprehensible, Nestorius replies, "Those who say these things are impious, and this opinion comes not from the orthodox."[11] His argument was that on Cyril's premises of the unity of the person, the impassable Son would come to possess a passable nature in order to suffer, thus proving that his own *ousia* ("nature") was not impassable in the union. Again, this indicates Nestorius's separation of the two natures. His was a commitment to a conjunction, not a union, and renders confession of *theotokos* impossible.

9. Nestorius, *Bazaar of Heracleides*, 47.
10. Nestorius, *Bazaar of Heracleides*, 296–97.
11. Nestorius, *Bazaar of Heracleides*, 164.

Thus, according to Nestorius, in connection with the cross, the Son "suffered not these things in his nature but made use therein of him who suffers naturally in his *schema* and in his *prosopon* that he might give him by grace in his *prosopon* a name more excellent than all names."[12] Here, the assumed humanity appears to be autonomous, in effect separate from the Son. It is the human nature that suffers. Being separate from the Son, the human nature is less than the Son and consequently a mere man, no different from Moses or any of the prophets.[13]

Sergey Trostyanskiy indicates that the crucial point is the identity of Christ, that is, exactly *who* is the subject of his actions. For Nestorius, the shared *prosopon* of divinity and humanity is the subject. The *prosopon* "is that of an external aspect of the Divine and human natures that came together to form a relational union. . . . The Word of God and the man Jesus of Nazareth are, so to say, placed alongside one another. It is the man who suffered human things humanly and the Word who did divine things divinely. Hence, both natures have their proper subjects and operations." There was no conflict in this for Nestorius, since these things "are not said of the same subject."[14]

Driver and Hodgson identify the main point of contention as Nestorius's claim that "the principle of union is to be found in the *prosopa* of the godhead and the manhood; these two *prosopa* coalesced in one *prosopon* of Christ incarnate."[15] They add: "His own theory can be stated almost in a dozen words. It is this: Christ is the union of the eternal Logos and the Son of Mary, the principle of the union being that the προσώπον of each has been taken by the other, so that there is one προσώπον of the two in the union."[16] It is a theory of prosopic union, a union of natures, rather than hypostatic union, a union in the person, in the case of Cyril.[17] Hence, Nestorius attacks Cyril for

12. Nestorius, *Bazaar of Heracleides*, 165.

13. See the comments of McGuckin in Cyril of Alexandria, *On the Unity of Christ*, trans. John Anthony McGuckin (St. Vladimir's Seminary Press, 1995), 34.

14. Sergey Trostyanskiy, "The Compresence of Opposites in Christ in St. Cyril of Alexandria's *Oikonomia*," *StPatr* 90 (2017): 3–23, here 4–5.

15. Nestorius, *Bazaar of Heracleides*, xxii.

16. Nestorius, *Bazaar of Heracleides*, xxii–xxiii.

17. Nestorius, *Bazaar of Heracleides*, xxiii.

confusing "the essential distinction between godhead and manhood, thus undermining the true humanity of Christ and dishonouring his divinity."[18] By his concern to preserve the humanity of Christ in view of the Creator-creature distinction, Nestorius rejected the union in favor of a conjunction.

For Nestorius, *prosopon* refers to an objectively real appearance of a thing. Deity and humanity both have their respective *prosopa*. But as Driver and Hodgson point out, two appearances of things that look alike are not one thing.[19] Again, Nestorius denies that he teaches two separate persons or two separate Sons,[20] but "Nestorius's theory . . . does not provide a real union."[21] The crux of the problem is that he has considered God and man to be incompatible. This renders incarnation problematic, threatening the gospel and the entire Christian faith.

There was a scholarly consensus in the last century that there were two schools of Christological thought at this time—that of Alexandria (Word-flesh), focusing on the person of the Son, and Antioch (Word-man), with a concern for the integrity of the two natures.[22] This was connected, so it was said, to two corresponding schools of biblical interpretation—a largely allegorical approach in Alexandria and a more literal one in Antioch, which foreshadowed modern historical-critical exegesis and consequently met with greater approval. It was the Antiochene school to which Nestorius was assigned, albeit as a more extreme exemplar of it. One still finds this accepted today. In fact, as Donald Fairbairn and others have demonstrated, the Antiochenes were largely only three persons, all of whom were then or later condemned as heretics for their Christological teaching.[23] Both

18. Nestorius, *Bazaar of Heracleides*, xxiv.

19. Nestorius, *Bazaar of Heracleides*, 415–16.

20. Nestorius, *Bazaar of Heracleides*, 20–21, 53, 147, 158, 165, 189–90, 218–19, 238, 246–47, 310–11, 318, 416.

21. Nestorius, *Bazaar of Heracleides*, 419.

22. Grillmeier, *Christ* passim; Kelly, *Doctrines*, 280–309; Jaroslav Pelikan, *The Christian Tradition: A History of the Development of Doctrine*, vol. 1, *The Emergence of the Catholic Tradition (100–600)* (University of Chicago Press, 1971), 244–46.

23. Donald Fairbairn, *Grace and Christology in the Early Church* (Oxford University Press, 2003).

allegorical and literal exegesis were practiced at both places. Here is a classic instance of a mythology of coherence, an attempt to impose a picture on historical texts that would appear coherent for a later readership without addressing the possible complexity of its own situation.[24] As with all such schematisms, it can distort as well as clarify, its weaknesses eventually telling against it.

Cyril of Alexandria

Since this is not strictly an exercise in history as such but rather theology, we will devote far greater space to Nestorius's chief opponent, Cyril of Alexandria (378–444).[25] This is because he had, and continues to have, by far the greatest impact on orthodox Christology of any single player, being "one of the most profound and subtle of the Church's theologians," as John McGuckin describes him.[26] Not only did he mount the decisive Christological rebuff to Nestorius, but as we will see in chapter 6, all significant discussions on Christology for the hundred or more years afterward concerned how best to interpret his thought. For now, we will consider his writings leading up to the decisive Council of Ephesus (431).

Before the eruption of the Nestorian controversy, Cyril wrote of the incarnation at some length in his celebrated *Commentary on the Gospel of John*.[27] The early date is evident by there being no mention of Nestorius in the entire commentary. Commenting on John 1:11–12, Cyril wrote that the Word "joined what is human to himself by means of the flesh that was united to him, and on the other hand was joined by nature to him who had begotten him, since he was by nature God. Thus what is servile rises up to the level of sonship through participation in him who is Son in reality, called and, as it

24. Quentin Skinner, "Meaning and Understanding in the History of Ideas," in *Visions of Politics*, vol. 1, *Regarding Method* (Cambridge University Press, 2002), 59–97, here 67–72.

25. For Cyril, see Cyril, *Unity of Christ*; John A. McGuckin, *St. Cyril of Alexandria and the Christological Controversy: Its History, Theology, and Texts* (St. Vladimir's Seminary Press, 2004); Prestige, *Fathers and Heretics*, 150–79; Kelly, *Doctrines*, 317–23; Norman Russell, *Cyril of Alexandria* (Routledge, 2000); Thomas G. Weinandy, *The Theology of St. Cyril of Alexandria: A Critical Appreciation* (T&T Clark, 2003), 23–74.

26. Introduction to Cyril, *Unity of Christ*, 32.

27. Extracts from this commentary are found in Russell, *Cyril*.

were, promoted to the rank which the Son possesses by nature."[28] The Word is thus by nature God and has actively taken what is human into union, such that it now possesses the same rank as he.

This is the logical order of Cyril's case:

1. The Son is eternally God, one with the Father and the Spirit, equal in power and glory.
2. He has taken human nature into personal union, such that it is now his.
3. All his actions, recorded in the Gospels, are actions of the Son, according to either nature.
4. The assumed humanity, by virtue of the union, now has the same rank.[29]

Cyril comments on John 1:14, "the Word became flesh," that "sacred Scripture often refers to the entire living creature by the word 'flesh' alone." Against Apollinaris, he writes that to say that this relates only to the flesh "unendowed with a soul" would be absurd, for John's expression is a synecdoche, the whole understood by the part.[30] He adds that the Word really became flesh, a human being. It was not an indwelling, as in the case of the prophets. The Word did not abandon his own proper nature, since "the divine is far removed from any kind of change or alteration into something else." Rather, the Word dwelt in flesh, having his own particular body.[31] There was one reality, not two, since the divine nature is immutable, "not susceptible of change into anything else, but always remaining the same."[32]

After Nestorius's views became known, in spring 430 Cyril produced his *Five Tomes Against Nestorius*,[33] which were not widely

28. Cyril of Alexandria, *The Commentary on St. John*, trans. Philip Pusey, vol. 1, Library of Fathers of the Holy Catholic Church 43 (Oxford: James Parker, 1874), 93b; Russell, *Cyril*, 102–3.

29. This is crucial for understanding the issues raised in Appendix A.

30. Cyril, *St. John*, 1:94e; Russell, *Cyril*, 104.

31. Cyril, *St. John*, 1:95e; Russell, *Cyril*, 106.

32. Cyril, *St. John*, 1:97c; Russell, *Cyril*, 107.

33. This can be found in *PG*, 76:9–248. The more recent critical text is in *ACO*, below. English extracts are in Russell, *Cyril*, 130–74.

circulated but kept in reserve, a tactic later used by Oliver Cromwell, according to his famous advice to "trust God, and keep your gunpowder dry." Cyril was genuinely shocked by Nestorius's opposition to *theotokos*, "not out of any special devotion to the Virgin, but because of his own emphasis on God the Word made flesh as the one personal subject in Christ and as the one to whom we are united in holy communion."[34] In response to Nestorius's claim that "Christ was not truly God but rather a God-bearing man,"[35] Cyril replied that "we have been taught to worship not a God-bearing man but an incarnate God."[36] If he were an ordinary man like us, how could he be Lord of all?[37] He cited Nestorius himself, who said, "That God passed through from the Virgin Mother of Christ I have been taught by the divine Scriptures, but that God was born from her I have not been taught anywhere," to which Cyril replied, "What is this 'passed through' if it does not indicate the birth?"[38]

Nestorius, Cyril remarked, not only opposed calling Mary *theotokos* and the idea that she has given birth to Emmanuel, who is God, but also repeated that Jesus Christ is "a God-bearing man and not truly God, a man conjoined with God." On the other hand, Cyril unequivocally asserted the unity of Christ, that Jesus of Nazareth *is* the eternal Word, the Son, one of the Trinity. He continued: "We say that the Word begotten essentially from God the Father became as we are and took flesh and became man, that is, he took to himself a body from the holy Virgin and made it his own. For that is how he will truly be one Lord Jesus Christ, that is how we worship him as one, not separating man and God, but believing that he is one and the same in his divinity and his humanity (ἕνα καὶ τὸν αυτὸν εἶναι πιστεύοντες, ὡς ἐν θεότητι καὶ ἀνθρωπότητι), that is to say, simultaneously both God and man."[39] Nestorius, however, "divides

34. Richard Price, "The Council of Chalcedon (451): A Narrative," in *Chalcedon in Context: Church Councils 400–700*, ed. Richard Price and Mary Whitby (Liverpool University Press, 2011), 70–91, here 70.

35. *ACO*, I.2.3.18; Russell, *Cyril*, 136.

36. *ACO*, I.2.3.20; Russell, *Cyril*, 138.

37. *ACO*, I.2.3.20; Russell, *Cyril*, 138–39.

38. *ACO*, I.1.6.32; I.2.3.20–21; Russell, *Cyril*, 140.

39. *PG*, 76:60; *ACO*, I.1.6.32; Russell, *Cyril*, 141.

the natures completely and sets each apart, saying that they did not truly come together. . . . He divides up the sayings in the Gospels assigning them sometimes exclusively to the Word alone and sometimes exclusively to the man born from a woman."[40] To the contrary, the only-begotten, "being God by nature, became man, not simply by a conjunction, as he himself says, that is conceived of as external or incidental, but by a true union (ἕνωσιν ἀληθῆ) that is ineffable and transcends understanding. In this way he is conceived of as one and only and every word befits him and everything will be said as from one person. For the incarnate nature of the Word is immediately conceived of as one after the union (μία . . . μετὰ τὴν ἕνωσιν)."[41] The natures of the Word and the flesh are different, but "Christ is nevertheless conceived of as one from both (εἷς ἐξ ἀμφοῖν), the divinity and humanity having come together in a true union."[42]

Cyril used an analogy drawn from wood and fire, "for when fire has entered into wood, it transforms it by some means into its own glory and power, while remaining what it was. . . . For Godhead and flesh are different in their nature, yet the body was the Word's own (ἴδιον ἦν τοῦ Λόγου τὸ σῶμα); the Word that was united to it was not separated from the body."[43] If he is like Moses or Cyrus, how can one avoid concluding that he has the same status as they do?[44]

In all this, Cyril did not ignore the difference between humanity and divinity, but was adamant that "the Word of God, having partaken of flesh and blood, is still thought of as a single Son and is called such," whereas "you [Nestorius] are caught speaking of two Christs and dividing man and God into their separate identities. And you attempt to demonstrate that one is the object of action and the other the subject."[45] In short, Cyril concluded, Nestorius "divides the one Christ and Lord Jesus into man and God separately and individually."[46]

40. *ACO*, I.1.6.32–33; Russell, *Cyril*, 141–42.
41. *PG*, 76:60; *ACO*, I.1.6.33; Russell, *Cyril*, 142.
42. *PG*, 76:61; *ACO*, I.1.6.33; Russell, *Cyril*, 142.
43. *PG*, 76:64; *ACO*, I.1.6.34; Russell, *Cyril*, 143.
44. *ACO*, I.1.6.41; Russell, *Cyril*, 147.
45. *ACO*, I.1.6.43; Russell, *Cyril*, 150.
46. *ACO*, I.1.6.47; Russell, *Cyril*, 157.

Thus, he applies the high priesthood to the man, detached from the only-begotten Word of the Father, on the grounds that it is man who suffers, since God is impassable.[47] For Nestorius, Christ is divided into two persons, for "he who suffers is a separate subject, and he who is life-giving is another."[48] On the contrary, Cyril maintained that "just as he remained God in his humanity, so too in the nature and pre-eminence of deity he was nonetheless man. Therefore in both these Emmanuel was at the same time both one God and man."[49]

Cyril, with the premise of Christ's unity, argued that Nestorius threatened not only the unity of Christ's person but also the incarnation, denying a real participation by the Son of God in our humanity. The two natures, it seemed, were more like two pieces of board held together by glue. Cyril stressed that salvation was a work of God, that the man Jesus could not defeat sin and death by his human nature alone. To do this, the eternal Logos assumed into *union* the human nature of Christ.[50]

In his *Second Letter to Nestorius*, Cyril stated that the Word "united to himself, in his hypostasis, flesh enlivened by a rational soul, and in this way became a human being." While the natures were different, there is an "unspeakable and unutterable convergence into unity, one Christ and one Son out of two." To reject this personal union is to fall into the error of positing two Sons. It was not that he was an ordinary human being upon whom the Logos came, for "we do not worship a human being in conjunction with the Logos, lest the appearance of a division creep in. . . . No, we worship one and the same, because the body of the Logos is not alien to him but accompanies him even as he is enthroned with the Father." The Word did not unite himself to a human person. The virgin Mary is *theotokos*, since it is *the Word* that united himself to this human body and soul.[51]

47. *ACO*, I.1.6.58; Russell, *Cyril*, 160.
48. *ACO*, I.1.6.60; Russell, *Cyril*, 164.
49. *ACO*, I.1.6.61; Russell, *Cyril*, 164.
50. See Meyendorff, *Christ*, 18–19.
51. Leo Donald Davis, *The First Seven Ecumenical Councils (325–787)* (Liturgical Press, 1990), 149–50; Richard A. Norris Jr., *The Christological Controversy* (Fortress Press, 1980), 131–35, esp. 133.

Thomas Weinandy remarks that Cyril made "a true christological breakthrough" in this letter by asserting that the union occurred within the person of the Word. Thus, "the incarnational act does not bring about a union of natures, but rather it is the act by which the humanity is united substantially to the person (*hypostasis*) of the Word."[52] Cyril distinguished between the person and the person's nature. Consequently, as Weinandy states, "there is a change or newness in the mode of existence of the Son, though not a change or newness within the natures. The Son now newly exists as man."[53] Hence, "Jesus is the *person* of the Son *existing* as man."[54]

In his *Third Letter to Nestorius*, Cyril again stressed the personal union of the Word with the flesh. All expressions in the Gospels refer to *the one incarnate person of the Word*. Mary is *theotokos* because she "gave birth after the flesh to God who was united by *hypostasis* with flesh," man ensouled with a rational soul.[55] Cyril adds twelve anathemas to this letter. In these, he declares that "if anyone will not confess that the Emmanuel is very God, and that therefore the Holy Virgin is the Mother of God (*theotokos*), inasmuch as in the flesh she bore the Word of God made flesh . . . ; let him be anathema." He insists, *inter alia*, that it is the Word who suffered, was crucified, and died *according to the flesh*.[56] For Cyril, the Word who existed before the incarnation is the same person after the incarnation, now enfleshed. This union excludes division but does not eliminate difference.

We will look more closely at these anathemas and at Cyril's explanation and defense of them, since they created a huge stir. Nestorius himself was fuming. Others, like Theodoret, who wanted to preserve the distinctness of the human nature, were greatly perturbed.

52. Thomas G. Weinandy, "Cyril and the Mystery of the Incarnation," in *The Theology of St. Cyril of Alexandria: A Critical Appreciation*, ed. Thomas G. Weinandy and Daniel A. Keating (T&T Clark, 2003), 23–54, here 41.

53. Weinandy, "Cyril," 42.

54. Weinandy, "Cyril," 43 (italics original).

55. Edward Rochie Hardy, ed., *Christology of the Later Fathers*, Library of Christian Classics (Westminster Press, 1954), 349–54, esp. 352–53.

56. Hardy, *Christology of the Later Fathers*, 354; Davis, *First Seven Ecumenical Councils (325–787)*, 150–51; Henry R. Percival, *The Seven Ecumenical Councils of the Undivided Church: Their Canons and Dogmatic Decrees*, *NPNF*[2] (repr., T&T Clark, 1997), 206.

In his *A Defense of the Twelve Anathemas Against Theodoret,*[57] written after 430 in response to the furor that had arisen as a result of his earlier letters but before the Council of Ephesus, Cyril again emphasized to Theodoret, whom he strongly suspected of having Nestorian sympathies, that the Word is not subject to change, so that no such change or mixture can be deduced from his becoming flesh as in John 1:14. The flesh was genuinely united to the Word such that the Nestorian phrase "mother of the man" is pointless.[58] "What we affirm, then, is that the Word of God the Father took upon himself the holy and animate flesh and was truly united to it without confusion, and that he then came forth from the womb as a man, while also remaining truly God. It is on this basis that we call the holy virgin 'Mother-of-God.'"[59]

The resulting union was at the level of concrete existence (*hypostasis*), the Word genuinely united to a human nature without change or confusion, a single Christ, the same individual being both God and man.[60] The union was genuine, unmixed, consisting of a human body and rational soul.[61] To distribute sayings in the New Testament between two persons separate from each other is impossible, since the Lord Jesus Christ is one, a single individual, both deity and humanity applicable to him.[62]

Thus, Cyril countered Theodoret's insistence that since God cannot suffer, it was the man who suffered.[63] He did so by agreeing that it is impossible for God to suffer in his own nature but insists that the Word "made the passable body his very own, the result of which is that one can say that he suffered by means of something naturally passable, even while he himself remains impassable in respect of his own nature." Thus we can say that the Word suffered

57. *PG*, 76:385–452. *ACO*, 1.1.7.33–65, is the main critical text.

58. In Daniel King, trans., *St. Cyril of Alexandria: Three Christological Treatises*, Fathers of the Church 129 (Catholic University of America Press, 2014), 89–91; *PG*, 76:393–97.

59. *PG*, 76:396; King, *Three Christological Treatises*, 90.

60. *PG*, 76:400; King, *Three Christological Treatises*, 93.

61. *PG*, 76:405; King, *Three Christological Treatises*, 97.

62. *PG*, 76:409; King, *Three Christological Treatises*, 102.

63. King, *Three Christological Treatises*, 85–86.

in the flesh, was crucified in the flesh, tasted death in the flesh, and became the firstborn from the dead, because as God he is both Life and the Life-Giver.[64] In contrast, Theodoret was close to Nestorius in refraining from applying all the statements in the Gospels to the Word.[65] Throughout, his insistence on the immutability of the Son prevented his predicating ascriptions of weakness to him. Indeed, he denied that "he who was formed by the Holy Spirit and anointed by it was himself God the Word, who is co-essential and co-eternal with the Spirit. Rather, it was the human nature that was taken up by the Word in these latter days."[66]

It is hard to see, in the light of this, how Theodoret could give credible testimony to incarnational union; he was a hair's breadth from Nestorius. Paul Clayton comments that "Antiochene Christology was rooted in the concern to maintain the impassability of God the Word, and is consequently a two-subject Christology."[67] Moreover, Theodoret insisted that to say that one of the Trinity died on the cross was Arian, since the Word would be mortal and changeable in his being and so less than God.[68] Again, he held that it was not the Word who is our High Priest but the human nature; "it was the nature that was taken from us for our sake, not the one who for our salvation had taken it."[69] Thus, it was not the form of God that suffered but rather the form of a servant, the man, the one whom God had taken up—"it is not the one who had life in himself who is killed. It is the one who possesses the mortal nature."[70]

Cyril answered the possible objection that his own position would be demeaning to the Word by stating:

64. *PG*, 76:449–51; King, *Three Christological Treatises*, 128–30.

65. King, *Three Christological Treatises*, 101–2.

66. King, *Three Christological Treatises*, 116.

67. Paul B. Clayton, *The Christology of Theodoret of Cyrus: Antiochene Christology from the Council of Ephesus (431) to the Council of Chalcedon (431)* (Oxford University Press, 2007), v.

68. Clayton, *Christology of Theodoret*, v–vi.

69. King, *Three Christological Treatises*, 118.

70. King, *Three Christological Treatises*, 129.

> Someone will object that it is belittling and inappropriate that God the Word should cry out, or be afraid of death, that he should pray against taking the cup of suffering or be appointed to the office of priesthood. Yes, I would agree. Such things are somewhat ignoble by comparison with the transcendent divine nature and glory, but it is precisely in them that we can see the poverty that he willingly endured for us. Whenever you find the dishonor arising from his self-emptying to be a problem, wonder all the more greatly how much the Son loves us; you say it is something mean, but he willingly did it for your sake. He wept like a man to protect your own tears. For salvation's sake he was afraid and at times allowed his flesh to suffer as it ought to, so that he might render us less fearful; . . . in his humanity he was called weak, so that he might put a stop to your weakness.[71]

Cyril's *Explanation of the Twelve Chapters* was written at Ephesus in 431 to guide the bishops at the council that was called to settle the matter. He was more irenic here compared to other writings, since his aim was to secure their support in condemning Nestorius. He wanted to focus on areas in which he could secure agreement. It was also written in response to the continued outcry following his *Third Letter to Nestorius* of November the previous year, with its twelve anathemas.

Norman Russell points out that the prime thing for Cyril was that there is "only a single subject for all the words and actions attributed to Christ, namely, the Word made flesh," for otherwise he could not save us.[72] Anathema 2 stresses this.[73] There was no change to the nature of the Word, since it is the same Word who took flesh from the virgin and made it his own. He is one and the same subject before and after the union.

> What then does "manifested in the flesh" mean? It means that the Word of God the Father became flesh, not by a change or alteration

71. King, *Three Christological Treatises*, 122–23.
72. Russell, *Cyril*, 176.
73. Russell, *Cyril*, 179.

> of his own nature, . . . but because having made the flesh taken from the holy Virgin his own, one and the same subject is called the Son, before the incarnation as the Word still incorporeal and after the incarnation as the same Word now embodied. That is why we say that the same subject is simultaneously both God and man, not dividing him conceptually into a human being with a separate individual identity and God the Word also with a separate identity, that we may exclude any idea of two Sons, but acknowledging that one and the same subject is Christ and Son and Lord.[74]

Anathema 3 condemns any who divide the *hypostases* after the union by a conjunction and not a union.[75] Thus, in Anathema 4, the same applies to those who take statements in the Gospels and apply them on the one hand to a man, "conceived of as separate from the Word of God," and on the other to God.[76] Consequently, Cyril affirms, the Son willingly entered our condition, "not abandoning what he is but remaining God even in this state while not disdaining the limitations of the human condition. Therefore everything relating to his divinity and everything relating to his humanity belong to him . . . [and] all the sayings in the Gospels, both those with a human colouring and indeed those appropriate to God, we therefore assign to a single *prosopon*," since Christ is a single Son. Those who divide the *prosopa* inevitably consider him to be two Sons.[77]

Anathema 9 is directed against any who say that Christ was glorified by the Spirit, as something alien to himself, and that he so used the power of the Spirit to cast out demons "instead of saying that the Spirit by which he also performed the miracles is his own." This is "because he possesses the Holy Spirit, which is from him and essentially innate within him, as his own property."[78]

Anathema 11 is against those who deny that the flesh and blood of Christ are life-giving. Cyril insisted that the assumed flesh is

74. Russell, *Cyril*, 179–80; *ACO*, I.1.5.18.
75. *ACO*, I.1.5.18; Russell, *Cyril*, 180.
76. *ACO*, I.1.5.19; Russell, *Cyril*, 181.
77. *ACO*, I.1.5.20; Russell, *Cyril*, 182.
78. *ACO*, I.1.5.23; Russell, *Cyril*, 186.

life-giving "because it became the Word's own flesh," referring immediately to John 6:57. "Since Nestorius and those who think like him ignorantly weaken the power of the mystery [of the sacrament], that is why this anathema has rightly been drawn up."[79]

Anathema 11

If anyone does not acknowledge that the Lord's flesh is life-giving and belongs to the Word of the Father himself, but say that it belongs to someone else who is joined to him on the basis of rank or simply possesses a divine indwelling, instead of saying that it is life-giving, as we have said, because it became the personal property of the Word who is able to endow all things with life, let him be anathema.

Explanation

We celebrate the holy and life-giving and bloodless sacrifice in the churches,[80] not in the belief that the offering is the body of an ordinary man like ourselves, and similarly with the precious blood, but instead accepting that it has become the very own body and blood of the Word who endows all things with life. For ordinary flesh cannot endow with life. The Saviour himself testifies to this when he says: The flesh is of no avail; it is the Spirit that gives life (John 6:63). Because it became the Word's own flesh it is therefore regarded as life-giving and actually is so. As our Lord himself said, "As the living Father sent me, and I live because of the Father, so he who eats me will live because of me" (John 6:57). Since Nestorius and those who think like him ignorantly weaken the power of the mystery, that is why this anathema has been drawn up.[81]

Cyril was saying that the Word assumed human nature into union such that it became his, with the result that he, the Word, is the subject of all references to Jesus in the Gospels, in accordance with

79. *ACO*, I.1.5.25; Russell, *Cyril*, 188.
80. This is a reference to the sacrament of the Lord's Supper.
81. *ACO*, I.1.5.24–25; Russell, *Cyril*, 188.

his natures. From this Cyril maintained that the flesh and blood of the Word is itself life-giving. This would be borne out biblically by the central theme of John, seen in statements such as John 1:4, "in him was life," and 1:14, "the Word [who is God] became flesh," reference to his resurrection in chapter 2, the new life in chapter 3, the living water in chapter 4, and his having life in himself in chapter 5. Again, in chapter 6 we have the feeding of the five thousand, his being the living bread from heaven who will raise us at the last day, immediately preceding the reference to eternal life through eating his flesh and drinking his blood. To crown it all, in chapter 11, before raising Lazarus from the dead, Jesus declares, "I am the resurrection and the life." This is supported by Paul in 1 Corinthians 15:45, "the last Adam [resurrected] became life-giving Spirit," and by the two post-glorification appearances in Acts 9 and Revelation 1. Hence in the Lord's Supper, we feed on Christ and drink his blood in a noncorporeal manner. Since he is life-giving, the Supper is the occasion of life-giving transformation. In contrast, Nestorius's false Christology weakened the sacrament.[82]

Capping it all, Anathema 12 reads, "If anyone does not acknowledge that the Word of God suffered in the flesh, and was crucified in the flesh, and experienced death in the flesh, and became the first-born from the dead, seeing that as God he is both life and life-giving, let him be anathema."[83] "The Word of God the Father is impassable and immortal" and "endows all things with life and is superior to corruption." Yet "he made his own the flesh that is receptive of death, that by means of that which is accustomed to

82. Along similar lines, the memorialist view of the Lord's Supper prevalent among evangelicals coheres with a position that entails either (1) that there is no participation in the flesh and blood of Christ in the Supper, or (2) that if there is such participation, the flesh and blood of Christ are not life-giving. John Calvin wrote that such a view would render the sacrament "frivolous and useless," and John Knox "utterlie damn[ed] the vanitie" of those who held the sacrament to be purely symbolic. Knox was never knowingly understated. John Calvin, *Short Treatise on the Holy Supper of Our Lord and Only Saviour Jesus Christ*, in *Calvin: Theological Treatises*, ed. J. K. S. Reid (Westminster Press, 1954), 146; Scots Confession art. 21 (1560), in Philip Schaff, *The Creeds of Christendom* (Baker, 1966), 3:467–70.

83. *ACO*, I.1.5.25; Russell, *Cyril*, 188.

suffering he might take these sufferings to himself on our behalf . . . and deliver all of us from both corruption and death, having as God endowed his body with life and become 'the first-fruits of those who have fallen asleep' (1 Cor. 15:20) and the first-born from the dead." Hence, "the Lord of glory himself suffered in the flesh, according to the Scriptures (1 Peter 4:1)."[84] In short, the Word suffered and died in the flesh, in a human manner, but in doing so, such sufferings were his own. This Nestorius could never accept, but the incarnation required it and Cyril effectively expressed it.

The Council of Ephesus (431)

It may be best to draw a veil over the confused proceedings, with rival camps using physical intimidation in an attempt to secure their aims. Cyril is one of the church's greatest theologians but also, it is often claimed, one of its most effective thugs.[85] God works in mysterious ways his wonders to perform. The details are readily available in the literature. The accusations are not proved.

The council expelled Nestorius from the episcopal office and the priesthood,[86] declaring that Christ's humanity, wholly human, was appropriated by the Word as his own, and so forms the basis for our own salvation.[87] A conjunction between deity and humanity —existing side by side—is not incarnation and could not save us. With Nestorius exiled, his followers were forced to flee and eventually made huge inroads eastward, into Mesopotamia and as far as China.[88] Nestorius wrote in exile his *Bazaar of Heracleides*, to which we referred above.

After Ephesus, Cyril reached an agreement with the see of Antioch, reconciling after their deep antagonism. Faced by the misgivings of some of his supporters over this accord, Cyril wrote letters to reassure them. Among these is a letter to Succensus, explaining

84. *ACO*, I.1.5.25; Russell, *Cyril*, 189.
85. *Hoc genus theologi mei est! Nihil melius muscularis christianitatis superat!*
86. Davis, *First Seven Ecumenical Councils (325–787)*, 160.
87. Meyendorff, *Christ*, 21.
88. Stephen Neill, *Christian Missions* (Penguin, 1964), 5–96, 126, 132.

his thoughts on the two natures.[89] Here Cyril spoke the language of two natures for the only time on record. He made clear that he considered the humanity and deity to be distinct, while ensuring that we neither separate nor divide them. At this time, as Cyril Hovorun emphasizes, Cyril needed to distinguish himself from Apollinaris and his fatally truncated view of the humanity,[90] since some alleged that he did not do full justice to the assumed humanity. Hovorun comments that Cyril's term for the particular in Christ was *physis* ("nature"), not the more common *hypostasis* ("person"), meaning by it "the singular reality of the incarnated Logos, full of life, dynamism, and salvation" and "one incarnate nature of the Word of God."[91] His focus was on the single reality of Christ. This became a source of confusion. What did Cyril really mean? Talk of "one incarnate nature" led to a range of misunderstandings in the next century, which were overcome only with great difficulty. We will refer to these in the next two chapters. The evidence supports Cyril's using "nature" for what we would call "person." At the same time, Cyril, in his second letter to Succensus, wrote that "if one and the same is conceived as complete God and complete man, consubstantial with the Father according to his godhead, but according to his manhood consubstantial with us, where is this completeness, if the human nature did not subsist?"[92]—in short, if the human nature was not truly his. This was to dispel the rumor that Theodoret had encouraged that he was a closet Apollinarian. As Cyril had remarked, this was utter rubbish.

Eutyches[93]

Before long, a fresh crisis arose, generated by Eutyches from Alexandria, whom J. N. D. Kelly calls an "aged and muddle-headed

89. Cyril, *Epistola ad Succensum*, 3–6, in *Cyril of Alexandria: Select Letters*, ed. and trans. Lionel R. Wickham, Oxford Early Christian Texts (Oxford University Press, 1983), 74–77, 87–89.

90. Cyril Hovorun, *Eastern Christianity in Its Texts* (T&T Clark, 2022), 500–501.

91. Hovorun, *Eastern Christianity*, 500, 504.

92. *ACO*, 1.1.6.160, 14–16, quoted in Benjamin Gleede, *The Development of the Term* ἐνυπόστατος *from Origen to John of Damascus* (Brill, 2012), 49.

93. See Grillmeier, *Christ*, 1:520–57; Pelikan, *Christian Tradition*, 1:263–66.

archimandrite."[94] Eutyches was an extreme exponent of Cyrilline Christology, without Cyril's theological sophistication. Unfortunately, we do not have direct records of Eutyches's teaching other than through his opponents and the council that rejected him. For Eutyches, before the incarnation Christ was of two natures, but after it he is one nature, one Christ, one Son, in one *hypostasis* and one *prosopon*. Christ's flesh was not identical with ordinary human flesh, since Eutyches thought this would entail the Word's assuming an individual man, thus destroying the union. Behind this, he understood nature to mean concrete existence—so Christ could not have two natures or he would have two concrete existences and so be divided.[95] Thus, Eutyches had an overpowering emphasis on the unity of Christ's person, exactly the opposite of Nestorius. Whereas Nestorius had sought to uphold the distinctness of the two natures and so threatened the unity of Christ, Eutyches so underlined Christ's unity that he blurred the distinctness of the two natures, his humanity swamped by his deity—although to be fair, he did insist on the full and complete humanity. His ideas raised similar problems to those of Apollinaris, for our salvation depends on the reality of the incarnation, of a real assumption of unabbreviated humanity by the Son of God. If Christ were not truly and fully man, we could not be saved, for only a second Adam could undo the damage caused by the first.

The Council of Chalcedon (451)

Eventually Marcian, the emperor, called a council to be held at Nicaea, but switched to Chalcedon, across the Bosphorus, because of invasions by the Huns. Pope Leo sent three legates.[96] The bishops reaffirmed Cyril's *Second Letter to Nestorius* and Pope Leo's *Tome*, addressed to the council. A commission was appointed to draw up a

94. Kelly, *Doctrines*, 331.

95. See Kelly, *Doctrines*, 330–34; Davis, *First Seven Ecumenical Councils (325–787)*, 171.

96. For the Council of Chalcedon, see R. V. Sellers, *The Council of Chalcedon: A Historical and Doctrinal Survey* (SPCK, 1953), 209ff.; Kelly, *Doctrines*, 338–43; Davis, *First Seven Ecumenical Councils (325–787)*, 180–82; Percival, *Seven Ecumenical Councils*, 243–95.

doctrinal statement. In composing the Definition, the bishops drew on a variety of sources, Leo's *Tome* the single most decisive contributor, even though there were more quotations from Cyril.[97] The Definition clearly distinguishes between one person and two natures:

> Therefore, following the holy Fathers, we all with one accord teach men to acknowledge one and the same Son, our Lord Jesus Christ, at once complete in Godhead and complete in manhood, truly God and truly man, consisting also of a reasonable soul and body; of one substance with the Father as regards his Godhead, and at the same time of one substance with us as regards his manhood; like us in all respects, apart from sin; as regards his Godhead, begotten of the Father before the ages, but yet as regards his manhood begotten, for us and for our salvation, of Mary the Virgin, the God-bearer; one and the same Christ, Son, Lord, Only-begotten, recognized in two natures, without confusion, without change, without division, without separation; the distinction of natures being in no way annulled by the union, but rather the characteristics of each nature being preserved and coming together to form one person and subsistence, not as parted or separated into two persons, but one and the same Son and only-begotten God, the Word, Lord Jesus Christ; even as the prophets from earliest times spoke of him, and our Lord Jesus Christ himself taught us, and the creed of the Fathers has handed down to us.

That Christ subsists in two natures is a decisive rejection of Eutyches. At the same time, it also insists that Christ is not divided or separated into two persons, as the Nestorian heresy implied.

The anti-Nestorian stance is evident in a number of ways. The repetition of the phrase "the same" and the reaffirmation of the virgin Mary as *theotokos* are two obvious points. The Definition denies that Christ is parted or separated into two persons, but rather asserts that the two natures "come together to form one person and subsistence," echoing Cyril's *Second Letter to Nestorius*. In all these, it

97. Pelikan, *Christian Tradition*, 1:263–64; Sellers, *Chalcedon*, 209–10.

clearly affirms the unity of the person of Christ. On the other hand, the Definition equally repudiates Eutyches. Christ is "complete in manhood"; he is "of one substance with us." The distinction of natures is in no way annulled by the union. There are also clear restatements of opposition both to Apollinarianism, in that Christ has "a reasonable soul and body," and also to Arianism, in that Christ is "of one substance with the Father."

Above all, the famous four privative adverbs together form the central hinge of the Definition.[98] The incarnate Christ is "*in two natures, without confusion, without change*." This is a rejection of Eutyches. The union neither changes Christ's humanity into anything else nor absorbs it into the divinity. At the same time, the natures are "*without division, without separation*." By this it is impermissible so to focus on the natures so as to undermine the personal union, as Nestorius had done. These four adverbs outlaw both Nestorianism and Eutychianism.

The council also anathematizes those who talk of two natures of the Lord before the union but only one afterward. This is directed at Eutyches, probably at the behest of Pope Leo and the papal legates.[99] It was to cause problems later, for the Monophysites were accustomed to think of "nature" as synonymous with what we would now call "person" and so considered Chalcedon a capitulation to Nestorius. Yet the problem was exacerbated by a lack of knowledge of Greek by the Latins, who had pressed this point. Taking *physis* (Greek) to mean *natura* (Latin), it seemed to Leo and his legates that the Alexandrian mantra of one incarnate nature (*physis*) of the Logos was a heretical belief in only one *natura*. It failed to appreciate that the Greeks used *physis* and *hypostasis* interchangeably. Another century passed before Emperor Justinian I brought a clear distinction between these two terms. In reality, the real objection in this anathema is, as R. V. Sellers observes, to Eutyches' false interpretation of the formula, not to Cyril's position, which was not in view.[100] It was in defense of the gospel that the council rejected any idea that Christ's humanity

98. The words in question are adverbs in Greek.
99. Sellers, *Chalcedon*, 224–26.
100. Sellers, *Chalcedon*, 226.

was truncated or absorbed by deity; if that had been so, we could not be saved.

We will see in chapter 6 that the Definition contained a range of ambiguities. It was clearly couched in a dualist mode that posed far more problems for many followers of Cyril than it did for Nestorius. In exile, Nestorius considered himself vindicated by Chalcedon. It was to take several generations of controversy and debate to resolve the issues that the council raised.

In the West—Augustine

We need to refer to Augustine (354–430), given his impact on the Latin church. But he died only two years after Nestorius hit the headlines and over twenty years before Chalcedon. He makes only cursory references to the incarnation, with nothing new to contribute. He provided a brief summary in his *Enchiridion*,[101] which, since there is a reference to the death of Jerome, was composed after 420. There is virtually nothing on John 1:14 in his homilies on John, preached from around 416, again well before the Nestorian controversy.[102] His attention in his homilies on John 1 was mainly directed to the Manichees. In the *Enchiridion*, there are references to the flesh (John 1:14), meaning the whole man, for "no part was wanting in that human nature which he put on, save that it was a nature wholly free from every taint of sin."[103] This was a probable reference to the Apollinarian heresy, indicating an awareness of the controversies of the Greek church. But he did not dwell on it at length. Since Augustine's career and life had all but ended when the crisis over Nestorius erupted in the East, it is not surprising that Augustine does not have anything of great significance to write.

101. Augustine, *Enchiridion*, 34–30; *NPNF*[1], 3:249–51.
102. *NPNF*[1], 7:13–18.
103. Augustine, *Enchiridion*, 34; *NPNF*[1], 3:249.

5

Touchstones of Christological Orthodoxy

Over the course of the controversies on the person of Christ, the following terms and formulae became accepted as legitimate expressions of the orthodox doctrine. Some aroused more debate than others and took time to gain approval, while some others appeared problematic if not understood in the way that was intended. In order to foster intelligibility in the two more difficult and dense chapters that follow, we list them here with some explanatory comments.

Theotokos

The first such term is the most widely known and the one that was at the center of the original controversy. As Karl Barth argued, this one Greek word meaning "God-bearer" "amounts to a test of the proper understanding of the incarnation of the Word, that as Christians and theologians we do not reject the description of Mary as the 'mother of God' but in spite of its being overloaded with the so-called Mariology of the Roman Catholic Church, we affirm and approve of it as a legitimate expression of christological truth."[1]

Theotokos makes a twofold assertion. On the one hand, it refers to the one born who, in being and status, was and is God. On the other hand, he was a child and Mary was his mother, so that he was

1. Karl Barth, *CD*, II/1:138.

genuinely human. Mary's conception was from the Holy Spirit. The birth was a normal human birth following a normal human process of nine months' gestation, yet the child born was God's Son, eternally one with the Father. Rejection of what *theotokos* signifies is rejection of the biblical doctrine of the incarnation.

Thus, Mary is quite rightly called "the mother of God." To her was accorded the greatest privilege that it is possible to imagine for a human being to be given, short of regeneration. God the Trinity—the Father, the Son, and the Holy Spirit—entrusted her with the care and nurture of the Son. Of course, she was assisted throughout by the grace and power of God, the work of the Spirit; we saw that the Gospel of Luke, in its early chapters, abounds in references to the Spirit's presence and power. But Mary was trusted by God to feed and change his Son, the Creator of the universe, who is life itself!

Yet the attention of Scripture is directed not toward her but to her son. Barth is emphatic that Mary is subsidiary, a servant: "as Luther understood it . . . , the greatness of the New Testament figure of Mary consists in the fact that all the interest is directed away from herself to the Lord." Thus, she is an indispensable figure in Bible proclamation.[2] Yet veneration of Mary of the kind that is too evident in the Roman church is to be rejected.[3] From the truth of the affirmation of *theotokos* the other formulae follow.

"Union According to Hypostasis"

This is the phrase used by the neo-Chalcedonians, Leontius of Jerusalem in particular, in opposition to the idea that union was according to nature, bringing about a union of the two natures. Instead, they argued that the union was according to person, the person of the Logos taking human nature into union, such that the integrity of both natures was preserved, unmixed and unaltered, in the one person.

If the union established in the incarnation were according to nature, there would have been one of two consequences. The first

2. Barth, *CD*, II/1:139–40.
3. Barth, *CD*, II/1:143.

possible result would be a merging of divine and human natures into a hybrid, a form of ontological soup. This would entail a third entity, a mixture that would be identical with neither of the two natures. In that case, Christ would be neither God nor man. Moreover, it could not be so because it would entail a change of nature in God, contrary to his immutability.[4] The second possibility would involve the human nature's being conjoined to the divine, a conjunction rather than a union. This was effectively the position of Nestorius and also the seemingly inevitable tendency of some of the Dyophysite defenders of Chalcedon, such as Leontius of Byzantium. If that were the case, the person of Christ would be an addition to two autonomous or semiautonomous natures, a *tertium quid*.

The accepted formula "union according to hypostasis," as used by Leontius of Jerusalem and the neo-Chalcedonians, asserted that union took place in the person (*hypostasis*) of Christ. The human nature was thereby assumed into union by Christ himself, a union in his divine person, in which there was no change in his divine nature. Behind this was the basic premise that God had created humanity for this purpose, fully compatible, made in his own image, the image that is found in Christ.

This is well expressed by Thomas Aquinas: "Although in God nature and person are not really distinct, yet they have distinct meanings . . . inasmuch as person signifies after the manner of something subsisting. And because human nature is united to the Word, so that the Word subsists in it, and not so that his nature receives therefrom any addition or change, it follows that the union of human nature to the Word of God took place in the person, and not in the nature."[5]

Enhypostatos

This doctrine that emerged in the time leading up to Constantinople II (A.D. 553) went hand in hand with its twin, *anhypostatos*, and became a crucial premise for the whole of theology. By *anhypostatos* is signaled the fact that the human nature of Christ has no independent

4. See on this Thomas Aquinas, *ST*, 3.2.1, *responsio*.
5. Aquinas, *ST*, 3.2.2, reply obj. 1.

existence of its own. It did not preexist the incarnation; the Son did not take a preexistent human nature into union. Nor does it exist side by side with the person of Christ as some form of adjunct. Its common designation as "the impersonal humanity" can be misleading. That phrase was intended to assert that the assumed human nature is not a person additional to the person of the Son, for it has no autonomous existence.

This is where *enhypostatos* comes in. Human natures are always anchored in the specific persons to whom they belong. That should be obvious. There are no "human natures" floating around in the ether that are not personal. Consequently, the human nature of the Son was taken into union in such a way that it is the Son's own human nature. The person of the Son—the "who"—has himself two natures, divine and human.

Against the idea that this means that the Son has a truncated humanity, on the grounds that there is no human person, is again the underlying factor that God created the human race to be fully compatible with himself on a finite level. The incarnate Son is fully human because God created our race for this very purpose. The union, far from crushing the humanity, perfectly expresses it. Therefore, the supreme and purest manifestation of humanity is in Jesus Christ.

John Meyendorff writes of Leontius of Jerusalem that he established "the absolute distinction between hypostasis and nature,"[6] with *hypostasis* signifying the personal subject, answering to the question "who?" It is, as Dennis Ferrara states, "to acknowledge that the sole such personal subject in Christ is the eternally preexistent hypostasis of the Word and Son of God, and thus that Christ's humanity has no independent, personal existence of its own; that, despite its consciousness and freedom, this human nature is not a personal 'who,' but exists precisely as the humanity of this divine subject. It is to acknowledge, accordingly, that Jesus Christ is not a human but a divine person, 'one of the holy Trinity,' as

6. John Meyendorff, *Christ in Eastern Christian Thought* (St. Vladimir's Seminary Press, 1975), 77.

II Constantinople says."[7] It must be recognized as "the Church's own authoritative interpretation of Chalcedon, one which compels us to read Chalcedonian dyophysitism in light of Christ's primordial unity as divine subject."[8]

Underlying it was a deep soteriological concern—who is it who can save humanity? At root is the question of salvation. The leading figures in these discussions were bishops, not academics. Their daily task was the care of the churches under their jurisdiction. Nor, ultimately, was this a solution confined to the Eastern church. Constantinople II was approved by Rome, in the person of Pope John II, and the doctrine of *enhypostatos* was taken over into the Latin church, as expressed—*inter alia*—by Aquinas.[9]

"One of the Trinity Suffered According to the Flesh"

It followed from all that we have discussed that this formula, known as the Theopaschite formula, eventually became received orthodoxy.[10] It was the final victory for Cyrilline Christology, which was also canonized at Constantinople II.[11]

It needs to be clearly distinguished from the third-century heresy of Patripassianism, which was modalist, holding that the Father suffered and died on the cross.

Aloys Grillmeier points to Proclus, patriarch of Constantinople in the fifth century, as the first to mention the Theopaschite formula. Many of the Dyophysite supporters of Chalcedon in the late fifth and early sixth centuries were unable to accept the formula, since they feared that it compromised the impassability of God. These

7. Dennis M. Ferrara, "'Hypostatized in the Logos': Leontius of Byzantium, Leontius of Jerusalem and the Unfinished Business of the Council of Chalcedon," *LS* 22 (1997): 311–27, here 324–25.

8. Ferrara, "Hypostatized in the Logos," 325.

9. Aquinas, *ST*, 3.2.2–3.

10. See Aloys Grillmeier, *Christ in Christian Tradition*, vol. 2, *From the Council of Chalcedon (451) to Gregory the Great (590–604): Part Two: The Church of Constantinople in the Sixth Century*, trans. Theresia Hainthaler and John Cawte (Mowbray, 1995), 317–43; J. A. McGuckin, "'The Theopaschite Confession' (Text and Historical Context): A Study in the Cyrilline Re-Interpretation of Chalcedon," *JEH* 35, no. 2 (1984): 239–55; Patrick T. R. Gray, *The Defense of Chalcedon in the East (451–553)* (Brill, 1979), 136–39.

11. McGuckin, "Theopaschite Confession," 243.

concerns gave the Monophysites added fuel for their reservations about Chalcedon.[12] We saw in chapter 4 and we will see again in chapter 6 how it was present in Cyril's *Third Letter to Nestorius*, canonized at Constantinople II.

The rationale behind the formula flows from the previous commitments. The person of the incarnate Christ is one. The Incarnate One is the same as the eternal Son, since it is the Son who has assumed human nature into union while remaining unchanged. All attributions are therefore to be made to the person of the Son, for it is persons who act, not natures. Consequently, it is the person of the Son who suffered and died. But since God cannot suffer or die, since he cannot be acted on or injured by any outside force, inasmuch as he is the sovereign Creator of all, the Son underwent these depredations in accordance with his human nature. He experienced *human* suffering, *human* death, *human* burial. "One of the Trinity suffered according to the flesh." He also knows *human* resurrection, transfiguration, and glorification! Christ has suffered in the flesh. To deny any of these attributions is to jettison the faith.

"One Incarnate Nature of God the Word"

At first sight, this formula would seem to be heretical, infringing the statement of Chalcedon that the person of Christ has two natures, divine and human. In fact, Cyril and those who came in his wake were using "nature" as a synonym for "person," emphatically insisting that the incarnate Son is not divided, as Nestorius had maintained, but is one person. Rather, God the Word became incarnate and is the personal subject of all actions in Jesus' life, including those recorded in the Gospels. The reference to "*incarnate* nature" indicates that he had assumed humanity into union and thus was God the Word, now incarnate as man.

We need to remember that at the time these debates were taking place, there was much linguistic confusion. Indeed, the formula had been used earlier by Arius and Apollinaris to support their own heretical ideas. It could be, and was, also used by the Monophysites.

12. Meyendorff, *Christ*, 64–65.

As Leontius of Jerusalem insisted, however, this was no reason to abandon it and fail to use it to express the true doctrine. Christopher Beeley remarks that "where the [second] council [of Constantinople] employs single-nature language . . . as in the phrase 'one nature of God the Word made flesh' it insists that it must agree with the doctrine of Chalcedon, in particular the idea that Christ is a union of divine and human natures *by hypostasis* (2 Const. 27 anathemas 3–4)."[13] Much later, Aquinas cited favorably canon 8 of Constantinople II on this very point: "If anyone proclaiming one nature of the Word of God to be incarnate does not receive it as the fathers taught, viz., that from the divine and human natures (a union in subsistence having taken place) one Christ results;—but endeavors from these words to introduce one nature or substance of the divinity and flesh of Christ:—let such a one be anathema."[14]

On this, Leontius of Jerusalem, in *Against the Monophysites: Testimonies of the Saints*, wrote that "one has to reject utterly all who say 'one incarnate nature of the Word of God' in a sense intended by heretics." He adds that one should accept all who take the formula to mean that the Word's nature was united by *hypostasis* to another nature (flesh) and to all who confess a duality of natures united according to *hypostasis* to show one person out of both.[15] The word "incarnate," Leontius argued, meant completeness of manhood. But we do not separate the natures, for they are undivided, nor do we sever the one Christ into two persons.[16] Leontius's opponents objected that Nestorius used the expression "two natures in Christ," which Leontius also used. Leontius replied: "Yes but he used many scriptural expressions. Moreover, the Arians were the first to use 'one incarnate nature of the Word'! Should this prevent us using it? No!"[17]

13. Christopher A. Beeley, *The Unity of Christ: Continuity and Conflict in Patristic Tradition* (Yale University Press, 2012), 295.

14. Aquinas, *ST*, 3.2.1, reply obj. 1.

15. Quoted in Patrick T. R. Gray, *Leontius of Jerusalem: Against the Monophysites: Testimonies of the Saints and Aporiae* (Oxford University Press, 2006), 57. For the original, *PG*, 86:1820c–d.

16. Gray, *Testimonies*, 59, 69; *PG*, 86:1812a, 1821b.

17. Gray, *Testimonies*, 107; *PG*, 86:1852d.

Summing it all up, Leontius adds—and this is the crux—that "if you'll join us in confessing the tried and true doctrines, saying both 'one incarnate nature of God the Word' and that there are two natures of Christ united in his one hypostasis, and if you don't repudiate the Council, and Leo, and ourselves, then we for our part will anathematize even an angel from heaven sooner than you."[18]

18. Gray, *Testimonies*, 141; *PG*, 86:1881b.

6

The Interpretation of Chalcedon

Introduction

We might be inclined to think that with the settlement of the controversies over the teachings of Nestorius and Eutyches at Ephesus and Chalcedon, calm waters would lie ahead, allowing the church to get on with its work. As we know from our own experience, life is not like that. The following century was to be marked by continued discord. The questions thrown up at this time are crucial ones and have been largely overlooked outside the Eastern church, where the issues continued to arise, were real and live, and aroused intense antagonisms.

Chalcedon was never intended to be the final verdict on Christology. As R. V. Sellers points out, "it allows deductions to be made from its dogmatic decisions, and, in effect, encourages enquiry into the mystery."[1] "It is intended to explain just one definite question of the church's Christology, indeed the most important one. It does not lay claim to having said all that may be said about Christ." It was far from innovative, but rather was in line with the preceding tradition.[2] Yet it left a good deal of unfinished business on the table.

As mentioned above, Chalcedon has been regarded in the Western church as effectively the *terminus ad quem* of orthodox

1. R. V. Sellers, *The Council of Chalcedon: A Historical and Doctrinal Survey* (SPCK, 1953), 350.

2. Aloys Grillmeier, *Christ in Christian Tradition*, vol. 1, *From the Apostolic Age to Chalcedon (451)*, ed. John Bowden, 2nd rev. ed. (John Knox Press, 1975), 550.

Christological discussion. This is particularly so in Protestant and evangelical circles, in which the later ecumenical councils, Constantinople II (553), Constantinople III (680–81), and Nicaea II (787), have received neither the attention nor the weighting that is their due. Additionally, the impact of this neglect has been compounded by an inherent ambiguity in the Definition of Chalcedon. The references to "the same" Lord Jesus Christ, stressing his personal identity as the eternal Son of God, are offset by the language of two natures coming together to form one person, which many saw as implying the priority of the natures, thus granting concessions to Nestorius. Dennis Ferrara calls this "a studied parallelism, . . . a profound tension."[3]

The eventual resolution of the crisis at the second Council of Constantinople in 553 involved recognizing that the Son assumed his human nature into personal union, the humanity having no other existence (*enhypostasis*). This underlined the personal identity of Jesus of Nazareth with the eternal Son of the Father; the one who lay in the manger, who hung on the cross, who was conceived in the womb and rose from the tomb, was and is one of the Trinity and now has his own human nature, body and soul.

Ferrara indicates the problem well when he writes: "It is not surprising that the profound traditional doctrine of the enhypostasis of Christ's humanity in the person of the eternal Logos should experience widespread and not so benign neglect. Not the least sign of this neglect is the tendency to 'freeze' the account of patristic Christology at the Council of Chalcedon and to treat subsequent developments, among which the enhypostasis stands pre-eminent, more or less as mop up operations without decisive import for the interpretation of Chalcedon itself."[4] This lacuna needs to be corrected. It is encouraging that this is happening.[5]

3. Dennis M. Ferrara, "'Hypostatized in the Logos': Leontius of Byzantium, Leontius of Jerusalem and the Unfinished Business of the Council of Chalcedon," *LS* 22 (1997): 311–27, here 317.

4. Ferrara, "Hypostatized in the Logos," 311.

5. Stephen J. Wellum, *God the Son Incarnate* (Crossway, 2016), 313–24; Donald Fairbairn, *Grace and Christology in the Early Church* (Oxford University Press, 2003); Robert Letham, *Systematic Theology* (Crossway, 2019), 490–522; Thomas Brand, *Intimately Forsaken: A Trinitarian Christology of the Cross* (Palgrave Macmillan, 2024).

The century following Chalcedon is perhaps the most crucial period in the formulation of the orthodox and, at root, biblical doctrine of the person of Christ. There is no avoiding the fact that the discussions that arose are among the most difficult to follow and to grasp. The basic issue was the ambiguity of Chalcedon, as expressed above. The solution was to affirm with greater clarity the fact that the human nature of the Son was neither an appendage to who he is nor some independent entity. Rather, since the Son took human nature into union, that human nature is his own. The result is not a union of two natures, which suggests a mixture of some sort, but a union of the human nature *in* the person of the Son.

Criticisms of Chalcedon

In modern times, Chalcedon has come under attack from a number of angles. Adolf von Harnack argued that the stress on two natures intruded elements into Christianity of Greek philosophy, with its dualism, its focus on the spiritual, and its denigration of matter, turning it away from what he regarded as the pure teaching of the gospel on the Father, the supreme value of the soul, and ethics. It was an inherently dualist construction, part of a historic abandonment of the biblical view of the world.[6] It is hard to see any validity in this criticism. The very idea of the incarnation was anathema to the generality of Greek philosophy, which viewed the material as decidedly inferior to the spiritual. While special terms derived from Greek philosophy were used by the fathers, they were given new meaning to express the reality for which they stood.[7] Moreover, as we will see, the conclusion of the sixth-century debates vindicated a unitive Christology.

In tandem with this has been a more recent claim that Chalcedon replaced the dynamic of the Bible by a static ontological view

6. Adolf von Harnack, *What Is Christianity?*, trans. Thomas Bailey Saunders, 4th ed. (Williams and Norgate, 1923), 43ff., 55ff.; Adolf von Harnack, *History of Dogma*, trans. James Millar (London: Williams and Norgate, 1897).

7. Thomas F. Torrance, *Theology in Reconstruction* (Eerdmans, 1965), 30–45; Paul L. Gavrilyuk, *The Suffering of the Impassible God: The Dialectics of Patristic Thought* (Oxford University Press, 2004), 1–16, 176–79. I am grateful to Sherman Isbell for pointing me to the Gavrilyuk book, the whole effect of which is to undermine the Harnack thesis.

of Christ. The fathers, it has been argued, started with Christology "from above" with the premise of the eternal deity of the Son, unchangeable and impassable, and, in doing so, relegated history and the humanity to a subordinate role. Instead, we are told, we are to begin with the historical record of Jesus of Nazareth; it is this that is to govern our thought on Christology.[8] It is easy to see how such thinking has been influenced by Immanuel Kant and his dualistic division between the phenomenal and the noumenal, which restricted knowledge to the observable realm, what was apparent to the senses. This line of thought was subjected to a penetrating critique by Colin Gunton.[9]

Thomas Weinandy addresses another criticism of Chalcedon, or rather the Christology of Cyril that was the dominant influence, citing John Macquarrie, Donald M. Baillie, R. Haight, John Knox, and J. A. T. Robinson as examples. He states that "the critics argue, in keeping with their accusation that Cyril minimizes the significance of Christ's humanity, that if Christ is a divine person and not a human person, then he is not fully human, for something that is essential to being fully human, that is, human personhood, has now been discarded."[10] This charge was also leveled at some of Cyril's supporters. We have already seen that this is misplaced. We will discuss it further shortly.

Above all, and central to the controversies of the following century, a pressing criticism in the immediately following years after Chalcedon argued that the Definition conceded too much to Nestorius and Nestorianism. This was a common view among many followers of Cyril and was expressed with particular vehemence among the Monophysites led by Severus of Antioch. But the repeated phrase "the same" in the Definition tends to belie this criticism,

8. Wolfhart Pannenberg, *Jesus—God and Man*, trans. Lewis L. Wilkins (Westminster Press, 1968) passim, esp. 11–14.

9. Colin E. Gunton, *Yesterday & Today: A Study of Continuities in Christology* (Eerdmans, 1983).

10. Thomas G. Weinandy, "Cyril and the Mystery of the Incarnation," in *The Theology of St. Cyril of Alexandria: A Critical Appreciation*, ed. Thomas G. Weinandy and Daniel A. Keating (T&T Clark, 2003), 23–54, here 44.

indicating the personal identity of Jesus as the eternal Son. Again, this will occupy us later in this chapter.

Nevertheless, it is true that Chalcedon failed to do justice to some real concerns of the Cyrillians. The point that "the distinction of natures being in no way annulled by the union but rather the characteristics of each nature being preserved and coming together" could be taken to mean that human attributes must be predicated only of the human nature, and the divine of the divine. This sounded Nestorian to these people. It gave the impression that Christ was some form of schizoid, for whom some things could be related only to one part of him and other things to another part. Their strong concern for the unity of Christ seemed to have been given short shrift.[11]

Moreover, Chalcedon left the concept of the personal union unclear. For instance, it did not explicitly specify the personal identity of Jesus, *who* exactly it was who had suffered and been crucified. Nor did it say—a vital theme for Cyril's supporters—that the deification of man began in the union of Christ's humanity with his divinity. It also appeared that the two natures were seen as prior to the person, for they were said to come together to form the person. This would make Christ's person distinct from the eternal Son and so destroy the incarnation. The Monophysites later thought that Chalcedon was soft on Nestorianism again by asserting "two natures after the union," precisely because it made no mention of the hypostatic (personal) union. Chalcedon satisfied the West but not much of the East.[12]

There is some disagreement on the nature and scope of the Definition of Chalcedon.[13] Following the general consensus, Oliver Crisp argues that it was mainly negative, outlawing heresy and

11. Sellers, *Chalcedon*, 224.

12. Sellers, *Chalcedon*, 256–60; Leo Donald Davis, *The First Seven Ecumenical Councils (325–787)* (Liturgical Press, 1990), 187; John Meyendorff, *Christ in Eastern Christian Thought* (St. Vladimir's Seminary Press, 1975), 28; Jaroslav Pelikan, *The Christian Tradition: A History of the Development of Doctrine*, vol. 1, *The Emergence of the Catholic Tradition (100–600)* (University of Chicago Press, 1971), 265–66.

13. See Sarah Coakley, "What Does Chalcedon Solve and What Does It Not? Some Reflections on the Status and Meaning of the Chalcedonian Definition," in *The Incarnation*, ed. Stephen T. Davis, Daniel Kendall, and Gerald O'Collins (Oxford University Press, 2002), 143–63.

identifying the boundaries for reflection while leaving a wide area of ambiguity.[14] He argues that it does not give us a complete account of the person of Christ or of his natures and is ambiguous because it was more concerned to rule out what was not orthodox than to make positive statements.[15] It does not say what a person is or what a nature is, nor does it address how someone fully human can be of the identical being as God. It is minimalist.[16] Its positive comment, Crisp contends, is limited to affirming that Christ is one person who has two natures that retain their integrity, are distinct, and are united in the person of Christ.[17] On the other hand, Donald Fairbairn argues against Chalcedon's being a negative statement and presses the point that the Definition of Chalcedon has on eight occasions the phrase "the same one" or "one and the same," stressing that the personal identity of Jesus Christ is the eternal Son.[18]

Central to Chalcedon and what had led up to it was the realization that the incarnation is essential for our salvation. "Whatever is not assumed cannot be healed," wrote Gregory of Nazianzus (330–89).[19] Unless Christ had come in our own flesh and blood, we could not be saved. The gospel was at stake. An appearance of God in human form was not enough. An assumption of human nature that remained separate from personal union with God would have left us with a divine messenger or a highly inspired man, not a Savior. Only the union established in the incarnation could avail. Thus, the supreme mystery of the incarnation can be summed up in the following way: The eternal Son of God took into union a human nature created in the womb of the virgin Mary by the Holy Spirit. This union continues for the whole of eternity, so that the humanity is permanently united to the Son, and remains human; it

14. Oliver D. Crisp, "Some Desiderata for Models of the Hypostatic Union," in *Christology, Ancient and Modern: Explorations in Constructive Dogmatics*, ed. Oliver D. Crisp and Fred Sanders (Zondervan, 2013), 19–41.

15. Crisp, "Some Desiderata," 26.

16. Crisp, "Some Desiderata," 27.

17. Crisp, "Some Desiderata," 29.

18. Donald Fairbairn, "The One Person Who Is Jesus Christ: The Patristic Perspective," in *Jesus in Trinitarian Perspective: An Introductory Christology*, ed. Fred Sanders and Klaus Issler (B&H Academic, 2007), 80–113.

19. Gregory of Nazianzus, "Ep. 101," *PG*, 37:181c.

is the humanity of the Son of God. As T. F. Torrance remarks, "As Cyril of Alexandria used to point out with reference to the burning bush, just as the bush was not consumed by the fiery presence of God, so the humanity of Christ is not consumed by his deity."[20]

The Long-Term Impact of Cyril's Christology

Over the years that followed, the Christological debates in the Greek church through to the seventh century were dominated by Cyril.[21] Cyril Hovorun comments that "as a result, all posterior Christological debates would continue not between supporters and adversaries of Cyril . . . but between factions interpreting Cyril."[22] In order to understand these controversies, we need to take another look at Cyril's Christology, focusing this time on his later thought. At the same time, it is important to recognize that his focus on a unitive Christology, with the focus on the one person of Christ, was consistent throughout his career, from long before his conflict with Nestorius and back at least to the time he became a bishop in 412.[23]

Perhaps Cyril's best known work on Christology, *Quod unus sit Christus* (*On the Unity of Christ*),[24] was written later in the 430s, possibly after 440, as the dust had begun to settle and the heat of the Nestorian controversy to subside. With the condemnation of Nestorius behind him, this treatise reflects Cyril's mature thinking, couched in the form of a dialogue.

Cyril explained his understanding of Christ's becoming man. It was not by being changed into flesh—his usual word for humanity as such—and ceasing to be God, nor was it by mixture or blending of deity and humanity. Rather, he made the assumed humanity, including a rational soul, his own. "He was God in an appearance

20. Thomas F. Torrance, *Incarnation: The Person and Life of Christ* (Paternoster, 2008), 9.

21. There is precious little evidence of his domination in later Eastern Orthodoxy outside Christology.

22. Cyril Hovorun, *Eastern Christianity in Its Texts* (T&T Clark, 2022), 503.

23. This is demonstrable in the case of his *Festal Letters*; see Jonathan Morgan, "The Unity of Christ in Cyril of Alexandria's *Festal Letters*," *SJT* 77, no. 2 (2024): 163–74.

24. Cyril of Alexandria, *On the Unity of Christ*, trans. John Anthony McGuckin (St. Vladimir's Seminary Press, 1995).

like ours, and the Lord in the form of a slave."[25] Again, "he took what was ours to be his very own so that we might have all that was his."[26] Cyril asked, "How could his body possibly give life to us if it were not the very own body of him who is life?"[27] This occurred with no divestiture of deity, for "the Word who is God came down out of heaven and entered our likeness . . . while ever remaining what he was."[28] The Son was made man "in order to reconstitute our condition within himself; first of all in his own body."[29] For Cyril, this was necessary for our salvation, construed as deification,[30] since "he came down into our condition solely in order to lead us into his own divine state."[31] How could he do this unless "appropriating a human body to himself in such an indissoluble union that it has to be considered as his very own body and no one else's"?[32]

Cyril offsets the possible accusation that deity and humanity might be confused as in a mixture of some sort by explaining that "the term 'union' in no way causes the confusion of the things it refers to, but rather signifies the concurrence in one reality of those things that are understood to be united. Surely it is not only those things that are simple and homogeneous which hold a monopoly over the term 'unity' for it can also apply to things compounded out of two, or several, or different kinds of things."[33] He then talks of the wickedness of Nestorians in dividing the incarnate Son and speaking of a conjunction, not a union, "something that any other man could have with God."[34] "Emmanuel must not be separated out into a man, considered as distinct from God the Word,"[35] for the

25. *PG*, 75:1261; Cyril, *Unity of Christ*, 54–55.
26. *PG*, 75:1268; Cyril, *Unity of Christ*, 59.
27. "τίνι γὰρ τρόπω ζωοποιὴσειεν ἂν τὸ σῶμα αὐτοῦ, εἰ μὴ ἐστιν ἰδιον αὐτου, ὁς ἐστι ζώη." *PG*, 75:1269; Cyril, *Unity of Christ*, 60.
28. "μεμένηκεν ὑπερ ἦν." *PG*, 75:1269; Cyril, *Unity of Christ*, 61.
29. *PG*, 75:1272; Cyril, *Unity of Christ*, 62.
30. See also Hovorun, *Eastern Christianity*, 502–3.
31. *PG*, 75:1272; Cyril, *Unity of Christ*, 63.
32. *PG*, 75:1275; Cyril, *Unity of Christ*, 63.
33. *PG*, 75:1285; Cyril, *Unity of Christ*, 73.
34. *PG*, 75:1285; Cyril, *Unity of Christ*, 74.
35. *PG*, 75:1289; Cyril, *Unity of Christ*, 76.

incarnation entails "an indissoluble union."[36] As a consequence of the incarnation, "this inseparable union has become the personal property of the one assuming."[37]

Therefore, "there is one Son and one nature even when he is considered as having assumed flesh endowed with a rational soul."[38] At first sight, this might seem alarming, conjuring up thought of a radical Monophysitism. But what Cyril means by "nature" is clear from what follows; he is using *physis* ("nature") for *hypostasis* ("person"). Thus, "he has made the human element his own (Αὐτοῦ γὰρ, ὡς ἔφην, γέγονε τὸ ἀνθρώπινον). . . . The same one is at once God and man." In the same place, he adds: "Godhead is one thing, and manhood is another thing, considered in the perspective of their respective and intrinsic beings, but in the case of Christ they come together in a mysterious and incomprehensible union without confusion or change. The manner of this union is entirely beyond conception,"[39] "an indivisible union beyond all conception."[40]

This impacts our language about Christ. Cyril indicated that "after the union (I mean with the flesh) even if anyone calls him Only Begotten, or God from God, this does not mean he is thought of as being separated from the flesh or indeed the manhood. Similarly if one calls him a man, this is not to take away the fact that he is God and Lord."[41] Settling the matter and dispelling any remaining concern, Cyril emphatically asserted that "if anyone says that when we speak of the single nature of God the Word incarnate and made man we imply that a confusion or mixture has occurred, then they are talking utter rubbish."[42]

While this is a mystery beyond our understanding, "it was not impossible for God . . . to make himself capable of bearing the

36. "εἰς ἕνωσιν αδιάτμητον." *PG*, 75:1289; Cyril, *Unity of Christ*, 77.
37. "ἕνωσιν αδιάσπαστον." *PG*, 75:1288; Cyril, *Unity of Christ*, 75.
38. *PG*, 75:1289; Cyril, *Unity of Christ*, 77.
39. *PG*, 75:1289; Cyril, *Unity of Christ*, 77.
40. "πρὸς ἕνωσιν ἀδιάτμητον, καὶ τὴν ὑπὲρ νοῦν." *PG*, 75:1292; Cyril, *Unity of Christ*, 78.
41. *PG*, 75:1292; Cyril, *Unity of Christ*, 78.
42. Cyril, *Unity of Christ*, 79; *PG*, 75:1292.

limitations of manhood,"[43] since nothing is impossible for him. "God the Word did not change even when he assumed flesh endowed with a rational soul."[44] He did not empty himself of anything, since "one cannot see anyone emptied out there, but on the contrary someone fulfilled."[45] "The Word was made man as we are, but was not changed."[46]

Cyril made some important comments on the relationship between Adam and the race, and between the second Adam and the new humanity, relating to ancestral / original sin. Citing Romans 5:14, he wrote that from the sin of Adam, "the effects of God's anger passed into the whole of human nature as from the original rootstock, that is Adam," found in corruption and the consequent judgment. In this, he drew a connection between Adam and the whole human race, largely based on the polluted human condition and the wrath of God expressed in judgment. "In the same way, however, the effects of our new first-fruits, that is Christ, shall again pass into the entire human race. The all-wise Paul confirms this for us when he says, 'For if many died because of the transgression of one, how much more' (Rom. 5:15) shall many come to life because of the righteousness of one. And again, 'as all men die in Adam, so shall all be made alive in Christ' (1 Cor. 15:22)."[47] Here he envisaged a relationship between Christ and the whole human race, coextensive with the Adamic relation, in this case based on the life-giving righteousness of Christ overcoming the nexus of transgression communicated from Adam.

Following Irenaeus and Athanasius, Cyril agreed that the Son of God must become man so that man might become divine.[48] This is closely allied to the cross and supports Cyril's conviction that Jesus must be truly God.[49] At root, the Son of God assumed into union a whole man, body and soul, flesh denoting the weakness and

43. Cyril, *Unity of Christ*, 79; *PG*, 75:1293.
44. *PG*, 75:1304; Cyril, *Unity of Christ*, 88.
45. *PG*, 75:1304; Cyril, *Unity of Christ*, 91.
46. *PG*, 75:1309; Cyril, *Unity of Christ*, 92.
47. *PG*, 75:1325–28; Cyril, *Unity of Christ*, 106.
48. Weinandy, *Cyril*, 24.
49. Weinandy, *Cyril*, 25.

vulnerability of fallen humanity.[50] Even the Son's humanity needed to be sanctified.[51] This statement of Cyril, one suggests, is acceptable in the light of Jesus' conception by the Spirit and the sanctification that occurred there and then (Luke 1:34–35), sanctification in this sense signifying separation or dedication to God. Cyril meant that the Son must come to exist as man, establishing an ontological union between the Son of God and his humanity. This was the only way that humanity could be saved and divinized. This does not mean that the Word was changed into flesh, since the unchangeable Son formed an ontological union without involving any change in himself.[52]

To recapitulate, for Cyril everything spoken of Jesus in the Gospels refers to the Word, "for there is only one Son, the Word who was made man for our sake. I would say that everything refers to him, words and deeds, both those that befit the deity, as well as those that are human."[53] While weakness and hunger cannot be attributed to the Word in eternity, not yet made flesh, before the self-emptying, yet "just as we say that the flesh became his very own, in the same way the weakness of that flesh became his very own in an economic appropriation, according to the terms of the unification."[54] This follows from the fact that Christ is in no way divided.[55] Therefore, attributes of both deity and humanity are predicable of the Son, from all he did as man to raising the dead. These are all acts of the Son of God acting as man, his deity and humanity engaged.[56] As Weinandy expresses it, in Cyril's thought "Jesus is one ontological entity, and the one ontological entity that Jesus is is the divine person of the Son of God existing as a complete and authentic man."[57]

50. Weinandy, *Cyril*, 26.

51. Weinandy, *Cyril*, 27.

52. Weinandy, *Cyril*, 28.

53. "φαίην ἂν εἶναι πάντα αὐτοῦ, λόγους τε καὶ πραγματα, τά τε θεοπρεπῆ καὶ προσέτι τὰ ἀνθρώπινα." *PG*, 75:1328; Cyril, *Unity of Christ*, 107.

54. "Ωσπερ γὰρ ἰδιαν αὐτοῦ τὴν σάρκα γενέσθαι φαμὲν, οὕτω πάλιν αὐτοῦ κατʼ οἰκείωσιν οἰκονομικὴν, καὶ κατά γε τὸν τῆς κενώσεως τρόπον, τὰς τῆς σαρκὸς ασθενείας." *PG*, 75:1328; Cyril, *Unity of Christ*, 107.

55. Cyril, *Unity of Christ*, 108.

56. Weinandy, *Cyril*, 29–30.

57. Weinandy, *Cyril*, 30.

He adds that the communication of idioms is the hermeneutical key to unlock Cyril's Christology. Thus, "the Son who was *homoousion* with the Father was the same Son who 'became incarnate of the Virgin Mary.'"[58] Christopher Beeley comments that "the idea of Christ's hypostatic union is Cyril's most distinctive contribution to the technical terminology of Christian theology,"[59] which he called "the concurrence into one reality."[60] Nestorius's denial of *theotokos* negated such an understanding of the incarnation.

The communication of idioms demanded that Jesus be one existing entity. It also required that the one entity that Jesus is be the Son of God existing as incarnate. This is the truth behind the *mia physis* formula (literally "one nature," but used for "one person").[61] What did Cyril mean by this? He did not mean one quiddity (one "what") but rather one entity, or reality (one "who").[62] He drew on the imagery of body and soul in one person, not as a model for the incarnation but rather as an illustration of the communication of idioms.[63] Consequently, we do not apportion statements about Jesus to one or the other nature, respectively, dividing them into separate categories. The unique Christ has no duality.[64] The Gospels witness that there is one subject or person. The divinity and humanity are united in that one person to form the one nature of Christ (in terms of entity or "who," not quiddity or "what") as body and soul form one human being.[65] The union is "natural" in the sense that it is "according to nature,"[66] not that the natures are united so as to form a third thing but rather so as to bring about one reality.[67] In other

58. Weinandy, *Cyril*, 31.

59. Christopher A. Beeley, *The Unity of Christ: Continuity and Conflict in Patristic Tradition* (Yale University Press, 2012), 259.

60. Beeley, *Unity of Christ*, 260.

61. Weinandy, *Cyril*, 32.

62. Entity, entailing existence, from *sum, esse*, "to be," in this case personal existence and thus meaning "who," referring to the person; quiddity, from *quis, quid*, meaning "what," referring to the nature of a thing and so to the natures of Christ.

63. Weinandy, *Cyril*, 33.

64. Weinandy, *Cyril*, 34.

65. Weinandy, *Cyril*, 35.

66. Weinandy, *Cyril*, 37.

67. Weinandy, *Cyril*, 38.

words, Cyril used *physis* in two different ways, here in this sense for one entity or person, and also for both divine and human natures in the sense of nature or quiddity. In short, in Weinandy's words, "the one reality or entity (*mia physis*, Greek) is that of the Word incarnate (*tou logou sesarkomene*)." Again, the formula contained within it not only the assertion of the one person of Christ but also the manner of the one subject's existence; "the subject (the who) of the *mia physis* is the Word. The manner or mode of the Word's existence as *mia physis* is as man." Therefore, all statements in the Gospels refer to the single person of the Word incarnate.[68] This is because "the one entity of Christ (*physis*) is none other than the one divine person or subject (*prosopon/hypostasis*) of the Son existing as incarnate. . . . The one entity of Jesus is the Word existing as man."[69] The translation that best articulates Cyril's meaning is "the one incarnate nature/ person of the Word." Against Nestorius's idea of a conjunctive union, Cyril insisted that the union is hypostatic (*kath' hypostasin*).[70] For Cyril, the *mia physis* formula captured all three elements. "It said it all." Yet the formula needs to be understood in a Cyrillian context. Often, critics have not appreciated this.[71]

In refuting criticisms—which largely, in suggesting that Cyril undermined the humanity, are hostile or opposed to the deity of Christ—Weinandy affirms that only if the identity of Jesus as the Son of God is maintained can one speak of an authentic and true incarnation.[72] Cyril held that divine attributes cannot be predicated of the human nature, and vice versa, but that attributes of both natures are predicated of the person.[73] For Cyril, it is the Son of God who suffers, and he suffers *as man*; "for Cyril what is truly at issue is not that the Son of God suffers as God in a divine manner, but that the Son of God suffers as man in a human manner."[74] The eternal,

68. Weinandy, *Cyril*, 38.
69. Weinandy, *Cyril*, 39.
70. Weinandy, *Cyril*, 39.
71. Weinandy, *Cyril*, 41.
72. Weinandy, *Cyril*, 45.
73. Weinandy, *Cyril*, 46.
74. Weinandy, *Cyril*, 49.

almighty, impassable Son actually experienced as a weak human being the full reality of *human* suffering and death.[75]

Contrary to Apollinaris, "this is not a soulless flesh . . . but flesh animated with a rational soul, and in all respects one factor (*prosopon*) with it."[76] "We say that these human things are his by an economic appropriation (οἰκονομικῶς), and along with the flesh all things belonging to it" such that "the Word is made one with it [the flesh]."[77] In short, it is incarnation, not a conjunction such as Nestorius taught. Yet "he did not suffer in the nature of the godhead, but in his own flesh" such that "the Word was alive even when his holy flesh was tasting death (Ἔζη γὰρ ὁ Λόγος καὶ γευομένης θανάτου τῆς ἁγία αὐτοῦ σαρκὸς), so that when death was beaten and corruption trodden underfoot the power of the resurrection might come upon the whole human race."[78] That is why, Cyril affirmed, we can say that the Word of God the Father himself suffered in the flesh for our sake (φαμὲν τὸν ἐκ θεοῦ Πατρὸς Λόγον, σαρκὶ παθεῖν δι᾽ ἡμᾶς).[79]

> And since on this account he wished to suffer, even though he was beyond the power of suffering in his nature as God, then he wrapped himself in flesh that was capable of suffering, and revealed it as his very own, so that even the suffering might be said to be his because it was his own body which suffered and no one else's.[80]

The manner of the economy allows him to choose to suffer in the flesh and not to suffer in the Godhead. He remains "the life-giving power of the Father . . . naturally resplendent in all the dignities of the one that begot him, even when he became flesh."[81] "The Word remained what he was even when he became flesh, so that he who

75. Weinandy, *Cyril*, 53; Thomas G. Weinandy, *Does God Suffer?* (University of Notre Dame Press, 2000).

76. *PG*, 75:1329; Cyril, *Unity of Christ*, 109.

77. *PG*, 75:1332; Cyril, *Unity of Christ*, 110.

78. *PG*, 75:1337; Cyril, *Unity of Christ*, 115.

79. *PG*, 75:1340; Cyril, *Unity of Christ*, 115–16.

80. *PG*, 75:1341; Cyril, *Unity of Christ*, 118.

81. *PG*, 75:1344; Cyril, *Unity of Christ*, 119.

is over all, and yet came among all through his humanity, should keep in himself his transcendence of all and remain above all the limitations of the creation."[82]

Cyril addresses the question of how the same one can both suffer and not suffer. "He suffers in his own flesh, and not in the nature of the Godhead (Σαρκὶ τῇ ἰδία παθών, καὶ οὐ θεότητος φύσει). The method of these things is altogether ineffable." Recognizing its limitations, he uses the analogy of fire and iron, the iron heated by the fire but remaining as it was.[83] In this way, the only way, the flesh of Christ becomes life-giving "even though by its own nature it was subject to the necessity of corruption, except that it became the very flesh of the Word who gives life to all things." Fire contacts things that are not hot, energizing and heating them. So "in an even greater degree the Word who is God can introduce the life-giving power and energy of his own self into his very own flesh."[84] Thus "we confess that it has become entirely the personal body of the Word of the Father . . . animated with a rational soul."[85]

According to Weinandy, Cyril established three things. First, he distinguished between person, who Christ is, and nature, the manner or mode of his existence. He is eternally God, who now also exists as man. Second, the incarnation involves neither a change in the Son nor a mixture of natures but rather a new mode of existence, as man. Third, it is the one person of the Word or Son who now exists as man.[86] The repetition of the phrase "the same" in the Definition of Chalcedon indicates that Cyril's Christology was definitive. Weinandy adds that "to read the Chalcedonian creed other than through the eyes of Cyril is to misread it."[87] Unfortunately, this has happened widely.

82. *PG*, 75:1356; Cyril, *Unity of Christ*, 129.

83. *PG*, 75:1357; Cyril, *Unity of Christ*, 130.

84. "πῶς οὐ μᾶλλον ἐνίησι θεὸς ὢν ὁ Λόγος τῃ ἰδίᾳ σαρκὶ τὴν ζωοποιὸν ἑαυτοῦ δύναμιν καὶ ἐνέρειαν." *PG*, 75:1361; Cyril, *Unity of Christ*, 132–33.

85. *PG*, 75:1361; Cyril, *Unity of Christ*, 133.

86. Weinandy, *Cyril*, 42.

87. Weinandy, *Cyril*, 43–44. For an extensive discussion of the question of paradox in Cyril's Christology, see Sergey Trostyanskiy, "The Compresence of Opposites in Christ in St. Cyril of Alexandria's *Oikonomia*," *StPatr* 90 (2017): 3–23, who concludes that for Cyril, "opposing characteristics are predicated of the same subject and exist in the same subject, but not in the same sense" but in a single operation, since they are fully unified.

Post-Chalcedon Divisions

Before the Council of Ephesus, the controversy was between Cyril and Nestorius, then spilling over into the overreaction of Eutyches. As we have observed, after Chalcedon, turmoil emerged over the interpretation of Cyril. Cyril's Christology was definitive for the church, but the presenting question became how to understand it.

A corresponding problem surrounded the ambiguities in Chalcedon itself, with the strong suspicion that it had given tacit support to Nestorianizing tendencies by its *parallel* focus on the two natures and the one person, and its expression that these two natures had come together to form one person, suggesting an ontological priority to be accorded to the natures. Let us remind ourselves of the relevant section of the Definition:

> our Lord Jesus Christ, at once complete in Godhead and complete in manhood, truly God and truly man, . . . of one substance with the Father as regards his Godhead, and at the same time of one substance with us as regards his manhood, . . . recognized in two natures, without confusion, without change, without division, without separation; *the distinction of natures being in no way annulled by the union, but rather the characteristics of each nature being preserved and coming together to form one person and subsistence.*

These discussions were crucial; in the West, and especially in Protestant circles, they have largely been ignored. Beeley remarks: "It has long been customary in some circles to think of the Council of Chalcedon as the great watershed in the definition of Christological orthodoxy. In fact, the council of 451 led to even greater divisions . . . , and . . . it arguably brought more problems than solutions."[88]

At the same time, classifications into groups that are at loggerheads can be only approximate; views develop and change, adherents come and go, contexts are altered. Moreover, later scholars impose categories on the past in order to provide greater clarity, whereas at the time such clarity may or may not have existed. Quentin Skinner

88. Beeley, *Unity of Christ*, 285.

calls this "the mythology of coherence."[89] We should bear this in mind in what follows.

The Monophysites[90]

This was the most significant grouping to emerge from the middle of the fifth century, significant in the sense that their presence and claims proved catalytic for further developments that did not necessarily affirm the central ideas that they held. It is now widely agreed that the Monophysites were fundamentally in support of Cyrilline Christology. They were not Eutychian. Overall, the Monophysites reacted to an interpretation of Chalcedon that gave undue prominence to the two-natures dogma at the expense of the unity of Christ's person, the single subject of the incarnation.

In particular, two passages in Leo's *Tome*, effectively canonized by Chalcedon, were held by Monophysites to be indisputably Nestorian, where "Leo so separates, and personalizes, what is divine and what is human in Christ that the hypostatic union is dissolved."[91] Leo had stated that the properties of both natures are "kept intact and come together in one person, lowliness is taken on by majesty, weakness by power, mortality by eternity, and the nature which cannot be harmed is united to the nature which suffers."[92] He added that "it is execrable to say that after 'the Logos was made flesh' the nature which was in him is one in number."[93] In this Leo betrayed his unfamiliarity with Greek and with the course of the controversy. He also commented that "one and the same mediator between God and human beings, the human being who is Jesus Christ, can at one and the same time die in virtue of the one nature and, in virtue of the other, be incapable of death."[94] Beeley considers that Leo speaks of Christ "as a combination of two acting subjects . . . envisioning the

89. Quentin Skinner, "Meaning and Understanding in the History of Ideas," in *Visions of Politics*, vol. 1, *Regarding Method* (Cambridge University Press, 2002), 64–72.

90. On the various groups, see Patrick T. R. Gray, *The Defense of Chalcedon in the East (451–553)* (Brill, 1979), 53–79.

91. Sellers, *Chalcedon*, 266.

92. Richard A. Norris Jr., *The Christological Controversy* (Fortress Press, 1980), 148.

93. Norris, *Controversy*, 154.

94. Norris, *Controversy*, 148.

divine Son doing certain things and the human Jesus doing others."[95] As a result, the final version stated that Christ is recognized "*in* two natures" rather than "*out of* two natures," as the original draft before the acceptance of Leo's *Tome* had claimed.[96] It appears that the natures are viewed as subjects of action.[97] Furthermore, the hypostatic union went unmentioned. Deep concerns had been expressed at Chalcedon over the orthodoxy of Leo's *Tome*.[98] Consequently, many of Cyril's followers were loath to accept Chalcedon. Moreover, they strongly held to the personal identity of the incarnate Christ with the preexistent Son, and this the council, in their eyes, did not explicitly affirm,[99] although the repeated phrase "one and the same" must be borne in mind in response to this claim.[100] Consequently, "the West supported it, but many in the East rejected it."[101] The Christology of the Western church has been colored by this perceived ambiguity ever since.[102] Given its basic premises, "we see that monophysitism was partially justified in its opposition to the Council of Chalcedon."[103]

Severus (c 465–538)

Severus of Antioch was perhaps the leading Monophysite theologian of the late fifth century. No one of comparable ability was

95. Beeley, *Unity of Christ*, 275.

96. See Andrew Louth, *John Damascene: Tradition and Originality in Byzantine Theology* (Oxford University Press, 2002), 150.

97. Demetrios Bathrellos, *The Byzantine Christ: Person, Nature, and Will in the Christology of Saint Maximus the Confessor* (Oxford University Press, 2004), 176.

98. Richard Price, "The Council of Chalcedon (451): A Narrative," in *Chalcedon in Context: Church Councils 400–700*, ed. Richard Price and Mary Whitby (Liverpool University Press, 2011), 75–76.

99. Davis, *First Seven Ecumenical Councils (325–787)*, 196–97.

100. Price correctly recognizes that since the majority on the committee that finalized the wording at Chalcedon and the majority of assembled bishops that approved it were Cyrillian and unlikely to have rejected his teachings, it is absurd to suggest that the Definition of Chalcedon was anti-Cyrillian. It is equally clear, however, that it was something of a compromise to which many Cyrillians could not give their support and that it left the door open to interpretations that would run counter to their interests. See Price, "Chalcedon," 81.

101. Louth, *John Damascene*, 151.

102. Beeley, *Unity of Christ*, 276.

103. I. A. Dorner, *History of the Development of the Doctrine of the Person of Christ*, trans. D. W. Simon (Edinburgh: T&T Clark, 1861), 3:119.

able to withstand him. His basic premise, together with his associates, was the ontological identity between the eternal Son and the incarnate Son, which we saw to be the keystone of Cyril's theology.

Severus, in common with many others, considered that since "no nature ever works unless it subsists in a person," a nature cannot exist of itself but must be instantiated in a *hypostasis*.[104] Another from the same camp, Timothy Aelurus, asserted that "the nature does not exist without the hypostasis, nor the hypostasis without the person; therefore, if there are two natures, there are also necessarily two persons."[105] It therefore followed, in Severus's thought, that those who affirmed, with Chalcedon, that Christ has two natures must also conclude that he is two *hypostases*, and thereby be Nestorian. Hence, the Monophysites—or Miaphysites, as they preferred to be called—held that since Christ is one person, it followed, on their premises, that he has one nature. Thus, Severus wrote that "we do not affirm that he is known in two natures, as the synod of Chalcedon declared as dogma, putting the expression 'indivisibly' into its declaration as a kind of apology. . . . It is in the nature of a contradiction to say concerning the one Christ that on the one hand there are two natures, but on the other one hypostasis. For the person who speaks of 'one hypostasis' necessarily affirms one nature as well." Consequently, Severus

104. "οὐ γὰρ ἐνεργεῖ ποτε φύσις οὐχ ὑφεστῶσα προσωπικῶς," in *Doctrina Patrum de incarnatione Verbi: Ein Griechishes Florilegium aus der Wende des 7. und 8. Jahrhunderts*, ed. Basileos Phanourgakis and Evangelos Chrysos (Aschendorff, 1981), 310.

105. "Car le nature n'existe pas sans l'hypostase ni l'hypostase sans la personne (προσωπον); si donc il y a deux natures il y a deux personnes." Timothy Aelurus, *Contre Chalcedoine*, ed. and trans. F. Nau, *PO*, 13.2.228–29. Underlying this assumption was the Cappadocian theory that had paved the way for the resolution of the Trinitarian crisis of the fourth century. This theory, originally propounded by Basil, reserved *ousia* for the one being or nature of God and *hypostasis* for the three persons, on the basis of the relationship between the universal and the particular. Thus, every *ousia* is instantiated in particular *hypostasis*. Consequently, if Christ is held to have two natures (*physeis*), it was concluded that there would be two persons (*hypostaseis*), which of course was entirely unacceptable. On this overall development, see Johannes Zachhuber, *The Rise of Christian Theology and the End of Ancient Metaphysics: Patristic Philosophy from the Cappadocian Fathers to John of Damascus* (Oxford University Press, 2020), 1–144.

called Chalcedon "a deception."[106] Hovorun correctly states that Chalcedon never accepted the sort of unity that Severus maintained was logical. Yet Severus did not deny the real humanity but argued that divinity and humanity were not two realities, for the reality of Christ is one.[107] Christ had no distinct human nature; rather, his one nature took on the characteristics of humanity, while the Word and the flesh are not changed into the other.[108] He referred to "one composite nature" rather than "one composite person."[109] He never said that Christ was a single essence (*ousia*), since that would undermine the humanity so that he could not be one with us.[110] In Christ, *physis* ("nature") and *hypostasis* ("person") are synonymous, since Christ is concretely unique and participates in the essence (*ousia*) of God and in the essence (*ousia*) of man.[111] But the *physis* and the *hypostasis* are not precisely identical; rather, the latter is the concrete instantiation of the former.[112] It is possible, then, for Severus to agree that Christ is made "out of two natures" but that these can be contemplated only by the mind, since there has occurred an unbreakable union.[113] But as Hovorun remarks, Severus was strongly opposed to the number "two" in Christology and to anything that even slightly suggested duality.[114] Here, a problem had been bequeathed by Chalcedon's silence on the "hypostatic union." It never *explicitly* identified the *hypostasis* of the incarnate Son with the *hypostasis* of the eternal Son.[115]

Around 515, a group emerged from these ranks, dubbed Aphthartodocetists,[116] who argued that Jesus by nature was incapable

106. Severus, *Ad Nephalium II*, in *Severus of Antioch*, by Pauline Allen and C. T. R. Hayward (Routledge, 2004), 59–60, 63, 64. See also Davis, *First Seven Ecumenical Councils (325–787)*, 209.

107. Hovorun, *Eastern Christianity*, 525.

108. Severus, *Letter to Oecumenius*, in *PO*, 12.2.176–77.

109. Hovorun, *Eastern Christianity*, 527.

110. Meyendorff, *Christ*, 41.

111. Meyendorff, *Christ*, 41.

112. Zachhuber, *Rise of Christian Theology*, 125–33.

113. Meyendorff, *Christ*, 42.

114. Hovorun, *Eastern Christianity*, 527.

115. Davis, *First Seven Ecumenical Councils (325–787)*, 215; Meyendorff, *Christ*, 44.

116. This is a useful term to know because its use could easily deter unwanted conversationalists at cocktail parties.

of suffering and dying or in any way undergoing corruption or decay. He is without blemish or spot. Some among them thought he could experience such things, but only by a free decision of his own. This produced a response from Leontius of Byzantium, about whom more will follow. This theory combined with a commitment to the two-natures doctrine, *aphtharsia* ("incorruption") beginning at conception. These people were not Docetists, for their distinctive position was not related to the human nature as such but rather to its relation with the divinity. In the end, for them the actual suffering of Christ occurred as a result of a miracle. In practice, this left little place for the reality of the incarnation.[117]

The Monophysites in general objected to their being labeled as "Monophysites" because it lumped them together with Eutyches, whom they—just as the Chalcedonians—opposed. They preferred to be called Miaphysites, which identifies their adherence to the formula "one nature" but differentiates them from Eutyches.

The Nestorians

Nestorius's followers were at the opposite end of the Christological spectrum. They no longer posed a direct threat, since they had been banished from the empire by the Council of Ephesus in 431. Nestorians traveled beyond the imperial bounds to Mesopotamia and eventually to China, planting churches throughout and creating a wide body of Christian literature.[118] It is possible that through interaction with exiled Nestorians, a garbled report of Mary's being called "the mother of God" came to the ears of Arab tradesmen on their travels and so filtered into the proposals of Muhammad.[119]

The Dyophysites

These were supporters of Chalcedon, particularly in its assertion of the two natures. Ranged against the Monophysites, by this strong

117. Aloys Grillmeier, *Christ in Christian Tradition*, vol. 2, *From the Council of Chalcedon (451) to Gregory the Great (590–604): Part Two: The Church of Constantinople in the Sixth Century*, trans. Theresia Hainthaler and John Cawte (Mowbray, 1995), 214–17.

118. Stephen Neill, *Christian Missions* (Penguin, 1964), 95–96.

119. Robert Letham, *The Holy Trinity: In Scripture, History, Theology, and Worship*, rev. and expanded ed. (P&R Publishing, 2019), 535–39.

focus on the two natures they gave some credence to the latter's claim that Chalcedon had adopted a quasi-Nestorian position. Indeed, it was from these sources that many readings of that council came in the decades following, thereby impacting long-term interpretations of it. These people have in the past been classified as "Antiochenes," as exponents of a "Word-man" Christology, the Word's uniting to himself a man. But there is scant evidence that such views were characteristic of, still less peculiar to, Antioch, or even that there was such a distinctive school of thought beyond a handful of figures, all of whom were to have works they composed condemned for heresy. As in all such categories imposed by later scholars, there is almost as much distortion as truth. Nevertheless, these scholarly paradigms linger, and it would by no means be stretching a point to say that in recent times much scholarship in the West, and Protestantism in particular, has assumed that a strong parallel focus on the two natures is a true representation of classic Christology.

Some of the Dyophysite spokesmen had a clear sympathy with aspects of Nestorius's Christology. Theodoret was a typical example. We commented on Theodoret in chapter 4.[120] Patrick Gray notes of those who followed Theodoret that they balked at the Theopaschite formula, "one of the Trinity suffered in the flesh." Among other things, from their base in Constantinople they considered that Chalcedon had endorsed their stress on the two natures. On this basis, the formula "one hypostasis of the Word made flesh" did not make sense.[121] Gray agrees that Theodoret never taught the Nestorian doctrine of two Sons—in reality opposing it—but yet insisted on two natures, refused Theopaschism, had no concrete term for the unity in Christ other than *prosopon*, and divided Christ's activities "as if they were separate subjects."[122] He concludes that these attitudes led the Scythian monks to call this group Nestorian defenders of Chalcedon.[123]

120. See Paul B. Clayton, *The Christology of Theodoret of Cyrus: Antiochene Christology from the Council of Ephesus (431) to the Council of Chalcedon (451)* (Oxford University Press, 2007).

121. Gray, *Defense of Chalcedon in the East*, 81.

122. Gray, *Defense of Chalcedon in the East*, 83–84.

123. Gray, *Defense of Chalcedon in the East*, 89.

Leontius of Byzantium (?–544 at latest)[124]

As the years passed and the sixth century was well and truly established, Leontius became the most prominent of these Dyophysites.[125] He suggested that when he was young he had been influenced by Nestorians but had extricated himself from their clutches through the grace of God.[126] Some have argued that he was an Origenist, but for this there is no evidence. Hovorun writes that "not a single passage in the surviving large bulk of Leontius' writings betrays a hint of Origenism."[127]

While there is agreement that Leontius was a Dyophysite, stressing the two natures, some have gone so far as to consider him to teach a *tertium quid,* a third thing in addition to the deity and humanity, and thus to be close to heterodoxy. Gray, for example, wrote that Leontius held to "two hypostases in two natures united in a single third hypostasis."[128] The root of this was his use of the comparison of general and particular that Basil had adopted in his discussion of the Trinity. It suggested that the natures were two separate or highly distinct things. From this, Leontius employed the analogy of the union of body and soul, which assumes that the person is some additional amalgam of the two. Besides, he used only two of the four

124. Brian E. Daley, ed., *Leontius of Byzantium: Complete Works* (Oxford University Press, 2017), 3–12.

125. In recent decades, the previously little-known figure John of Caesarea, or John the Grammarian (dates uncertain), has come to light as pivotal in the development of sixth-century Christology. See Zachhuber, *Rise of Christian Theology*, 189–202.

126. *PG*, 86:1357–60; Daley, *Leontius of Byzantium*, 414–15; Gray, *Defense of Chalcedon in the East*, 90.

127. Hovorun, *Eastern Christianity*, 548–49. Daley agrees that there is no evidence of the influence of Origen on Leontius and suggests that the group with which he was associated did not share Origen's distinctive views, being labeled "Origenists" due to their intellectual curiosity and critical thinking at a time when this was perceived as threatening, particularly to a bishop such as Cyril of Skythopolis, the main recorder of events, who wanted order and unity. Daley, *Leontius of Byzantium*, 14–15. The only reference to Origen in Leontius's extant works refers to the Nestorians, that "they do not admire Origen," and implies that he shared this assessment (Τὸν δὲ 'Ὀριγένην οὐ θαυμάζουσιν), *PG*, 86:1:1377c, in his *Deprehensio et Triumphus super Nestorianos*, 41; Daley, *Leontius of Byzantium*, 438–39. While this refers to the Nestorians' views of Origen, the implication is that Leontius shared them.

128. Gray, *Defense of Chalcedon in the East*, 94; *PG*, 86:1277–80; Daley, *Leontius of Byzantium*, 132–35.

central Chalcedonian adverbs, ignoring "without division, without separation."[129] He wrote of a union of two natures (*henosis kat' ousian*) rather than the motto of the neo-Chalcedonians, union according to *hypostasis* (*henosis kat' hupostasin*), union in the person. Gray adds that he does this "because *he is talking about the union of two things, not simply with each other or in one another, but in a third thing*."[130] On this basis, Christ is "an independent essence," "an indeterminate reality between God and man."[131] It was by no means accidental, Gray proposes, that Leontius of Jerusalem attacked this notion in his *Contra Nestorianos*.[132]

John Meyendorff takes a similar tack. He observes that Leontius attempts to tread a middle course between Nestorius and Eutyches, between Theodoret and the Aphthartodocetists. In doing so, his body-soul analogy lays him open to the charge that he has posited two *hypostases*, since he understands *hypostasis* as "existence by itself."[133] Nor does he ever say that the Logos is the subject of the incarnation.[134] For Leontius, this *hypostasis* is "not that of the pre-existent Logos but that of Christ, formed at the time of the incarnation, finding itself in 'essential union' with the Logos, and 'made of' natures, which are its parts."[135] Aloys Grillmeier agrees with Meyendorff's assessment.[136] Leontius writes that "the Word is in a complete humanity (ὁ τρόπος δηλαδὴ τῆς ἑνώσεως, οὐσιωδῶς ἀλλ' οὐ σχετικῶς γεγονώς· ὡς εἶναι ἐν τῇ τελείᾳ ἀνθρωπότητι τὸν Λόγον, ὅπερ ἐν ημῖν ὁ ἔσω ἄνθρωπος)."[137] With the basis in the two natures, it is not possible to identify Jesus of Nazareth with the eternal Logos, since it is the composite *hypostasis*, designated as Christ,

129. Gray, *Defense of Chalcedon in the East*, 97.

130. Gray, *Defense of Chalcedon in the East*, 98–99 (italics original).

131. Gray, *Defense of Chalcedon in the East*, 101–2. Ferrara agrees with this analysis. Ferrara, "Hypostatized in the Logos," 315.

132. *PG*, 86:1560; Gray, *Defense of Chalcedon in the East*, 103.

133. Meyendorff, *Christ*, 62.

134. Meyendorff, *Christ*, 64.

135. *PG*, 86:1293–96, 1305; Daley, *Leontius of Byzantium*, 160–61, 175; Meyendorff, *Christ*, 66.

136. Grillmeier, *Christ*, 2:187.

137. *PG*, 86:1379c; Daley, *Leontius of Byzantium*, 444–45.

who is the subject of the incarnation. It is quite possible, however, that Leontius had simply not thought through the implications of what he was saying.

As we have mentioned, one of the most prominent features of Leontius's Christology was his sharp distinction between nature and *hypostasis*, for which he relied in great measure on the distinction between general and particular that Basil had adopted in the Trinitarian crisis of the previous century, a move that at that time had contributed toward its eventual resolution. It had helped toward clarifying the relation between the one indivisible being of God and the three *hypostases* ("persons").[138] But this became problematic for the Christological issue. According to Benjamin Gleede, for Leontius a nature is not without *hypostasis* just as a body is not without shape. But since a body is not shape itself, so a nature is not without at least one *hypostasis* but is not identical to *hypostasis*.[139] The term "nature" is not convertible with *hypostasis*. For Leontius, "nature" means "being," not individualized, self-sufficient being. "Nature" signifies species, *hypostasis* individuals. "Nature" reveals the general character of a thing, *hypostasis* the individual.[140] Natures necessarily exist in *hypostases* and make them what they are.[141] By itself, one is inclined to think that this suggests two *hypostases*, with another needed to establish a union of sorts.[142]

138. Grillmeier, *Christ*, 2:189–93.

139. Benjamin Gleede, *The Development of the Term* ἐνυπόστατος *from Origen to John of Damascus* (Brill, 2012), 66.

140. Gleede, Ἐνυπόστατος, 66.

141. Gleede, Ἐνυπόστατος, 67.

142. Referring to Anastasius I of Antioch, Gleede highlights two problems. First, if *hypostasis* consists of certain properties, why should not the human properties constitute a human *hypostasis* distinct from the Logos? The answer, following Leontius, is that only the actual configuration of the divine and human properties constitute the *hypostasis*, since the human properties are common and not distinctive of any particular individual. Second, how can this "conglomeration" be reconciled with the simplicity of God? This was to be answered by Leontius of Jerusalem, who argued that the Son assumed the human properties into the distinct Trinitarian relations particular to himself. Gleede considers that this can be done only if the eternal Son is shown to be identical with the incarnate Son. This had been the brunt of Cyril's arguments, but Gleede seems to have overlooked the fact. Gleede, Ἐνυπόστατος, 121–22.

Moreover, in contrast to the Cappadocians, who had moved away from philosophical terminology to talk in more straightforward language about the Trinity, Leontius engaged in extensive lexicographical and philosophical discussion.[143] As Grillmeier remarks: "Leontius of Byzantium was intensively occupied with contrasting nature and *hypostasis* linguistically and conceptually. . . . He is dependent on the Cappadocian theology of the Trinity, but also on the language of the philosophers."[144] Leontius, however, does introduce a new idea—*enhypostatos*—referring to existing in something, in another *hypostasis*. By this the human nature of Christ could be said to exist in the person of Christ as his human nature. At the same time, it would have no other existence apart from being the humanity of Christ.[145]

143. Beeley, *Unity of Christ*, 289–91.

144. Grillmeier, *Christ*, 2:192.

145. "Hypostasis, gentlemen, and the hypostatic are not the same thing, just as essence and the essential are different. For the hypostasis signifies the individual, but the hypostatic the essence; and the hypostasis defines the person by means of peculiar characteristics, while the hypostatic signifies that something is not an accident, which has its being in another and is not perceived by itself. Such are all qualities, those called essential and those called non-essential; neither of them is the essence, which is a subsistent thing—but is perceived always in association with an essence, as with color in a body or knowledge in a soul. He then who says, 'There is no such thing as an anhypostatic nature,' speaks truly; but he does not draw a correct conclusion when he argues from its being not-hypostatic to its being an hypostasis. . . . There could never be, then, an anhypostatic nature—that is, essence. But the nature is not a hypostasis, because it is not a reversible attribution; for a hypostasis is also a nature, but a nature is not also a hypostasis; for nature admits of the predication of being, but hypostasis also of being-by-oneself, and the former presents the character of genus, the latter expresses individual identity. And the one brings out what is peculiar to something universal, the other distinguishes the particular from the general. To put it concisely, things sharing the same essence are properly said to be of one nature, and things whose structure of being is common; but we can define as 'hypostasis' things which share a nature but differ in number, or things which are put together from different natures, but which share reciprocally in a common being. I say that they share being, not as if they completed one another's essence, as happens with essences and with things that are essentially predicated of them—which are called qualities—but insofar as the essence and nature of each is not considered by itself but with the other, to which it is joined and assimilated. One finds this in various things, not least in the case of soul and body, whose hypostasis is common but each of whose natures is individual, with a different way of being." *Contra Nestorianos et Eutychianos*, 1; *PG*, 86:1277C–1280B; the translation above is from Daley, *Leontius of Byzantium*, 133–35.

Later, this would be integrated into a paradigm in which the *hypostasis* of Christ is identical to the *hypostasis* of the Logos, positing the Logos as the single subject in the incarnation.[146] Leontius himself was unable to take that step.[147]

The Neo-Chalcedonians

These were determined followers of Cyril who rightly understood Chalcedon to have attempted to express his Christology, with the repeated "the same" in its Definition, indicating the identity of the eternal Logos with the incarnate Logos and, by entailment, the single subject in Jesus of Nazareth. They had that in common with many of the Monophysites but, at the same time, were willing to accept Chalcedon if it could be interpreted along clearly Cyrillian lines. This is the group, such as it was, that eventually proved winners. We will examine the thought of the leading figure, Leontius of Jerusalem. Fairbairn points out that the questions raised were integrally related to the issue of the relation between divine and human action in salvation. The issue whether Christ was in reality the Son of God or merely a man indwelt by God the Son reflected the issue whether God is the author of salvation or rather whether human effort attains it.[148]

The Scythian Monks

In 518, a group of monks in Scythia, led by John Maxentius,[149] made representations to Rome in an attempt to broker an agreement

146. Meyendorff, *Christ*, 67–68.

147. Grillmeier, *Christ*, 2:185–229, disagrees with the claim that Leontius proposed a *tertium quid*. He lists the arguments in favor of the idea but argues that his aim was to justify the two-natures formula (188–89) and that his focus was not on the one *hypostasis* (198). In his work against the Aphthartodocetists, he was concerned to stress the true humanity of Christ (221). This was so, one agrees, but his choice of opponents is indicative of the direction from which he came, although here one must bear in mind that he wrote at a time when the Miaphysites were the most dominant. Zachhuber acknowledges the possibility of a *tertium quid*. Zachhuber, *Rise of Christian Theology*, 213–14.

148. Donald Fairbairn, Introduction to *Fulgentius of Ruspe and the Scythian Monks: Correspondence on Christology and Grace*, trans. Rob Roy McGregor and Donald Fairbairn, Fathers of the Church 126 (Catholic University of America Press, 2013), 6, 14–21.

149. See John Maxentius, *Professio brevissima Catholicae fidei*, in *CCSL* (Brepols, 1953), 85A:33–36.

that would reconcile as wide a range as possible to Chalcedon, interpreted through a strongly Cyrillian lens. In particular, they hoped for reconciliation with the Monophysites and also with the Dyophysite views of Rome (influenced by Leo's *Tome*). They had written to Fulgentius of Ruspe to secure his agreement. John used the slogan from Cyril's twelfth anathema against Nestorius, "one of the Trinity suffered in the flesh" (*unus de trinitate carne passus est*).[150] Behind it was an addition by Peter the Fuller, patriarch of Antioch, to the trisagion prayer—"Holy God, holy Mighty, holy immortal, have mercy upon us"—of the clause "who was crucified for us," which, Fairbairn remarks, had caused "a firestorm of protest."[151] John McGuckin makes it very clear that the term "Theopaschite formula" that identifies the slogan was not coined by the monks but by their critics, the Acoemetae monks, and that they had no connection whatsoever with the Patripassian heretics of the third century.[152] The Scythian monks are particularly noted for bringing this matter into the forefront of debate. While their immediate plans for reconciliation were not fulfilled, the long-term impact was great, since eventually Cyril's letter and their main arguments were canonized at Constantinople in 553.

McGuckin summarizes the main points of their presentation, found in their *Letter to the Bishops of North Africa in Exile in Sardinia*. First, they appealed throughout to the authority of tradition—scriptural, apostolic, and patristic—to support their case, with copious citations from Cyril, Gregory of Nazianzus, and others. Second, they stressed that Christ is *composite*, implying complete unity in his incarnate person, thus avoiding Monophysitism. Third, the Theopaschite formula is not found explicitly but is the foundation of the whole document, and Cyril's twelfth anathema is explicitly

150. The Maxentian confession is found in *PL*, 63:83–92, and the letter to Fulgentius as Letter 16 of his correspondence in *PL*, 65:442f. McGuckin provides a translation in J. A. McGuckin, "'The Theopaschite Confession' (Text and Historical Context): A Study in the Cyrilline Re-Interpretation of Chalcedon," *JEH* 35, no. 2 (1984): 239–55.

151. McGregor and Fairbairn, *Fulgentius and the Scythian Monks*, 9–10.

152. McGuckin, "Theopaschite Confession," 239.

quoted. Fourth, the doctrine of grace follows Augustine, with divine grace preceding the human will and all inclinations of the will to good coming from God. Fifth, they held to a restrained Augustinian doctrine of predestination.[153]

They assert that "the phrase, 'one incarnate nature of God the Word' signifies nothing other than two natures ineffably united, . . . for indeed, when one uses the word 'incarnate,' one thereby implies both the perfection of humanity and the manifestation of our essence."[154] Therefore, the incarnation brought no change to the Word himself: "The full and perfect God the Word, even after He had assumed flesh, suffered no increase or diminution but rather by His union brought ineffable glory to that nature He assumed."[155] Indeed, "even after the mystery of the Incarnation the Trinity continues to abide because the same God the Word, even with His own flesh, is one of the Trinity. And this is not because His flesh is of the substance of the Trinity but because it is the flesh of God the Word who is one of the Trinity."[156] "And for this reason we profess that God the Word suffered in the flesh, was crucified in the flesh, and was buried in the flesh, in accordance with the blessed Cyril when he says: 'If anyone does not confess that God the Word suffered in the flesh, tasted death in the flesh, and was made the firstborn from the dead, even as He is God the life and the life-giver, then let him be anathema.'"[157]

Leontius of Jerusalem (485–543)

Leontius's most important work for our purposes is his vast *Contra Nestorianos*, written against those who say that there are two

153. McGuckin, "Theopaschite Confession," 246–47.

154. "Quasi aliquid aliud quam duas naturas ineffabiliter unitas una dei verbi natura incarnata significet." *CCSL*, 85A:159; Scythian Monks, *Letter*, 3, in McGregor and Fairbairn, *Fulgentius and the Scythian Monks*, 26–27; McGuckin, "Theopaschite Confession," 248.

155. McGuckin, "Theopaschite Confession," 249.

156. "Non quod caro eius sit de substantia trinitatis, sed quia caro dei verbi est, qui est unus ex trinitate." *CCSL*, 85A:162; McGuckin, "Theopaschite Confession," 250; McGregor and Fairbairn, *Fulgentius and the Scythian Monks*, 31.

157. *CCSL*, 85A:162; McGuckin, "Theopaschite Confession," 250; McGregor and Fairbairn, *Fulgentius and the Scythian Monks*, 31.

hypostases of Christ.[158] This was formerly thought to be the work of his Byzantine namesake, but more recent scholarship has established that it is his own work.[159]

Gray remarks that this Leontius was "the outstanding neo-Chalcedonian theologian of the first half of the sixth century."[160] A strong case could be made for his being the outstanding theologian of that era regardless of which group, or which century, he is thought to belong to. Grillmeier puts his finger on the difference between Leontius of Jerusalem and his namesake of Byzantium. Leontius of Byzantium had written opposing Severus, the Monophysite, supporting the two-natures formula, while Leontius of Jerusalem opposed the Nestorians' radical separation of the two natures, being committed to the Cyrilline doctrine of the hypostatic union, with the identity of the Logos incarnate with the eternal Logos, something that the Byzantine could not do.[161] Grillmeier concludes: "For this reason each of them places the accent in a different place: Leontius of Jerusalem extends the understanding of the one *hypostasis*, while

158. Gray, *Defense of Chalcedon in the East*, 122–23; *PG*, 86:1400–1901.

159. See Grillmeier, *Christ*, 2:271–312; Meyendorff, *Christ*, 73–82; Gray, *Defense of Chalcedon in the East*, 122–41; Gleede, Ἐνυπόστατος, 122–37; Davis, *First Seven Ecumenical Councils (325–787)*, 231–32. Dirk Krausmüller, "Leontius of Jerusalem: A Theologian of the Seventh Century," *JTS* 52 (2001): 637–57, has proposed, contrary to the overwhelming consensus of twentieth-century scholarship, that Leontius belonged to the seventh century rather than the sixth. This claim has not gone uncontested. Patrick T. R. Gray, *Leontius of Jerusalem: Against the Monophysites: Testimonies of the Saints and Aporiae* (Oxford University Press, 2006), 38–40. To my mind, he fits better into the earlier time; the progression of thought seems to me to suggest this.

Indeed, Zachhuber comments on the huge uncertainties surrounding the dates of the leading figures: "Most of the relevant texts during this period cannot easily be dated or assigned to a known author. . . . In some cases even their inclusion in this broad chronological bracket is speculative. . . . We are dealing with a story of intellectual history largely detached from other developments due to our almost complete lack of historical context for most of the relevant texts." Zachhuber, *Rise of Christian Theology*, 218. Such huge gaps in knowledge suggest caution in the face of radically new hypotheses. Either way, whether Leontius was alive before Constantinople II (553) or in the next century does not unduly alter the question of the development of Christological thought. We will proceed on the basis of the widely accepted assumption that he lived at the earlier time.

160. Gray, *Defense of Chalcedon in the East*, 122.

161. Grillmeier, *Christ*, 2:288.

Leontius of Byzantium builds up the two-natures teaching. The real advance which appears to have been achieved consists in the fact that the concept of *enhypostasis* or insubsistence has emerged formally and is used to explain the unity of the subject in Christ, in the duality of the natures."[162] We will discuss *enhypostatos* shortly. Ferrara agrees with Meyendorff and Gray, contra Beeley, that it is this Leontius that is primary originator of the doctrine of *enhypostasis*.[163]

In his *Contra Nestorianos*, Leontius speaks of the natures "united in one hypostasis." The one-nature formula, "one incarnate nature of God the Word," he saw as fully compatible with Chalcedon, although, as Gray acknowledges, "the use of the word 'nature' admittedly causes confusion."[164] Perhaps the most distinctive feature of Leontius's Christology, one that chimes with Cyril, is the formula "union according to hypostasis" (ἕνωσις κατ' ὑπόστασιν). Contrary to the Nestorians, there is no preexistent human nature that becomes united to the Word, as if the natures are prior to the person and so form the person. Rather, the eternal Son or Logos is the subject of the incarnation. There is continuity between the eternal Son and the incarnate Son, for they are one and the same in terms of personal identity.[165] If Jesus were a mere man, he would have a *hypostasis* of his own, and consequently there would be two *hypostases*, a conjunction of sorts, not a union.[166] As Gray argues of Leontius's argument, since the Word is the sole subject, he takes into union a human nature, which has as its own *hypostasis* the *hypostasis* of the Word.[167] In essence, this is the doctrine of *enhypostatos*.

Behind this was the need to counter the assumption that the presence of a nature required the existence of a comparable *hypostasis*, such that Jesus, having two natures, would thereby, of necessity, have two corresponding *hypostases*, which is what both the Nestorians and the Monophysites held to be the case, albeit from diametrically opposed

162. Grillmeier, *Christ*, 2:288–89.
163. Ferrara, "Hypostatized in the Logos," 318; Meyendorff, *Christ*, 53.
164. Gray, *Defense of Chalcedon in the East*, 125–26.
165. *PG*, 86:1552.
166. *PG*, 86:1748.
167. Gray, *Defense of Chalcedon in the East*, 127.

positions. Leontius, in response to this, maintained that a nature that does not have its own *hypostasis* can be hypostatized in another nature.[168] For this, Leontius held that "nature" is an abstraction and must exist in a concrete *hypostasis*. In other words, there can be no such thing as a human nature floating around apart from distinct and particular embodiment. This is normally in a particular human person, but it can also be in another *hypostasis*. For him, *hypostasis* was "that which shows the concrete, individual thing and is set off from all other things."[169] *Hypostasis* is the foundation, the underlying reality, the real subject, and not the product.[170] In short, as Grillmeier remarks, "the humanity of the Saviour does not have a subsistence of its own, but from the very beginning subsisted in the *hypostasis* of the Logos."[171] Clearly, Leontius operated with the basic premise that man was created in the image of God and, allowing for the vast disparity between Creator and creature, was made by God to be compatible with himself. As part of this premise was a coordinate assumption that what is unattainable from the side of man is perfectly manageable on the part of God, given his creating of man in his image. Thus, the union is *in* the *hypostasis* of the Son, the Logos, the Word. It is not a merging of natures, but a union according to *hypostasis*, the assumption of human nature into union in the Word.

Leontius therefore says that "God the Word, the Son of the Father became Christ not by removal from what he was or had but rather by

168. Gray, *Defense of Chalcedon in the East*, 129; *PG*, 86:1561. Leontius considered *hypostasis* to mean "one indivisible subject." Kenneth Paul Wesche, "The Christology of Leontius of Jerusalem: Monophysite or Chalcedonian?," *SVTQ* 31 (1987): 65–95, here 71. In the same place, Wesche elaborates: "Already we have uncovered some basic characteristics of hypostasis: it may be constituted of several natures, or one nature, of several properties or one. Its constitution may be simple or composite, it may be particular or common; but the hypostasis itself is simple and not composite. It is that in which the simple or composite constitution is observed and as such it is distinguishable in thought from the nature and its properties."

169. *PG*, 86:1509D, Zachhuber's translation, in Zachhuber, *Rise of Christian Theology*, 260.

170. Wesche, "Leontius of Jerusalem," 73. "It is a particular [thing], but *not* a particular nature, or else tritheism would result from the three Trinitarian hypostases being autonomous or independent" (74).

171. Grillmeier, *Christ*, 2:283; *PG*, 86:1568.

addition of what he did not have" (Οὐ γὰρ ἐπι ἀναιρέσει τῶν ὄντων αὐτῷ, ἀλλὰ προσκτήσει τῶν οὐκ ἐνόντων, γέγονε Χριστὸς ὁ θεὸς Λόγος καί Υἱὸς τοῦ Πατρός).[172] This follows from the fact that God is able by his will to unite the nature of the creature to himself, which created nature is unable to do.[173] It occurs by "the superaddition of the new nature" (περισσεύει γὰρ καὶ τοῖς παρὰ τὸ θεῖον χαρακτηρίσμασι συναχθεῖσι τῇ προσλήψει τῆς καινοτέρας φύσεως).[174]

Leontius compares the union of natures with the relation of fire and steel. These are joined, preserved in the *hypostasis* of one of them without the destruction of either.[175] Thus, the natures are united in Christ, not in a union of *hypostases* but union in the Word's *hypostasis* (ἐν τῇ ὑποστὰσει τοῦ Λόγου καταφαίνεται).[176] In short, this union does not eradicate the distinction of the natures (οὐδὲν οὖν ἐκ τῶνδε ἡμῖν ἡ τοῦ προσώπου ἕνωσις τὴν διαφορὰν τῶν φύσεων λυμαίνεται).[177] Gray concludes that Leontius's view of *hypostasis* gives "a different category for viewing the Christological union from the category of nature used to view the Christological duality."[178] Johannes Zachhuber remarks that "the thrust of his argument is to justify how the Son's hypostasis can stay the same while admitting a second nature. Insubsistence Christology in Leontius, therefore, not only explains why Christ's humanity can have reality without a hypostasis of its own, but also why the addition of another *ousia* does not cause any ontological disruption in the pre-existent hypostasis of the Logos."[179]

An important question arises: How did Leontius avoid the riposte that Christ has no particular *human* identity, since the Word assumed into union a human nature, not a human person or *hypostasis*? As he wrote, "the Word out of our nature assumed a particular nature into his own hypostasis. The coming together of natures was therefore

172. *PG*, 86:1501.

173. Grillmeier, *Christ*, 2:283; *PG*, 86:1501, 1593.

174. *PG*, 86:1552–53.

175. Gray, *Defense of Chalcedon in the East*, 133–34.

176. *PG*, 86:1512–13.

177. *PG*, 86:1748.

178. Gray, *Defense of Chalcedon in the East*, 135. See also Zachhuber, *Rise of Christian Theology*, 257–74.

179. Zachhuber, *Rise of Christian Theology*, 263–64.

according to/in the hypostasis" (οὕτω φαγμὲν τὸν Λόγον ἐκ τῆς ἡμετέρας φύσεως εἰς τὴν ἰδίαν ὑπόστασιν προσλαβέσθαι φύσιν ἰδικήν τινα; κατὰ τὴν ὑπόστασιν οὖν ταῖς φύσεσιν ἡ σύνθεσις . . . ἐκ τῶνδε γὲγονεν).[180] The reason is, as Gray states, that before the incarnation, there was no particular human subject (Jesus), only a general abstract category of "our nature." But every nature is concretized in a *hypostasis* when it begins to exist. In assuming our nature, the Word made it his particular humanity.[181] As Cyril had stressed, it is his own human nature, his own body and soul.[182]

Leontius includes a defense of the Theopaschite formula, which was important for him—"one of the holy Trinity suffered and was crucified according to the flesh" (ἐκ τοῦ ἕνα λέγειν τῆς ἁγίας Τριάδος τὸν σταυρωθέντα καὶ παθόντα).[183] Gray again points out that the divine nature can have suffering predicated of it because it is the *hypostasis* that suffers, one of the Trinity.[184] In general terms, we must say that it is a person that suffers, not a nature. Yet a person suffers according to his own nature. I, not my nature, am writing this, but I am writing in accordance with my human nature. Consequently, suffering is properly predicated of the Word *because his suffering was in his own human nature*. This is necessary for salvation.[185]

Gray sums up well in stating that Leontius accepts the necessity of Chalcedon's two-natures formula, roots his thought in the Word as the one subject of the incarnation, and demonstrates that Chalcedon's one-*hypostasis* formula is both Cyrillian and Dyophysite. The key for him, Gray thinks, is that the *hypostasis* is a concrete individual entity.[186]

180. *PG*, 86:1485.

181. Gray, *Defense of Chalcedon in the East*, 135.

182. Gleede points to Leontius's argument that the two natures subsist in the same *hypostasis*. One of them—the human nature—is not anhypostatic in an independent sense, but they are both enhypostatic in the one *hypostasis*. This in itself establishes the integrity of both natures. *PG*, 68:1561; Gleede, Ἐνυπόστατος, 130, 132–33.

183. Gray, *Defense of Chalcedon in the East*, 136; *PG*, 86:1544.

184. Gray, *Defense of Chalcedon in the East*, 137.

185. Gray, *Defense of Chalcedon in the East*, 138.

186. Gray, *Defense of Chalcedon in the East*, 139.

Leontius provided the solution that could never be found in the work of his Byzantine namesake. Ferrara argues this, in reflecting that the Byzantine's Christology "opens itself to the charge of conceiving Christ's person as a 'result' of the union of natures, a position peremptorily excluded by Leontius of Jerusalem's doctrine of insubsistence."[187]

The Emperor Justinian (482–565, Emperor from 527)[188]

Justinian was not only emperor but a theologian in his own right. His imperial policy was directed toward securing unity based on an acceptance of Chalcedon interpreted in alignment with Cyril.[189] In 533, he issued two decrees, one based on the formula proposed by the Scythian monks, "one of the Trinity suffered," and the second on the formula "union by hypostasis," proclaiming both as necessary parts of the Chalcedonian and orthodox faith. In this he was supported by Pope John II.[190] It was a genuine attempt to secure agreement and reconciliation.

One of the problems of Chalcedon in the eyes of the Monophysites was its acceptance of two allies of Nestorius—Theodoret of Cyrus and Ibas of Edessa. As we saw, Theodoret defended Chalcedon with the language and ideas of the "Antiochenes" and had been at loggerheads with Cyril.[191] In 544, Justinian made a further edict, condemning certain writings of Theodoret and Ibas, not their persons, since both had been restored at Chalcedon and had renounced Nestorius.[192] This was part of the attempt to encourage Cyrillians to fall into line and

187. Meyendorff, *Christ*, 53–54; Ferrara, "Hypostatized in the Logos," 320.

188. For a detailed discussion of Justinian's own writings, see Grillmeier, *Christ*, 2:315f. As an irrelevant aside, for an account of Pope Vigilius's dramatic rooftop escape from Constantinople, see Davis, *First Seven Ecumenical Councils (325–787)*, 239. I am surprised that, to my limited knowledge, a movie has not been made of this.

189. On Justinian, see Kenneth Paul Wesche, *On the Person of Christ: The Christology of Emperor Justinian* (St. Vladimir's Seminary Press, 1991), 10–22; Meyendorff, *Christ*, 47–84; Gray, *Defense of Chalcedon in the East*, 154–70; Grillmeier, *Christ*, 2:315ff. and passim. What a remarkable change it would be if that were the policy of the U.S. President or the British Prime Minister.

190. Gray, *Defense of Chalcedon in the East*, 57.

191. Gray, *Defense of Chalcedon in the East*, 64.

192. Gray, *Defense of Chalcedon in the East*, 65.

come to the anticipated agreement. In this he was, as Gray remarks, "a consummate politician[,] . . . also a theologian of some ability."[193] He understood Chalcedon as primarily excluding heresies rather than making a constructive Christology and, as his plan indicates, understood the one-nature formula to be orthodox, as long as it was interpreted in harmony with Cyril.[194] In his major works, *Contra Monophysitas* and *Contra Nestorianos*, Justinian says nothing new but accepts that the union is in the *hypostasis*, since the Word is not united to a man, and agrees that the Word is the subject of the incarnation.[195] In short, he accepted the teaching of Leontius of Jerusalem, but did so in a guarded manner that was calculated to win over those who were otherwise sitting on the fence. In this, he himself reflected the overall sense of the church, present at Chalcedon, although ambiguously expressed, and widely held by the majority since.[196]

In his *Edict on the True Faith* of 551,[197] Justinian expresses as orthodox doctrine the formula "one of the holy trinity was incarnate":[198]

> We affirm that the union has taken place in the *hypostasis* ('Η δὲ καθ' ὑπόστασιν ἕνωσις δηλοι). But the *hypostatic* union means that the Divine Logos, that is to say one *hypostasis* of the three divine *hypostases,* is not united to a man who has his own *hypostasis* before [the union], but that in the womb of the Holy Virgin the Divine Logos made for himself, in his own *hypostasis,* flesh that was endowed with a reasonable and intellectual soul, i.e. human nature.[199]

He acknowledges that "the same one in the flesh is passable, and in his divinity he is impassable. For he who took upon himself

193. Gray, *Defense of Chalcedon in the East*, 154.
194. Gray, *Defense of Chalcedon in the East*, 155–57.
195. Gray, *Defense of Chalcedon in the East*, 154–60.
196. Gray, *Defense of Chalcedon in the East*, 162–68.
197. See Wesche, *Christology of Justinian*, 163–98.
198. *PG*, 86:995; Wesche, *Christology of Justinian*, 164.
199. *PG*, 86:997; Wesche, *Christology of Justinian*, 166. In this and the following notes, I have used the translation of Wesche, which does not reference the Greek. I have added the original where it is significant.

suffering and death is not someone other than the Logos, but the impassable and eternal Logos of God himself submitted to being born in human flesh, and he accomplished all things."[200] He adds, "So we never refer to the human nature of Christ by itself, nor did it ever possess its own *hypostasis* or *prosopon*, but it began to exist in the *hypostasis* of the Logos (ἀλλ' ἐν τῇ ὑποστάσει τοῦ Λόγου τὴν ἀρχήν τῆς ὑπαρξεῶς ἐλαβεν)."[201] "And so, presenting this doctrine of union, we confess one Christ, one Son, one Lord, who is the Logos of God, who was incarnate and became man; and we worship him together with the Father and the Holy Spirit."[202]

Constantinople II (A.D. 553)

This council represented a move toward the more unitive Christology of Cyril, as Beeley remarks, in which Christ is the single individual who is the Word of God, "a primarily divine subject who has been made flesh, not a compound or a hypostasis that contains both natures. Both Christ's divine acts and his human suffering belong to 'the same one,' the Word of God[,] . . . 'one of the holy Trinity.'"[203]

The final session on June 2 condemned the three chapters, works of Theodore, Ibas of Edessa, and Theodoret, now considered heretical,[204] in fourteen anathemas. Anathema 12 condemned "the most impious Theodoret," not as a person but in terms of his rejected writings. Anathema 13 condemned Theodoret's writings against Cyril's twelve anathemas, and his writings against the Council of Ephesus that had anathematized Nestorius. This was an attempt to reconcile the Monophysites to Chalcedon by disassociating Chalcedon from its "Nestorian" defenders.[205] The council's condemnation of Theodore of Mopsuestia was in effect a defense of the Cyrillian

200. *PG*, 86:995; Wesche, *Christology of Justinian*, 165.
201. *PG*, 86:1011; Wesche, *Christology of Justinian*, 179.
202. *PG*, 86:1013; Wesche, *Christology of Justinian*, 180.
203. Beeley, *Unity of Christ*, 294–95.
204. These were written by Theodore of Mopsuestia, Ibas of Edessa, and Theodoret of Cyrrhus, whom we encountered earlier.
205. Gray, *Defense of Chalcedon in the East*, 69–70.

view of God the Word's suffering in the flesh.[206] Grillmeier agrees that the question of the three chapters is an intensely intricate one, central to which was a major question "whether the Council [of Chalcedon] could be completely cleared of the suspicion of encouraging Nestorianism."[207]

Gray remarks that this was not a new movement. It was conservative, "the most articulate representation of a position widely held by the conservative majority in the church since 433."[208]

The defense of Chalcedon by the neo-Chalcedonians was not the product of a school but the coming of age of a tradition alone true to the spirit of Chalcedon, since it was the majority position there, the tradition of Cyril, now canonized by the whole church, "the tradition of thinkers who, as Cyrillian and Chalcedonians, interpret Chalcedon as fundamentally Cyrillian."[209]

The theological substance of the council is contained in the Canons, produced in the eighth and final session.[210] In Canon I, there is a confession of the Trinity, using *ousia-hypostasis*, but there is no reference to "the Cyrillian-Severan synonymous use of *physis-hypostasis*."[211] Canon II ascribes two births to the Logos, one eternally from the Father and the other *of the same who came down from heaven* from the *theotokos*, a clear canonization of the Logos as the single subject of the incarnation. It includes an anathema against any who deny the eternal generation of the Son by the Father.

Consequently, Canon III affirms that all statements relating to the incarnate Son are to be taken to refer to his person and not to be divided up on the basis of supposed separated natures. Thus, "the God-Logos who works miracles and the Christ who suffered should not be separated as 'each and other,'" for it is "one and the same Jesus Christ, our Lord, the Word, who became flesh and a human

206. Gray, *Defense of Chalcedon in the East*, 72.

207. Grillmeier, *Christ*, 2:444.

208. Gray, *Defense of Chalcedon in the East*, 168.

209. Gray, *Defense of Chalcedon in the East*, 169.

210. *ACO*, 4.1.240–44; Richard Price, trans., *The Acts of the Council of Constantinople of 553* (Liverpool University Press, 2009), 2:120–26; cf. 1:143–47; Grillmeier, *Christ*, 2:446–51.

211. Price, *Constantinople 553*, 2:120; Grillmeier, *Christ*, 2:446.

being. To him as one and the same being belong the miracles and the sufferings voluntarily borne in the flesh."[212]

From this, Canon IV makes a very important conclusion. *Inter alia*, it states that "if anyone does not accept the teaching of the holy fathers that the union occurred of the Word of God with human flesh which is ensouled by a rational and intellectual soul, and that this union is by synthesis or person, and that therefore there is only one [Lat: composite] person, namely the Lord Jesus Christ, one member of the holy trinity: let him be anathema."[213] Here the putative "Antiochene" Christology is anathematized. The union predicated by that alleged school would be "only accidental and not substantial." In short, the canon canonizes union *kat' hypostasin* and not according to nature.[214]

Canon V insists that "the incarnation is conceived entirely from the one *hypostasis* of the Son." There is no additional *hypostasis*.[215] Canon VI vehemently reasserts the *theotokos*. Canon VII and Canon VIII outlaw any consideration of the two natures as separate, while affirming that they remain distinct in the union: "If anyone proclaiming one nature of the Word of God to be incarnate does not receive it as the Fathers taught, viz., that from the divine and human natures (a union in subsistence having taken place) one Christ results;—but endeavors from these words to introduce one nature or substance of the divinity and flesh of Christ:—let such be anathema." This, again, is a reaffirmation of Chalcedon, understood from Cyrillian Christology.[216] Thus, in Canon IX "the one act of worship is directed to the incarnate God-Logos with his flesh."[217]

Canon X comes to the crux of the Theopaschite formula, canonizing it in asserting, "If anyone does not confess his belief that our Lord Jesus Christ, who was crucified in his human flesh, is truly God and the Lord of glory (1 Cor. 2:8) and one of the members of

212. Grillmeier, *Christ*, 2:447; Price, *Constantinople 553*, 2:120.

213. Grillmeier, *Christ*, 2:447; Price, *Constantinople 553*, 2:120–21.

214. Grillmeier, *Christ*, 2:448. The Antiochene "school," such as it was or was not, tends to be favored among conservative evangelicals and Reformed.

215. Price, *Constantinople 553*, 2:121; Grillmeier, *Christ*, 2:449.

216. See the reaffirmation of this canon by Thomas Aquinas, *ST*, III.2.1.

217. Grillmeier, *Christ*, 2:449–51; Price, *Constantinople 553*, 2:121–23.

the holy Trinity: let him be anathema."[218] McGuckin comments that the canonization of the Theopaschite formula was the final victory for Cyrilline Christology.[219] It was ratified by Pope John II.[220]

Grillmeier sums up and concludes that the main concepts and intent of Chalcedon were strengthened. The one *hypostasis* was anchored in the preexistent Logos "as the ultimate subject." Moreover, "this one *hypostasis* of the human nature which did not exist in itself was formally the event of the incarnation, or, seen from above, the self-communication of this Logos hypostatically to the ensouled flesh, by the Logos creating this flesh for himself."[221] Or, as Steven Duby remarks of the Son, "he brings it about that his ὑπόστασις is now a ὑπόστασις of not only eternal deity but also the human nature that he assumes."[222]

Torrance remarks, "It is only because Christ himself is personally God that his human speech and actions, and his human forms of thought are also divine revelation."[223] *Enhypostasia* "is a very careful way of stating that we cannot think of the hypostatic union statically,"[224] for in terms of soteriology it involves a once-for-all union of God and man in Christ *and also* a living union in Christ.[225] He writes of *anhypostasia* and *enhypostasia* as "a sort of 'theological algebra' to help us work out the 'inner logic' in christology more consistently and purely. . . . Together [they] do not themselves contain the 'stuff' of christology, but they may be, rightly used, theological instruments or lenses through which we may discern more deeply and clearly the ontological structures of the incarnation."[226]

Richard Price has a perceptive discussion of the theology of Constantinople II and concludes that "so far from narrowing or distorting

218. Price, *Constantinople 553*, 2:123; Grillmeier, *Christ*, 2:451.

219. McGuckin, "Theopaschite Confession," 243.

220. Grillmeier, *Christ*, 2:340–41.

221. Grillmeier, *Christ*, 2:456–57.

222. Steven J. Duby, *Jesus and the God of Classical Theism: Biblical Christology in the Light of the Doctrine of God* (Baker Academic, 2022), 153.

223. Torrance, *Incarnation*, 193.

224. Torrance, *Incarnation*, 84.

225. Torrance, *Incarnation*, 85.

226. Torrance, *Incarnation*, 233.

the vision of Chalcedon, [it] imported a welcome clarification."[227] Leo Donald Davis reflects that "the work of the neo-Chalcedonians was crowned with success in an ecumenical council."[228] Later, in 681, Constantinople III affirmed Constantinople II together with the preceding four councils.[229]

The far-reaching nature of these conclusions is pointedly expressed by I. A. Dorner. He writes, "If the Son of God be indissolubly and eternally united with humanity, . . . if humanity is construed as a constituent element of his person, then humanity is introduced within the sphere of the Trinity; for the incarnation is represented as an expression, not merely of the activity, but also of the very being of the Son of God." In the same place, he concludes that there is no alteration of the inner life of God, but the Son became what he was not before, while what he was before did not undergo any change.[230]

To reinforce these decrees, the emperor composed the following hymn, to be sung in all the churches. We sang it on more than one occasion in my church in Wales:

O Word immortal of eternal God,
Only-begotten of the only Source,
For our salvation stooping to the course
Of human life, and born of Mary's blood:
In equal honour with the Holy Ghost,
and with th'eternal Father glorified.

Sprung from the blessed virgin womanhood
Of her who bare you, God immutable,
Incarnate, made as man with man to dwell,
And condescending to the bitter cross:
In equal honour . . .

227. Price, *Constantinople 553*, 1:75.

228. Davis, *First Seven Ecumenical Councils (325–787)*, 245.

229. See G. L. C. Frank, "The Council of Constantinople II as a Model Reconciliation Council," *Theological Studies* 52 (1991): 636–50. Meyendorff, *Christ*, 47–60, thinks it inexplicable how Harnack could accuse the church of Hellenizing the faith when the various writings condemned by this council were rejected precisely because of the Hellenizing philosophy that undergirded them.

230. Dorner, *Development*, 3:127.

Save us, O Christ our God, for you have died
To save your people to the uttermost,
And, dying, trampling death in victory;
One of the ever blessed Trinity:
In equal honour . . .[231]

231. Justinian (483–565), "O Word Immortal of Eternal God," in *The English Hymnal*, ed. Ralph Vaughan Williams (Oxford University Press, 1933; alt. 2023), no. 325; tune: YORKSHIRE (a brisk *andante*).

7

Person and Nature, Action and Will

The Threat of Monoenergism and Monotheletism

In the seventh century, a new crisis erupted. Initially the issue was whether Christ had one activity or two—divine and human—and it eventually reached a crescendo over whether he had one will or two. Monoenergism and Monotheletism both proceeded on the premise of the unity of Christ's person, with their perceptions that therefore activity and volition were attributable to the person, rather than the nature. From the recognition that Christ is a single subject, it moved on to posit a single activity. "The axiom, shared by pro- and anti-Chalcedonians, that both divine and human activities have the same subject, was interpreted as implying the single activity (ἐνέργεια) of Christ."[1] This was similar to the understanding of Severus and some Monophysites that God the Word is one incarnate nature; it appeared that two sources of action and two volitional centers would entail two persons and would therefore be heretical, a form of Nestorianism. In sum, the issues of Christ's *energeia* and will were "among the most important challenges that Christology was ever to face."[2]

Sophronius, a Palestinian patriarch, opposed this and thus laid the groundwork for the comprehensive solution later presented by

1. Cyril Hovorun, *Eastern Christianity in Its Texts* (T&T Clark, 2022), 557.

2. Cyril Hovorun, *Will, Action and Freedom: Christological Controversies in the Sixth Century* (Brill, 2008), 3. On the controversy overall, see Leo Donald Davis, *The First Seven Ecumenical Councils (325–787)* (Liturgical Press, 1990), 258–79; John Meyendorff, *Christ in Eastern Christian Thought* (St. Vladimir's Seminary Press, 1975), 144–48.

his disciple, Maximus the Confessor. Sophronius agreed that Christ was the single subject of all his activities but also affirmed that he acts in accordance with his two natures and that his theandric (divine-human) activities were composite.[3] The leading figure among the Dyothelites, who affirmed two sources of action and two wills, was Maximus the Confessor (580–662). Their basic assumption was that will is a predicate of nature. While there is clearly one acting and willing subject—the person of the incarnate Son—he wills and acts according to his natures. Consequently, Maximus affirmed that Christ had two wills.

In a celebrated debate in 645 with Pyrrhus, the former archbishop of Constantinople,[4] Maximus argued that if will is related to *hypostasis* ("person"), then God would have three wills. On the contrary, the person of Christ willed in accordance with his natures, "and if he has two natures, then he surely must have two natural wills, the wills and essential operations being equal in numbers to the natures."[5] Pyrrhus thought that the single will of Christ was "gnomic"—connected with an ability to reason based on limited knowledge. Maximus rejected this "gnomic will," since, he argued, Christ never had an opinion based on limited knowledge and rational deliberation, because his will was perfect. Given the assumption of a single will, a gnomic will would entail that Christ was a mere man. Without a human will, salvation would not be possible.[6] Andrew Louth remarks that "the errors of Christological heresy arise from the confusion of these terms: either confusion between the definitions of nature and person . . . or confusion over the natural will and the hypostatic (or personal) or 'gnomic' will, in the case of the monothelites."[7]

3. Hovorun, *Eastern Christianity*, 558.

4. For a discussion of the debate, see I. A. Dorner, *History of the Development of the Doctrine of the Person of Christ*, trans. D. W. Simon (Edinburgh: T&T Clark, 1861), 3:179–81.

5. Maximus, *Disputatio cum Pyrrho*, 13–15; Andrew Louth, *Maximus the Confessor* (Routledge, 1996), 169; Hovorun, *Eastern Christianity*, 571.

6. Hovorun, *Eastern Christianity*, 571–73.

7. Andrew Louth, *John Damascene: Tradition and Originality in Byzantine Theology* (Oxford University Press, 2002), 167.

The Lateran Council of 649 strongly opposed Monotheletism. It was "an update to the first neo-Chalcedonian council, held in Constantinople in 553[,] . . . the highest theological point in polemics against monotheletism." It "professed an intrinsic connection between Christ's two natures and his natural wills."[8] Nevertheless, hostilities continued. The controversy was exceptionally divisive. With the general coarsening of society, punishments became ever more barbaric. Maximus was publicly mutilated, his right hand cut off and his tongue removed, hence his being called Confessor. There was not a final and lasting settlement until the Third Council of Constantinople in 680–81.

The Issues at Stake

Both Monoenergism and Monotheletism sprang out of neo-Chalcedonianism, but they were not necessary to the latter, for Dyothelites were also from the same source. It was another dispute arising from the common Cyrilline basis of what had become orthodox Christological doctrine,[9] "an extraordinary case study in the profound role of a single pericope—the agony of Christ in Gethsemane (Matt. 26:36–42 *et par.*)—in shaping a historic doctrinal commitment of the Church."[10] This famous passage was the focus of many questions. Jesus prayed, "My Father, if it be possible, let this cup pass from me; nevertheless, not as I will, but as you will." Did this suggest that the Son had a different will from the Father? That would be contrary to the indivisibility of God, whose will is one, since he has but one nature. Was this expressive of a dialogue between the human will of the Son, as he faced the grim and horrific ordeal before him, and the divine will, which he shared with the Father? This was the position of the Dyophysites.

Demetrios Bathrellos comments, "The key question of the controversy was whether there is one will in Christ corresponding to his person, or two wills corresponding to his natures, and . . . this

8. Hovorun, *Eastern Christianity*, 575.

9. Hovorun, *Will, Action and Freedom*, 3.

10. Paul M. Blowers, *Maximus the Confessor: Jesus Christ and the Transfiguration of the World* (Oxford University Press, 2016), 157.

question . . . cannot be dealt with adequately unless a thorough study of the notions of person, hypostasis, nature, and essence is offered."[11] There were precedents for talk of a single energy in Christ, but these were all from sources that the ecumenical councils had condemned: Apollinarianism, Nestorianism, and Monophysitism.[12]

Putting it in perspective, Monotheletism did not have widespread appeal but was restricted to the elite, and there was no real agreement among its adherents. Technical words often meant different things to different people.[13] Furthermore, there was no outstanding thinker to give these views traction.[14] As Bathrellos remarks, they were "a small team of rather amateur theologians," motivated more by politics than Christian doctrine. Moreover, he adds, later discussion of the issue has been clouded, since most of those who have written on the subject have been Roman Catholics, who have been understandably sensitive to the orthodoxy of Pope Honorius, who succumbed to Monotheletism and was condemned as a heretic by Constantinople III in 681.[15] In short, the implications of the dispute have not been satisfactorily aired until fairly recently.

Monothelites tended to think of the human will as fallen and corrupt, and therefore contrary to the divine will. Therefore, from that commitment, it was unacceptable to posit a human will in Christ.[16] Moreover, because the human will is corrupt, it was considered unsustainable to them for their opponents to propose a natural will (a will based in nature as created), since that too would be corrupt.[17] They insisted that there would have been an inevitable conflict within the person of Christ.[18] In fact, as Bathrellos correctly suggests, Monotheletism was an exaggerated stress on redemption

11. Demetrios Bathrellos, *The Byzantine Christ: Person, Nature, and Will in the Christology of Saint Maximus the Confessor* (Oxford University Press, 2004), 6.
12. Hovorun, *Will, Action and Freedom*, 163.
13. Hovorun, *Will, Action and Freedom*, 164.
14. Hovorun, *Will, Action and Freedom*, 165.
15. Bathrellos, *Byzantine Christ*, 60–61.
16. Hovorun, *Will, Action and Freedom*, 164.
17. Hovorun, *Will, Action and Freedom*, 165.
18. Hovorun, *Will, Action and Freedom*, 126.

as exclusively a work of God. The issue highlighted the importance of Christ's saving us as the *incarnate* God.[19]

The Dyothelites, for their part, denied a corrupt will in Christ, since it would be contrary to his divinity. They also opposed the idea of a gnomic will, entailing deliberation, vacillation, and choice between alternative moral possibilities. Rather, they maintained, Christ's human will was in full accord with his divine will, willing humanly what the divine will willed. Behind this was their denial that the human will *as such* was inherently corrupt. Corruption had entered with the fall, but the natural will, *as created*, was free from corruption.[20] According to Cyril Hovorun, "even after the dyothelites had explained to [the Monothelites] that they should not accept a corrupted will, but one that was natural and in concord with the divinity, the monothelites insisted that this was impossible. For them conflict between the two wills was inevitable because the human will was by definition liable to sin and corruption."[21] This is borne out by the writings of the leading Monothelite figures, Sergius of Constantinople, Pope Honorius, Pyrrhus, and Macarius of Antioch.[22]

The Dyothelites put the question into a clearly soteriological context. They asserted that neither Christ's human nature nor his will or *energeia* was corrupted, since "only that which is against nature (παρὰ φύσιν) opposes the will of God." It is not Christ's will but ours that is corrupted by sin. "In order to be healed, this nature had to be adopted by Christ."[23] If the Monothelites were right, Christ would have condemned his creation as inherently corrupt or failed to heal our will of its corruption, depriving us of salvation.[24] This was a reiteration of Gregory of Nazianzus's dictum that "whatever has not been assumed cannot be healed." Indeed, the Monothelites were forced to the absurd claim that because of the inherent corruption of the human will, Adam before the fall did not have a human will but

19. Bathrellos, *Byzantine Christ*, 71.
20. Hovorun, *Will, Action and Freedom*, 165.
21. Hovorun, *Will, Action and Freedom*, 127.
22. Bathrellos, *Byzantine Christ*, 72–82.
23. Hovorun, *Will, Action and Freedom*, 128.
24. Bathrellos, *Byzantine Christ*, 151.

only a divine will, receiving his own will only after he had sinned.[25] This would entail, bizarrely, that Adam's divine will had sinned! As John of Damascus later wrote in his treatise *On the Two Wills in Christ*, "if [Christ] did not assume a human will, he did not become perfectly human. If he did not assume a human will, he did not heal that which first suffered in us. For the unassumed is unhealed, as the theologian Gregory said. For what was it that fell save the will? What was it that sinned save the will?"[26]

As a consequence of the fall, according to the Monothelites, Adam and all who follow have a gnomic will, one that engages in deliberation and free choice. This is what Christ would have had, they supposed, if he had a human will based in his *hypostasis*. Hence, they rejected it. Maximus, on the other hand, denied that Christ had a gnomic will, on the grounds that the will would have instinctive and contrary inclinations associated with the passions as well as rational ones, and so would entail ignorance and doubt, since deliberation involves a conflict of some kind with sin and corruption and is inherently imperfect.[27]

In summary, the Monothelites held that will is attributable to *hypostasis* ("person"). Therefore, Christ has one will. To assert two wills would entail two persons and be Nestorian. The Dyothelites, on the other hand, maintained that will is an attribute of nature. Therefore, Christ, who is a single willing agent, wills according to both his divine and human natures, and so has two wills, which were not in conflict. There is a distinction, they insisted, between the ability to will, inherent to nature, and the act of willing, which is an act of the person. Hovorun compares this to the ability to speak and the act of speaking.[28] Thus, the human will of Christ, belonging to his nature, "was modelled, moved, and actualized in particular acts of human willing by the divine person of the Logos in obedience to the Father."[29]

25. Hovorun, *Will, Action and Freedom*, 129–30.

26. Quoted in Louth, *John Damascene*, 169.

27. Blowers, *Maximus*, 158–62 (but see the whole section, 135–66); Bathrellos, *Byzantine Christ*, 176; Hovorun, *Will, Action and Freedom*, 134–35.

28. Hovorun, *Will, Action and Freedom*, 144–45.

29. Bathrellos, *Byzantine Christ*, 185.

Various proposals have been advanced about the possible sources for the Monothelite position, mostly implausible.[30] The most convincing suggestion was made by Archbishop Kallistos Ware (Timothy Ware), who indicated its commonality with Apollinarianism, in adopting a truncated view of Christ's humanity.[31] Bathrellos comments that the orthodox reaction to Apollinaris had probably not been thoroughly assimilated by the church. He establishes, with detailed references, that "not only the theology and the argumentation, but even the very wording of some Apollinarian passages, are strikingly similar to some monothelite passages, as if passages of the Apollinarians had been inserted into the texts of the monothelites."[32] There may have also been a connection with the Monophysites, for neither group took cognizance of Gregory of Nazianzus's dictum that whatever is not assumed cannot be healed.[33] Whatever the background, "the disputes enriched the Church's theological tradition immensely."[34]

The Contribution of Maximus the Confessor

Early Writings

Writing in the mid-630s before he entered the fray as the leading opponent of Monotheletism and advocate for orthodox Christology, Maximus wrote *Ambiguum 5* to argue that the expression "theandric energeia" in Denys the Areopagite "did not imply a single activity but the unity of the two *energeiai*."[35] Rather, the two *energeiai* are known in and through each other.[36] He wrote that the oneness of the theandric *energeia* "was related to Christ by virtue of his being the single subject of activities, but it also retained an element of duality and relationship

30. The main suggestions are succinctly scrutinized in Bathrellos, *Byzantine Christ*, 89–98.

31. Kallistos Ware, "Christian Theology in the East, 600–1453," in *A History of Christian Doctrine*, ed. Hubert Cunliffe-Jones and Benjamin Drewery (T&T Clark, 1978), 181–225, here 188.

32. Bathrellos, *Byzantine Christ*, 96.

33. Bathrellos, *Byzantine Christ*, 98.

34. Hovorun, *Will, Action and Freedom*, 166.

35. Louth, *Maximus*; the text is found in 171–80, here 171.

36. Hovorun, *Will, Action and Freedom*, 116.

to the two natures."[37] In this *Ambiguum*, Maximus developed a distinction between will as a faculty of nature (θέλησις, θέλημα) and will as the object of volition (θέλητον, θεληθέν). Both have the same object, the salvation of the world. The divine will is by nature saving, while human wills are by nature saved. Therefore, "the human and divine wills are not conflated into one when targeted onto the same object."[38]

Maximus's Christology

Maximus's opposition to the Monothelites' attribution of a gnomic will to Christ is important. Paul Blowers and Robert Wilken remark that in *Ad Thalassium 21* and *42*, Maximus traces the legacy of the fall of Adam, concerning which he notes that we inherit not only Adam's own sin but also that generic sin. Thereby "the ambiguity of embodied, historical existence reveals itself . . . [*inter alia*] in the stunted 'gnomic' will (γνώμη)." This contrasts with the natural will (θέλησις φυσική) given at creation for communion with God and the free choice Adam had before the fall. The gnomic will has to deliberate. This would entail a struggle with doubt, and with contrary impulses associated with the passions, lust for pleasure and fear of death. Maximus, however, insisted that "the incarnate Christ assumes the whole legacy of human fallenness while not wavering from the divine initiative toward the deification of creation." Indeed, the incarnation "is the lens through which to interpret the protology and teleology of the universe."[39]

In his celebrated *Ad Thalassium 60*, Maximus "locates the incarnation within a trinitarian matrix. The three persons foreknew the incarnation and shared mutually in its realization: the Father approving it, the Son properly carrying it out, the Spirit co-operating in it."[40] In 60.2, referring to 1 Peter 1:20, where Christ is said to have been foreknown before the foundation of the world, Maximus

37. Hovorun, *Will, Action and Freedom*, 117.

38. Hovorun, *Will, Action and Freedom*, 125.

39. Paul M. Blowers and Robert Louis Wilken, trans., *On the Cosmic Mystery of Jesus Christ: Selected Writings from St. Maximus the Confessor* (St. Vladimir's Seminary Press, 2003), 32–33.

40. Blowers and Wilken, *Cosmic Mystery*, 34. See also Blowers, *Maximus*, 146–48.

writes of this as "the mystery of Christ," "obviously the ineffable and incomprehensible union according to hypostasis of divinity and humanity. This union brings humanity into perfect identity, in every way, with divinity, through the principle of hypostasis, and from both humanity and divinity it completes the single composite hypostasis, without creating any diminishment due to the essential difference of the natures."[41] In this union, "their natural difference remains inviolate. . . . The natures retained their integrity in every way, neither nature disowning anything properly its own because of the union."[42]

Bathrellos remarks that Maximus protected the integrity of the human nature of Christ. It "made it possible to regard the human history of Jesus as recapitulating and rewriting our history, not as a history of human rebellion against God but as a history of loving obedience to him." The attribution of two wills did not, in Maximus's thought, imply personal division or sinfulness. "Maximus insisted on the unity of the person of the enfleshed Logos. For him, the Logos assumed our natural self-determining will and deified it. . . . In fact, according to Maximus's Chalcedonian logic, the unity between the divine and human wills must be stressed as much as their distinction. This unity is implied by the unity of the two natures that bear the two wills in the one person of the Logos." His determination was "to emphasize their unity while respecting their distinction."[43] Again, "For Maximus, the willing and acting subject . . . is the person of the incarnate Logos," with the result that "the incarnate Logos wills the divine and the human [deeds] and performs as God and as man divine and human acts."[44] In *Ambiguum 4*, Maximus states that there is no division between the two natures, for Christ acted uniquely as a single agent (ὢν αὐτὸς ἕνωσις ἦν

41. Maximos Constas, trans., *St. Maximos the Confessor: On Difficulties in Sacred Scripture: The Responses to Thalassios* (Catholic University of America Press, 2018), 427; *CCSG*, 22:73.

42. Constas, *Ad Thalass.*, 428; *CCSG*, 22:73, 75.

43. Bathrellos, *Byzantine Christ*, 173–74.

44. Bathrellos, *Byzantine Christ*, 182. See also *Opusculum 7*, in Louth, *Maximus*, 180–91.

ἀσύγχυτος).[45] Again, in *Ambiguum 5,* he writes that "the human nature, united without confusion to the divine nature, is completely penetrated by it (δι' ὅλου περικεχώρηκε), with absolutely no part of it remaining separate from the divinity to which it was united, having been assumed according to hypostasis (καθ' ὑπόστασιν),"[46] and later, "He completed the plan of salvation on our behalf in a 'theandric' (θεανδρικῶς) manner, . . . in a way that was simultaneously divine and human."[47]

Indeed, Maximus stresses that there was no conflict between the assumed human will and the divine will, since the natural will is not corrupt, because Christ did not have a gnomic will. In the Gethsemane prayer, Jesus handed over his natural will to the divine will. Thus, he willed as man what the divine will (the one will of the Father, the Son, and the Spirit) willed, even when this entailed his own death. In short, Dyotheletism maintains Christ's ontological and ethical unity. The subject of willing is one, since the two natures are borne by one and the same person. The wills are distinct but not opposed, and they are borne by the one indivisible person.[48] Jesus had a natural, healthy fear of the horrifying reality of the destruction of life, not the irrational dread that we have; he "learned obedience through the things that he suffered" (Heb. 5:8).[49] Maximus uses the analogy of a sword heated by fire. The heat of the fire is diffused through the sword, and the iron becomes burning hot through the union with the fire. The iron gets a cutting edge through the union with the fire. Yet neither the heat nor the iron undergoes change. In the incarnation, the divine and human are united in the *hypostasis* of the Word. Neither is displaced, nor does either function independently after the union, for the union is indissoluble.[50] Both these

45. Maximos Constas, ed. and trans., *On Difficulties in the Church Fathers: The Ambigua: Maximos the Confessor*, vol. 1, Dumbarton Oaks Medieval Library (Harvard University Press, 2014), 29.

46. Constas, *Ambigua*, 45.

47. Constas, *Ambigua*, 51.

48. Maximus, *Opusculum 7; PG*, 91:80–81; Blowers, *Maximus*, 163; Bathrellos, *Byzantine Christ*, 194.

49. Blowers, *Maximus*, 238.

50. Constas, *Ambigua*, 55, 57.

factors, the single subject and his willing according to his natures, are essential (*Opusculum 8*, 105a).[51] Bathrellos concludes that "a via media cannot be endorsed. Dyotheletism is right: monotheletism is wrong."[52]

The Relationship Between Incarnation and Deification

Deification or, better, *theosis* was central to the soteriology of the Greek church and was by no means alien to the Latins. It held that salvation consists in transformation by the Holy Spirit "from one degree of glory to another," in being "partakers of the divine nature." It had roots as far back as Irenaeus and, before him, in the New Testament. Maximus's Christology would not be properly intelligible without reference to it. Jean-Claude Larchet notes that most of Maximus's texts relate to the divinization of man but that others speak at the same time (*en même temps*) of the divinization of the whole creation. Others speak of beings in general.[53] In this divine design in divinization, all three divine persons are integrally involved.[54]

The context of both incarnation and deification is this. Man is the mediator and unifier of all beings. The first man failed in this mission —hence the necessity of the incarnation.[55] Christ began to unify man. Man occupies first place in the plan of God. Christ restores man to God, with a view to the reunion of the whole creation (*Le Christ restaure l'homme en lui-même pour le rendre de nouveau capable de jouer son rôle de médiateur, d'accomplir la mission de réunir en lui, entre eux, et à Dieu tous les êtres de la création*).[56]

Maximus bases divinization entirely on the incarnation of the Word. It also has the same schema as the incarnation (*précisément*

51. Bathrellos, *Byzantine Christ*, 197.

52. Bathrellos, *Byzantine Christ*, 205.

53. Jean-Claude Larchet, *La Divinisation de l'Homme Selon Saint Maxime le Confesseur* (Les éditions du Cerf, 1996), 105.

54. See Maximus, *Ad Thalassium*, 2; *PG*, 90:272ab; *CCSG*, 7:51, 7–23; English translation in Constas, *Ad Thalass.*, 97–99; *Ad Thalass.*, 13; *PG*, 90:293d–296c; *CCSG*, 7:95, 9–17; Constas, *Ad Thalass.*, 123–25; Larchet, *Maxime le Confesseur*, 106.

55. Maximus, *Ambiguum*, 41; *PG*, 90:1092cd–1093a; Louth, *Maximus*, 156–62.

56. Larchet, *Maxime le Confesseur*, 110–11.

correspond à l'union en lui des natures, et à leur périchorèse). Moreover, the assumption of humanity in the incarnation corresponds to the divinization of man (*Maxime veut aussi souligner qu' à l'inhominisation véritable et intégrale du Verbe correspond une divinisation véritable et intégrale de l'homme, et que de même que le Verbe assume la plénitude de l'humanité, l'homme divinisé reçoit la plénitude de la divinité*).[57]

Samuel Korb agrees with Larchet that Maximus held to the integral connection of incarnation with deification, and the identity of the two in a reciprocal and nuanced manner. This was based, *inter alia*, on the church's being the body of Christ and thus partaking in his own identity as the Word. Incarnation and deification are linked; the one is the prelude and necessary basis for the other.[58] This is borne out by Maximus's own writings, and the cosmic and soteriological structure of his theology.[59] For him, in Torstein Tollefsen's words, "the creation of this kind of world, in all its sumptuous variety, even if fallen to corruption, is not made to be annihilated, but rather to participate in the universal transfiguration and glorification."[60] Creation and salvation are inextricably linked, "seamlessly connected aspects of the single divine initiative, or *energeia*, God's urge to share his glory with an 'other.'"[61]

In *Ambiguum 7*, as Larchet remarks, the connection Maximus makes between incarnation and divinization is pervasive. Here, "man will remain wholly man in soul and body, owing to his nature, but will become wholly God in soul and body owing to the grace and splendour of the blessed glory of God (ὅλος μὲν ἄνθρωπος μένων κατὰ ψυχὴν καὶ σῶμα διὰ τὴν φύσιν καὶ ὅλος γινόμενος θεὸς κατὰ ψυχὴν καὶ σῶμα διὰ τὴν χάριν)," concerning which Maximus comments that "nothing more splendid or sublime can be

57. Larchet, *Maxime le Confesseur*, 381.

58. Samuel Korb, "Whole God and Whole Man: Deification as Incarnation in Maximus the Confessor," *SJT* 75, no. 4 (2022): 308–18.

59. Blowers and Wilken, *Cosmic Mystery*, 20–21.

60. Torstein F. Tollefsen, "Christocentric Cosmology," in *The Oxford Handbook of Maximus the Confessor*, ed. Pauline Allen and Bronwen Neil (Oxford University Press, 2015), 308–20, here 319.

61. Blowers, *Maximus*, 139.

imagined."[62] Divinization is the goal of the entire cosmos. Underlying this is the reality that God created us in such a way that we are similar to him. Before the ages, he determined that we should exist in him. He gave us the ability to make use of our natural power, but man voluntarily chose to reject this plan. So God introduced another way in its place, more marvelous and befitting than the first, the supremely mystical sojourn of God among human beings.[63] Thus, the Son, in taking into union a full human nature, with a human will, "did not come to debase the nature which he himself, as God and Word, had made, but he came that that nature might be thoroughly deified."[64] Blowers and Wilken refer here to "Maximus's integrative cosmic vision in which the economies of creation-deification, on the one hand, and (postlapsarian) intervention-redemption, on the other, merge as one dramatic plot whose 'thickness' and internal connections can only truly be discerned from the standpoint of the mystery which *is* Jesus Christ 'the mystery hidden throughout the ages' (Col. 1:26) that discloses the providence and judgment of God operative in the *logoi* of creation."[65] They also point out that "'Christ' and 'the mystery of Christ' are one and the same thing, in the sense that the whole universal mystery of salvation and deification is recapitulated deep within the composite hypostasis of the incarnate Logos."[66] In this, Maximus is saying that the incarnation in itself is revelatory of the entire redemption, not only of humanity but also of the whole cosmos.[67]

In *Ad Thalassium 22*, a pregnant writing, Maximus describes in 22.2 "God's ineffably good plan" made before all the ages "for him

62. Constas, *Ambigua*, 112–13, text and Constas translation; Larchet, *Maxime le Confesseur*, 110. These words were used by John Calvin in his commentary on 2 Peter 1:4.

63. Constas, *Ambigua*, 133.

64. *Opusculum 7*, in Louth, *Maximus*, 185.

65. Blowers and Wilken, *Cosmic Mystery*, 26. Blowers refers in a note also to *Ad Thalass. 60*.

66. Blowers and Wilken, *Cosmic Mystery*, 26n41.

67. On this great theme, see Andrew Louth, "The Place of *Theosis* in Orthodox Theology," in *Selected Essays*, vol. 2, *Studies in Theology*, ed. Lewis Ayres and John Behr (Oxford University Press, 2023), 178–90.

to be mingled, without change, with human nature through a true union according to hypostasis, uniting human nature, without alteration, to himself (ᾗ δὲ ἦν αὐτὸν μὲν ἀτρέπτως ἐγκραθῆναι τῇ φύσει τῶν ἀνθρώπον διὰ τῆς καθ' ὑπόστασιν ἀληθοῦς ἑνώσεως, ἑαυτῷ δὲ τὴν φύσιν ἀναλλοιώτως ἑνῶσαι τὴν ἀνθρωπίνην), so that he could become man—in a manner known to him—and at the same time make man God through union with himself (θεὸν δὲ ποιήσειε τῇ πρὸς ἑαυτὸν ἑνῶσαι τὸν ἄνθρωπον), and thus he wisely divided the ages, determining that some would be for the activity of his becoming man, and others for the activity of making man God."[68] In Scholia 1 on this work, Maximus insists that there is no mixture of natures in Christ—the mingling he mentions in the main text is itself qualified by his comments that no change or alteration occurred to the natures in the union.[69] In short, history is divided into two epochs. The first was to prepare the world for the incarnation; the second was to prepare man for divinization. Both are set in a cosmic context. Both are centered in Christ the Son.

Again, in *Opusculum 7*, Maximus wrote, "For he did not come to debase the nature which he himself, as God and Word, had made, but he came that that nature might be thoroughly deified which, with the good pleasure of the Father and the co-operation of the Spirit, he willed to unite to himself in one and the same *hypostasis*, with everything that belongs to it, apart from sin."[70] As Blowers sums up, "time and eternity have converged in Jesus Christ, and in him the fullness of divine embodiment and the fullness of creaturely deification have arrived, and the Church now dwells in the 'meantime' until the full effects of Christ's recapitulative work are revealed,"[71]

68. *CCSG*, 7:137; Constas, *Ad Thalass.*, 150–51.

69. "The union according to hypostasis of the Word with the flesh revealed the ineffable purpose of the divine counsel in that it did not mix the divine essence with the flesh (Ἡ πρὸς τὴν σάρκα τοῦ λόγου καθ' ὑπόστασιν ἕνωσις . . . ἐν τω μὴ φύραι τη ἑνώσει τῆς σαρκὸς τὴν οὐσίαν), but rather showed forth one hypostasis of the Word even in his becoming flesh, so that the flesh might remain flesh according to its essence and become divine according to the hypostasis." *CCSG*, 7:143; Constas, *Ad Thalass.*, 154.

70. Translation by Louth, *Maximus*, 185.

71. Blowers, *Maximus*, 141.

adding later, "Christ's work is an eschatological achievement from within the Adamic history, completing the Old Adam as he realizes the New Adam."[72]

Constantinople III (A.D. 680–81)

Eventually, Emperor Constantine IV summoned an ecumenical council,[73] which met from November 7, 680, until September 16, 681, with extensive breaks. Hovorun comments that the council condemned Monoenergism and Monotheletism in "a thorough vindication of Maximus's Christology." It "employed the full set of Maximus' arguments" and affirmed the two activities and two wills in Christ.[74] Its results were approved by Rome and thus "promoted [the language of the neo-Chalcedonians] as a Christological *lingua franca*," ending the neo-Chalcedonian civil war.[75]

The Acts of the Council state that in the first session, the papal legates added their weight against the Monothelites, referring to "certain novelties in expression, contrary to the orthodox faith" that had been introduced over the preceding forty-six years, as "a depraved opinion." The Monothelites, for their part, insisted that they had not introduced anything new but had taught nothing other than "whatever we have received from the holy ecumenical synods."[76]

72. Blowers, *Maximus*, 144. I. A. Dorner made an important criticism of Maximus's Christology, arguing that "what part the historical Christ takes in such a general process of deification is hard to say," for Christ is reduced to a mere theophany, with the historical significance of his person destroyed. Dorner, *Development*, 3:232–33. Of course, Dorner's own context must be taken into account when evaluating these criticisms, located as it was in the nineteenth century with its intense historicizing and its interest in organism and development, springing from romanticism.

73. In the view of the Greek or Eastern church, an ecumenical council is one that receives the approval of both the Eastern and Latin churches. Since Rome claims universal jurisdiction over the entire church, it views its own councils as ecumenical by definition. This book accepts the Greek position. On Constantinople III, see Henry R. Percival, *The Seven Ecumenical Councils of the Undivided Church: Their Canons and Dogmatic Decrees*, *NPNF*[2] (repr., T&T Clark, 1997), 327–53, and Davis, *First Seven Ecumenical Councils (325–787)*, 279–89.

74. Hovorun, *Eastern Christianity*, 577.

75. Hovorun, *Eastern Christianity*, 578.

76. Percival, *Seven Ecumenical Councils*, 327.

A letter from Pope Agatho affirmed that in the Latin church, "we equally detest the blasphemy of division and commixture. For when we confess two natures and two natural wills, and two natural operations in our one Lord Jesus Christ, we do not assert that they are contrary or opposed one to the other . . . , nor as though separated in two persons or subsistences. . . . This is the apostolic and evangelic tradition, . . . the pure expression of piety[,] . . . taught by the Holy Ghost through the princes of the apostles[,] . . . the living tradition of the apostles of Christ, which the church holds everywhere."[77] Later in the same letter, Agatho explained it in these terms: "Since, as the truth of the Christian faith holds, the will is natural, where the one nature of the holy and inseparable Trinity is spoken of, it must be consistently understood that there is one natural will, and one natural operation. But when in truth we confess that in the one person of our Lord Jesus Christ the mediator between God and men, there are two natures . . . even after his admirable union, just as we canonically confess the two natures of one and the same person, so too we confess his two natural wills and two natural operations."[78]

The Definition of Faith was produced in the eighteenth session. It confessed that it followed the five preceding ecumenical councils in their Christological affirmations, introducing nothing new. It is worth quoting its key assertions:

> We likewise declare that in him are two natural wills and two natural operations indivisibly, incontrovertibly, inseparably, inconfusedly, according to the teaching of the holy Fathers. And these two natural wills are not contrary the one to the other (God forbid!) as the impious heretics assert, but his human will follows and that not as resisting and reluctant, but rather as subject to his divine and omnipotent will. For it was right that the flesh should be moved but subject to the divine will, according to the most wise Athanasius. For as his flesh is called and is the flesh of God the Word, so also the natural will of his flesh is called and is the

77. Percival, *Seven Ecumenical Councils*, 330–31.
78. Percival, *Seven Ecumenical Councils*, 333.

> proper will of God the Word, as he himself says: "I came down from heaven, not that I might do mine own will but the will of the Father which sent me!" where he calls his own will the will of his flesh, inasmuch as his flesh was also his own. For as his most holy and immaculate and animated flesh was not destroyed because it was deified but continued in its own state and nature, so also his human will, although deified, was not suppressed, but was rather preserved according to the saying of Gregory Theologus: "His will [i.e., the Savior's] is not contrary to God but altogether deified."[79]

> His two natures shone forth in his one subsistence in which he both performed the miracles and endured the sufferings. . . . Although joined together yet each nature wills and does the things proper to it and that indivisibly and inconfusedly. Wherefore we confess two wills and two operations, concurring most fitly in him for the salvation of the human race.[80]

Recent Monothelite Revival

Garrett DeWeese

Garrett DeWeese, together with a group of analytic philosophers, proposes a consideration of what he terms a contemporary model that draws on psychological and analytic philosophical sources, advocating one will in Christ.[81] Others, including William Lane Craig, have taken a similar line.[82]

As he addresses this particular issue, DeWeese presents a rather shallow treatment of the ecumenical councils, without recourse to primary sources, with only a cursory passing reference to Maximus

79. Percival, *Seven Ecumenical Councils*, 345.

80. Percival, *Seven Ecumenical Councils*, 346.

81. Garrett J. DeWeese, "One Person, Two Natures: Two Metaphysical Models of the Incarnation," in *Jesus in Trinitarian Perspective: An Introductory Christology*, ed. Fred Sanders and Klaus Issler (B&H Academic, 2007), 114–53.

82. William Lane Craig, "The Incarnation," in *Philosophical Foundations for a Christian Worldview*, by J. P. Moreland and William Lane Craig (InterVarsity Press, 2003), chap. 6. See also Richard Sturch, *The Word and the Christ: An Essay in Analytic Christology* (Oxford University Press, 1991).

and nothing on his thought.[83] Throughout he argues on the basis of human personhood as it is understood in contemporary terms. There is an assumption that without reference to the fall and sin, human volition and divine are in necessary conflict, something that sounds rather similar to the original Monothelites. He ignores Maximus's distinction between a gnomic will, which Maximus rejects as alien to Christ, and a natural will, which he accepts. The latter, as created, is without sin, and as a result there is no conflict. Underlying DeWeese's case is an inadequate treatment of the divine and human, missing the point that humanity as created by God was fully compatible with him, and in the eschaton will be fulfilled in its total conformity to God.[84]

DeWeese compares two models, one of which he terms the Dyothelite model and the other a contemporary model, based on psychological and philosophical premises. The latter, which he appears to prefer, although not absolutely, argues that will is a predicate of person, rather than nature, since it is persons who will. This is what Severus on the one hand and the Monothelites on the other both assumed, although reaching opposite conclusions —a specific nature requires a specific person. In DeWeese's case, it yields one will in Christ and three in God, a clear case of tritheism. He writes, "On the contemporary model there are three wills (i.e., three faculties of volition) in the Trinity and one in Jesus Christ."[85] It misses the point that in the classic orthodox Christological doctrine, there is certainly one active agent, but that agent acts and wills in accordance with his natures.[86] But DeWeese also accepts the validity of the Dyothelite model and considers both to be within the parameters of Chalcedon. This seems to me to be at best a tenuous and dangerous prevarication, a striking example of postmodern perspectivalism, in which truth is to be assessed primarily in relation to particular contexts, cultures, and persons,

83. DeWeese, "Two Metaphysical Models," 118–25.

84. DeWeese, "Two Metaphysical Models," 133.

85. DeWeese, "Two Metaphysical Models," 150.

86. See Steven J. Duby, "Inseparable Operations and the Human Operation of Christ," *SJT* 77, no. 2 (2024): 115–25. Although not specifically dealing with the Monothelite controversy, this is a very clear discussion on the issues that underlie it.

no doubt to be discarded by later thinkers in favor of their own contemporary predilections.

Melvin Tinker (1955–2021)

In similar vein to DeWeese and Craig, Tinker, in his otherwise excellent and highly accessible book on Christology, retrieves and supports a modified form of Monotheletism. He relies on Fred Sanders's "Chalcedonian box,"[87] using it in such a way as to make Chalcedon determinative of all that follows, whereas Chalcedon did not and could not address the issues that came after. Moreover, as we noted, Chalcedon created as many problems as it solved and appeared to a large slice of the church to have made concessions to Nestorianism in talking about two natures coming together to form one person, implying the ontological priority of natures over persons. DeWeese recognizes this, but Tinker does not.

In this one relatively small section of his book, Tinker argues, as did the Monothelites, that will is a predicate of person and not nature and so Christ had one will: "Since a *person* has a mind and a will and a nature does not, Christ had *one* mind and *one* will which belonged to the divine person."[88] The corollary of this is that God has three wills, since will is a predicate of person, according to Tinker and those he cites. Again, as with DeWeese, this is hardly distinguishable from tritheism. The argument does not follow. A person, as we have seen, is a particular and unique manifestation of a nature, and so the one person of Christ is a perfect exemplification of both deity and humanity.

Tinker has a simplistic view of the ecclesiastically authorized position of Dyotheletism. He charges it with Nestorianism because he thinks it entails two persons. This it would do only on the supposition that Tinker presents, with which the Monothelites agreed, that

87. A phrase Sanders uses that draws attention to the crucial four adverbs in the Definition of Chalcedon, asserting that Christ is "without division or separation, without confusion or mixture." Sanders does not use this formula in the way that Tinker does.

88. Melvin Tinker, *Veiled in Flesh: The Incarnation—What It Means and Why It Matters* (Inter-Varsity Press, 2019), 131 (italics original).

will is a predicate of person, which none of the councils accepted. He also misses the point that for Constantinople III Christ is one active agent, who wills in accordance with his natures. There is no inherent internal conflict, since he is sinless. Man was made to be compatible with God, being in his image, and because of Jesus' own unique personal identity, he cannot be said, even on Tinker's assumptions, to be divided into two persons. The charge of Nestorianism was exactly what the Monothelites adopted to contend against the orthodox.[89]

Tinker cites DeWeese approvingly, but misunderstands the councils and consequently misrepresents Dyotheletism and Constantinople III, accusing both of Nestorianism by their insistence on two wills.[90] He then proceeds to present a view of the event in Gethsemane that seems perfectly in harmony with what he is purporting to oppose![91] This seems to stem, in my mind, from the lack of attention given to post-Chalcedonian developments in Western thought, with the consequent muddled thinking.

This leads Tinker to posit only two effective alternatives: either (1) two wills, stemming from two natures, but since natures do not exist apart from persons it entails two persons, as in Nestorianism, or (2) one will because one person, operating as human with the divine will in the subconscious or preconscious. He does not appear to grasp that the classic doctrine is that (1) persons act, not natures as such, and (2) persons act in accordance with their nature; therefore, (3) Jesus Christ is the one active agent, and (4) he acts and wills in accordance with his natures, which are twofold. In short, Tinker appears to have similar assumptions to Severus and the Monothelites: a particular nature requires a particular person. This aberrant Christology has gained a strong foothold, together with extensive approval, in contemporary conservative evangelicalism.[92]

89. I write this with some sadness, because of Tinker's fine qualities and work, including having been, until his death, a staunch defender of the faith while facing significant opposition.

90. Tinker, *Veiled in Flesh*, 137.

91. Tinker, *Veiled in Flesh*, 137–38.

92. As the range of well-known names who endorsed Tinker's book attests. See further on Monotheletism Stephen J. Wellum, *God the Son Incarnate* (Crossway, 2016), 338–48.

8

Consolidation in East and West

Following the tumultuous years when the doctrine of Christ was heavily contested, mainly in the Greek church, attention largely turned to other areas. John of Damascus is the most significant theologian in the East after Maximus, while Thomas Aquinas, who frequently cites him, is the most dominant figure in the Latin church.

John of Damascus (675–749)

John was a synthesizer of patristic theology, a major figure in the Eastern church, and thus an authoritative source. He is particularly important because of his clear articulation of *perichoresis*, mutual indwelling, and its application to the hypostatic union. The idea and the term had been used before in Christology, but John was the first to apply it to the Trinity, and he gave especially incisive voice to its Christological application.[1] It asserted that in their particular contexts, the two natures of Christ and the three persons of the Trinity mutually and comprehensively indwell one another in such a way as to occupy the same infinite divine space.[2]

1. This should be distanced from a recent use of *perichoresis*, which diverges widely from its meaning in the fathers. In this modern use, it has been seen as a dance of equals, giving almost an autonomy to the three Trinitarian *hypostases*, a form of social Trinitarianism akin to a human family, bordering at times on tritheism. Moreover, some have used the idea to embrace almost everything, which has the tendency to debase and even empty the term of meaning, or to push it toward panentheism or even pantheism.

2. Gerald Bray, *The Doctrine of God* (Inter-Varsity Press, 1993), 158.

John was fully in line with the post-Chalcedonian developments that we have explored, "fully within the so-called Cyrilline Chalcedonian tradition," according to Andrew Louth.[3] John wrote that "we confess also that there is one incarnate nature of God the Word [in the way Cyril used it], expressing by the word 'incarnate' the essence of the flesh, according to the blessed Cyril."[4] John stated that "although we hold that the natures of the Lord permeate one another, yet we know that the permeation springs from the divine nature."[5] In short, in the incarnation the person of the Son is the single active agent, and he takes into union a human nature that becomes his and that has no existence apart from that union. Vassa Kantouma (née Conticello) describes his *The Orthodox Faith*, a later extraction from a larger work, *The Fount of Knowledge*, as "a synthesis of Maximian theology."[6]

Charles Twombly points to the asymmetric nature of *perichoresis* in the Damascene's thought. Since the incarnation is a divine initiative, the divine nature is "the source and controlling center of indwelling."[7] If the humanity were equally active, the two natures "coming together" (in the language of Chalcedon), it would point to Nestorianism, but in contrast, if the divinity swamped the human nature and reduced it to quiescence, it would be "the virtual reduction of the incarnate Logos to one nature."[8] Twombly observes that in John's writings, God pervades the creation, remaining unaffected by that which he indwells, and so the relation of the Logos to his own humanity is in some way analogous.[9]

3. Andrew Louth, *John Damascene: Tradition and Originality in Byzantine Theology* (Oxford University Press, 2002), 157.

4. John of Damascus, *On the Orthodox Faith*, 3.7; *NPNF*², 9/2:52.

5. John of Damascus, *On the Orthodox Faith*, 3.7; *NPNF*², 9/2:52. See Louth, *John Damascene*, 174–75 and 157–79, for an account of the Damascene's Christology overall.

6. Vassa Kantouma, *John of Damascus: New Studies in His Life and Works* (Ashgate/Variorum, 2015), V. 14.

7. Charles C. Twombly, *Perichoresis and Personhood: God, Christ, and Salvation in John of Damascus* (Pickwick Publications, 2015), 54.

8. Twombly, *Perichoresis*, 55.

9. Twombly, *Perichoresis*, 55.

John makes very clear at the start of book 3 of *The Orthodox Faith* that the incarnation is an action of the indivisible Trinity, all three *hypostases* integrally at work: "God being perfect becomes perfect man, and brings to perfection the newest of all new things, the only new thing under the sun, through which the boundless might of God is manifested. For what greater thing is there, than that God should become man? And the Word became flesh without being changed, of the Holy Spirit, and Mary the holy and ever-virgin one, the mother of God."[10] He adds that "the divine Word was not made one with flesh that had an independent existence. . . . He unreservedly in his own subsistence took upon himself through the pure blood of the eternal virgin a body of flesh animated with the spirit of reason and thought. . . . So that he is at once flesh, and at the same time flesh of God the Word, and likewise flesh animated, possessing both reason and thought."[11] The two natures are united without change or alteration. Christ does not have a compound nature, but the two are distinct, for "though he is constituted of these different parts he is yet the same," for "we cannot speak of one nature made up of divinity and humanity, as we do in the case of the individual made up of soul and body. . . . And therefore we hold that there has been a union of two perfect natures, one divine and one human; . . . one and the same subsistence."[12]

Twombly summarizes John's account of the patristic consensus in writing that nature "is that form of substance embodied in a particular species and gives that species the traits associated with it." Hence, when thinking of nature, "species, and not individuals within species, are the principal focus." On the other hand, *hypostasis* or person is "a particular manifestation of some species."[13] Thus,

10. John of Damascus, *Orthodox Faith*, 3.1; *NPNF*², 9/2:45; Boniface Kotter, *Die Schriften Des Johannes von Damaskos. Herausgegeben Vom Byzantischen Institut der Abtei Scheyern*, 6 vols. (Walter de Gruyter, 1969–2009), 2:106–8.

11. John of Damascus, *Orthodox Faith*, 3.2; *NPNF*², 9/2:46; Kotter, *Johannes von Damaskos*, 2:110, lines 26–31.

12. John of Damascus, *Orthodox Faith*, 3.2; *NPNF*², 9/2:47; Kotter, *Johannes von Damaskos*, 2:109–10.

13. Twombly, *Perichoresis*, 59.

the Word appropriates to himself all the attributes of humanity.[14] Yet we ourselves do not speak of his divinity in terms of humanity, nor vice versa, but we attribute to his person the attributes of both. This is because the two natures are preserved, after the union, in the one compound subsistence or person, united without confusion, distinguished without separation, interpenetrating one another but not transmuted into one another, for Christ is one.[15]

In a crucially important passage, John affirms the far-reaching consequences of the incarnation.

> Thus, therefore, we confess that the nature of the Godhead is wholly and perfectly in each of its subsistences, wholly in the Father, wholly in the Son, and wholly in the Holy Spirit. Wherefore also the Father is perfect God, the Son is perfect God, and the Holy Spirit is perfect God. In like manner, too, in the incarnation of the Trinity of the one God the Word of the Holy Trinity, we hold that in one of its subsistences the nature of the Godhead is wholly and perfectly united with the whole nature of humanity, and not part united to part. . . . But we shall not be driven to hold that all the subsistences of the holy Godhead, to wit the three, are made one in subsistence with all the subsistences of humanity. . . . But we hold that to the whole of human nature the whole essence of the Godhead was united. For God the Word omitted none of the things which he implanted in our nature when he formed us in the beginning, but took them all upon himself, body and soul both intelligent and rational, and all their properties. For the creature that is devoid of these is not man. But he in his fulness took upon himself me in my fulness, and was united whole to whole that he might in his grace bestow salvation on the whole man (ὅλον γὰρ ὅλος ἀναλαβέ με, καὶ ὅλος ὅλῳ ἠνώθη, ἵνα ὅλῳ τὴν σωτηρίαν χαρίσηται). For what has not been taken cannot be healed.[16]

14. John of Damascus, *Orthodox Faith*, 3.3; *NPNF*², 9/2:48.

15. Kotter, *Johannes von Damaskos*, 2:118–19; John of Damascus, *Orthodox Faith*, 3.5; *NPNF*², 9/2:49.

16. John of Damascus, *Orthodox Faith*, 3.6; *NPNF*², 9/2:50; Kotter, *Johannes von Damaskos*, 2:120, lines 16–121, line 37.

Consequently:

> We hold, moreover, that our nature has been raised from the dead and has ascended to the heavens and taken its seat at the right hand of the Father: not that all the persons of men have risen from the dead and taken their seat at the right hand of the Father, but that this has happened to the whole of our nature in the subsistence of Christ. Verily, the divine apostle says, "God hath raised us up together and made us sit together in Christ."[17]

John maintains that in the event of the incarnation, three things happened at the same time: (1) our nature was assumed into union by the Logos, (2) it came into being, for it had no existence apart from this assumption, and (3) it was deified by the Word.[18] "The Mother of God in some marvellous manner was the means of fashioning the Framer of all things," for "he existed in the Word himself from the beginning of the conception."[19] On his coming into being in other than the normal way, without a human father, John defends this by pointing out that the Son and the Spirit come from the Father in different ways but are the same God. Furthermore, Adam, Eve, and Seth each had a different origin.[20] Therefore, "the very subsistence of God the Word was changed into the subsistence of the flesh, and the subsistence of the Word, which was formerly simple, became compound . . . in two perfect natures."[21]

Twombly reflects that *perichoresis* ("mutual indwelling") has a dynamic character missing from *enhypostatos*.[22] But this is most likely a matter of perspective. *Perichoresis* is the form that *enhypostatos* takes in the incarnate Christ. The Logos personalizes (*enhypostatos*)

17. John of Damascus, *Orthodox Faith*, 3.6; *NPNF*², 9/2:51; Kotter, *Johannes von Damaskos*, 2:122.

18. John of Damascus, *Orthodox Faith*, 3.12; *NPNF*², 9/2:56–57; Twombly, *Perichoresis*, 66.

19. Kotter, *Johannes von Damaskos*, 2:133–36; John of Damascus, *Orthodox Faith*, 3.12; *NPNF*², 9/2:57.

20. Twombly, *Perichoresis*, 68; John of Damascus, *Orthodox Faith*, 1.8.

21. *NPNF*², 9/2:51; John of Damascus, *Orthodox Faith*, 3.7.

22. Twombly, *Perichoresis*, 70.

the assumed humanity and, in doing so, indwells. In Twombly's words, in the Damascene's thought *perichoresis* "functions as a magnet drawing various iron filings together into a coherent pattern."[23] The basis, however, is *enhypostasis*, both natures having one and the same subsistence (person), always without division or separation.[24]

Thus, John remarks, "he did not do divine deeds divinely—for he did not work miracles as naked God but through touch and stretching out his hands—nor did he work human deeds humanly —for it was not as a mere human being that he endured the passion that saved the world—but being God and having become human he manifested a certain new and strange theandric activity, divine but working through the human, human but assisted by the divine, and showing the signs of the divinity coexistent with it (καινὴν τινα καὶ ξένην θεανδρικὴν ἐνέργειαν ἐπεδειξατο, θείαν, ἀλλά δι' ἀνθρηωπίνης ἐνεργοῦσαν, ἀνθρωπίνην, ἀλλὰ τῇ θείᾳ ἐξυπηρετουμένην, καὶ τὰ τῆς συνυφεστηκυίας αὐτῃ θεότητος ἐμφαίνουσαν σύμβολα)."[25]

John, like Maximus, connects the incarnation with deification. In the incarnation, as he wrote, "the flesh of the Lord received the riches of the divine energies through the purest union with the Word."[26] This does not mean a change of nature (ὡς οὐ κατὰ μεταβολὴν φύσεως), but rather "the permeation of the natures through one another, just as we saw that burning permeated the steel."[27]

John affirms strongly the conciliar decree on Dyotheletism.[28] "Since . . . Christ has two natures, we hold that he has also two natural wills and two natural energies. But since his two natures have one subsistence, we hold that it is one and the same person who wills and energizes naturally in both natures (ἕνα καὶ τὸν αὑτόν φαμεν θέλοντά τε καὶ ἐνεργοῦντα φυσικῶς κατ' ἀμφω) . . .

23. Twombly, *Perichoresis*, 74.

24. John of Damascus, *Orthodox Faith*, 3.9; *NPNF*², 9/2:53.

25. John of Damascus, *On the Two Wills in Christ*, 47.27–33, in Kotter, *Johannes von Damaskos*, 4:228. Translation by Louth, *John Damascene*, 171–72.

26. John of Damascus, *Orthodox Faith*, 3.17; *NPNF*², 9/2:66; Kotter, *Johannes von Damaskos*, 2:156.

27. John of Damascus, *Orthodox Faith*, 3.17; *NPNF*², 9/2:65; Kotter, *Johannes von Damaskos*, 2:155, lines 3–4, 7–8.

28. John of Damascus, *Orthodox Faith*, 3.17; *NPNF*², 9/2:66.

and moreover that he wills and energizes without separation but as a united whole."[29] Accordingly, Christ's wills are natural, not personal; otherwise, the three persons of the Trinity would differ in will and operation.[30]

As to the question of how a human mind could be said to will if there is not a human person, John reiterates the enhypostatic teaching that it is the human will of the person of the Logos.[31] Thus, "the subsistence of God the Word in itself became the subsistence of the flesh (Αὐτὴ γὰρ ἡ ὑπόστασις τοῦ θεοῦ λόγου ἐγένετο τῇ σαρκὶ ὑπόστασις)."[32] Union is different from incarnation, since "union signifies only the conjunction, but not at all that with which union is effected . . . [, whereas] incarnation . . . signifies that the conjunction is with flesh, . . . with man."[33] As Twombly remarks, "*perichoresis* provided a way of bringing contraries together in union without violating their final differences. If there is a mutual indwelling of human and divine natures in Christ, then there must also be a mutual indwelling of wills as well, since dogmatic opinion posited that the wills resided in the natures. [Consequently,] in the relationship of mutual indwelling, both the human nature and the human will were deified without being transformed into something else."[34]

Thomas Aquinas (1225–74)

Aquinas affirmed in the medieval Latin context the developed Christology of the Greek patristic tradition. He frequently cited John of Damascus in support. His is perhaps the most concentrated and

29. John of Damascus, *Orthodox Faith*, 3.13–14; *NPNF*², 9/2:57; Kotter, *Johannes von Damaskos*, 2:136–37.

30. John of Damascus, *Orthodox Faith*, 3.14; *NPNF*², 9/2:57; Kotter, *Johannes von Damaskos*, 2:137–44.

31. Johannes Zachhuber, *The Rise of Christian Theology and the End of Ancient Metaphysics: Patristic Philosophy from the Cappadocian Fathers to John of Damascus* (Oxford University Press, 2020), 291–93, 300; John of Damascus, *Orthodox Faith*, 3.17; *NPNF*², 9/2:65–66; Kotter, *Johannes von Damaskos*, 2:156–57.

32. John of Damascus, *Orthodox Faith*, 3.11; *NPNF*², 9/2:55; Kotter, *Johannes von Damaskos*, 2:131, lines 14–15.

33. John of Damascus, *Orthodox Faith*, 3:11; *NPNF*², 9/2:55.

34. Twombly, *Perichoresis*, 82.

sustained reflection in the West, given that Augustine's comments were relatively sparse, the Nestorian crisis only arising in the last few months of his life and in a remote area and language.

Thomas Weinandy summarizes the chief planks of Aquinas's Christology, in its affirmation of the conciliar tradition: "It is *truly the divine Son of God* who is man. . . . It must be *truly man* that the Son of God is. . . . The Son of God must *truly be* man."[35] Aquinas confirms that "Christ is one ontological reality / supposit ['thing' / quiddity] and that the one ontological reality / supposit that Christ is is the one person / hypostasis of the Son existing as man."[36] Consequently, the Son did not become a different person when he became incarnate, for if that had been the case, it would not have been the person of the Son who became man. But he did acquire a new mode of existing, as man, because the humanity was ontologically united to him in his existence as God.[37] Thus, it is truly the Son who is man.[38]

It is often overlooked that Aquinas was principally a biblical commentator. Right at the start of his massive *Summa theologiae*, he maintains the supremacy of Scripture over all the opinions of the philosophers and all the teachings of the church fathers.[39] As Dominic Legge states, "Aquinas's thought springs from the rich and fertile soil of sacred Scripture, which he quotes often."[40] In commenting on Aquinas's discussion of why the Son became incarnate, Legge remarks that "Aquinas's theology of Christ is not only suffused by his trinitarian doctrine which is everywhere present, but his treatment of Christ is the central movement in the whole symphony of his account of God in himself (*theologia*) and how God, having created creatures out of his goodness, draws them back into himself."[41] In short, the

35. Thomas G. Weinandy, "Aquinas: God IS Man: The Marvel of the Incarnation," in *Aquinas on Doctrine: A Critical Introduction*, ed. Thomas G. Weinandy, Daniel A. Keating, and John P. Yocum (T&T Clark, 2004), 67–89, here 68–69 (italics original).

36. Weinandy, "Aquinas: God IS Man," 73.

37. Weinandy, "Aquinas: God IS Man," 74.

38. Weinandy, "Aquinas: God IS Man," 78.

39. Thomas Aquinas, *ST*, 1a.1.8.

40. Dominic Legge, *The Trinitarian Christology of St. Thomas Aquinas* (Oxford University Press, 2017), 66.

41. Legge, *Trinitarian Christology*, 61.

incarnation is an absolutely vital part of the wider reality of God's purpose for the whole creation.

The Mode of Union of the Word Incarnate

Legge comments that "Word" means something proceeding from another.[42] In commenting on John 1:3, Aquinas argues that it is proper to the Word that the Father works through him, since "the Son never causes anything in the Father; rather, he receives from him [speaking of the hypostatic relations]." There is one divine action—from the Father through the Son in the Holy Spirit.[43]

In the wake of the conciliar developments, Aquinas rejects union according to nature, that is, of one nature with another. He adds that it is impossible that the union took place in the natures because it would produce either a mixture or a combination. The divine nature is immutable and cannot be changed into flesh.[44] Rather, the union took place in the person (following Cyril, Leontius of Jerusalem, and Constantinople II—the received doctrine that was passed on through Maximus and the Damascene). "Whatever adheres to a person is united to it in person." The Word did not unite to himself human nature in general but "in an individual," as John of Damascus says; "otherwise every man would be the Word of God"—thus, union is in the person. "Therefore, although this human nature is a kind of individual in the genus of substance, it has not its own personality because it does not exist separately, but in something more perfect, viz. in the person of the Word. Therefore the union took place in the person."[45] After the incarnation, Christ is composite—one *hypostasis* composed from two natures.[46]

Assumption and union are not the same. Assumption implies the action, whereas union implies the relation. Assumption implies becoming, whereas union implies having become. Since the Son of

42. Legge, *Trinitarian Christology*, 64; Aquinas, *ST*, 1a.34.3.

43. Thomas Aquinas, *Commentary on the Gospel of St. John* (Magi Books, 1980), 52, lecture 2, sections 76–77; Legge, *Trinitarian Christology*, 65.

44. Aquinas, *ST*, 3a.2.1.

45. Aquinas, *ST*, 3a.2.2.

46. Aquinas, *ST*, 3a.2.4.

God assumes human nature into himself, we can say that the Son of God is man. But the human nature is assumed, and we cannot say that the Son of God is human nature.[47] Citing Augustine (*De praedestinatione sanctorum,* 15), Aquinas stresses that there were no preceding merits to the union, which follows from the human nature's not preexisting the assumption but rather having been conceived in the womb of the virgin.[48]

The Mode of Union on the Part of the Person Assuming

Aquinas addresses the question whether one person can assume a created nature without the involvement of another and concludes that this is not the case. He states that "assumption implies two things, viz. the act of assuming and the term of assumption. Now the act of assumption proceeds from the divine power, which is common to the three persons, but the term of the assumption is a person. . . . Hence what has to do with action in the assumption is common to the three persons; but what pertains to the nature of the term belongs to one person in such a manner as not to belong to another; for the three persons caused the human nature to be united to the one person of the Son."[49] Thus, all three Trinitarian persons were equally involved, but only one person assumed the human nature. Legge remarks that this is "of capital importance both for Christology and for trinitarian theology." It brings the affirmation of the inseparability of the works of the Trinity together with the fact that Christ is the incarnate Son and that he only is the Son and not the Father or the Spirit.[50] The human nature terminates in the person of the Son alone, taken up into the personal unity of the Son, into his very being.[51]

Following this is the issue whether each of the divine persons could have assumed human nature. Aquinas concludes that if the Son could do so, then so could the Father and the Holy Spirit.[52] Legge

47. Aquinas, *ST*, 3a.2.8.
48. Aquinas, *ST*, 3a.2.11.
49. Aquinas, *ST*, 3a.3.4.
50. Legge, *Trinitarian Christology*, 104.
51. Legge, *Trinitarian Christology*, 106.
52. Aquinas, *ST*, 3a.3.5.

is correct that Aquinas is talking here of the divine nature / essence. Since all three are equally and comprehensively one, it follows that each could do so.[53] Later, however, Aquinas considers that it was "fitting" that only the Son be incarnate; there he speaks in terms of hypostatic order and properties.[54] Aquinas presents three reasons why it was more fitting that the Son became incarnate, rather than any other divine person.[55]

The first factor is the hypostatic order, seen in creation. Aquinas argues that "as all things were created by the Word, so they should be recreated through the Son's incarnation."[56] He uses an analogy, originally used by Athanasius, of an architect who has in mind what he wants to produce, together with an act of will to build it. If the thing produced gets damaged, the architect has the resources to correct it and bring it to the design he has for it. Since all things were created in and by the Word, he has an affinity with the whole of creation, a unique fit. Even more, the Word has an affinity with the human race. The fact that Scripture uses the name "Word" indicates a rational nature, which is also the distinguishing mark of humans. Thus, the incarnate Word and humans are the image of God.[57] Indeed, the Father always acts through the Word.[58]

A second factor is that power and wisdom are appropriated to the Son. The Son's personal property is "begotten wisdom," and as such, he is the source of all human wisdom.[59]

53. Legge, *Trinitarian Christology*, 106.

54. Aquinas, *ST*, 3a.3.8.

55. On an Anselmian basis, God always does what is best. If that is so, it follows that it was necessary that the Son, rather than the Father or the Holy Spirit, become incarnate, not out of necessity from some external force (which is impossible), but from fittingness of nature.

56. Aquinas, *ST*, 3a.3.8.

57. "Rursus, affinitas quaedam videtur maxime Verbi ad humanam naturam; homo enim propriam speciem sortitur secundum quod rationalis est; Verbum autem rationi affine est; unde apud Graecos Λόγος verbum et ratio dicitur. Convenientissime igitur Verbum rationali naturae unitum est; nam et propter affinitatem praedictam divina Scriptura nomen imaginis et Verbo attribuit et homini; dicit enim Apostolus de Verbo quod est *imago Dei invisibilis* (*Coloss.* 1:15), et idem de homine dicit quod *vir imago et gloria Dei est* (1 Cor. 11:7)." Thomas Aquinas, *SCG*, 4.42.

58. Aquinas, *ST*, 3a.3.8; Aquinas, *St. John*, 48–52, lecture 2, on John 1:3, 48–52, sections 68–77. See Legge, *Trinitarian Christology*, 68–70.

59. Legge, *Trinitarian Christology*, 74–75.

A third factor is the end or purpose of the hypostatic union. The end goal is that the church and its members be predestined to be conformed to the image of the Son. Since Adam had sinned by seeking knowledge wrongfully, it was through the knowledge imparted by the Word that recovery comes. As the first creation was made through the Word and in the Word, it was fitting that the second creation be brought about by the Word.[60]

Legge comments: "The incarnation is ordered not only to the satisfaction for sin . . . but also to the restoration of the whole order of creation, through the supreme union—personal, not by participation—of the immutable and perfect Word with a weak and changeable human nature. This union orders human nature to God, its immutable perfection. To be sure, Thomas regards the fall of human nature by sin as prompting the extraordinary remedy, but his accent here is not on the collapse or the details of the repair work (i.e., satisfaction, redemption), but on the restoration of creatures to the ultimate end for which they were made, the perfect and immutable perfection which is God himself."[61] Here there are definite echoes of the cosmic scope of salvation that was at the heart of Maximus's Christology, incarnation and deification integrally related with effects on the individual, the church, humanity, and the whole of creation.

Moving on to the details of the Son's incarnate life, Aquinas denies that Christ had faith. Faith is the evidence of things not seen, but as Aquinas thought, Christ knew and saw everything and so had no need of faith.[62] The same applies to hope.[63] Nor could the grace of Christ increase, since he was the only-begotten of the Father, full of grace and truth.[64] This seems at first sight to diminish

60. Aquinas, *ST*, 3.3.8.

61. Legge, *Trinitarian Christology*, 72. Aquinas is referring here to deification. John Calvin writes on 2 Peter 1:4 that the goal of the gospel is to make us, sooner or later, like God. *Calvin's Commentaries: The Epistle of Paul the Apostle to the Hebrews and the First and Second Epistles of St. Peter*, trans. William B. Johnston (Eerdmans, 1963), 330. Aquinas does not mean that the ultimate end is for humans to cease to be humans and become God.

62. Aquinas, *ST*, 3a.7.3.

63. Aquinas, *ST*, 4a.7.4.

64. Aquinas, *ST*, 3a.7.12.

the genuineness of Christ's humanity and be contrary to the clear statements in the New Testament that he grew in wisdom (Luke 2:52), learned obedience (Heb. 5:8), and so forth. But this is not the whole picture; Aquinas states that Christ did advance in acquired or empiric knowledge, since this is human wisdom, the effect of knowledge, while the habit of (infused) knowledge did not increase, since from the beginning he had perfect infused knowledge of all things, just as his divine knowledge could not increase. He brings these strands together: "Both the infused knowledge and the beatific knowledge of Christ's soul were the effects of an agent of infinite power, which could produce the whole at once; and thus in neither knowledge did Christ advance; since from the beginning he had them perfectly. But the acquired knowledge of Christ is caused by the active intellect which does not produce the whole at once, but successively; and hence by this knowledge Christ did not know everything from the beginning, but step by step, and after a time, i.e., in his perfect age; and this is plain from what the Evangelist says, viz. that he increased in knowledge and age together."[65] This leaves the question of how the acquired knowledge could exist on its own terms if, at the same time, he had perfect infused knowledge. Aquinas does not explore this question, which may not have been an issue for him and his contemporaries.

Aquinas agrees that "it was fitting for the Son of God to assume flesh subject to human infirmities, in order to suffer and be tempted in it and so bring succor to us." Since it was to satisfy for the sin of the human race that he came into the world, to do this he had to take on himself the punishment due to the other. Citing Isaiah 53:4, he says that otherwise he would not have seemed to be true man, but to have imaginary flesh.[66] How necessary were these sufferings? They were not necessary by necessity of constraint, brought about by an external agent, but they arose from natural necessity resulting from natural principles—the necessity of death and other defects[67] and the divine decision that this be so. He did not contract these bodily

65. Aquinas, *ST*, 3a.12.2, reply obj. 2.
66. Aquinas, *ST*, 3a.14.1, *sed contra.*
67. Aquinas, *ST*, 3a.14.2.

defects from some external necessity, since that is the question at hand, for he "received human nature without sin"—and death is connected with sin (Rom. 5:12)—but he freely assumed them.[68] In short, it was a free decision of God, all three persons involved, and the sufferings and weaknesses that Christ bore he took on voluntarily in order to fulfill his eternal purpose.

That leads on immediately to the question whether the soul of Christ was passible, capable of suffering. He refers to Psalm 87:4 (88:4, Eng.) and its rendering "my soul is filled with evils." A soul may suffer in two ways, he argues. It can have a bodily passion, through being hurt, in which sense Christ's body was passible and mortal. It can also have an animal passion, in its operations, which are proper to the soul. These too Christ had, since he had everything relating to human nature.[69] But there was a difference compared to us. Christ's passions throughout were guided by reason.[70] Hence, he suffered pain, sorrow, fear, and wonder.[71] The same applied to anger. Anger—referring to John 2:17—is an effect of sorrow with a desire for revenge. Sorrow was in Christ; seeking revenge was not, since it goes beyond the bounds of reason and is sin. Yet there is a desire for revenge that seeks justice, zealous anger, and "such was the anger that was in Christ."[72]

In view of the reality of the incarnation and following from these discussions, Aquinas affirms the legitimacy of saying, "God is man." Philippians 2 states that "he who is in the form of God is man. Now he who is in the form of God is God. Therefore God is man." Moreover, "the proposition 'God is man' is admitted by all Christians, yet not in the same way by all." Some do so falsely or heretically, while

68. Aquinas, *ST*, 3a.14.3.

69. See Augustine, *City of God*, 14.9.

70. Aquinas, *ST*, 3a.15.4.

71. Aquinas, *ST*, 3a.15.5–8.

72. Aquinas, *ST*, 3a.15.9. On the theme of this paragraph, see Paul Gondreau, *The Passions of Christ's Soul in the Theology of St. Thomas Aquinas*, Beiträge zur Geschichte der Philosophie und Theologie des Mittelalters, Neue Folge 61 (Aschendorff, 2002), 166–89, 221–27; Kevin Madigan, *The Passions of Christ in High-Medieval Thought: An Essay on Christological Development* (Oxford University Press, 2007). I thank Sherman Isbell for these references.

adherents to Manichaeism and Nestorianism cannot do so at all.[73] Furthermore, the reverse is also true—man is God, as in Romans 9:5, where Paul writes that "Christ according to the flesh" is "God over all."[74] This is a case in which the *communicatio idiomatum* are applicable, with attributes of deity and humanity being equally attributable to the person of Christ because of the hypostatic union.

Aquinas reiterates the conciliar decree of Constantinople III on the two wills of Christ. The human will is in conformity with the divine will because it "had a determinate mode from the fact of being in a divine hypostasis, i.e., it was always moved in accordance with the bidding of the divine will."[75] Thus, for Aquinas, in Legge's words, "Christ's humanity bears the Son's personal property."[76] It reflects the fact of the Son's filial relation to the Father in the indivisible Trinity, receiving everything from him, here expressed in his mission as incarnate. To equate the mission with the eternal relation would lead to subordinationism, but to distance the two, thereby asserting that the incarnate state bore no relation to the eternal relations, would point to modalism. Aquinas obviously does neither.

Aquinas writes at length on the incarnate Christ as the Son of the Father and, as man, making the Father known. He considers it fitting for Christ to pray for himself, *inter alia*, "to show that the Father is the author both of his eternal procession in the divine nature, and of all the good that he possesses in the human nature. Now just as in his human nature he had already received certain gifts from his Father, so there were other gifts he had not yet received but which he expected to receive."[77] Legge points to this, indicating that at every point, whatever Christ had was from the Father in his incarnate state, and since this was a mission, it indicated his eternal reliance on the Father.[78] Aquinas expands, "For he came in the manner in which he was sent by the Father, by whom he was

73. Aquinas, *ST*, 3a.16.1.
74. Aquinas, *ST*, 3a.16.2.
75. Aquinas, *ST*, 3a.18.1–4. See Legge, *Trinitarian Christology*, 112–13.
76. Legge, *Trinitarian Christology*, 112.
77. Aquinas, *ST*, 3a.21.3.
78. Legge, *Trinitarian Christology*, 112–13.

sent, i.e., he was made flesh."[79] Aquinas paraphrases Jesus' prayer to the Father: "Everything I have I have from you. 'Now they know, that all things which you have given me,' that is, to your Son in his human nature, 'are from you: we saw his glory, glory as it were of the only begotten of the Father' (John 1:14), that is to say, we saw him as having everything from the Father."[80] All of Christ's human actions reveal the Son as Son and the Father as principle and so lead us to the Father.[81] As man, Christ is the way to the Father (John 14:6), and the Father draws us (6:44–45). As God, Christ draws us to the Father (Matt. 11:26; John 14:6; 17:6).[82] This follows from Aquinas's "always being careful to maintain this strict correspondence between the Son's eternal procession and his visible mission."[83]

On John 5:19, "the Son can do nothing of his own accord, but only what he sees the Father doing," Aquinas rejects applying statements such as this to the assumed human nature and argues that they refer to the eternal relations, to his origin as begotten from the Father, "as if to say: I am equal to the Father, but in such a way as to be from him, and not he from me; and whatever I may do, is in me from the Father."[84] This revelation of the Father follows, since "the Father was not in the flesh in such a way that it was joined to him to constitute one person, but he was in the incarnate Word because they had one and the same nature, and the Father was seen in the incarnate Christ."[85] Elsewhere he adds that "Christ wished to make his Godhead known through his human nature."[86] Legge again sums up: "Christ's actions are truly the actions of the

79. Aquinas, *St. John*, 83, lecture 7 on John 1:14, section 165.

80. Aquinas, *Commentary on the Gospel of John Chapters 9–21*, trans. Fabian R. Larcher (Aquinas Institute for the Study of Sacred Doctrine, 2013), 366, on John 17:7, lecture 2, section 2199.

81. Aquinas, *John 9–21*, 267, on John 14:6, lecture 6, section 1958.

82. Aquinas, *St. John*, 372, on John 6:41–46, lecture 5, section 936. These statements are based on the Father's being the principle (*principium*) of the Trinity, the source of the personal relations and of the external works. They do not denote subordination but rather refer to the eternal order (*taxis*) of the persons in the indivisible Trinity.

83. Legge, *Trinitarian Christology*, 115.

84. Aquinas, *St. John*, 298, on John 5:19, lecture 3, section 747.

85. Aquinas, *John 9–21*, 238, on John 14:7, lecture 2, section 1881.

86. Aquinas, *ST*, 3a.40.1.ad1.

Son; they are properly from the Father insofar as Christ's human nature participates in the filial mode of the Son's personal action. In themselves, when they are known for *what they truly are* they reveal the Son and hence the Father."[87] It is precisely the enhypostatic assumption of human nature that undergirds the reality of Christ *as man* revealing to us the nature of God.

87. Legge, *Trinitarian Christology*, 122.

9

Reformation Issues

Christology was not a major issue between the Reformers and the Roman church. Both accepted the classic Christological dogma as it had been worked out in the fifth, sixth, and seventh centuries. The only slight question surrounded John Calvin's attribution of *autotheos* ("aseity") to the Son, in his opposition to the Italian anti-Trinitarian Valentine Gentile. We will discuss this later. The main area of concern related to the differences between the Lutheran and the Reformed, which were related to their respective views on the Eucharist.

The Communication of Attributes

Martin Luther

As Paul Althaus remarks, Luther "expressly accepts the great ecumenical creeds of Greek and Latin theology. Apart from individual concepts he expresses no criticism of the traditional christological dogmas."[1] Luther's grasp of the twin dogmas of *anhypostasia* and *enhypostasia* is clear and important for his Christology, for it forms the basis for his peculiar ideas of the *communicatio idiomatum*.

The classic doctrine of the *communicatio idiomatum* was grounded on the conclusion of the ecumenical councils that the *person* of the Son is the active agent in all his works, from the miracles to the

1. Paul Althaus, *The Theology of Martin Luther*, trans. Robert C. Schultz (Fortress Press, 1966), 179.

sufferings, the womb, tomb, and resurrection. Consequently, attributes of both deity and humanity are predicable of the person of Christ. In the light of this established recognition by the whole church, Luther's adaptation of the *communicatio idiomatum* was a novelty. But it was founded on an orthodox base, as he wrote; "since the divinity and humanity are one person in Christ, the Scriptures ascribe to the divinity, because of this personal union, all that happens to humanity, and vice versa. And in reality it is so. Indeed, you must say that the person (pointing to Christ) suffers and dies. But this person is truly God, and therefore it is correct to say: the Son of God suffers. Although, so to speak, the one part (namely, the divinity) does not suffer, nevertheless the person, who is God, suffers in the other part (namely, in the humanity)."[2] He used a number of analogies in support. The king's son is wounded when only his leg is wounded; Solomon is wise, whereas it is only his soul that is wise; Peter is gray, although only his head is gray.[3] So the person of Christ is crucified according to his humanity.[4] There is a problem with this, as with many other analogies. A single leg, gray hair, and wisdom are accidents, not indispensable to being a human person, whereas the human nature of Christ was indispensable to his being our Savior.

The main issue was the new turn taken by Luther. He contended that Christ possessed the full range of divine attributes according to his human nature. These were communicated to his humanity by virtue of the hypostatic union. Thus Christ, according to his human nature, possessed the attributes of divine majesty. In short, in addition to divine attributes being predicated of the person, which was a commonplace, they were, for him, transmitted to the human nature.

Luther's interpretation of Philippians 2:6f. illustrates his argument. Earlier exegetes had understood Paul's reference to Christ's emptying himself to refer to his preexistence and his decision in eternity to take the form of a servant. Luther, however, considered that it was pointing to Christ in his incarnate state and therefore

2. Martin Luther, *Confession Concerning Christ's Supper* (1528); *LW*, 37:210.
3. Luther, *Confession*, *LW*, 37:211.
4. Luther, *Confession*, *LW*, 37:211.

to his constantly emptying himself throughout his earthly life.[5] He was "unwilling to use his rank against us, unwilling to be different from us," and "although he was free . . . he made himself servant of all [Mark 9:35]."[6] This is an ongoing self-emptying leading to the cross.[7] Luther's stress on the *genus majestaticum*—the divine attributes' being communicated to the humanity of Christ—was the assumption underlying his view of Christ's self-emptying in history. It is true, as Althaus argued, that the *genus majestaticum* was balanced by Luther's acceptance of the *genus tapeinoticon*—God in Christ sharing weakness, suffering, and humiliation.[8]

Famously, this impacted Luther's doctrine of the real presence of Christ in the Lord's Supper, whereby he held emphatically that the body and blood of Christ are present corporeally in, with, and under the bread and wine, due to their partaking of the divine attribute of omnipresence. Christ's flesh is not fleshly—under the curse of God and requiring rebirth—but spiritual, since Christ was born of the Holy Spirit, and so it is God's flesh that gives life to all who eat it in faith.[9]

Luther's basic Christological thought was that there is no God apart from Christ.[10] From this, the omnipresence of Christ's humanity follows. The right hand of God is not to be located in one place but is everywhere: "Where is the Scripture which limits the right hand of God in this fashion to one place?" he asks.[11] Citing Psalm 139, Luther states: "The Scriptures teach us . . . that the right hand of God is not a specific place in which a body must or may be . . . but is the almighty power of God, which at one and the same time can be nowhere and yet must be everywhere. . . . For if it were at some

5. Martin Luther, "Two Kinds of Righteousness" (1519); *LW*, 31:301–2; Martin Luther, "Freedom of a Christian" (1520); *LW*, 31:366.

6. Luther, "Two Kinds of Righteousness," *LW*, 31:301.

7. Luther, "Two Kinds of Righteousness," *LW*, 31:300–303.

8. Althaus, *Theology of Martin Luther*, 196–98.

9. Martin Luther, *That These Words of Christ, "This Is My Body," Still Stand Firm Against the Fanatics* (1527); *LW*, 37:98–100, 124. See also Luther, *Confession*, *LW*, 37:236–38.

10. Luther, *This Is My Body*, *LW*, 37:56.

11. Luther, *This Is My Body*, *LW*, 37:56.

specific place, it would have to be there in a circumscribed and determinate manner . . . so that it cannot meanwhile be at any other place. But the power of God cannot be so determined and measured, for it is uncircumscribed and immeasurable, beyond and above all that is and may be. . . . On the other hand it must be essentially present at all places, even in the tiniest tree leaf."[12] From this, Luther concludes that Christ—at the right hand of God—is present at the same time in heaven and in the Supper, for "it is contrary neither to Scripture nor to the articles of faith for Christ's body to be at the same time in heaven and in the Supper."[13]

He attacks Huldrych Zwingli's idea of *alloiosis*, understanding the biblical language as a figure of speech, in which in a reference to one nature we also understand the other, or when we name both yet we understand only one.[14] What is needed, Luther fumed, "is Scripture, and sound reasons, not [Zwingli's] snot and slobber."[15] He strongly defended himself against the claim that he mingled the natures; rather, he replied, his opponents threatened to divide the person.[16] Yet Luther may have misunderstood Zwingli, thinking that he had confined the right hand of God to a single space in heaven.[17]

Given that Luther held that the divine attribute of omnipresence was communicated to Christ's humanity, thus facilitating his corporeal presence in the Lord's Supper wherever it was held, it is important to realize that he considered there to be three forms of presence. First, an object is locally or *circumscriptively* in a place, where the object and the space fit precisely. This applies to people and all other visible entities, who occupy particular locations. Second, an object is present *definitively* or in an uncircumscribed way, where it can occupy more room or less. Such was the risen Christ, whose body was transformed so that he passed through the gravestone and through locked doors. Angels too are not confined to particular spaces. Third,

12. Luther, *This Is My Body*, *LW*, 37:57.
13. Luther, *This Is My Body*, *LW*, 37:55.
14. Luther, *Confession*, *LW*, 37:209–10.
15. Luther, *Confession*, *LW*, 37:212.
16. Luther, *Confession*, *LW*, 37:212–13.
17. Luther, *Confession*, *LW*, 37:213.

God alone occupies places *repletively*, being present in all places at all times, filling them while not being measured by any one. The result of this is that we cannot confine our thoughts on the presence of Christ to one mode of presence only.[18] Since the risen Christ was present definitively, Luther remarked, it makes sense to take "this is my body" as it stands.[19] Wherever Christ is, he is present as God and as man; if this were not so, he would be divided.[20] Rather, he is one person with God, besides which there is nothing higher.[21] Since he is one indivisible person with God, wherever God is, he must be also. This is a mystery known only to God; Luther wrote about it only to show "what crass fools our fanatics are."[22] So he raves, "Get out of here, you stupid fanatic, with your worthless ideas!"[23] Luther expressed these ideas vehemently at the Colloquy of Marburg (1529), where he came into sharp conflict with Zwingli.[24]

Huldrych Zwingli

Zwingli's stress was on God rather than man, so in Christology it is on Christ as God. Whereas Luther emphatically asserted the unity of Christ's person, Zwingli distinguished sharply between the two natures. This led Luther to accuse him of holding that a mere man had died for us, effectively Nestorianism.[25] This sharp distinction—almost separation—between the natures is clear in Zwingli's *Commentary on True and False Religion* (1525). There he wrote that Christ is our salvation according to his divine nature, not according to his humanity,[26] and so in John 6 he refers the flesh and blood simply to the gospel, the eating and drinking to faith.

18. Luther, *Confession*, *LW*, 37:215–16.
19. Luther, *Confession*, *LW*, 37:217.
20. Luther, *Confession*, *LW*, 37:218.
21. Luther, *Confession*, *LW*, 37:221–22.
22. Luther, *Confession*, *LW*, 37:223.
23. Luther, *Confession*, *LW*, 37:220.
24. See, for the record of the debate, B. J. Kidd, ed., *Documents Illustrative of the Continental Reformation* (1911; repr., Clarendon Press, 1967), 247–55.
25. W. P. Stephens, *The Theology of Huldrych Zwingli* (Clarendon Press, 1986), 111.
26. Huldrych Zwingli, *Commentary on True and False Religion*, ed. Samuel Macaulay Jackson and Clarence Nevin Heller (1929; repr., Labyrinth Press, 1981), 204.

"This, then, is the third sure mark that Christ is not speaking here of sacramental eating; for he is only in so far salvation unto us as he was slain for us; but he could be slain only according to the flesh and could be salvation bringing only according to his divinity."[27] Much of this section is devoted to establishing that John 6 does not refer to sacramental eating, but in doing so, he comes close to the Nestorianism of which he was accused by Luther and of the consequences for the Supper that, as Cyril had indicated in his explanation of his eleventh anathema, were integral to Nestorius and his followers.[28] It follows that Zwingli regards the phrase "this is my body" to mean that this *signifies* the body.[29] In the clash with Luther, Zwingli so stressed the two-natures distinction that accusations of Nestorianism were hardly surprising.[30]

On the *communicatio idiomatum*, Zwingli argued that attributions to one of the natures of what is accomplished by the other are a figure of speech on the basis of the unity of the person of Christ and do not represent an actual transfer of attributes.[31] His most usual word in this connection was *alloiosis*, indicating that when we refer to one nature we also understand the other, or when we name both yet we understand only one. Consequently, Zwingli resisted Luther's belief in the ubiquity of Christ's humanity. This points to the root of the clash with Luther. While Luther held together the two natures to an extent that it was questionable whether he had done justice to the humanity, Zwingli distinguished them to the point that his grasp of the unity of the person was weak. This clash underlay the sacramental controversy.

In an early work, his *Exposition of the Articles* (1523), Zwingli held that the Eucharist strengthens faith, but he had abandoned this position when he wrote his *Commentary on True and False Religion* (1525).[32]

27. Zwingli, *True and False Religion*, 205.

28. Zwingli, *True and False Religion*, 199–211. For Cyril's eleventh anathema in his *Third Letter to Nestorius*, see chapter 4, page __. ### **Need page number** ###

29. Zwingli, *True and False Religion*, 226–30.

30. Stephens, *Zwingli*, 113–14.

31. Zwingli, *True and False Religion*, 205.

32. Stephens, *Zwingli*, 222.

His main argument in the debate at Marburg was focused on the ascension. For him, the body of Christ could be in only one place. After the ascension, he is at the right hand of God, *in loco*. Therefore, he cannot be corporeally present in the Eucharist. Neither can the omnipotence of God or the will of Christ make his body ubiquitous.[33] Repeatedly Zwingli had recourse to what he thought was the clear meaning of John 6:63, "the Spirit gives life, the flesh profits nothing." But he read this text, as he did wider theological issues, through the lens of his neo-Platonism that made it difficult for him to see how material entities could be the channel of spiritual realities.[34] He agreed that Christ is present in the Supper but could not accept that this was in a bodily form.[35] Christ's body is human and has human characteristics, and so is bound by the limitations of space and time.

In his short treatise *On the Lord's Supper* (1526), Zwingli accentuated the human nature, treating the two natures as virtually autonomous. He considers that Christ experiences this or that according to his natures rather than his person.[36] Accordingly, the ascension is in Christ's human nature only, so he is now absent and his body and blood cannot be present in the sacrament.[37] Only Christ's divine nature is ubiquitous, or else he would have had no need to ascend. Consequently, the body of the ascended Christ is in one place and cannot be present simultaneously in the Supper.[38] Therefore, the clause "this is my body" is a trope.[39] Geoffrey Bromiley agrees that "Zwingli did tend towards that isolation of the distinctive natures or aspects both of Christ himself and also of the Word and sacraments."[40]

These differences over the *communicatio idiomatum* highlight the significantly different Christologies of the two Reformers, which, in

33. Stephens, *Zwingli*, 238.

34. Robert Letham, "Baptism in the Writings of the Reformers," *SBET* 7, no. 2 (Autumn 1989): 21–44.

35. Stephens, *Zwingli*, 252.

36. G. W. Bromiley, ed., *Zwingli and Bullinger* (Westminster Press, 1953), 212.

37. Bromiley, *Zwingli and Bullinger*, 214–15.

38. Bromiley, *Zwingli and Bullinger*, 219–22.

39. Bromiley, *Zwingli and Bullinger*, 222–27.

40. Bromiley, *Zwingli and Bullinger*, 183.

turn and *inter alia*, impact their views of the Eucharist. Luther and Zwingli famously clashed at the Colloquy of Marburg (1529). The Lutherans and Reformed parted company on this issue, and subsequent colloquys at Malbronn (1564) and Montbéliard (1586), aimed at some kind of understanding, also reached an impasse.

James Atkinson pointed out that Luther was almost Eutychian, mingling divine and human, whereas Zwingli bordered on Nestorianism.[41] Luther had a strong doctrine of the hypostatic union; Zwingli's focus was on the distinctiveness of Christ's humanity, although his overall concentration was on his deity. K. J. Drake argues that in his writings after Marburg, Zwingli moved away from his earlier Nestorian tendency and developed a clearer and more robust understanding of the hypostatic union.[42] His attempt to exonerate Zwingli from the charge of Nestorianism before that, in his use of *alloiosis*, only partially succeeds. Drake's insistence that Zwingli was working from a Chalcedonian base overlooks the ambiguities in Chalcedon to which we referred earlier. For both Chalcedon and Zwingli, at the forefront were the two natures. To suggest, as Zwingli did, that the union was in any way to be seen as a figure of speech was at best a singularly questionable proposal.[43]

Lutheranism After Luther

Following Luther, two main strands of thought emerged. Johannes Brenz (1499–1570), while his views went through various stages,[44] in his main work on Christology, *De Personali Unione Duarum Naturam in Christo* (1561),[45] held that when the Word became flesh, all the majesty of his deity was poured into his human nature, the communication of divine attributes to the human nature of Christ beginning from

41. James Atkinson, *Martin Luther and the Birth of Protestantism* (1968; repr., John Knox Press, 1982), 269.

42. K. J. Drake, *The Flesh of the Word: The* Extra-Calvinisticum *from Zwingli to Early Orthodoxy* (Oxford University Press, 2021), 104–17.

43. Drake, *Flesh of the Word*, 70–71.

44. Richard Cross, *Communicatio Idiomatum: Reformation Christological Debates* (Oxford University Press, 2019), 101–16.

45. Johannes Brenz, *De Personali Unione Duarum Naturarum in Christo, et Ascensu Christi* (Tubingae: Ulrici Morhardi, 1561), 4–15.

conception. This occurred, he wrote, because of the inseparable union of deity and humanity.[46] He reasoned that the divine person and the human nature are the same person.[47] He held that "if the Son of Man has divine properties, so too must the human nature," such that "the human *nature* communicates its attributes to the divine *person*," while "the divine *person* communicates its (divine) attributes, some or all of them, to the human *nature*," and as a corollary, "any divine attribute possessed by the whole Christ—the person along with the human nature—must be possessed by the human nature."[48] The power that Christ was given after the resurrection he had beforehand.[49] Such ideas run up against the evidence of the Gospels that Christ shared our sorrows, griefs, and weaknesses, was hungry and thirsty, knew bereavement and disappointment, was in one place at one time, and expressed ignorance of certain future events. Johannes Brenz, aware of the problems, insisted that humanity is not changed into divinity, since the properties of both natures remain.[50] Moreover, he came to restrict the divine attributes that were communicated to the assumed human nature.[51] In terms of geometrical space, Christ is not everywhere.[52] The ascension was not to another corporeal place but was to the omnipotence and majesty of God.[53]

On the other hand, Martin Chemnitz (1522–86) produced a more subtle construction than Brenz and avoided some of his most evident weaknesses.[54] His *De Duabus Naturis in Christo* (1578),[55] and its English translation *The Two Natures of Christ* (1971),[56] was the most careful exposition of the Lutheran position.

46. Brenz, *De Personali Unione*, 4–7b.
47. Cross, *Communicatio Idiomatum*, 112; Brenz, *De Personali Unione*, 24.
48. Cross, *Communicatio Idiomatum*, 96.
49. Brenz, *De Personali Unione*, 7b.
50. Brenz, *De Personali Unione*, 11b; Cross, *Communicatio Idiomatum*, 111.
51. Cross, *Communicatio Idiomatum*, 145–52.
52. Brenz, *De Personali Unione*, 12a.
53. Brenz, *De Personali Unione*, 15a–b.
54. For some errors of Brenz, see Cross, *Communicatio Idiomatum*, 97.
55. Martin Chemnitz, *De Duabus Naturis in Christo: De Hypostatica Earum Unione: De Communicatione Idiomatum, et de Aliis Questionibus* (Lipsiae: Ramba, 1578).
56. Martin Chemnitz, *The Two Natures in Christ*, trans. J. A. O. Preus (1578; repr., Concordia, 1971).

Chemnitz considered there to be a threefold aspect to the communication of attributes. The first type, resulting at once from the hypostatic union, entails the attribution of properties of Christ's natures to his person *in concreto*, known as the *genus idiomaticum*.[57] Second are things attributed to the person according to both natures, when each nature performs in communion with the other what is proper to them, the *genus apotelesmaticum*.[58] Chemnitz's third category, the *genus maiestaticum*, is the most significant for our purposes. This is that "countless supernatural qualities and qualities even contrary to the common condition of human nature are given and communicated to Christ's human nature."[59] By this Christ, according to his human nature, is different from other humans in general or the saints in particular.[60]

According to Chemnitz, Scripture testifies that the humanity assumed in the incarnation retains its essential attributes but because of the hypostatic union is exalted above every name and given all power in heaven and earth, so that the flesh is life-giving.[61] Since Christ's divine nature dwells personally in the assumed nature, it would be blasphemous to think that in this hypostatic union the humanity of Christ had received nothing beyond its essential attributes, powers, and faculties. Scripture asserts that Christ was anointed above his fellows. These infused gifts are not the essential attributes of the divine nature but are *his workings outside the divine nature* infused into the human nature so that they inhere in it formally, habitually, and subjectively, an instrument suitable for the deity.[62] Omnipresence flows from this.[63] There are echoes here of the distinction between the essence of God and his workings expounded by the Cappadocians in the Trinitarian crisis of the fourth century, later in Orthodox theology expressed by Gregory

57. Chemnitz, *Two Natures*, 215–31.
58. Chemnitz, *Two Natures*, 231–40.
59. Chemnitz, *Two Natures*, 241–42. See Drake, *Flesh of the Word*, 218–19.
60. Drake, *Flesh of the Word*, 220.
61. Chemnitz, *Two Natures*, 243–44.
62. Chemnitz, *Two Natures*, 247–48.
63. Drake, *Flesh of the Word*, 221.

Palamas as a distinction between essence and energies. Chemnitz reinforces his comments by extensive citations from the church fathers.[64] These gifts are not only created, finite, or habitual gifts but the very attributes of the divine nature of the Christ, attributes belonging to the deity itself but given according to the assumed human nature. So Christ, according to his human nature, has been given omnipotence, which properly belongs to the divine nature.[65] The divinity has the kind of communion with the humanity that fire has when it communicates its essence and heat to burn iron, without any commingling. The glory of the only-begotten did not always reveal itself in its fullness through the assumed flesh at the time of his humiliation, but when the humiliation was laid aside *after the resurrection*, Christ was exalted according to the human nature and so entered glory.[66] Here there are echoes of Cyril's eleventh anathema against Nestorius's denial that the flesh and blood of Christ are life-giving, and of Paul's statement that the second Adam, risen from the dead, is "life-giving spirit" (1 Cor. 15:45). Chemnitz writes of a "real communication" of divine attributes, in distinction from a purely verbal communication, while at the same time distancing himself from an "essential" communication. In this way, he could say that Christ's humanity is really and truly omnipresent while not being essentially omnipresent—not omnipresent in itself, as it is intrinsically, but omnipresent according to the hypostatic union, by virtue of the communication. In this, Chemnitz saw the communication of divine attributes to the humanity as an act of Christ's will rather than a necessary element of the incarnation.[67]

Chemnitz was clear that there is no mixture or change in either nature.[68] The divine attributes communicated to the humanity are not possessed essentially by the human nature; otherwise, the divine nature would be commuted. Properties of one nature cannot become the properties of the other. Any idea of this essential

64. Chemnitz, *Two Natures*, 248–56.
65. Chemnitz, *Two Natures*, 259.
66. Chemnitz, *Two Natures*, 263–64.
67. Drake, *Flesh of the Word*, 221.
68. Chemnitz, *Two Natures*, 267.

communication of divine attributes must be rejected. There is no equalization of natures, no communication of essences or natures.[69] On the other hand, Chemnitz also rejected any denial that the majesty is communicated to the assumed nature, with the corollary that the humanity in the hypostatic union has no share in divine attributes. He also opposed the claim that the divine attributes relate only to the person and are given verbally to Christ only as man, the humanity having no communion in them at all.[70] Antiquity is united on this, he claimed,[71] while the Reformed have been evasive, saying that these gifts were given to the person of Christ but not to the human nature, as if the person exists outside the united natures, so that the person had something that either or both natures did not have.[72]

Chemnitz agreed that this is a mystery, received by us in faith.[73] It takes place through interpenetration, like fire in heated iron,[74] the whole majesty of Christ's deity shining forth in the humanity, working with it and through it so that the assumed nature can give life and rule over all things, with no commingling.[75] He cited the fathers profusely—Athanasius, Cyril, Luther, Justin, Ambrose, Eusebius, Theodoret, Cyril, Leo, and Constantinople III.[76] In sum, the communication flows out of the hypostatic union, not the other way around. This safeguards against the idea that the whole Trinity became incarnate.[77]

A. B. Bruce thought that Chemnitz has probably no theoretical difference from the Reformed.[78] In fact, I suggest, Chemnitz had a better grasp of the classic doctrine of the incarnation than Zwingli and many of the Reformed. His basic premise was the hypostatic union, rather than the two natures, a perspective in keeping with

69. Chemnitz, *Two Natures*, 270.
70. Chemnitz, *Two Natures*, 278–79.
71. Chemnitz, *Two Natures*, 280–82.
72. Chemnitz, *Two Natures*, 283.
73. Chemnitz, *Two Natures*, 288–89.
74. Chemnitz, *Two Natures*, 292.
75. Chemnitz, *Two Natures*, 293.
76. Chemnitz, *Two Natures*, 294–312.
77. Chemnitz, *Two Natures*, 305.
78. A. B. Bruce, *The Humiliation of Christ* (T&T Clark, 1905), 98.

Cyril and the ultimate patristic Christological resolution. His view of ubiquity was nuanced too. Christ *is able to be present* when, where, and how he pleases. This is a hypothetical or optional omnipresence, as Bruce calls it.[79] Chemnitz sees it as a logical deduction from the hypostatic union, after which the Logos is not outside the flesh. It follows that Christ's human nature is always intimately and inseparably present to the Logos, with the possibility of being present at will to any part of the creation.[80] Chemnitz maintained that in his state of humiliation, from cradle to cross, from womb to tomb, Christ only occasionally used these gifts but after his ascension entered their full use. Brenz, on the other hand, thought that in possessing these gifts from conception, he used them furtively.[81]

The Formula of Concord (1576)

The differences between Brenz and Chemnitz were the focus of heated debate within Lutheranism. The Formula of Concord attempted a resolution, with Chemnitz prominent. The result, in article 8, had all the hallmarks of a compromise. Opposing positions were placed side by side, and troublesome questions passed over in silence. No distinction was made between essential and accidental properties of the human nature. The underlying problems were unresolved.[82]

Article 8[83] stated the question in controversy, "whether the divine and human nature in the attributes of each are in mutual communication REALLY, that is, truly and in every fact and deed, in the person of Christ, and how far that communication extends." The sacramentarians, or the Reformed, the Formula claimed, consider that neither nature communicates to the other anything proper to it, but that the communication is purely nominal. This supposes that God has nothing in common with humanity, nor humanity with divinity, a charge of effective Nestorianism.

79. Bruce, *Humiliation of Christ*, 99.
80. Bruce, *Humiliation of Christ*, 100.
81. Bruce, *Humiliation of Christ*, 101–2; Drake, *Flesh of the Word*, 145–52.
82. Bruce, *Humiliation of Christ*, 104–6.
83. Philip Schaff, *The Creeds of Christendom* (Baker, 1966), 3:147–59.

Positively, the Formula affirmed that the natures are personally united so completely that the Son of God and Son of Man are one and the same. The natures are not mingled or changed but retain their own essential attributes. Therefore, the divine attributes of omniscience, omnipresence, and omnipotence never become attributes of the humanity. On the other hand, the union is not a conjunction whereby neither nature has anything personally in common with the other, for it is the highest communion that God has with man—like glowing iron, body and soul. Due to the personal union with the Son, God is man and man is God. Mary bore not a mere man but the true Son of God, and is rightly called the Mother of God. It was not a mere man that suffered and died but the person of the Son of God. He suffered according to his human nature, assumed into the unity of his divine person. According to his human nature, the Son of Man is exalted to the right hand of God. All this is classic orthodox Christology.

In his humiliation, Christ divested himself of his divine majesty and did not always use it until after the resurrection, when he laid aside the form of a servant, but not the human nature. Therefore, now he is omniscient, omnipotent, and omnipresent not only as God but also as man. Hence he can be present in his body and blood in the Supper according to the mode of the right hand of God. This presence is not physical but is true and substantial.

In turn, the Formula repudiated, *inter alia*, the position that the personal union is only a figure of speech and that the *communicatio idiomatum* is only verbal, without any corresponding reality. It rejected the notion that the humanity has become infinite and so is everywhere present with the divine nature, or that it has been made equal to the divine. It denied the claim that it is impossible for Christ to be in more places than one with his body, that humanity alone suffered for us and the Son of God had no communication with the human nature, or that he is present to us only by his divinity. It also rejected those who assert that the Son does not accomplish omnipotent works in and with his humanity, and that according to his humanity he is incapable of the properties of the divine nature, that the power given to Christ according to his humanity has no communication with the omnipotence of God, that there are limits on what he can know, so that Christ even now does not have a perfect knowledge of God and his works and cannot know what has been from eternity, what is everywhere, and what will be to eternity.

Heinrich Schmid sums up Lutheran Christology—while concentrated later than 1600—"a real communion of both natures is thereby asserted, in consequence of which the two natures sustain no merely outward relations to each other"[84] but "a true and real impartation and communion."[85]

Bruce makes some telling criticisms. Why, he asks, is the communication not reciprocal? He correctly points to its being one way, from divine to human, for there is no corresponding claim that attributes of Christ's humanity are communicated to his deity.[86] This, he says, threatens the humanity of Christ, for the humiliation, while soteriologically necessary, is Christologically impossible.[87] This is evident, I suggest, since Christ, if even only potentially omnipresent, omnipotent, and omniscient according to his humanity, can hardly be said to have been in a state of humiliation! As Bruce concludes, in its zeal for the deification of Christ's humanity, the Lutheran Christology robs us of the incarnation.[88] This is telling in connection with Brenz's ideas that the communication of divine attributes was from conception; it is less so with Chemnitz's more careful distinction between the time before and after the resurrection.

Strikingly, Philip Melanchthon (1497–1560) moved to a Reformed position over the years. In his 1521 *Loci Communes*, he wrote nothing on the person of Christ, since he was concerned with the works of Christ and the immediate issues in the Reformation. He discussed the bodily ascension in his commentary on Colossians, while expounding the third chapter.[89] The 1555 *Loci* are clearly Reformed,

84. Heinrich Schmid, *The Doctrinal Theology of the Evangelical Lutheran Church*, 3rd ed. (1899; repr., Augsburg Press, 1961), 309.

85. Schmid, *Doctrinal Theology*, 310.

86. Bruce, *Humiliation of Christ*, 106–7.

87. Bruce, *Humiliation of Christ*, 107–12.

88. Bruce, *Humiliation of Christ*, 113–14.

89. Philip Melanchthon, "Enarratio Epistolae Pauli ad Colossenses Praelecta" (1556), in *Operum Omnium* (Wittenberg: Zacharia Schürerio et eius Sociis, 1601), 4:358.

especially in the section *De Coena Domini*.[90] He rejected the communication of attributes from one nature to another.[91]

Reformed Christology

Bruce summed up the characteristics of Reformed Christology in contrast to the Lutheran in its stress on the reality of Christ's humanity and the state of humiliation.[92] As in orthodox Christology, Christ had two natures, a twofold mind, and a twofold will. In virtue of the hypostatic union, whatever is said of Christ is said of his person, sometimes in respect of both natures, sometimes in respect of one or the other. In terms of the divine nature, the difference is between concealment in the state of humiliation and open manifestation after the ascension. In his exaltation, the humanity lost some accidental properties—hunger, thirst, and the like—while others are perfectly developed—glory, majesty, strength, wisdom, and virtue—and the essential properties retained.[93]

Bruce thought that the differences from Lutheran Christology relate to the nature of the union. The Lutherans accused the Reformed of viewing the natures as being like two pieces of plywood glued together without any real communion. The Reformed, for their part, stressed the communication of charisms—wisdom and virtue as qualities produced by the Logos through his Spirit.[94] Bruce's questions were these: How does this do justice to the union? Why should not these graces result from the union of the Logos with the humanity? Why should they be communicated in a roundabout way by the Holy Spirit? Does this not make the union itself purely external?[95] This is a pressing matter, as we will see, for it raises the specter of Nestorianism.

Prominent in Reformed Christology is the Son's emptying (*exinanition*), applied to his divine nature, not by divestiture but by

90. Philip Melanchthon, *Loci Communes Theologici* (1555; repr., Basel: Ioannem Operinum, 1562), 41–44, 402–17.

91. Clyde L. Manschreck, trans. and ed., *Melanchthon on Christian Doctrine: Loci Communes 1555* (Baker, 1965), 34.

92. Bruce, *Humiliation of Christ*, 114–16.

93. Bruce, *Humiliation of Christ*, 118–20.

94. Bruce, *Humiliation of Christ*, 120–23.

95. Bruce, *Humiliation of Christ*, 124.

concealment (*occultatio*). From this arose the idea of a double life of the Logos—the *logos totus extra Jesum* and the *logos totus in Jesu* —one unaffected by the incarnation, another self-controlled in the man Jesus Christ.[96]

John Calvin (1509–64)

In his *Institutes*, Calvin asked why it was necessary for the mediator to be God and become man. He related the incarnation to the whole of redemption: "The situation would surely have been hopeless had the very majesty of God not descended to us, since it was not in our power to ascend to him. Hence, it was necessary for the Son of God to become for us 'Immanuel, that is, God with us' [Isa. 7:14; Matt. 1:23], and in such a way that his divinity and our human nature might by mutual connection grow together (*ut mutua coniunctione eius divinitas et hominum natura inter se coalescerent*)."[97] Here *coalesco* implies the ontological priority of the natures rather than the person, which runs counter to the eventual conclusions of Constantinople III and has a Nestorian ring to it. So Christ took "what was ours as to impart what was his to us, and to make what was his by nature ours by grace."[98]

Calvin continued, drawing the indissoluble connection between incarnation and atonement:

> The second requirement of our reconciliation with God was this: that man, who by his disobedience had become lost, should by way of remedy counter it with obedience, satisfy God's judgment, and pay the penalties for sin. Accordingly our Lord came forth as true man and took the person and name of Adam in order to take Adam's place in obeying the Father, to present our flesh as the price of satisfaction to God's righteous judgment, and, in the same flesh, to pay the penalty we had deserved. In short, since neither as God alone could he feel death, nor as man alone could he overcome it, he coupled human nature with divine that to

96. Bruce, *Humiliation of Christ*, 125–26.
97. John Calvin, *Institutes*, 2.12.1; *OS*, 3:437.
98. Calvin, *Institutes*, 2.12.2.

> atone for sin he might submit the weakness of the one to death; and that, wrestling with death by the power of the other nature, he might win victory for us.

Thus, in the same place, "our common nature with Christ is the pledge of our fellowship with the Son of God; and clothed with our flesh he vanquished sin and death together that the victory and triumph might be ours."[99]

Later, Calvin expounded the *communicatio idiomatum*. Christ was free from all corruption not just because he was born of the virgin but

> because he was sanctified by the Spirit that the generation might be pure and undefiled as would have been true before Adam's fall. . . . Here is something marvelous: the Son of God descended from heaven in such a way that, without leaving heaven, he willed to be borne in the virgin's womb, to go about the earth, and to hang upon the cross; yet he continually filled the world even as he had done from the beginning!

Calvin stressed that the Son was not restricted to the human nature he assumed into union but that he transcended it. This is what Lutherans were to call the *extra Calvinisticum*.[100]

Calvin's stress was on the two natures, however, to the extent that he appears to flirt with Nestorianism. Christ's divinity is so joined and united with his humanity (*ita coniunctam unitamque humanitati divinitatem*) that each retains its distinctive nature unimpaired, and yet these two natures constitute one Christ (*ex duabus illis unus Christus constituatur*).[101] Calvin appears to equalize the natures, with the possible implication that the humanity existed prior to the union insofar as the union is formed out of the two. This impression is reinforced by his considering the *communicatio* to be merely a figure of speech. In the same section, he wrote that Scripture sometimes attributes to Christ what applies solely to his

99. Calvin, *Institutes*, 2.12.3.
100. Calvin, *Institutes*, 2.13.4.
101. Calvin, *Institutes*, 2.14.1.

humanity, sometimes what belongs to his divinity, sometimes what embraces both natures but fits neither alone. "And they so earnestly express this union of the two natures that is in Christ as sometimes to interchange them. This figure of speech is called by the ancient writers 'the communicating of properties.'" What Calvin called a "figure of speech" the Lutherans considered a reality.

While Calvin considered that passages that comprehend both natures at once set forth Christ's true substance most of all—such as John 1:29; 5:21–23; 8:12; 9:5; 10:11; 15:1—he remarks, puzzlingly, that "the name 'Lord' exclusively belongs to the person of Christ only in so far as it represents a degree midway between God and us (*Nec alio respectu peculiariter in Christi personam competit Domini nomen, nisi quatenus medium gradum statuit inter Deum et nos*)."[102] Besides being an astonishing and rather disturbing comment, it seems that Calvin thought the person is a union of two natures rather than an action of the eternal Son in assuming human nature.

This tendency is particularly evident in Calvin's comments on 1 Corinthians 15:27. There he stated that at the end, Christ "will transfer it [the kingdom] in some way or other (*quodammodo*) from his humanity to his glorious divinity,"[103] as if the natures have some degree of autonomy and are active agents in themselves. It is this that lies at the root of the Reformed's attributing the union of natures and the works performed by Christ to the Holy Spirit rather than to the union established in the Son himself, for if the incarnation was simply a coalescence of two natures, the union is subsequent to the natures, almost a conjunction, and so requires an outside agent to effect and maintain it. The proximity to Nestorianism is clear.

Calvin agreed with Zwingli that the human body of Christ is in one place, in heaven. In his *Second Defence of the Pious and Orthodox Faith Concerning the Sacraments in Answer to the Calumnies of Joachim Westphal* (1556), he wrote, with a play on words, that to say as Westphal does that "the body which the Son of God once assumed, and

102. Calvin, *Institutes*, 2.14.3.

103. John Calvin, *Calvin's Commentaries: The First Epistle of Paul the Apostle to the Corinthians*, ed. Thomas F. Torrance and David W. Torrance, trans. John W. Fraser (Eerdmans, 1960), 327.

which . . . he raised to heavenly glory is ατοπος, (without place) is indeed very ατοπος, (absurd)."[104] Rather, Calvin said, "in order to gain possession of Christ he must be sought in heaven," since "the body . . . which he once offered in sacrifice, must now be contained in heaven, as Peter declares."[105] This is so because the body, while it is "carried above the heavens is exempt from the common order of nature, it does not however cease to be a true body."[106] He differed from Zwingli in that Christ "not only fills heaven and earth, but also miraculously unites us to himself in one body, so that the flesh, though it remains in heaven, is our food." Westphal had argued that Calvin shut Christ up in heaven as Zwingli did.[107]

In reply, Calvin argued that "if believers would find Christ in heaven, they must begin with the word and sacraments."[108] Thus, "Christ, by the incomprehensible agency of his Spirit, perfectly unites things disjoined by space, and thus feeds our souls with his flesh, though his flesh does not leave heaven, and we keep creeping on the earth."[109] So Calvin went beyond Zwingli in asserting that the distance between Christ's body in heaven and us on earth is overcome by the Holy Spirit. In distinction from Luther and the Lutherans, however, this feeding does not occur in direct relation to the incarnation, to the hypostatic union and the communion of natures resulting from it, but by the distinct agency of the Spirit. Union with Christ is not a consequence flowing directly from the incarnation.

In his *Clear Exposition of Sound Doctrine Concerning the True Partaking of the Flesh and Blood of Christ in the Holy Supper in Order to Dissipate the Mists of Tileman Heshusius* (1561), Calvin was even clearer. Here he attributed the life we receive to the flesh of Christ, with the Spirit as the agent who effects this. Hence, he says that the flesh Christ

104. Henry Beveridge, ed., *Selected Works of John Calvin*, vol. 2, *Tracts and Letters, Part 2* (1849; repr., Baker, 1983), 282.

105. Beveridge, *Tracts and Letters*, 2:285.

106. Beveridge, *Tracts and Letters*, 2:290.

107. Beveridge, *Tracts and Letters*, 2:295.

108. Beveridge, *Tracts and Letters*, 2:296.

109. Beveridge, *Tracts and Letters*, 2:299.

assumed is life-giving, since it is the source of spiritual life for us,[110] a clear Cyrillian theme. While the body of Christ is absent in terms of place, we have a real spiritual participation in it, "every obstacle from distance being surmounted by his divine energy."[111] Calvin acknowledged that it is incomprehensible to us how the body of Christ is in one place but yet the person of Christ is omnipresent.[112] He mentioned his adoption of the scholastic dictum *totus ubique sed non totum*, "the whole Christ everywhere but not wholly." Hesshus, he maintains, perverts what he had said by stating that the human nature is everywhere, and Christ's human nature can exist in different places wherever he chooses.[113] On the contrary, "to our having substantial communion with the flesh of Christ there is no necessity for any change of place, since, by the secret virtue of the Spirit, he infuses his life into us from heaven. Distance does not at all prevent Christ from dwelling in us, or us from being one with him, since the efficacy of the Spirit surmounts all natural obstacles."[114] From Scripture it is clear that the body of Christ is finite. "We deny not that the whole and entire Christ in the person of the mediator fills heaven and earth. I say whole, not wholly (totus, non totum) because it were absurd to apply this to his flesh. The hypostatic union of the two natures is not equivalent to a communication of the immensity of the Godhead to the flesh, since the peculiar properties of both natures are perfectly accordant with unity of person."[115]

Citing previous work, Calvin stated that while the humanity of Christ is in heaven, the right hand of God does not signify a place but rather the power that the Father has given Christ to rule the cosmos. "For Christ by his ascension to heaven entered on the possession of the dominion given him by the Father." He is far removed in terms of bodily presence, "yet fills all things . . . by the agency of his Spirit."[116]

110. Beveridge, *Tracts and Letters*, 2:507.
111. Beveridge, *Tracts and Letters*, 2:510.
112. Beveridge, *Tracts and Letters*, 2:514.
113. Beveridge, *Tracts and Letters*, 2:515.
114. Beveridge, *Tracts and Letters*, 2:518–19.
115. Beveridge, *Tracts and Letters*, 2:557–58.
116. Beveridge, *Tracts and Letters*, 2:558–59.

"For wherever the right hand of God, which embraces heaven and earth, is diffused, there the spiritual presence of Christ himself is present by his boundless energy, though his body must be contained in heaven, according to the declaration of Peter."[117] As a parting shot, Calvin retorted that "when he [Hesshus] says that certain properties are common to the flesh of Christ and to the Godhead, I call for a demonstration which he has not yet attempted."[118]

Extra Calvinisticum

Calvin's insistence, shared by the Reformed, that the Son is not confined to the humanity he assumed was to be dubbed by the Lutherans "that most damnable Calvinistic beyond (*extra-Calvinisticum*)." Yet it was hardly an innovation. David Willis, investigating Calvin's sources, unearthed extensive evidence from patristic and medieval writers[119] to conclude that it represented "a consensus of the ancient fathers."[120] Indeed, he adds, "the term 'extra-Calvinisticum' is not an exclusive mark distinguishing the Christology of Calvin from other Christologies of the one Catholic Church. . . . Rather, the doctrine sustains the correct Catholic interpretations of the Biblical witness to Christ."[121] He considers that "the fact is that the 'extra-Calvinisticum' is a medium for expressing the unity of the person of Jesus Christ without displacing mystery with speculation."[122] Consequently, "the 'extra-Calvinisticum,' because of its widespread and ancient usage could just as well be called the 'extra-Catholicum.'"[123]

Notwithstanding this, the pressure of debate may have driven Calvin on occasion to the type of unguarded comment to which we have drawn attention. It appears that the Lutherans had a stronger

117. Beveridge, *Tracts and Letters*, 2:561.

118. Beveridge, *Tracts and Letters*, 2:561.

119. For instance, he cites Lombard, Aquinas, Duns Scotus, Occam and Biel, Lefevre, Augustine, Origen, Theodore of Mopsuestia, and Athanasius. Edward David Willis, *Calvin's Catholic Christology: The Function of the So-Called Extra-Calvinisticum in Calvin's Theology* (Brill, 1966), 26–58.

120. Willis, *Calvin's Catholic Christology*, 49.

121. Willis, *Calvin's Catholic Christology*, 99.

122. Willis, *Calvin's Catholic Christology*, 100.

123. Willis, *Calvin's Catholic Christology*, 153.

grasp of the patristic doctrine of the hypostatic union as this had come to expression in the sixth century at Constantinople II, but the Reformed had understood better the distinctness of the natures. Forces of controversy, however, have a habit of polarizing opinions.[124]

More recently, Andrew McGinnis unearthed an even wider range of patristic and medieval authors who held that the incarnate Son also existed *extra carnem* ("beyond the flesh"), including Origen, Eustathius of Caesarea, Athanasius, Eusebius of Caesarea, Ephrem the Syrian, Gregory of Nyssa, Augustine, Peter Chrysologus, Cyril, Theodoret, Fulgentius of Ruspe, John of Damascus, Peter Lombard, Thomas Aquinas, and Gabriel Biel. McGinnis himself focuses on Cyril and Aquinas, good choices because of their own respective influences and their stature as exponents of Christology.[125]

Calvin's position was substantially adopted by Pietro Martire Vermigli and Theodore Beza and became standard in the Reformed churches. This is hardly surprising, given its being in all salient features the same as the historic catholic teaching of the church, East and West.

Pietro Martire Vermigli (1499–1562)

Vermigli's Christology was unfolded in his *Dialogus de Utraque in Christo Naturae* (1561).[126] Vermigli was keenly aware of the reality of Christ's humanity in its postascension state. The dialogue accurately portrays the differences between the two confessions. He insists that we cannot remove mass, size, bodily disposition, parts, features, and limbs, which are part of the human makeup, from the body of Christ. The human body is abolished when one takes away such things.[127]

124. See further Heiko Oberman, "The 'Extra' Dimension in the Theology of Calvin," *JEH* 21, no. 1 (1970): 43–64.

125. Andrew M. McGinnis, *The Son of God Beyond the Flesh: A Historical and Theological Study of the Extra-Calvinisticum* (Bloomsbury, 2014). On Cyril, 15–45; Aquinas, 47–72; Lutheran and Reformed, 73–92; decline of interest in the *extra carnem* until the end of the nineteenth century, 125–48; Barth and retrieval, 149–79.

126. Pietro Martire Vermigli, *Dialogus de Utraque in Christo Natura: Illustratur & Coenae Dominicæ Negotium,Perspicuisque . . . Testimoniis Demonstratur Corpus Christi Non Esse Ubique* (Tiguri: C. Froschoverus, 1561).

127. Peter Martyr Vermigli, *The Peter Martyr Library*, vol. 2, *Dialogue on the Two*

Vermigli affirmed the adherence of the Reformed churches to the first six ecumenical councils. His notional Lutheran interlocutor replied that Vermigli didn't want to affirm their consequences. Since the deity and humanity are inseparable in the one person of Christ, wherever the Godhead is there is the humanity. Vermigli rejected these conclusions; they exhibit the flaw of equivocation. The Lutheran, he said, understands the human nature as though the whole of the divine nature were included in it or as though the human nature were filled out and spread out equally with the divine. This is not far from Eutyches, who held to only one nature.[128] Rather, Vermigli believed that the humanity is inseparable from the divinity, so that "it in no wise restricts the divinity within its own narrow limits nor so expands itself so that it fills every place where the divinity exists." The Lutheran opponent cannot avoid a commingling between the natures. He thinks the person is torn apart if the deity is held to be where the humanity is not present. But, Vermigli maintained, while the body of Christ is in heaven and no longer dwells on earth, still the Son of God is in the church and everywhere: "he is never so freed from his human nature that he does not have it engrafted in him and joined in the unity of his person in the place where the human nature is."[129]

Vermigli used a variety of arguments—the relationship of head to body, the orbits of planets—to argue that the unity of things is not destroyed when there is an intervening spatial distance. He denied that this means setting the deity off from the humanity. The divine nature is everywhere by virtue of its immensity and always has the humanity conjoined to it. But the humanity is not present in every place that the divinity fills. The divine Word fills all things, but the humanity hypostatically united to it is confined to its own place. The Lutheran countered by claiming that this means that Vermigli posits two persons, one *hypostasis* where the humanity is

Natures in Christ, trans. and ed. John Patrick Donnelly, Sixteenth Century Essays and Studies 31 (Thomas Jefferson University Press and Sixteenth Century Journal Publishers, 1995), 12.

128. Vermigli, *Dialogue*, 23.

129. Vermigli, *Dialogue*, 24.

united to the deity and another where the deity is spread outside the human nature.[130] Vermigli had none of this. The unity of the person is retained in such a way that the properties of the natures remain distinct, but not mixed.[131] He preached neither a separation of the deity from the humanity nor vice versa, he insisted. Wherever the human nature is, it is sustained in the divine person. The deity is not limited by the human body, since it fills all things.[132]

On the properties of the natures in Christ, Vermigli made copious references to the church fathers,[133] Cyril, John of Antioch, Leo, Theodoret, Ambrose, and Augustine.[134] He referred to Cyril's speaking of Christ's dying according to his humanity, the nature that the Word made its own through the incarnation, suffering, and dying.[135] He cited Augustine, writing to Dardanus,[136] that scriptural statements are proper to one of Christ's natures so that they cannot be attributed to the other without allowances for their manner of speaking.[137] Further, he indicated that Cyril's *Fifth Dialogue on the Trinity*[138] warns against attributing to Christ's humanity qualities uniquely belonging to the Godhead, or human attributes to the divine nature. Instead, Cyril urged his readers to "cultivate a terminology that distinguishes and befits each one."[139]

From this, Vermigli discussed the Lutheran commitment to ubiquity.[140] The Lutheran asks whether, if we grant to the humanity, because of the hypostatic union, life-giving, sanctifying power, why not ubiquity? Vermigli replies that while such faculties do not destroy human nature but perfect it, it is impossible to make humanity coextensive with the Godhead without making it infinite

130. Vermigli, *Dialogue*, 24–25.
131. Vermigli, *Dialogue*, 26.
132. Vermigli, *Dialogue*, 28.
133. Vermigli, *Dialogue*, 39–89.
134. Vermigli, *Dialogue*, 51–59.
135. Vermigli, *Dialogue*, 61–65.
136. *PL*, 33:835.
137. Vermigli, *Dialogue*, 66; *PL*, 33:835.
138. *PG*, 75:973.
139. Vermigli, *Dialogue*, 67.
140. Vermigli, *Dialogue*, 89–107.

and so destroying it.[141] The opponent insisted that Lutherans do not believe that the human nature is everywhere intrinsically. Instead, the Word communicates that power to it in the hypostatic union. Citing Brenz, the body of Christ does not fill all things as a human body but as an assumed body. Vermigli responded by stating that the divine *hypostasis* does not rob the assumed body of being a real human body.[142] The Lutheran then mentioned the three types of ubiquity held by Luther: *localem*, *repletivam*, and *personalem*. After the incarnation, it necessarily follows that the humanity assumed into the unity of Christ's person is everywhere by a personal ubiquity (*ubiquitate personali*). Vermigli thought this very strange.[143]

Vermigli wrote that Christ is not human in heaven before the ascension. The Lutherans must show that Christ could have ascended according to his humanity if he was already present there. After all, someone who is everywhere doesn't have anywhere to go! The divine *hypostasis* of Christ could not ascend because he was infinite and already occupied everything. But the humanity has fixed dimensions and truly ascended into heaven. His body was not in the tomb. Christ was not with Lazarus when he died. For the Lutherans, given their notion of ubiquity, the ascension was only in appearance and for display.[144]

On the life-giving flesh of Christ, received in the Supper, Vermigli strongly echoed Cyril. The flesh of Christ is life-giving in virtue of its having been taken into union and glorified. The faculty of giving life is not a property of the human nature; it is intrinsic to deity. But Christ's flesh is joined to his divine nature (*Christi caro secum habet coniunctam naturam divinam*). Therefore, while we do not worship the flesh, we worship the Son of God, with his flesh (*nil obstat quo minus una cum Filio Dei etiam cuius caro adoretur, quam de ventre virginis assumpsit*).[145] The primary reference of things predicated of

141. Vermigli, *Dialogue*, 89.
142. Vermigli, *Dialogue*, 90.
143. Vermigli, *Dialogue*, 91.
144. Vermigli, *Dialogue*, 107–11.
145. Pietro Martire Vermigli, *Dialogus de Utraque in Christo Natura* (Tiguri: C. Froschoverus, 1575), 45b.

Christ is to his person (*ipsa persona*); then, following that, according to natures (*deinde animo prudenter contemplandae sunt duae naturae ac proprietates distribuendae, ut illis conveniunt*). Hence, he is the Son of God according to the seed of David on the one hand and the Lord of glory crucified on the other.[146]

After the Colloquy of Malbronn (1564), the Lutherans called their opponents *Calviniani* rather than *Zwingliani*.[147] At Malbronn, Olevian introduced the figure of Antwerp and the ocean to defend the Reformed position, the ocean representing the Son of God, who exists also beyond the bounds of the flesh he assumed.[148]

The Colloquy of Montbéliard (1586)

The Christological issues increasingly assumed prominence in this controversy, since it was there that the underlying sacramental differences lay. As Jill Raitt observes, "From the Maulbronn Colloquy 1564 through the bitter battles about the meaning of *kenōsis* in the first quarter of the seventeenth century, discussions of the Lord's Supper, which meant discussions of the manner of Christ's presence, became christological arguments."[149] At Montbéliard, the chief antagonists, Jacob Andraeus for the Lutherans and Theodore Beza for the Reformed, failed to reach agreement. For Andraeus, there was not much difference in Christ before and after the resurrection, because of the communication of divine attributes to the human nature.[150] To him, Reformed analogies, such as the comparison between Antwerp and the ocean, seemed incongruous.[151] Behind these lay the intention to state that the humanity is finite or it is not humanity, even when hypostatically united to the infinite Creator. From 1586, this *extra* was seen by the Lutherans as definitively Calvinist.[152] This meant that for the Lutherans, the Son does

146. Vermigli, *Dialogus* (1575), 44b–45.

147. Willis, *Calvin's Catholic Christology*, 11.

148. Willis, *Calvin's Catholic Christology*, 15.

149. Jill Raitt, *The Colloquy of Montbéliard: Religion and Politics in the Sixteenth Century* (Oxford University Press, 1993), 110.

150. Raitt, *Colloquy of Montbéliard*, 84.

151. Willis, *Calvin's Catholic Christology*, 16–18.

152. Willis, *Calvin's Catholic Christology*, 18.

not exist beyond the bounds of the assumed humanity, which in turn entails the humanity's ubiquity.

Theodore Beza (1519–1605)

We will consider Beza's comments on the debates at Montbéliard.[153] Beza strongly reacted to the calumny that he acknowledged only a verbal *communicatio idiomatum* in Christ, not a real one.[154] It is verbal, he wrote, only insofar as it is a form of predication (*genus praedicationis*) on account of the unity of the person, by which concrete attributes of either nature are attributed to the indivisible person. We call Chemnitz's claim, he said, that the gifts communicated to the humanity of Christ are immense to be *falsam, impiam & blasphemam*.[155] He denied that the hypostatic union negates the human nature or that the divine properties are communicated to it. Christ's elevation to the right hand of God is not the result of the incarnation as such but occurred at the end of the time of humiliation. The presence of Christ's flesh in the Eucharist is due to the words of institution, not to the hypostatic union. The substance of Christ's body is now in heaven and absent from earth. Beza accused Andraeus of confusing and mixing the deity and humanity.[156] Christ's humanity receives nothing from the divinity, nor vice versa.[157] This sounds close to Nestorianism, as unsatisfactory as the Lutheran position, more a conjunction of two natures than an incarnation.

Karl Barth has an important discussion on these issues, including copious references to fathers who held that the Word existed beyond the limits of the flesh that he had taken into union.[158]

153. Theodore Beza, *Ad Acta Colloquii Montisbelgardensis Responsionis*, 3rd ed. (Geneva: Ioannes le Preux, 1589), 79–80, 163–67.

154. Beza, *Responsionis*, 17–18.

155. Beza, *Responsionis*, 80.

156. Beza, *Responsionis*, 164.

157. Beza, *Responsionis*, 167.

158. Karl Barth, *CD*, II/1:163–70. He references Athanasius, *De incarn*, 17; Gregory of Nyssa, *Orat. Cat*, 10; Augustine, *Civ Dei*, 9.15.2. "When he chose to be in the form of a servant, and lower than the angels, that he might be our mediator, he remained higher than the angels, in the form of God." *NPNF*[1], 2:174; John of Damascus, *Ekdos*, 3.7; Thomas Aquinas, *ST*, 3:5:2, ad.1.

He thought, however, that "the Reformed failed to show convincingly how far the *extra* does not involve the assumption of a twofold Christ . . . and therefore a dissolution of the natures and the hypostatic union. . . . In short it cannot be denied that the Reformed *totus intra et extra* offers at least as many difficulties as the Lutheran *totus intra*."[159]

McGinnis draws attention to a revival of interest in the *extra carnem* in the past century after a period of eclipse.[160] This renewed focus was instigated by Barth (151–55), although he was somewhat equivocal about its validity.[161] It has been alleged that Barth denied the *logos asarkos*, that the Son is also beyond the flesh, but this cannot be sustained. McGinnis refers to Darren Sumner[162] and Bruce McCormack, the latter of whom correctly argued that Barth considered that Jesus Christ did not reject the *Logos asarkos/Logos ensarkos* distinction.[163] What is distinctive about Barth is that he uses humiliation and exaltation as simultaneous rather than successive periods, which enables him to take this position, with the result that the Son is never limited to human form and never ceases to rule the universe. This has backing from the settled conclusion of the one identical subject of the incarnation, that Jesus of Nazareth, in terms of personal identity, is the eternal Son of the Father, seen in the repeated phrase "the same" in the Definition of Chalcedon.

Calvin and the Son as *Autotheos*[164]

Later in his career, Calvin was forced by disputes with Italian anti-Nicenes to assert the deity of the Son and the Holy Spirit in the

159. Barth, *CD*, II/1:170.

160. McGinnis, *Son of God Beyond the Flesh*. See Myk Habets, "Putting the 'Extra' Back into Calvinism," *SJT* 62, no. 4 (2009): 441–56.

161. McGinnis, *Son of God Beyond the Flesh*, 151–55; cf. Barth, *CD*, I/2:165, IV/1:181.

162. Darren O. Sumner, "The Twofold Life of the Word: Karl Barth's Critical Reception of the *Extra Calvinisticum*," *IJST* 15, no. 1 (2013): 42–57.

163. Bruce L. McCormack, "Seek God Where He May Be Found: A Response to Edwin Chr. Van Driel," *SJT* 60 (2007): 62–79.

164. The substance of this section occurred in Robert Letham, *The Holy Trinity: In Scripture, History, Theology, and Worship*, rev. and expanded ed. (P&R Publishing, 2019), 297–99.

strongest terms possible. His critics were Michael Servetus, George Blandrata, and Valentine Gentile. These, together with Faustus Socini and his nephew Laelio Socini, were the vanguard of what was to become the Socinian movement, which opposed virtually every major doctrine of the Christian faith. Gentile taught that the Father alone is *autotheos*, and so the Son and the Spirit are of a different essence from the Father. Calvin wrote in opposition to Gentile, in his *Impietas Valentini Gentilis Detecta et Palam Traducta*, where he frequently referred to the Son as *autotheos*, God of himself.[165] By this he opposed any idea that the Son receives his deity from the Father. Rather, he has his deity from himself, just as the Father does.

Calvin's claim raised opposition in Roman Catholic circles. Critics alleged that Calvin was failing to distinguish the Son from the Father, and so falling into Sabellianism, or else—if distinguishing them—he was arguing for another *principium* ("beginning") than the Father, thereby coming close to Manichaeism. But Rome's leading contemporary theologian and apologist, Robert Bellarmine, gave a measured assessment. He recognized that in terms of the classic Trinitarian dogma, Calvin was orthodox. He was introducing a novelty, but simply in terminology, the manner of speech (*modus loquendi*), while defending the true doctrine.[166] Calvin, Bellarmine agreed, erred in his manner of speech, particularly in *Institutes*, 1.13.19 and 23 and in his treatise against Gentile, where he called the Son *autotheos* and the phrase in the Creed of Nicaea (325), "God of God," a hard saying. "However, when I examine the matter and carefully scrutinize Calvin's thoughts I am not so bold to pronounce him to be in error, since he teaches the Son to be of himself in respect of essence, not of person, and he is seen to speak well that the person is begotten by the Father, and the essence not begotten . . . but to be from itself." The reason why Calvin said that the Son is *autotheos*, Bellarmine suggested, is that he was driven to it by Gentile, who constantly pronounced that the Father alone is *autotheos*, meaning that he alone had the uncreated, divine essence, the Son

165. *CO*, 9:368–70.

166. Robert Bellarmine, "Secunda Controversia Generalis de Christo," in *Disputationum de Controversiis Christianae Fidei Adversus Haereticos* (Rome, 1832), 1:307–10.

and the Spirit being of a different essence produced by the Father.[167] Bellarmine went on to make some heavy criticisms of Calvin and his disciples on other matters, but on these vital points he pronounced him in error only in his way of speaking.

What did Calvin mean by this term? On the premise of the orthodox Trinitarian teaching that God is one, and indivisible, it follows that all three persons are in themselves and together the one identical and undivided being of God. Thus, the Son cannot be said to derive his deity from the Father, while in terms of the relations of the three, the Son is from the Father. Gentile had argued that only the Father has deity of himself and that thus the other two persons are of a different essence from the Father. Calvin was not introducing anything radically new, for as we will see, he reinforced his opposition to Gentile with reference to the fathers. It is clear that Calvin expressed in the strongest way the full, unabridged deity of the three persons.[168]

The Essence and the Persons

Where does that leave the classic teaching that the Son is begotten by the Father from eternity? Gentile maintained that Calvin could not have his cake and eat it—he could not hold Christ to be *autotheos* and also confess the Niceno-Constantinopolitan faith, which asserted that he is "light of light, true God of true God." According to Gentile's thinking, eternal generation and procession were incompatible with the Son and the Spirit's being *autotheos*. Here Calvin had recourse to the equally classic teaching of Gregory of Nazianzus, followed by Augustine, that the creedal phrases are characteristics of the persons, not the essence. Behind this lies the fact that the persons are each and together identical with the one essence but that in terms of their relations, they are not identical to

167. Bellarmine, "Secunda Controversia," 1:307–8.

168. For an extensive and, to my mind, definitive assessment of Calvin's assertion that the Son is *autotheos* (God of himself), together with comprehensive discussion of secondary literature, see Richard A. Muller, "Trinity and the Son's Aseity: Formulation and Debate in Calvin and Reformed Orthodox y," in *Understanding the Divine in Early Modern Reformed Theology* (Reformation Heritage Books, 2024), 71–131. Especially important is the distinction drawn in Reformed orthodoxy, which Muller highlights, between generation and communication of essence.

one another. Here Calvin wrote of the relations that are peculiar to the several persons:

> Indeed, if we hold fast to what has been sufficiently shown above from Scripture—that the essence of the one God is simple and undivided, and that it belongs to the Father, the Son, and the Spirit; and on the other hand that by a certain characteristic the Father differs from the Son, and the Son from the Spirit—the gate will be closed not only to Arius and Sabellius but to other ancient authors of errors.[169]

Thus, for the Son, "with respect to his deity his being is from himself" and "whoever says that the Son has been given his essence from the Father denies that he has being from himself." The anti-Nicenes held that the Father alone has the being of God and imparts this essence to the Son. But, Calvin says, there is with respect to the essence no distinction between the Father and the Son.[170] Yet Calvin also says that we can still hold to the distinct eternal relations between the persons, since we do not separate the persons from the essence but rather distinguish them while they subsist in it. "Therefore we say that deity in an absolute sense exists of itself; whence likewise we confess that the Son since he is God, exists of himself, but not in respect of his Person; indeed, since he is the Son, we say that he exists from the Father. Thus his essence is without beginning; while the beginning of his person is God himself."[171]

Hence, for Calvin, the Word was eternally hidden in God before he was revealed in the creation of the world, but his *hypostasis* was distinct from the Father while he was of the same essence as the Father, "concealed in God."[172] Christ the Son is also distinct from

169. Calvin, *Institutes*, 1.13.22.

170. Calvin, *Institutes*, 1.13.23.

171. Calvin, *Institutes*, 1.13.25. Here Calvin cites Augustine in support, from his commentary on Psalm 109:13 (110:13, English), in *PL*, 37:1457, *NPNF*[1], 8:542ff., and *De trinitate*, bk. 5.

172. Calvin, on John 1:1–3. *Calvin's Commentaries: The Gospel According to St. John 1–10*, trans. T. H. L. Parker (Eerdmans, 1961), 7–10.

the Spirit. Commenting on John 14:16 and the phrase "another Comforter," he remarks that "there must be some property in which the Spirit differs from the Son so as to be another."[173] Thus, there is a distinction of persons in God. Unity of essence requires that what is of the essence of God is as much the Son's as the Father's. Therefore, the Son "is one God with the Father, yet is nonetheless to be distinguished in such a way that each has His own subsistence."[174]

This entails an order between the three that is in full harmony with their autotheotic status. As B. B. Warfield puts it, Calvin's conception of the Trinity "included a postulation of an 'order' in the Persons of the Trinity, by which the Father is first, the Son second, and the Spirit third. And it included a doctrine of generation and procession by virtue of which the Son as Son derives from the Father, and the Spirit as Spirit derives from the Father and the Son."[175] Whenever the name of God is mentioned, the Son and the Spirit are included as well as the Father. On the other hand, "where the Son is joined to the Father, then the relation of the two enters in; and so we distinguish among the persons." In doing so, the peculiar properties of the three persons carry an order within them. Since the Father is the beginning and the source, where he is mentioned together with the Son and/or the Spirit, the name of God is peculiarly applied to him.[176] This is why the Father is called the Creator—"it is by reason of the order between the persons." For this reason, it is improper (*improprie*) to call Christ the Creator in terms of the persons. Rather, he is to be called Creator when speaking of the divine essence.[177]

173. Calvin, on John 14:16. *Calvin's Commentaries: The Gospel According to St. John 11–21 and the First Epistle of John*, ed. Thomas F. Torrance and David W. Torrance, trans. T. H. L. Parker (Eerdmans, 1959), 81–82.

174. Calvin, on Hebrews 1:2–3. *Calvin's Commentaries: The Epistle of Paul the Apostle to the Hebrews and the First and Second Epistles of St. Peter*, trans. William B. Johnston (Eerdmans, 1963), 6–10.

175. B. B. Warfield, "Calvin's Doctrine of the Trinity," in *Calvin and Augustine*, ed. Samuel G. Craig (Presbyterian and Reformed, 1974), 244.

176. Calvin, *Institutes*, 1.13.20.

177. "Cur ergo creator dicitur pater, et hoc titulo seorsum ornatur? Nempe ratione ordinis, dum respicitur ad personas. . . . Si vere creator est Christus, neque id personae respectu: sequitur necessario referri hoc ad essentiam." *CO*, 9:369.

The Father as the *Principium* (Source)

Correspondingly, in keeping with the patristic and medieval teaching, Calvin regarded the Father as the beginning (*principium* or *origo*). To him "is attributed the beginning of activity, and the fountain and wellspring of all things; to the Son, wisdom, counsel, and the ordered disposition of all things; but to the Spirit is assigned the power and efficacy of that activity." In the same place, he adds that in all of God's works, the three work together (a dominant theme in Augustine) and that in these activities there is this clear order. Behind this lies a relational order. The Father is first, from him is the Son, and from both is the Spirit. For this reason, "the Son is said to come forth from the Father alone; the Spirit, from the Father and the Son at the same time."[178] Thus, it is permissible to say that "in respect to order and degree the beginning of divinity is in the Father."[179] "The Father is first in order, . . . the beginning and fountainhead of the whole of divinity."[180] As we saw, this is in respect to the persons.

This is very clear in Calvin's catechetical work, *Le Catechisme de l'Église de Genève* or in its Latin translation *Catechismus Ecclesiae Genevensis*, published in 1545, in question 19. Here he calls the Father the beginning or origin, the First Cause. Again, he is speaking of the relations of the persons, not the one divine essence or being.[181] In the draft he produced for the French Confession in 1559, a draft that was followed almost entirely except for his first few chapters, of which this is one, he says that the name of God is sometimes applied in particular to the Father, "since he is the principle and origin of his Word and his Spirit."[182]

178. Calvin, *Institutes*, 1.13.18.

179. Calvin, *Institutes*, 1.13.24.

180. Calvin, *Institutes*, 1.13.25.

181. "Pource qu'en une seule essence divine nous avons à considerer le Pere, comme le commencement et origine, ou la cause premiere de toutes choses" and in translation "Quoniam in una Dei essentia patrem intueri nos convenit, tanquam principium et originem, primamve rerum omnium causam." *OS*, 2:76–77; *CO*, 6:13–14.

182. "Et combien que le nom de Dieu soit quelque fois attribué en particulier au Pere, d'autant qu'il est principe et origine de sa Parole et de son Esprit." *OS*, 2:312. See also the *Expositio Impietatis Valentini Gentilis*, *CO*, 9:369.

The Eternal Generation of the Son

The distinction of the Son from the Father is not confined to creation and redemption. Nor is language referring to the Father's begetting the Son to be limited to the economic sphere only, although it is true that Calvin's focus normally lies there. Biblical passages referring to the generation of the Son usually point to the incarnate Son's resurrection, but nevertheless, before this "it is manifest that he was the only-begotten 'in the bosom of the Father.'"[183] Indeed, he is the Son "because the Word was begotten by the Father before all ages."[184] At the same time, Calvin is averse to speculating on what eternal begetting entails. Like Gregory of Nazianzus, he regarded this as a question beyond our capacities. These thoughts profit little, and involve useless trouble. The idea of Origen that there is a "continuous act of begetting" is foolish, since the relation is eternal.[185] Calvin's *focus* was on the economic activity of the divine persons. Thus, the quotation of Psalm 2:7 in Acts 13:33 refers to the resurrection of Jesus, by which he was visibly generated before human eyes. Nevertheless, this in no way negates the hidden generation (*illa arcana generatio*) that happened in eternity.[186] Both, we might add, are expressive of life, the inner life of the Trinity and that life in its human conquest of death. In his High Priestly Prayer in John 17, Christ indicated that since his glory is eternal, he always is. In so doing, the Son expressed a distinction between himself and the Father, "from which we infer that He is not only the eternal God but also the eternal Word of God begotten of the Father before the ages."[187] Also in *Le Catechisme de l'Église de*

183. Calvin, *Institutes*, 1.13.17.

184. Calvin, *Institutes*, 1.13.23–25.

185. Calvin, *Institutes*, 1.13.29. Warfield is wrong in lumping together all the "Nicene fathers" when he says that they were "accustomed to explain" eternal generation. We have noted how they overwhelmingly recognized this as an impenetrable mystery. See Warfield, "Calvin," 247.

186. *Calvin's Commentaries: The Acts of the Apostles 1–13*, trans. John W. Fraser (Eerdmans, 1965), 378; *Ioannis Calvini: Opera Exegetica: Volumen XII/1 Commentariorum in Acta Apostolorum Liber Primum*, ed. Helmut Feld (Droz, 2001), 389.

187. "Sed aeternum quoque Dei sermonem ex Patre ante secula genitum." Calvin, *John 11–21*, on 17:5.

Genève, 22, Calvin asserted that the eternal Word was begotten by the Father before all ages.[188]

Calvin brought this into focus most acutely in the very work where he stressed the Son as *autotheos*, the *Expositio Impietatis Valentini Gentilis*. Christ is the Son of God, since he is the Word of God begotten by the Father before all ages (*ante secula a patre genitus*), who is now made known in the flesh. The eternal Word relatively is the Son of God, and considered apart from the relations he is at the same time God.[189] In a crucial passage in which he reflected on the words of the Creed of Nicaea (325), "God of God," dropped by the Niceno-Constantinopolitan Creed in 381, Calvin weighed the views of the church fathers, particularly Athanasius, and concluded that the creed is speaking of the personal relations and does not imply any communication of essence or concomitant subordination.

> But the words of the Council of Nicea resound "God of God." This is a hard saying, I acknowledge. However, no one is better able to remove any ambiguity or a more capable interpreter than Athanasius who composed it. And certainly the counsel of the fathers was no other than that the Son in terms of origin is led out from the Father, in respect of his person, and in no way to oppose his being of the same essence and deity. And so, according to essence, he is the word of God without beginning, according to his person however the Son has a beginning from the Father.[190]

Again, shortly afterward he wrote that the Son "has his origin from the Father, as he is the Son; an origin not of time, nor of essence, both of which would be most absurd, but an origin strictly of order (*sed ordinis duntaxat*). Thus everything is said to be from the Father,

188. *OS*, 2:77; *CO*, 6:15–16.

189. *CO*, 9:370.

190. "Sed verba consilii Nicaeni sonant, Deum esse ad Deo. Dura loquutio, fateor, sed ad cuius tollendam ambiguitatem nemo potest esse magis idoneus interpres, quam Athanasius, qui eam dictavit. Et certe non aliud fuit patrum concilium, nisi manere originem quam ducit a patre filius, personae respectu, nec obstare quominus eadem sit utriusque essentia et deitas: atque ita, quoad essentiam, sermonem esse Deum absque principio: in persona autem filii habere principium a patre." *CO*, 9:368.

insofar as the relations of the persons are concerned."[191] Calvin has no quarrel with Gentile if all he were saying were that the Son has his origin from the Father in terms of begetting. The issue surrounds Gentile's denial that the Son is without origin in terms of the one divine essence.[192] In his *Defensio* (1545), written in reflection on the Caroli controversy, Calvin remarked that in terms of the relation, he has "continually proclaimed" that the Son is of the Father.[193] This, as he wrote in his draft for the French Confession, is because the persons have that which is characteristic of each, while the unique essence is indivisible.[194] To sum up Calvin's thoughts on the question, since he is God, the Son exists of himself, "but not in respect of his Person; indeed, since he is the Son, we say that he exists from the Father."[195]

John Owen and the Incarnate Son's Dependence on the Holy Spirit

John Owen advanced the claim that during his incarnate life and ministry, Jesus relied on the Holy Spirit to sustain and strengthen him, and to empower his work. Owen was followed later, in the nineteenth century, by Edward Irving, although Bruce McCormack argues correctly that this is typical of Reformed theology in contrast to the church fathers.[196]

The fathers generally considered that Jesus was sustained in his humanity and preserved from sin by the indissoluble hypostatic union, his humanity being suffused by divine qualities flowing from his divine person. Owen, on the other hand, sought to do justice to the reality of the incarnation. In this he argued that humans are dependent on the Holy Spirit for their relationship with God.

191. *CO*, 9:369.

192. *CO*, 9:375.

193. *CO*, 7:323–24.

194. "D'autant que chacun ha tellement ce qui luy est propre, quant à la Personne, que l'essence unique n'est point divisee." *OS*, 2:312.

195. Calvin, *Institutes*, 1.13.25.

196. Bruce L. McCormack, *For Us and Our Salvation: Incarnation and Atonement in the Reformed Tradition*, Studies in Reformed Theology and History (Princeton Theological Seminary, 1993), 17–22.

Since the eternal Son took into union a human nature and lived as man, so in his incarnate state he too lived in dependence on the Spirit. This was necessary in order to restore the image of God in man that was lost at the fall; first it had to be renewed in the incarnate Christ. What the Holy Spirit does in the mystical body of Christ, the church, he did first in his natural body.[197] I have written of this elsewhere.[198]

This claim has the advantage that it provides a paradigm for our own experience and finds biblical support in the portrayal of Christ's humanity in Hebrews (Heb. 2:10–11; 5:7–9). It also demonstrates the point that the Spirit was and is active in these ways and so, again, all Trinitarian persons act together inseparably. But it is not a case of two opposed realities. The very fact that the humanity assumed into union in the incarnation is the human nature of the eternal Son of the Father should be enough to establish that these things took place within the indivisible person of the incarnate Son. United to the Son by the Spirit by whom he was conceived, his human nature developed under the direction of the Spirit and was progressively deified in union with the Son by the same Spirit and so grew in his relation to the Father.[199] Again, the Holy Spirit is Christ's own Spirit, as we saw that Cyril stressed, so rightly understood the Spirit cannot be detached from Christ, the Son.

Still, it is hard to avoid seeing the danger of Nestorianism lurking in the background in Owen's proposal. It suggests that Jesus was dependent on something other than the union and thereby posits the idea that there was a need for such additional assistance. This opens the door to a fragile union between the Father and the Son. As we saw with Calvin (above), the incarnation is the Achilles' heel of Reformed theology. Its focus on the humanity can at times raise the specter of Nestorius. It yields a weaker grasp of the hypostatic union. Ironically, it also encourages a view of salvation as a form

197. John Owen, *Holy Spirit*, in *The Works of John Owen*, ed. William H. Goold, 16 vols. (Banner of Truth, 1965–68), 3:168–76.

198. Robert Letham, *The Work of Christ* (Inter-Varsity Press, 1993), 114–15; Robert Letham, *The Holy Spirit* (P&R Publishing, 2023), 128–30.

199. See Robert Letham, *Systematic Theology* (Crossway, 2019), 500–503.

of moral example. It is a possible outflow from the controversy with the Lutherans over the *extra Calvinisticum.* We remarked, in tandem with Bruce, that the Lutheran doctrine of the *communicatio idiomatum,* while it was a new one, nevertheless had a securer grasp of the hypostatic union than did the Reformed. It is an area in which the Reformed need to do some work. Some retrieval of the late patristic debates will by no means come amiss.

10

Post-Enlightenment Questions

Christological theory is in truth like the great cathedral. "It is ever beautiful for worship, great for service, sublime as a retreat from the tumult of the world, and it is for ever unfinished." The Christ whom any mind or group of minds can reproduce is not the infinite redeemer of the world.[1]

Kenōsis

From the late eighteenth century through the nineteenth, Western culture was marked by the impact of romanticism. The focus turned to humanity and its feelings, to development in the world around. In its wake came an eruption of interest in intellectual disciplines that focused on humanity. "Know then thyself, presume not God to scan, the proper study of mankind is man," wrote Alexander Pope.[2] Anthropology, sociology, history, psychology, psychiatry, economics, and biology all mushroomed. In music, in late Beethoven the classical structures seen in Mozart and Haydn were extended and eventually burst, introducing a greater emphasis on feeling. Development and organism became an important feature in philosophy with G. W. F. Hegel, in biology in the work of Charles Darwin, and in the new humanities generally. In theology, it surfaced in the developmental

1. H. R. Mackintosh, *The Doctrine of the Person of Jesus Christ* (T&T Clark, 1912), 300. The quotation within the quotation is not attributed by Mackintosh. Sherman Isbell informs me that it is from George A. Gordon, *The Christ of Today* (Boston: Houghton, Mifflin and Company, 1896), 168.

2. Alexander Pope, *An Essay on Man*, 1.

theories of John Henry Newman and in the sacramentalism of the Oxford movement, J. W. Nevin, and even the Plymouth Brethren. In a different way, it is seen in Herman Bavinck's motif of organism.[3]

Into this context, the reality and genuineness of the human life of the incarnate Son loomed large. There were real issues to consider, many that still need addressing even though the immediate causes of their original appearance have long passed. If we reject some of the proposals in the nature and form in which they were cast, it does not negate the fact that they were matters worth discussing, and that needed to be discussed. Perhaps the most well known and enduring is the *kenōsis* theory. Since, in the incarnation, one of the Trinity took human nature into union and lived as man, how did his infinite power, his omnipresence, and his comprehensive and perfect divine knowledge coexist with the human limitations he took on? How could these human features avoid being swamped? How could he know everything actual and possible in one act of cognition and yet genuinely be human, with limited knowledge? How could he be almighty and yet grow weary, get hungry, and die? Or, as Eric Mascall wrote, graphically, "There are obvious difficulties in supposing that, in the plain and obvious sense of the words, the human mind of the Babe of Bethlehem was thinking, as he lay in the manger, of the Procession of the Holy Ghost, the theorems of hydrodynamics, the novels of Jane Austen, and the Battle of Hastings."[4] Questions arise over the compatibility of the omniscience of deity with the limited knowledge of human nature; how can these coexist in one person? Will not the deity swamp the human limitations? These were issues considered among advocates of the *kenōsis* theory, the bulk of whom were seeking to operate in accordance with the teaching of Chalcedon.[5] This new idea was taken from the verb *kenōo*

3. See James Eglinton, *Trinity and Organism: Towards a New Reading of Herman Bavinck's Organic Motif* (Bloomsbury, 2012).

4. E. L. Mascall, *Christ, the Christian and the Church* (Longmans, Green and Co., 1946), 53.

5. See R. Sherman Isbell, *Understanding the Offer of the Gospel* (forthcoming), writing on the character of God manifested in the agency of Christ, where, in passing, post-Enlightenment *kenōsis* theories are contrasted with the language of Irenaeus and classic Reformed theologians.

("to empty") in Philippians 2:7, where Christ, being in the form of God, is said to have emptied himself, taking the form of a servant. But the theory was based on wider considerations than that passage.

Gottfried Thomasius

One of the early and most prominent exponents of *kenōsis* was the German Lutheran Gottfried Thomasius (1802–75).[6] Thomasius self-consciously sought to operate within the parameters of Chalcedon. He wrote that for the historical person of the God-man, we must suppose "a self-limitation of the divine"; otherwise, there would be a radical dualism between his world-ruling position that extends far over and above the human.[7] Thomasius maintained that the divine consciousness of the Son of himself and his universal governance does not coincide with his divine-human action in the state of humiliation.[8] If the Son had imparted the fullness of his divine lordship, it would have eradicated his inherent earthly limitation.[9] Rather, the Son of God gave himself over to the form of human limitation, "not a divesting of that which is essential to deity . . . but a divesting of the divine mode of being in favour of the humanly creaturely form of existence, . . . a renunciation of the divine glory which he had from the beginning with the Father."[10] Thus divesting himself, he appropriates humankind, imparting himself to it—"the deepest mystery of self-denying love."[11]

I suggest that there is a real sense in which something of this must be true. When the Son took human nature, he lived here on earth as man. Being God, he did not exploit his status or identity. He was incognito. To the eyes of those around him, he was simply the carpenter's son. Thomasius, however, writes of his "divesting" himself of the divine mode of being, a "renunciation" of the divine

6. Gottfried Thomasius, "Christ's Person and Work," in *God and Incarnation in Mid-Nineteenth Century German Theology*, ed. and trans. Claude Welch, Library of Protestant Thought (Oxford University Press, 1965), 32–101.

7. Mackintosh, *Jesus Christ*, 300.

8. Thomasius, "Christ's Person and Work," 47.

9. Thomasius, "Christ's Person and Work," 47.

10. Thomasius, "Christ's Person and Work," 48.

11. Thomasius, "Christ's Person and Work," 49.

glory. That goes far beyond a concealment in which the reality is there but is not manifested in its fullness.

Thomasius refers to Philippians 2:6–11, arguing that his questions are supported by the biblical presentation of the two states —human lowliness and Godlike glory—involving "an alteration that has gone on in the relation of the Son to the Father." This was not a surrender of the divine ego but "a divesting of a higher form of existence, a yielding of a God-like relation to a humanly limited and conditioned one."[12] The Son became something that he previously was not—human nature in consequence of sin.[13] According to John 17:5, Thomasius maintains, he relinquished the glory he had with the Father as the eternal Logos, something that he now "no longer has," a divesting of something proper to the deity of the Son.[14] Again, Paul in Philippians 2, he states, means the "divesting of an actual possession."[15] The Son emptied himself of the divine form of existence and assumed the other.[16] It appears on the surface that Thomasius considers the human Jesus as a distinct person from the Logos. That there is a huge contrast between "the form of God" and "the form of a servant" in verses 6–7 is clear; note the adversative "but." Yet Thomasius presented it as a change of one form of existence for another quite different one, something at least susceptible of interpretation along Nestorian lines.

Moving to Mark 13:32, Thomasius indicates that Christ acknowledges actual ignorance of a historical fact.[17] For Thomasius, to possess knowledge and not possess knowledge is inconceivable and impossible. He concludes that Jesus' statement requires the divestiture of omniscience.[18] Thomasius states that the Son will have this knowledge upon his exaltation, something he did not have in the days of his flesh. At that time, he did not exercise the lordship that the Father

12. Thomasius, "Christ's Person and Work," 50.
13. Thomasius, "Christ's Person and Work," 51.
14. Thomasius, "Christ's Person and Work," 51.
15. Thomasius, "Christ's Person and Work," 52.
16. Thomasius, "Christ's Person and Work," 53.
17. Thomasius, "Christ's Person and Work," 54.
18. Thomasius, "Christ's Person and Work," 55.

had—this applies to the whole historical life of Jesus.[19] In short, "the assumption of human essence does not by itself completely express the concept of incarnation, but that the latter must be conceived at the same time as divesting of the divine."[20]

It is plain that Thomasius thought that in the state of humiliation it was impossible for the Son to exercise distinctively divine attributes, since they would have been incompatible with his humanity and its limitations. Therefore, so he argued, he exchanged one form of existence—the divine—for another. At root, despite his protestations to the contrary, he appears to assume that deity and humanity are intrinsically incompatible. If that were so, would it not pose as much of a problem in the state of exaltation?[21] Moreover, his theory assumes a distinction between attributes essential to divinity and those that are capable of being divested and so are accidental. This runs contrary to the tradition, in which the divine attributes are identical to the divine essence, and so threatens or negates the simplicity of God—which is a vital matter but one on which we have neither time nor space to linger here.[22] Indeed, the problem reaches back to the debates in the early centuries; had Thomasius a proper grasp of Christ as a single subject, a single agent acting in both natures?[23]

Isaak Dorner

These proposals came under heavy criticism from the great Lutheran theologian Isaak Dorner (1809–84), who was possessed of vast knowledge together with incisive critical power and persuasive argumentation, and who took a moderating position

19. Thomasius, "Christ's Person and Work," 55.

20. Thomasius, "Christ's Person and Work," 56.

21. This is common to all kenotic theories. I have singled out Thomasius as one of the most prominent continental exponents, but there were a wide range, including J. August Ebrard (1818–88) and, in Britain, Charles Gore (1853–1932) and P. T. Forsyth (1848–1921). See Stephen J. Wellum, *God the Son Incarnate* (Crossway, 2016), 356–64.

22. For an excellent survey of a range of leading nineteenth-century continental exponents of *kenōsis*, see Thomas R. Thompson, "Nineteenth-Century Kenotic Christology: The Waxing, Waning, and Weighing of a Quest for a Coherent Orthodoxy," in *Exploring Kenotic Christology: The Self-Emptying of God*, ed. C. Stephen Evans (Oxford University Press, 2006), 74–111.

23. I thank Sherman Isbell for this last question.

between the liberal theology that had come to prominence and the Christian tradition.[24]

Evaluating Thomasius's theory, he understood it to assert that in his essence the Logos is capable of becoming, only the Father's having aseity.[25] This is what the Italian anti-Trinitarians argued at the time of John Calvin. In effect, it represents, as Dorner continued, the self-transmutation of the Logos into a man, "a theophany in human form."[26] It is, he contended, a form of Apollinarianism, in which the human reality is a body with which the divested Logos clothed himself,[27] with a return of the self-restored Logos to deity when the growth of the divested Logos reached its goal.[28] In this theory, the human and the humiliated Logos stand over against one another in parallel development. But parallels never meet. There is no unity of person.[29] In other words, Dorner effectively accused Thomasius of Nestorianism. The theory was not new, he maintained, for it was held by the Valentinians, some Apollinarians, and the Anabaptists. It was constantly rejected by the Lutherans in the Formula of Concord. In it there is no bond of union. It is a false path.[30] Dorner concluded that the "hypotheses of kenoticism [are] found to be in contradiction with the eighteen hundred year old Christology of the church."[31]

Dorner's own response to the *kenōsis* theory was a theory of development. He, as Thomasius, was operating within the same intellectual world that we mentioned. He wrote, "That not only the humanity of Jesus merely, but also his God-human living unity, was at first incomplete and in need of increase, is clear already beyond all contradiction."[32] According to Dorner, seeking to hold to the unity of

24. Isaak August Dorner, "System of Christian Doctrine," in *God and Incarnation in Mid-Nineteenth Century German Theology*, ed. and trans. Claude Welch, Library of Protestant Thought (Oxford University Press, 1965), 181–284.

25. Dorner, "Christian Doctrine," 191.

26. Dorner, "Christian Doctrine," 192.

27. Dorner, "Christian Doctrine," 192.

28. Dorner, "Christian Doctrine," 192.

29. Dorner, "Christian Doctrine," 193.

30. Dorner, "Christian Doctrine," 195.

31. Dorner, "Christian Doctrine," 196.

32. I. A. Dorner, *A System of Christian Doctrine*, trans. Alfred Cave and J. S. Banks (Edinburgh: T&T Clark, 1882), 3:332.

Christ's person, this development affected not merely the assumed humanity but the incarnate Son viewed as a whole.

The basis for this novel idea was the Son's corporeality and its obvious growth. Thus, "it is only the result of process that the body becomes the voluntary organ of the soul, nay, the mere organic side and manifestation of the personality."[33] The Logos as such cannot enter a state of potentiality, but the humanity has to subject itself to development. Moreover, the actuality of the Logos "extends beyond the human." Thus, the humanity cannot at once participate in the knowledge and will of God the Logos, who rules the world; "the unity of the God-human total personality was not perfect at the beginning."[34] Dorner denies that this entails a separation of natures; rather, the Logos is able to influence the growth of the God-human person.[35] "Thus the *unio* itself is not to be regarded as a rigid and motionless whole," for the growth of the humanity is the growth of the God-humanity. The God-human living unity is "not a complete unity unchangeably settled from the beginning."[36]

Dorner perceived the danger of interpreting the state of humiliation, of incarnate lowliness from conception to the cross, in terms of the state of exaltation, which took place after the resurrection. He considered that a developmental theory safeguarded the state of exaltation by recognizing that the limitations evident in Jesus' earthly life did not reflect on his eventual exaltation or the eternal sphere of the Logos. In other words, the state of humiliation is not to be equated with being human, or else that state would be made eternal and would thereby exclude the state of exaltation.[37] Dorner considered the incarnation to exhibit "a divine self-forgetfulness of love, which loses itself in its objects, and shuns nothing to save them, nay, surrenders itself to them in unreserved self-communion."[38] As we remarked, it is not hard to see in Dorner's argument the impact

33. Dorner, *System*, 3:332–33.
34. Dorner, *System*, 3:332.
35. Dorner, *System*, 3:333.
36. Dorner, *System*, 3:334.
37. Dorner, *System*, 3:337.
38. Dorner, *System*, 3:339.

of romanticism, with the idea of organism, anthropocentrism, development, and evolution that it entailed.

What this means for Christology overall is that Dorner begins with the two natures and argues against the priority of the person. Thereby, the *unio* is confirmed and established by the perfecting of the humanity, in self-consciousness and self-determination.[39] This is the opposite of Cyril and the tradition.[40] It is governed by the impetus of the nineteenth century's preoccupation with human-centered interests. So it exhibits many of that movement's problems. Dorner is attempting to wed this interest with Christological orthodoxy. His overall position is the healthy and correct view of Christ as the second Adam, the center of humanity, who brings creation to its destiny, for "only by the incarnation of the Logos in his totality as the divine image and world-centre is he possible, who is destined to be the historical universal middle-point of the world."[41] This entails the repudiation of an anthropocentric Christology.[42] It excludes two positions. The first is a *unio* complete from the beginning, admitting no further development; the second is a beginning that is no *unio* at all.[43] The first would preclude growth; the second would rule out preexistent deity.

H. R. Mackintosh

H. R. Mackintosh (1870–1936) was a leading Scottish theologian in the early twentieth century. He was a moderate exponent of the *kenōsis* theory, taking something of a mediating position. He wrote, "Every theory which accepts a real incarnation must deny that the lowliness of our life is incongruous with Godhead, and hold that, as it has been put, our Lord became 'representative of mankind not only on the sacrificial side but also on the side of human weakness.'"[44]

39. Dorner, *System*, 3:312–17.

40. Most, if not all, of the post-Enlightenment issues arose because of a failure to reckon with and assimilate the post-Chalcedonian conciliar decisions relating to person and nature. The neglect of that period has brought great damage in its wake.

41. Dorner, *System*, 3:324.

42. Dorner, *System*, 3:326.

43. Dorner, *System*, 3:331.

44. Mackintosh, *Jesus Christ*, 474.

Mackintosh here is offsetting criticisms of the basic assumption of the theory that humanity is in some way incompatible with deity, such that the latter must be retracted or divested in order for incarnation to occur.

Mackintosh regards Thomasius's theory of a distinction between essential and relative attributes of God, the latter (omnipotence, omnipresence, omniscience) incommunicable to humanity, as "not one which can be maintained."[45] Instead, with echoes of Dorner, he thinks the incarnate Son's own knowledge of his own identity developed over time, given the reality of his humanity, and suggests that only in mature manhood did he become aware of his divinity.[46] He suggests that Jesus, while impeccable, may not have been aware of this and so treated every temptation with full effort to resist—"the sphere of finitude had veiled in nescience his eternal relationship to the Father"—even though he had "a firmly based confidence of victory" because of the intimacy of his relation to the Father and of the crucial importance of his mission.[47] One wonders how that claim holds up in the face of Jesus' statement in Luke 2, when he was only twelve, about being about his Father's business. Rather, Mackintosh holds that divine qualities were "transposed," functioning in new ways, although it is not entirely clear what he means by this. Mackintosh concludes, "If then we see clearly that God and man are not definable as opposites, and that time is susceptible of eternity, it will not seem incredible that there should have existed in Christ, under conditions never again repeated, a gradual coalescence of life divine and human."[48] Mackintosh, while aware of problems with the *kenōsis* theory, was presenting a moderate and reserved example of it.

45. Mackintosh, *Jesus Christ*, 476. "Thus to talk of the abandonment of this or that attribute on the part of the eternal Son is a conception too sharp and crude, too rough in shading, for our present problem. God ceases to be God not merely when (as with Gess) there is a self-renunciation actually of the divine self-consciousness, but even when such qualities as omnipotence are parted with" (477).

46. Mackintosh, *Jesus Christ*, 480–81.

47. Mackintosh, *Jesus Christ*, 480–81.

48. Mackintosh, *Jesus Christ*, 503.

Karl Barth

Barth vigorously opposed the *kenōsis* theory. Any subtraction or weakening of the deity would, he said, throw doubt on the atonement, for Christ "humbled himself but he did not do it by ceasing to be who he is. . . . The word ἐκένωσεν in Phil. 2:7 certainly does not mean this. . . . The κένωσις consists in a renunciation of his being in the form of God *alone*," for "he did not treat his being in the form of God (τὸ εἶναι ἴσα θεῷ) as a robber does his booty."[49]

Barth considered the kenotic development of Thomasius and, in a more extreme form, Wolfgang Gess as "an open breach with the whole tradition of the church."[50] Gess held that the Son ceased to be God in the incarnation and returned to that status in his exaltation, a view described by A. E. Biedermann as "the complete *kenosis* of reason."[51] Barth is emphatic and correct in stating that "there are many things we can try to say in understanding the christological mystery but we cannot possibly understand or estimate it if we try to explain it by a self-limitation or de-divinisation of God. . . . If in Christ—even in the humiliated Christ on the cross of Golgotha—God is not unchanged and wholly God, then everything that we may say about the reconciliation of the world made by God in this humiliated one is left hanging on the tree."[52]

Indeed, "the mystery reveals to us that for God it is just as natural to be lowly as it is to be high,"[53] for "even in the form of a servant, which is the form of his presence and action in Jesus Christ, we have to do with God himself in his true deity."[54] Consequently, "if, then, God is in Christ, if what the man Jesus does is God's own work, this aspect of the self-emptying and self-humbling of Jesus Christ as an act of obedience cannot be alien to God."[55] Barth is right in speaking here of mystery. The truth of the matter is that the Son himself

49. Karl Barth, *CD*, IV/1:180 (italics mine).

50. Barth, *CD*, IV/1:182.

51. Quoted in Barth, *CD*, IV/1:182. Gess is considered favorably by Thompson, "Nineteenth-Century Kenotic Christology," 111.

52. Barth, *CD*, IV/1:183.

53. Barth, *CD*, IV/1:192.

54. Barth, *CD*, IV/1:193.

55. Barth, *CD*, IV/1:193.

remains unchanged in the incarnation. He was, is, and continues to be God. There is also the reality of the assumed humanity in its weakness and lowliness. This assumption is into the person of the Son such that it is *his* humanity, without diminishing or diluting his unabbreviated deity or the union established in the incarnation. See also the powerful criticisms of the theory by T. F. Torrance.[56]

Recent Developments

In recent years, there has been a revival of kenoticism by contemporary Christian theologians and philosophers, expressed in a variety of new ways.[57] From differing perspectives, prominent among these are J. P. Moreland and William Lane Craig,[58] Garrett DeWeese,[59] Cornelius Plantinga, Thomas R. Thompson,[60] C. Stephen Evans, and Stephen T. Davis.

The exponents of the new version of *kenōsis* all wish to maintain that Jesus of Nazareth is ontologically identical to the Logos, and that the Son does not relinquish any of his divine attributes in becoming incarnate. On the other hand, they do depart from the conciliar Christology in arguing that both the mind and will of the incarnate Son are to be predicated of the person, not the nature. Hence, there is a close connection between the new kenoticists and the revived Monotheletism to which we referred in chapter 7.[61] Exemplified in the case of Thompson and Plantinga, it entails a redefinition of the meaning of "person" that includes in its scope both divine and human

56. Thomas F. Torrance, *Incarnation: The Person and Life of Christ* (Paternoster, 2008), 76.

57. C. Stephen Evans, ed., *Exploring Kenotic Christology: The Self-Emptying of God* (Oxford University Press, 2006).

58. J. P. Moreland and William Lane Craig, *Philosophical Foundations for a Christian Worldview* (InterVarsity Press, 2003), 606–12.

59. Garrett J. DeWeese, "One Person, Two Natures: Two Metaphysical Models of the Incarnation," in *Jesus in Trinitarian Perspective: An Introductory Christology*, ed. Fred Sanders and Klaus Issler (B&H Academic, 2007), 114–53, here 144–46.

60. Thomas R. Thompson and Cornelius Plantinga, "Trinity and Kenosis," in *Exploring Kenotic Christology: The Self-Emptying of God*, ed. C. Stephen Evans (Oxford University Press, 2006), 165–89.

61. Wellum, *God the Son*, 380–81.

persons, yielding a radical social Trinitarianism.[62] DeWeese writes of person as a distinct center of knowledge, will, and action,[63] while Thompson and Plantinga do so in Boethian terms as, *inter alia*, an individual substance with discrete, untransferable individuality.[64] Applied to the Trinity, this invites charges of tritheism, since the divine persons would appear to be separable. Moreland and Craig are well aware of this criticism and spend a good deal of space defending themselves against it, in a way that seems to me to be less than convincing. They acknowledge that they are opposed to the doctrine of divine simplicity. Whatever merits their view, and the views of their colleagues, may have, and however laudable their intention, it is incontestable that they have deviated from the Christian tradition of the past millennium and a half.

A common denominator in these proposals is an acceptance of Monotheletism. In chapter 7, we remarked that the idea that Christ lacked a human mind and will is a major problem. It is akin to Apollinarianism, in which the Logos replaced the human soul in Jesus, eliciting the famous retort from Gregory of Nazianzus that "whatever is not assumed cannot be healed."[65] Moreland and Craig affirm Chalcedon, reject outright any divestiture of divine attributes, but, in interaction with psychoanalytic theory, argue that "the divine aspects of Jesus' personality were largely subliminal during his state of humiliation."[66] "Like an iceberg beneath the water's surface [they] lay submerged in his subconscious."[67] This, they concede, implies Monotheletism, so they interpret Jesus' prayer in Gethsemane as distinguishing the will of the Son from the will of the Father. Craig and Moreland's proposal points to three wills in God, which they accept, and thus tritheism.[68] Certainly, the full

62. Thompson and Plantinga, "Trinity and Kenosis," 172–81.

63. DeWeese, "Two Metaphysical Models."

64. Thompson and Plantinga, "Trinity and Kenosis," 178.

65. Gregory of Nazianzus, *Letter 101 to Cledonius*, in *St. Gregory of Nazianzus: On God and Christ: The Five Theological Orations and Two Letters to Cledonius*, trans. Frederick Williams and Lionel Wickham (St. Vladimir's Seminary Press, 2002), 158.

66. Moreland and Craig, *Philosophical Foundations*, 610.

67. Moreland and Craig, *Philosophical Foundations*, 611.

68. Moreland and Craig, *Philosophical Foundations*, 611.

human growth and development of Jesus, his genuine temptations, his expressions of ignorance of this or that, are genuine realities, vital for his saving work; he could not have known of the result of the forthcoming cricket series between England and Australia in 2025–26. But Craig and Moreland's case—self-consciously attempting to be orthodox by constructing a plausible explanation in today's world—puts the involvement of God in our lowly condition and in the excruciating sufferings of the cross to one side, consigned to the depths of the human subconscious. While not Nestorian, insofar as there are not two "persons," yet there is a clear lurch toward separation.

Ironically, in recent *kenōsis* discussions, there is a preference for speaking of the Son as having assumed human *properties*; while these are a necessary part of what it is to be human, they are not sufficient of themselves for a true human nature.

Additionally, Stephen Wellum remarks on the close connection of these arguments with Spirit-Christology, in which discussion proceeds from a focus on the Holy Spirit.[69] This tends to follow from a stress in *kenōsis* theories on the human nature of Christ. From this, they look to the Holy Spirit, rather than the hypostatic union itself, to uphold the humanity of Christ, hinting at a distance of sorts between the Son and the humanity he assumed. We referred earlier critically to the ideas of John Owen on this point, as we have done elsewhere.[70] It is generally stated that the Son occasionally, often rarely—some say never—exercised his divine attributes when he was incarnate, whether in his life on earth or even in governing the universe. Gerald Hawthorne wrote that Jesus exercises divine actions by the Holy Spirit, like other Spirit-empowered men. This would negate the *communicatio idiomatum*, the settled position of the church, that actions relating to either nature are both predicable of the person. Hawthorne considered that the incarnate Son acted "within the bounds of human limitations," while his divine attributes are

69. Wellum, *God the Son*, 382–83. See Robert Letham, *The Holy Spirit* (P&R Publishing, 2023), 91–99.

70. Letham, *Holy Spirit*, 128–30.

purely potential.[71] In contrast, Thomas Aquinas wrote that there is no potentiality in God.[72] Alarmingly, if Jesus was acting purely as man, then he is our example and cannot be our Savior, any more than can other Spirit-empowered men, such as Moses and Paul. This is what I consider the corollary of this position, but probably not something that any of its exponents would willingly endorse.[73]

Summary

The criticism of *kenōsis* theories made by William Temple was taken up by the classic liberal theologian Donald Baillie:

> I am not sure that a good reply has yet been made to the simple question asked by the late Archbishop of Canterbury in objection to the Kenotic theory. "What was happening," he asks, "to the rest of the universe during the period of our Lord's earthly life? To say that the infant Jesus was from his cradle exercising providential care over it all is certainly monstrous; but to deny this, and yet to say that the creative Word was so self-emptied as to have no being except in the infant Jesus, is to assert that for a certain period the history of the world was let loose from the control of the creative Word." It is vain to reply that the question presupposes a crude and false separation of the persons of the Trinity from each other, or to quote the sound principle *opera trinitatis ad extra sunt indivisa*. For the kenotic theory itself presupposes precisely such a separation, and could not even be stated without it. Thus any crudity or naïveté which may seem

71. Gerald F. Hawthorne, *The Presence and the Power: The Significance of the Holy Spirit in the Life and Ministry of Jesus* (Wipf & Stock, 2003), 208, quoted in Wellum, *God the Son*, 381–82.

72. Thomas Aquinas, *ST*, 1.9.2, *sed contra*.

73. I have written that modern evangelicalism is a variant form of Christianity. Robert Letham and Donald MacLeod, "Is Evangelicalism Christian?," *EQ* 67, no. 1 (January–March 1995): 3–33. More recently, I have concluded that in general—it is such an amorphous conglomeration and is well-nigh impossible to pin down—it has become a petri dish of heresies, given its uninformed view of the *sola Scriptura* slogan and its lack of familiarity with, and allegiance to, the ecumenical creeds and their rationales. Of course, this is a generalized conclusion that does not apply to many who identify themselves as "evangelicals."

> to characterize the Archbishop's question derives directly from the theory it is intended to criticize, since his method is that of a *reductio ad absurdum*. Is there any answer?[74]

In sum, the *kenōsis* theory has a Nestorian tendency, in focusing on the two natures and in abstracting the assumed humanity from the person. Yet, ironically, it is also rigidly Monophysite, since it considers the coexistence of unabbreviated deity and unabbreviated humanity impossible.[75]

A Major New Proposal

Bruce McCormack makes a weighty and radical proposal in his book *The Humility of the Eternal Son*.[76] This is a development from the debate that followed his controversial claims on the relationship between the Trinity and election, to which we referred in chapter 2 and elsewhere.

McCormack wants to avoid the conclusion drawn by his critics that by arguing that election is prior to God's being Trinity, and thus constitutes God as Trinity, he has eroded or abandoned God's freedom. Consequently, he now seeks to ground the doctrine of God Christologically. He asks what kind of God there must be if it is true that Jesus is Lord.[77] From this, he argues that since the fathers assumed as given the doctrines of divine immutability, impassability, and simplicity, Chalcedon is unable to reconcile the reality of Jesus' humanity with the eternal Logos. Since God was held to be impervious to change, one of two consequences follow. Either the assumed humanity could be only a mere instrument, passive, with the divine

74. D. M. Baillie, *God Was in Christ: An Essay on Incarnation and Atonement* (Charles Scribner's Sons, 1948), 95–96. Baillie was quoting William Temple, *Christus Veritas* (Macmillan, 1939), 142f.

75. Donald MacLeod, *The Person of Christ* (Inter-Varsity Press, 1998), 209–10. A valuable analysis of the *kenōsis* movement is found in Francis J. Hall, *The Kenotic Theory* (New York: Longmans, Green and Company, 1898), highly recommended by Professor John Murray, according to Sherman Isbell.

76. Bruce L. McCormack, *The Humility of the Eternal Son: Reformed Kenoticism and the Repair of Chalcedon* (Cambridge University Press, 2021).

77. McCormack, *Humility of the Eternal Son*, 2.

Logos the active agent, or else Jesus has no constitutive relation to the Logos. McCormack thinks Cyril's claim that the Word made the human properties "his own" is not sufficiently clear. He considers that it was intended in a purely figurative sense, for "how can the Word, who is impassable by nature, truly and really 'appropriate' human properties (and the human experiences they make possible) without ceasing to be what he is?"[78] There are clearly limits to how far the Word could go in allowing Jesus to function in a purely human manner. In short, McCormack writes, quoting a statement of John McGuckin's, the problem was "how the existence of a soul in Christ could be reconciled with a single-subject Christology."[79] If Jesus has a human mind, soul, and will, it appears to McCormack difficult to reconcile with the unity of the immutable person. The result was that the attributes of both natures had to be predicated of the person.[80]

McCormack seeks a resolution, and with it a repair of Chalcedon as his subtitle states, through the idea of the *receptivity* of the eternal Son. He builds on Barth's discussion in the *Church Dogmatics* to the effect that the Son's human obedience reflects his obedience in the Trinity.[81] This Barth based on God's self-revelation in the missions, the relations of the persons of the Trinity in history being a true reflection of who he is eternally. For Barth, with the tradition, the processions are necessary, while the missions reflect them and arise from a free decision of God.

The difference McCormack introduces is that the decisive moment in revelation is the earthly history of Jesus of Nazareth. It follows, according to his construction, that the missions are primary in relation to the processions. The missions disclose Jesus' receptivity to the Father and also the Son's receptivity to the man Jesus. He writes, "God is acted upon in this one human being because God unites himself with this one human and with him alone."[82] This sounds Nestorian,

78. McCormack, *Humility of the Eternal Son*, 46.

79. McCormack, *Humility of the Eternal Son*, 51, quoting John A. McGuckin, *St. Cyril of Alexandria and the Christological Controversy: Its History, Theology, and Texts* (St. Vladimir's Seminary Press, 2004), 183.

80. McCormack, *Humility of the Eternal Son*, 52.

81. Barth, *CD*, IV/1:192–204.

82. McCormack, *Humility of the Eternal Son*, 6.

the man Jesus the primary actor, the Son receptive. But McCormack at this point is indicating some possible results that may accrue on dispensing with immutability and impassability, as he is inclined to do. His aim is to construct an ontology of the Trinity that is grounded in God's self-revelation in Jesus Christ.[83] In this, he aims to get away from assumptions based on God in himself apart from his revelation.

For our purposes, this is a new angle on *kenōsis*. Whereas the kenotic theologians operated with the idea that in the incarnation the Son emptied himself by divestiture of divine attributes, McCormack argues that he emptied himself by being receptive to the human Jesus. There is some credibility to this position, since it aligns with Paul's comment that Christ emptied himself by "taking the form of a servant, and being made in the likeness of a [human] person," not by divestiture of aspects of deity but by assumption of humanity. McCormack seeks to identify with Cyril's Christology, with the single subject, and is critical of the dualism inherent in Chalcedon. Moreover, by basing his doctrine of God on the shared life experience of Jesus, McCormack claims that the path Jesus took is truly revelatory of what the Son is like.

Yet at root, McCormack's solution, as Alex Irving correctly identifies it, involves a union of two agents, for "McCormack's unified Christological subject is constituted by two agents who unite their distinct agencies to form a single activity."[84] The Son is receptive to the human agent; the Son is who he is by his receptivity to this human agent.[85] Despite McCormack's clear opposition to Nestorianism, he seems to accord a distinct, even primary, agency to the human. His favorable treatment of Owen's argument that the Spirit upheld and directed Jesus, rather than the Son who assumed the humanity into union, a postulation that we considered earlier, supports this.[86]

McCormack's discussion is extremely complex, and his configuration of the doctrines of the Trinity and election, of the nature of

83. McCormack, *Humility of the Eternal Son*, 6.

84. Alex Irving, "A Critical Assessment of Bruce L. McCormack's Christological Proposal," *SJT* 77, no. 2 (2024): 149–62, here 153.

85. Irving, "Critical Assessment," 154.

86. McCormack, *Humility of the Eternal Son*, 148, 250–51.

God and revelation, is all included and based on his Christological proposal. It is far too wide-ranging to do it justice in the space available here. Suffice it to say that he has no place for a doctrine of God that regards him as independent of his creation. God is free, but he is never free from his act of self-determination for us. By grounding his understanding of the Son (and God) in human history, McCormack reverses the classic position that the missions in human history are based on the processions in eternity, since he is emphatic that it is what happens in our world that determines who the Son is, for "the eternal personal identity of the Son is established in relation to the human Jesus."[87] Thus, the Son is united to Jesus eternally, which seems to undermine the integrity of history, and makes God dependent in some way on creation.

It seems to me that, as with so many other proposals that entail a departure from, or modification or repudiation of, classic affirmations, at root is an assumption of an incompatibility of God and humanity, such that in the incarnation there is an inherent conflict between the person of the Son and the human nature that is assumed. For us, so it is argued, it appears to make an almost intractable difficulty of understanding or of reconciling these conflicts. What is often missing is the realization that God created humans to be his partners and to be compatible with him on a finite level. Indeed, he made us with a primary view to the incarnation.

This is where, for all his questionable speculations, Sergei Bulgakov is helpful. Bulgakov argues that man as the image of God establishes both the divinity of man and the humanity of God. He refers to Acts 17:28 ("we are [God's] offspring"), to Ezekiel's vision of the glory of God in the form of "the image of heavenly manhood" (Ezek. 1:26), and to the Son of Man in Daniel 7:9–13. From this he concludes that the incarnation "is closely connected with this heavenly or eternal manhood. There is something in man which is directly related to the essence of God. It is no one natural quality, but his whole humanity, which is the image of God."[88]

87. Irving, "Critical Assessment," 158–60.

88. Sergius Bulgakov, *The Wisdom of God: A Brief Summary of Sophiology* (Williams and Norgate, 1937), 117–18.

Bulgakov develops this theme. "In view of the fall, [the incarnation's] . . . purpose extends beyond this [atonement] to the complete divinization of the creation, and the union of things in heaven and things on earth under the headship of Christ."[89] The creation of man underlies the incarnation. There is some inalienable characteristic in man by which the possibility of the incarnation is comprehensible.[90] He continues by stating, "We must infer that, since the person of the Word found it possible to live in human nature as well as in its own, therefore it is itself in some sense a human person too." In order to serve as person to manhood, the divine person of the Word must itself be human "or, more exactly, co-human." Its union with human nature corresponds to the original relation between them. Man on his side must be capable of receiving and making room for a divine person in the stead of the human. So "man's original mode of being is theandric."[91] "The incarnation thus appears to postulate, on its hypostatic side at least, some original analogy between divine and human personality, which yet does not overthrow all the essential difference between them." The personal spirit of man has its divine, uncreated origin from "the spirit of God" (Gen. 2:7). It is a spark of the divine. Man is made a partaker of the divine nature and capable of divinization.[92] Man is theandric—the Word is the everlasting God-man (cf. Rom. 5:15; 1 Cor. 15:47–49). "Thus it is possible for the person of the heavenly God-man, the Word, to become the person of a created human nature, and so realize its original God-manhood."[93] In short, it was natural for the Word to take the place of the human personality of the human nature of Christ. Thus, the union of the

89. Bulgakov, *Wisdom*, 125.

90. Bulgakov, *Wisdom*, 126.

91. Bulgakov, *Wisdom*, 129. See Geerhardus Vos, *Reformed Dogmatics*, 1:47–48 (III.14) (Lexham Press, 2014), who argues that as one in a set of "clear demands that a theological definition of person must satisfy" in formulating the doctrine of the Trinity: "2. It must have an element in itself that is common to divine and human personality. In Christology, specifically the divine person of Christ serves to represent the human person of the elect in the justice of God. If a point of likeness does not exist, then this could not happen."

92. Bulgakov, *Wisdom*, 129–30.

93. Bulgakov, *Wisdom*, 130–31.

two natures in Christ rests in their mutual relationship as two variant forms of divine and created Wisdom.[94] Bulgakov concludes that there is a *kenōsis* ("self-emptying") by Christ (cf. Phil. 2:7), but contrary to Protestant theories of *kenōsis*, our Lord never ceased to be God. The *kenōsis* occurred through "that unity of eternal and created manhood."[95] While thus united, the two natures remain distinct to eternity.[96]

What are we to make of all this? Amid much that is at best questionable, underlying Bulgakov's speculations lies his attestation to the reality that God created humanity to be compatible with him, with the incarnation of the Son the overwhelmingly dominant evidence for that. The incarnation is not, therefore, a sudden whim on the part of God, a plan B when all else had failed, a surprising and difficult intrusion. For God, it is perfectly natural, not in the sense of an outflow of his being, for it was a free and sovereign determination of his will, but rather because he created the human race with this in the forefront of his mind.

Calvin contended strongly for the incarnational life of the Son to entail a *krupsis*, a concealing of his deity. He wrote, commenting on Philippians 2:7: "Christ, indeed, did not renounce his divinity, but he kept it concealed for a time, that under the weakness of the flesh it might not be seen. Hence he laid aside his glory in the view of men, not by lessening, but by concealing (*supprimendo*) it." Further, "the abasement of the flesh was, nevertheless, like a veil, by which his divine majesty was covered."[97] In short, with Calvin we can affirm that the Son came among us incognito. If we were to have seen him in a crowd, there would be no way of knowing who he is. As John the Baptist cried, "among you stands one you do not know" (John 1:26). Charles Wesley wrote, "Veiled in flesh the Godhead see."[98]

94. Bulgakov, *Wisdom*, 132–33.
95. Bulgakov, *Wisdom*, 134.
96. Bulgakov, *Wisdom*, 141.
97. John Calvin, *Calvin's Commentaries: The Epistles of Paul to the Galatians, Ephesians, Philippians and Colossians*, ed. Thomas F. Torrance and David W. Torrance, trans. T. H. L. Parker (Eerdmans, 1965), 248, on Philippians 2:7; *In Pauli Apostolas*, 248.
98. Charles Wesley, "Hark! the Herald Angels Sing" (1739).

Jesus informed Peter that his confession that Jesus is the Christ was revealed to him by the Father and did not arise as a result of his own reason or intuition (Matt. 16:17). Donald MacLeod remarks that "as he hangs on the cross, bleeding, battered, powerless, and forsaken, the last thing he looks like is God. Indeed, he scarcely looks human."[99] As Paul wrote in Philippians 2:6–8, in becoming man the Son renounced any opportunity to use his divine power in his own interests while deploying it for the interests of others.

Peccability

Charles Hodge argued strongly for the possibility of Christ's sinning (peccability), while equally strongly affirming his sinlessness: "The sinlessness of our Lord, however, does not amount to absolute impeccability. It was not a *non posse peccare*. If he was a true man he must have been capable of sinning. That he did not sin under the greatest provocation; that when he was reviled he blessed; when he suffered he threatened not; that he was dumb, as a sheep before its shearers, is held up to us as an example. Temptation implies the possibility of sin. If from the constitution of his person it was impossible for Christ to sin, then his temptation was unreal and without effect, and he cannot sympathize with his people."[100] The argument states that being human entails the possibility of sinning. The existence of temptation too requires the possibility of succumbing. Moreover, it establishes Christ's obedience as exemplary and is the only foundation for his priestly sympathy. Barth took a similar position to Hodge: "[Christ] was not immune from sin. He did not commit it, but he was not immune to it."[101] This stems from Barth's commitment to Christ's taking a fallen nature and remaining sinless in that nature. Such an argument has become almost standard.

Mackintosh had a somewhat different nuance from Hodge. He distinguished between temptation and sin.[102] He stated: "For the completeness of the redeemer it is not essential that he should

99. MacLeod, *Person of Christ*, 218.
100. Charles Hodge, *Systematic Theology* (Eerdmans, 1977), 2:457.
101. Barth, *CD*, IV/1:216.
102. Mackintosh, *Jesus Christ*, 402–4.

undergo each individual temptation by which men may be assailed. What is essential is that he should be 'schooled' in temptation, should taste and see what it is to repel the approach of evil through a lowly trust in God."[103] He learned obedience, "for the holiness of Jesus was no automatic necessity of being. It was possessed only by being perpetually won anew."[104] "He was not absolved from painful effort. Sinless temptations may be the most severe. . . . The resistance of temptation may be torture to a good man, whereas a bad man yields easily. . . . None was ever tempted so subtly."[105]

In contrast to Hodge, William G. T. Shedd (1820–94) pointed to the immutability of Christ, as evidenced in Hebrews 13:8, and noted that the possibility of being overcome by temptation was incompatible with his omnipotence.[106] He also argued from the asymmetrical nature of the incarnation. Since the divine *person* of the Logos took a human *nature* into union, the human is directed by the divine. The omnipotent person of the Logos preserves the finite human nature from falling. "Consequently, Christ while having a peccable human *nature* in his constitution, was an impeccable *person*."[107] Anything else, Shedd argued, would mean disruption in the person of Christ, which is impossible as a result of the union.[108] He added that impeccability does not prevent temptability; indeed, the fiercest temptations will confront it because of its resistance. Because an army cannot be conquered does not mean that it cannot be attacked. "Temptability depends upon the constitutional *susceptibility*, while impeccability depends upon the *will*."[109]

Along similar lines, Oliver Crisp writes that "it is rather like an invincible pugilist battling it out in the ring with an opponent. The outcome is a foregone conclusion if our pugilist is invincible; but that does not mean that he does not have to put up a real fight in

103. Mackintosh, *Jesus Christ*, 402.
104. Mackintosh, *Jesus Christ*, 402.
105. Mackintosh, *Jesus Christ*, 403.
106. William G. T. Shedd, *Dogmatic Theology* (1888; repr., Zondervan, 1971), 2:331.
107. Shedd, *Dogmatic Theology*, 2:333.
108. Shedd, *Dogmatic Theology*, 2:334–36.
109. Shedd, *Dogmatic Theology*, 2:336.

the ring. Similarly, when Christ is tempted in the desert . . . he really feels the 'pull' of that temptation, he really wrestles with it, having fasted for forty days, although the outcome is certain."[110]

Bavinck hit the nail on the head when he argued that "Scripture . . . prompts us to recognize in Christ, not just an empirical sinlessness but a necessary sinlessness as well. He is the Son of God, the Logos, who was in the beginning with God and himself God. He is one with the Father and always carries out his Father's will and work. For those who confess this of Christ, the possibility of him sinning and falling is unthinkable. . . . For in that case either God himself would have to be able to sin—which is blasphemy—or the union between the divine and the human nature is considered breakable and in fact denied."[111] This, I suggest, is not only the majority position down through the years, despite the more modern preference for peccability, but is more in harmony with the wider theological context.

Fallen Human Nature?

Edward Irving (1792–1834)

Also in the first half of the nineteenth century, other questions arose relating to the impact of the incarnate state. What kind of nature was it that the Son assumed into union? Was it a sinless nature such as possessed by Adam before the fall? Was it a morally neutral nature? Or was it, as the Scots minister and theologian Edward Irving controversially posited, a nature just like ours today, a nature vitiated by the fall, sinful in itself?[112] Irving, for his pains, was deposed from the ministry of the Church of Scotland, forming his own denomination but not living for long thereafter.

Commenting on Hebrews 2:17, "made like his brothers in all things," Irving states, "The man who will put a difference between the flesh of Christ, in its natural constitution and laws, and the flesh

110. Oliver D. Crisp, *God Incarnate: Explorations in Christology* (T&T Clark, 2009), 133.

111. Herman Bavinck, *RD*, 3:314. For a fuller discussion, see Robert Letham, *Systematic Theology* (Crossway, 2019), 520–26.

112. Edward Irving, *The Orthodox and Catholic Doctrine of Our Lord's Human Nature* (London: Baldwin and Cradock, 1830).

of other men, doth, I think, directly gainsay the word of God . . . in respect of human nature; and that too suffering human nature, mortal human nature, and therefore human nature in the fallen state; for that is the subject of the Apostle's discourse."[113]

Irving went on to explain his reasoning: "We have unity of substance with the fallen Adam, through the inheritance of his guilty soul and sinful flesh. We have no community of substance with Adam unfallen. If Christ be common with Adam unfallen, he is not common with us. For Adam unfallen differeth from me in the same way, and perhaps in as far as I differ from the risen Son of Man; or from what I myself shall be, by God's mercy and grace, in the resurrection of the just."[114]

In order to effect deliverance, Irving argued, the captain who was to lead his brothers out of suffering into glory "was made of one substance with the sufferers" and calls them brothers and children to express the closest unity of substance.[115] No limit is placed on it, Irving maintained. The catholic church has never considered anything other than that "the constitution of his human nature was as the constitution of our human nature in all respects and in all conditions."[116] In all respects he was sinless, without guile, concupiscence, or any consideration of evil. The weight of all sin, death, devils, and corruption lay upon him "and yet prevailed not to incline his human will once to desist from his divine will: so mighty a work of God is incarnation."[117]

The expiation of sin and reconciliation, Irving continues, is derived from the fact that Christ "took sinful flesh, or fallen human nature, and upheld it holy against the devil, the world, and the flesh, and the influence of all these upon the mind." He stood immovable, "and so having met all sin, and all weakness, and all mortality, and all corruption, and all devils, and all creature-oppression, and all creature-rebellion, in his flesh; in his body, he strangled them there,

113. Irving, *Orthodox and Catholic Doctrine*, 5–6.
114. Irving, *Orthodox and Catholic Doctrine*, 6.
115. Irving, *Orthodox and Catholic Doctrine*, 6.
116. Irving, *Orthodox and Catholic Doctrine*, 7.
117. Irving, *Orthodox and Catholic Doctrine*, 7.

he did judgment upon them there, he resisted, he overcame, he captured them. They are no more valid, they are no more potent, they are no more valiant in the region of creation; the voice, the will, the act of him who heretofore withstood them in weak flesh, and expelled them out of sinful flesh, and destroyed their works of disease, of death, of temptation of every kind, shall do his pleasure with them in the judgment, and cast them into the lake of fire which the Father hath prepared for the devil and his angels."[118] Moreover, Christ was under the law, which must mean "to be put into the condition of a fallen creature,"[119] since the law was made for the unrighteous.[120]

Irving's eloquent case—one can only imagine his impact as an orator—betrays more than a whiff of Nestorianism. Christ was made under the law in terms of his human nature in itself "*as contemplated apart from the divine nature which upheld it*," apart from the person of the Son of God who wrought in it.[121] The orthodox and catholic doctrine insisted that the human nature assumed into union by the Son of God is not, and cannot ever be, contemplated apart from the person of the Son. Irving's argument requires the Nestorian heresy to sustain it.

Again, Irving needed to restrict the purpose of the incarnation to limits less than the holistic biblical witness will allow. Christ came in order to deal with sin and nothing else, he asserts. And where did he find it? In the flesh, fallen corrupt nature, and nowhere else.[122] In doing so, he brought in a righteousness as universal as the fall. The tenor of Irving's thought is to an objective universalism of sorts.[123] He continues, "I ask, in all Scripture, for a hint, or the shadow of a reason, to induce us to believe that Christ's flesh was different from ours."[124]

Irving's claim has far-reaching consequences for the atonement. It reduces the cross to a moral example. Paul is emphatic (Rom. 8:3) that the Son's assumption of flesh was for the proximate purpose of

118. Irving, *Orthodox and Catholic Doctrine*, 8.
119. Irving, *Orthodox and Catholic Doctrine*, 9.
120. Irving, *Orthodox and Catholic Doctrine*, 10.
121. Irving, *Orthodox and Catholic Doctrine*, 10 (italics mine).
122. Irving, *Orthodox and Catholic Doctrine*, 11–13.
123. Irving, *Orthodox and Catholic Doctrine*, 17.
124. Irving, *Orthodox and Catholic Doctrine*, 19.

making atonement. Indeed, Irving proceeds to unfold a distinctive doctrine of atonement: "Christ took our fallen nature, with all its natural and inherent propensities: and overcame these, and brought it into union with the Godhead, and hath fixed it there for ever by his resurrection."[125] This is an objective work for all humanity. Irving attacks the classic doctrine of penal substitution and propitiation as a distortion that cannot represent the love of God, other than to the elect.[126] The atonement, such as it is, is to be found in the incarnation and its consequences. Why, we may ask, did Christ need to die on the cross?

Later Advocates

Considering the nature of Christ's humanity, a century later Barth famously took up Irving's theory and gave it the impetus that it still has today. He asserted: "Jesus Christ is not a demigod. He is not an angel. Nor is he an ideal man. He is a man as we are, equal to us as a creature, as a human individual, but also equal to us in the state and condition into which our disobedience has brought us. And in being what we are he is God's Word."[127] Continuing, he adds that *sarx* ("flesh") is a description of neutral human nature. But what the New Testament calls *sarx* includes "the narrower concept of the man who is liable to the judgment and verdict of God, who having become incapable of knowing and loving God must *incur* the wrath of God, whose existence has become one exposed to death because he has sinned against God. Flesh is the concrete form of human nature marked by Adam's fall . . . exactly like us, even in our opposition to him [God]."[128] Christ "would not be man if he were not 'flesh' in this definite sense. . . . He was not a sinful man. But inwardly and outwardly his situation was that of a sinful man."[129] Indeed, "there must be no weakening or obscuring of the saving truth that the nature which God assumed in Christ is identical with our nature as

125. Irving, *Orthodox and Catholic Doctrine*, 88.
126. Irving, *Orthodox and Catholic Doctrine*, 98–100.
127. Barth, *CD*, I/2:151.
128. Barth, *CD*, I/2:151.
129. Barth, *CD*, I/2:152.

we see it in the light of the fall. If it were otherwise how could Christ really be like us?"[130] Throughout this section, Barth is insistent that Jesus never actually sinned. While "the Word of God, who assumes our human existence, assumes our flesh, exists in the place where we exist,"[131] nevertheless "in our state and condition he does not do what underlies and produces that state and condition, or what we in that state and condition continually do."[132]

T. F. Torrance took an almost identical line to Barth, the main difference being that he attempted to support it with reference to the Greek patristic tradition.[133] He wrote that "in becoming flesh the Word penetrated into hostile territory, into our human alienation and estrangement from God. When the Word became flesh, he became all that we are in our opposition to God in our bondage under law. . . . St. Paul declares quite plainly therefore that . . . he was made in the likeness of sinful flesh."[134] "If Jesus Christ did not assume our fallen flesh, then our fallen humanity is untouched by his work—for '*the unassumed is the unredeemed*,' as Gregory Nazianzen put it."[135] Torrance adds that the obedience of Christ "was not light or sham obedience. It was agonisingly real in our flesh of sin."[136] He presents an anachronistic interpretation of Gregory, using his ontological point to support Torrance's own ethical one.[137]

Evaluation

Those who have argued that Christ assumed a fallen human nature have often misused patristic sources, especially from Gregory of Nazianzus's *Letter to Cledonius*, "whatever is not assumed cannot be healed." But it addressed a different question—ontological, not

130. Barth, *CD*, I/2:153.
131. Barth, *CD*, I/2:155.
132. Barth, *CD*, I/2:155–56.
133. See Torrance, *Incarnation*, 61–64, 204–6.
134. Torrance, *Incarnation*, 61.
135. Torrance, *Incarnation*, 62.
136. Torrance, *Incarnation*, 64.
137. Torrance, *Incarnation*, 201–6. See Jason R. Radcliff, "Thomas F. Torrance: Historian of Dogma," in *T&T Clark Handbook of Thomas F. Torrance*, ed. Paul D. Molnar and Myk Habets (T&T Clark, 2020), 101–10, which he sees as both a strength and a weakness.

ethical. It was written against Apollinaris, who claimed that the Son took the place of a human mind in the incarnate Christ. Gregory was opposing an ontological claim, not asserting an ethical one, one of which he and his contemporaries could know not an inkling.[138] The issue in Gregory's day related to the identity of the incarnate Son's person—a very different issue. As an example of recent evangelical exponents of the theory, the otherwise outstanding book of John C. Clark and Marcus Peter Johnson comes into this category.[139]

The argument that by assuming humanity in its fallenness Christ redeemed it from where it actually is, or else he could not have saved us in our actual state as fallen human beings, is a protest against all tendencies to Docetism. An unfallen nature, it is held, would be detached from ourselves and our world. Rather, Christ acted in redeeming love from within our own nature, sanctifying it and offering it up to the Father. As we remarked elsewhere, this paints an appealing picture of Christ's living a sinless life within the precise conditions we are in, and thereby healing our humanity from within.

One of the main problems with this line of thought is that it requires a Nestorian separation of the human nature from the person of Christ; the Son is free from all contact with the realm of sin, but his assumed human nature is fallen. The Son's human nature never exists of itself, however, but is the human nature of the eternal Son, one of the Trinity, so the attribution of fallenness to that nature is a statement about Christ, the eternal Son. If so, he could not save us; he would be included in the sin of Adam and its consequences and would have needed atonement himself, if only for his inclusion in Adam's sin.

Even when, to offset these objections, it is affirmed that Christ's healing of the assumed human nature happened from the moment of conception, that immediately sets him apart from the rest of us and so undermines the argument that he must be exactly like us *qua* fallen.

138. "Whoever has set his hope on a human being without mind is actually mindless himself and unworthy of being saved in his entirety. The unassumed is the unhealed." Gregory of Nazianzus, *Letter 101 to Cledonius,* 158.

139. John C. Clark and Marcus Peter Johnson, *The Incarnation of God: The Mystery of the Gospel as the Foundation of Evangelical Theology* (Crossway, 2015). See my review in *Them* 40, no. 2 (August 2015): 334–36.

This does not mean that Christ assumed a human nature like Adam's before the fall. Rather, he lived in a state of humiliation, sinless and righteous but with a nature bearing the consequences of the fall in its mortality, its vulnerability, and its suffering—but not fallen. Furthermore, as we observed in chapter 3, the New Testament witness is that the incarnation is a new creation, the start of the new humanity, not a repristinization of the old. Christ is the second Adam, not the first. He does not restore; he elevates, sanctifies, and glorifies.

A basic premise for the idea that Christ had a fallen human nature is that anything other than a propensity to sin would diminish his humanity. Notwithstanding, a fallen nature is intrinsic to a *fallen* human being but is not definitive of, but incidental to, a human being. In fact, being human is being in relation to God as his image bearers. That was how Adam was first created and how the second Adam preeminently is. We gain our humanity by being *rescued* from sin and corruption, not by wallowing in it.

Furthermore, the claim that to sympathize effectively with us Christ needed to share our fallenness and corruption sounds rather like the argument that to counsel a person who has committed adultery, it is necessary first to have committed adultery oneself. No; rather, Christ's sympathy as High Priest is directly connected to his ability. His sympathy is *effective* sympathy. He sends us grace to help us in time of need. He is able to do so precisely because he has been tempted and emerged without stain. It is *his conquest of temptation* that qualifies him as our High Priest, not any possibility that he was subject to it.

While it is vital to integrate the atonement with the incarnation, the New Testament stresses that atonement was made by the blood of Christ, his life laid down in death. But instead of "redemption by his blood" (Eph. 1:7) and reconciliation by the death of the Son (Rom. 5:9–10), advocates of a fallen nature locate these realities within the being and life of our Mediator. It is hard to see the reason for the cross. R. P. C. Hanson categorized this kind of theory as redemption by "a kind of sacred blood-transfusion."[140]

140. With reference, disputably, to Athanasius. R. P. C. Hanson, *The Search for the Christian Doctrine of God: The Arian Controversy 318–381* (T&T Clark, 1988), 451.

Purely Functional Christology

Oscar Cullmann, in his *The Christology of the New Testament*, argued forcibly that the New Testament considered Christ purely in terms of the functions he performed, not in ontological terms based on his status as the eternal Son. After an extensive discussion of titles applied to Christ and the work he did, Cullmann concludes: "Because the first Christians see God's redemptive revelation in Jesus Christ, for them it is his very nature that can be known only in his work—fundamentally in the central work accomplished in the flesh. Therefore, in the light of the New Testament witness, all mere speculation about his natures is an absurdity. Functional Christology is the only kind which exists."[141] This was written nearly seventy years ago and bears the marks of its era.[142] But even at the time, it provoked strong opposition. Cullmann was forced to add a caveat shortly after publication. He assured his critics that he affirmed the historic creeds and had no intention of undermining the conclusions reached by the ecumenical councils.[143]

This argument would leave, at best, a truncated view of the Son. After all, his work depends for its efficacy on who he is, the Son of the Father who is also true man. Nevertheless, a similar mindset continues in other forms. Most particularly, it has been seen in what is called "Christology from below," in which the starting point and, effectively, the entire process of investigation is conducted on the basis of historical research that suspends judgment on who Jesus was and is, treating him as it would any historical figure. Colin Gunton subjected this methodology to extensive and incisive criticism, pointing out that in the end it leaves us with a Christ who is not quite God and not quite man, since it portrays him as a religious leader, a wonder worker, a sage or a prophet, out of the reach of

141. Oscar Cullmann, *The Christology of the New Testament* (SCM, 1959), 326.

142. Only a few years ago, however, after I had preached a sermon in Oxford on Colossians 1:15–20, a cleric approached me to argue what in effect was Cullmann's thesis.

143. Oscar Cullmann, "The Reply of Professor Cullmann to Roman Catholic Critics," *SJT* 15, no. 1 (1962): 36–43.

most people but yet not one with the Father.[144] From a similar perspective, Torrance repeatedly criticized exponents of these ideas as being unscientific insofar as they did not allow the object of inquiry to disclose the reality.

The Threat of Biblicism

The title of this section might raise the eyebrows of some; others might reach for their blood-pressure medication. Surely, it could be said, if we believe in the divine inspiration and supreme authority of Holy Scripture, how can biblicism be a bad thing? What we mean here by "biblicism" is the false idea that the post-Reformation slogan *sola Scriptura* excludes other authorities, including that of the church and its leading teachers. It tends toward a consistently literalistic interpretation of the Bible and relies exclusively on express statements of Scripture. This methodology is at odds with the historic position of the church, established in the fourth-century Trinitarian crisis and repeated many times thereafter, notably in Westminster Confession of Faith 1.4, which states that the whole counsel of God for God's glory, man's salvation, faith, and life either is expressly set down in Scripture or by good and necessary consequence may be deduced from Scripture. It is also refuted by the Thirty-Nine Articles of the Church of England, which in article 8 affirms that "the three Creeds, Nicene Creed, Athanasius' Creed, and that which is commonly called the Apostles' Creed, ought thoroughly to be received and believed; for they may be proved by most certain warrants of holy Scripture."

By following this biblicistic path, some in recent years have come to oppose classic teaching on the eternal generation of the Son and to propose that the Son is eternally subordinate to the Father. Others have taken the position that eternal generation should not be made the test of orthodoxy. While this does not directly relate to the incarnate Son, it does highlight a number of problems, largely stemming from ignorance of the historic debates. A number of conservative

144. Colin E. Gunton, *Yesterday & Today: A Study of Continuities in Christology* (Eerdmans, 1983), 10–55.

theologians rejected eternal generation on these biblicistic grounds in recent years, but some of them subsequently retracted their opposition; such a change is a hallmark of a wise and genuine Christian, for we all err at times and need grace to recognize and correct it.

The grounds on which these views developed were as follows. First, there was a truncated doctrine of Scripture. By this, I mean that express statements were required from the Bible to establish matters of doctrine. Since, so it was claimed, this was not present, these doctrines were regarded as speculative, going beyond Scripture and influenced by Greek philosophy. This hermeneutic, however, had been rejected by the church in the fourth century during the Trinitarian controversy. Gregory of Nazianzus, among others, appealed to the sense of Scripture, to its overall teaching with its entailments, together with the interrelationship between those entailments.[145] That this became the accepted standard for theological inquiry is evidenced by the consensus of the Reformation and post-Reformation confessions, such as Westminster Confession of Faith 1.4, as we mentioned above. Throughout history, the cry for express statements *only* has been the hallmark of heretics—the Socinians and the Jehovah's Witnesses being notable instances. The early Plymouth Brethren made the same mistake but eventually corrected themselves.

Second, perhaps as a result of this biblicistic emphasis, another influence was a lack of familiarity with the details and nuances of historical discussions. The mistaken interpretation of the post-Reformation slogan *sola Scriptura* has been used to distance the Bible from the past teaching of the church, missing the point that the church's past teaching was the result of sustained biblical exegesis over many generations. One seminary, when I was short-listed for a faculty position, provided me with a copy of its faculty manual before interview. I was amazed to find that there was not a single graduate module on anything before the Reformation. With such studied indifference, it is no surprise that the evangelical world is

145. Gregory of Nazianzus, *Oration 31 on the Holy Spirit*, 21–24; *PG*, 36:156–60; *St. Gregory of Nazianzus: On God and Christ: The Five Theological Orations and Two Letters to Cledonius*, trans. Frederick Williams and Lionel Wickham (St. Vladimir's Seminary Press, 2002), 133–36.

recapitulating many of the early heresies to the extent that claims to continuity with the historic church are increasingly problematic.[146] These problems might arise in any case, but this vast lacuna does nothing to inhibit them.

In short, our own understanding of the Bible, in all its many facets, needs to be checked with the classic confessions of the church. Luke commended the Berean believers for evaluating even the teaching of the apostle Paul (Acts 17:11). Since Luke was a regular member of Paul's traveling entourage and Paul would probably have known what Luke was writing, we may reasonably conclude that this had Paul's approval. Even more, Paul was present himself at the time those events took place! He was perfectly willing to submit his own apostolic teaching to the *consensus fidelium,* the agreement of the faithful. To impose our own ideas on the church of Christ, as though wisdom began with us, is contrary to Scripture and apostolic practice.

146. Letham and MacLeod, "Evangelicalism."

11

For Us and Our Salvation

We believe in one God
　　the Father Almighty,
　　maker of heaven and earth
　　and of all things visible and invisible;

And in one Lord Jesus Christ
　　the Son of God, the Only-begotten,
　　begotten by his Father before all ages,
　　　　Light from Light,
　　　　true God from true God,
　　begotten, not made,
　　consubstantial with the Father,
　　through whom all things came into existence,
　　who for us men and for our salvation
　　　　came down from the heavens
　　　　and became incarnate by the Holy Spirit and the Virgin Mary
　　　　and became a man,
　　　　and was crucified for us under Pontius Pilate
　　　　and suffered and was buried
　　　　and rose again on the third day in accordance with
　　　　　　　　the Scriptures
　　　　and ascended into the heavens
　　　　and is seated at the right hand of the Father
　　　　and will come again with glory
　　　　to judge the living and the dead,
　　　　and there will be no end to his kingdom;

And in the Holy Spirit,
the Lord and life-giver,
who proceeds from the Father,
who is worshipped and glorified together with the Father and the Son,
who spoke by the prophets;
And in one holy, catholic and apostolic Church;
We confess one baptism for the forgiveness of sins;
We wait for the resurrection of the dead and the life of the coming age. Amen.[1]

This chapter engages with what has been known as the work of Christ, which in reality is inseparable from his person. It involves all that he did in his incarnate life and ministry and all that he continues to do by the Holy Spirit. These elements have become known as the *historia salutis* (the "history of salvation") and the *ordo salutis* (the "order of salvation"). The former is a recital of the historical outworking of salvation, reaching its climax in the death of Christ, together with his burial, resurrection, ascension, and enthronement. The latter is the manner by which this is received by his elect, through the work of the Spirit in regeneration, justification, adoption, sanctification, and glorification (or, in Eastern terms, deification).

These are vitally important realities. We will not be addressing them in detail, or in themselves. In particular, we will approach the outworking of salvation from a different perspective. Our focus is specifically on the Son. In every aspect of the history and order of salvation, Christ is central, he it is who governs and directs them, and it is precisely in relation to him, the Christ, the eternal Son of the Father, that these wonders come to be. I have written elsewhere

1. Niceno-Constantinopolitan Creed (A.D. 381) (italics mine). This creed, commonly known as the Nicene Creed, has been confessed by both the Eastern and Western churches through the centuries. The text here is the translation of R. P. C. Hanson, taken from the Greek text of G. L. Dosetti, *Il Simbolo di Nicaea e di Costantinople*, 1967: R. P. C. Hanson, *The Search for the Christian Doctrine of God: The Arian Controversy 318–381* (T&T Clark, 1988), 816.

at some length about the atonement, union with Christ, and the *ordo salutis*,[2] and detailed resources in the literature can be explored.[3]

Christ Is Our Salvation

It is important to recall that Paul states that *Christ himself* is the gospel (Rom. 1:1–4) and that in union with him we are saved. In introducing himself to the church of Rome, Paul felt compelled to give an account of the gospel he preached, not only in view of his being a stranger to Rome but also because of the widespread opposition of the Judaizers. He refers to his own calling from God as an apostle, dedicated to the gospel of God, which, he says, concerns "[God's] Son, Jesus Christ our Lord" (Rom. 1:1–4). This is the central theme, the spine of this introductory paragraph. If we peel away its various subordinate clauses and arrive at the main clause—in bold type below—we reach this conclusion.

> **Paul**, a servant of Christ Jesus, called to be an apostle, **set apart for the gospel of God**, which he promised beforehand through his prophets in the holy Scriptures, **concerning his Son**, who was descended from David according to the flesh and was declared to be the Son of God in power according to the Spirit of holiness by his resurrection from the dead, **Jesus Christ our Lord**, . . . to all those in Rome. (Rom. 1:1–4, 7 ESV)

Paul, the gospel, and Christ are the themes, Christ being the chief and the end goal. Paul describes himself in three ways; a servant of Christ Jesus, called to be an apostle, and set apart for the gospel of God (Rom. 1:1). In turn, the gospel was promised beforehand through the prophets in the Holy Scriptures, the Old Testament as we now know it (v. 2). Finally, the gospel concerns God's Son, who is identified as Jesus Christ our Lord (vv. 3–4). Of him it is said that he "became of the seed of David according to the flesh" (my trans.),

2. Robert Letham, *The Work of Christ* (Inter-Varsity Press, 1993); Robert Letham, *Union with Christ: In Scripture, History, and Theology* (P&R Publishing, 2011); Robert Letham, *Systematic Theology* (Crossway, 2019), 440–68, 545–789.

3. John Murray, *Redemption Accomplished and Applied* (Banner of Truth, 1961).

and was designated, or appointed, Son of God with power by the Spirit of holiness at or since the resurrection of the dead (vv. 3–4), two stages in his incarnate experience. In this long and convoluted journey, all roads lead to Christ, with both Paul and the gospel under his authority and dominance.

Prominent here is the faithfulness of God. The good news is his; it is the gospel *of God*; he planned and effected it. He promised it over many centuries of the Old Testament, through the writings of the prophets and the covenants he made, through the twists and turns of Israel's rebellious history. In due course, the promise of the Abrahamic and Davidic covenant was realized in Jesus Christ, who was born, or became, of his seed. We know from the Gospel records and from history overall that his Davidic descent was never disputed by his enemies. While Joseph was not his biological father, Joseph was most definitely his legal father. God kept his promise. Moreover, the historical trajectory continued, and in due course Jesus Christ was raised from the dead, transformed in his assumed humanity, and designated Son of God with power by the Holy Spirit. So much Paul spells out elsewhere in 1 Corinthians 15.

Jesus Christ *is* the gospel, the good news. In Romans 1:3–4, Paul unequivocally identifies Jesus Christ as the Son of God. From pre-existence to conception to resurrection and glorification, he is one integral and identical person. Jesus of Nazareth is the same identical person as the eternal Son of the Father in the divine Trinity. He is good news because he has taken human nature into everlasting union—"man with God is on the throne"[4]—raised in power by the Spirit of God. Christ is himself the gospel because in himself he sums up all of God's covenantal dealings with the human race; God is God in Jesus Christ; we are his people in Christ and nowhere else. Hence, when elsewhere Paul writes of the gospel as Christ dying for our sins, being buried, and being raised from the dead on the third day (1 Cor. 15:3), this all hinges on who Christ is, one with the Father.[5]

4. Christopher Wordsworth, "See, the Conqueror Mounts in Triumph," in *The English Hymnal*, ed. Ralph Vaughan Williams (Oxford University Press, 1933), no. 145.

5. Others died, were buried, and were raised from the dead—Lazarus for one, among the various saints who appeared in Jerusalem (Matt. 27:51–54)—but the gospel is not about them.

Indeed, as T. F. Torrance argues, because of the indivisibility of the Trinity and the inseparability of its works, we cannot separate the Son from the Father or the Holy Spirit.[6] Furthermore, all that he has done is in union with us, in our flesh and blood, and so all the blessings that flow from the panorama of salvation are in and from him by our incorporation into him by the Spirit. Every particular element of the redemptive plan of God comes to expression in, and focuses on, Christ. The incarnation, life and ministry, death and resurrection are each and all clear evidences of his purpose to take humanity into union, having dealt with the questions of sin and death that humans had intruded onto the scene. All the elements of the salvation we receive—all the many words ending in *-tion*—are outflows of what Christ has done and who he is.

In Ephesians 2:14, Paul[7] underlines this by writing that in Christ the barriers between Jew and Gentile have been broken down. Christ himself is our peace. He has brought peace with God and peace among hitherto warring people. The entire first two chapters of Ephesians are directly relevant to this issue. In Ephesians 1:3–14, Paul, setting forth the whole sweep of redemption from election in eternity through the atoning death of the cross to its ultimate consummation, lists all its facets as comprehended in Christ, in him, in the beloved one.[8]

From this, more narrowly, Paul addresses the Corinthian church in 1 Corinthians 15:1–3, affirming that the gospel is focused on the death, burial, and bodily resurrection of Christ, for it is in union with him in these central events that we are delivered from sin and death, and transferred to the kingdom of God's Son. It was the bodily aspect of redemption, the resurrection in particular, that puzzled many at Corinth and was foolishness to the Greeks, and it is in this instance that the focus lay.

6. Thomas F. Torrance, *Incarnation: The Person and Life of Christ* (Paternoster, 2008), 164.

7. On the authorship of Ephesians, see my comments in Robert Letham, *The Holy Trinity: In Scripture, History, Theology, and Worship*, rev. and expanded ed. (P&R Publishing, 2019), 71–73.

8. Note the repetitive phrase "in Christ," "in him," or "in the beloved one." See Letham, *Holy Trinity*, 80–81, 184–85.

Leaving Paul for the moment, John wrote his Gospel for the purpose of convincing his readers that Jesus is the Son of God, so that they would receive life through him (John 1:1–18; 20:31). His first letter is predicated on the fact that he and the other apostles had seen Jesus Christ, the Word, had touched him, and could attest that he is the source of eternal life to all who believe, since he is life itself (1 John 1:1f.). As John records in Revelation, the risen and glorified Christ appeared to him and affirmed that he had conquered death and is the living one (Rev. 1:9–18).

Throughout the Gospel of John, the theme of life, eternal life, is to the forefront, and in each case it is to be sought and found in Jesus, the incarnate Son. "In him was life" (John 1:4). He is life itself. Not only is life in him, not merely is he the source of contingent, created life, but *he* is life. This follows from his being one with God eternally, since God is the living God. When humans sinned, rebelling against God, they chose death rather than life. Christ the Son came to give life in abundance (10:10, 28), granting eternal life to all who believe in him (1:12–13, 16). This is because he gives sonship to all who receive him. Sonship itself entails union and communion with the Father in Christ by the Spirit (17:3 and context) and thus participation in the life of God, the presence and possession of eternal life, as John indicates when he expresses his purpose in writing the Gospel (20:30–31); Jesus is the Son of God, the giver of life, and so those who receive him and are called the children of God thereby are in receipt of the selfsame status he has and the life he gives.[9]

Jesus creates life and the means to sustain and enhance it. At the wedding feast, he changes the water into vintage wine (John 2:1–10), not any wine but the best wine, wine that the wedding guests, in their state of inebriation (note μεθυσθῶσιν, v. 10), would be unable to fully appreciate. Moreover, when challenged by those offended at his conduct in the temple, Jesus claims authority over death; when his bodily temple is to be destroyed in death, he will raise it again to life (vv. 19–22).

9. See Clive Bowsher, *Life in the Son: Exploring Participation and Union with Christ in John's Gospel and Letters* (Apollos, 2023).

In conversation with Nicodemus, he insists that whoever believes in him will pass from death to eternal life (John 3:3–16), life that is a present reality as well as future consummation (v. 36), in quality as well as everlasting duration. He presents to the woman at the well in Samaria this prospect of water springing up to eternal life. Whereas water sustains both animal and human life, this water will sustain life both now and forever (4:13–14). It is found in him. This is reinforced by Jesus' healing of the official's dying son (vv. 46–54), effected at a distance with immediate result.

Again, in the following chapter Jesus restores the health of a chronically ill and paralyzed invalid (John 5:1–15) and claims that he has life in himself, given by the Father, will raise the dead from their graves, and gives life to all who hear his voice in faith (vv. 21–29). Indeed, when he miraculously feeds the five thousand with a superabundance of provisions, he is seen as the Creator of the means of human life (6:1–14). No wonder that he equates believing in him with receiving eternal life and identifies this as eating his flesh and drinking his blood, without which we cannot receive life (vv. 27–58). In our chapter 4, we saw how Cyril insists that the flesh and blood of Christ is life-giving and that whoever denies this has departed the faith.[10]

Moreover, the Holy Spirit brings an overflowing torrent of life, consequent on Jesus' ascension (John 7:37–39). Jesus predates Abraham as the living one (8:51–58), heals and gives sight to the blind (9:1–7), and lays down his life and takes it again in the resurrection (10:10–11, 17–18).

John 11 is the climax of all these events and declarations. There Jesus raises Lazarus from the dead, after four days in the tomb (John 11:21–44). One striking comment is repeated. Both Martha and Mary run to meet Jesus at intervals upon his arrival, he having delayed his departure by several days. The first thing they say, both of them, separately, is:

10. We noted then how Cyril connected this to the communion service. In the Supper, we "receive and feed on Christ," and to deny that is to deny the position of the historic church on the life-giving flesh and blood of Christ.

> "Lord, if you had been here, my brother would not have died." (John 11:21, 32)

Both recognize that Jesus would have healed Lazarus if he had arrived before he died. The astonishing fact that we can draw from this, on reflection, is that while a host of healings, a couple of resurrections, and the seeming banishment of disease are all recorded in the four Gospels, nowhere is anyone recorded as having died in Jesus' presence. Some, the criminals on the crosses, died after Jesus had laid down his own life. There are references to deaths occurring offstage, such as John the Baptist, away from Jesus. Animals die—the herd of pigs into which the legion of demons entered, although even there it is connected with the amazing healing and restoration of the demoniac. But no one died in Jesus' presence—how could they? Jesus is one of the Trinity come among us as man. He is life, the giver of life, the conqueror of death. "If you had been here, my brother would not have died." After all that, after the delay, what did Jesus do? He brought Lazarus back to life.

Britain is preeminent at pageantry. When Queen Elizabeth II died in 2022, her funeral procession demonstrated that to the hilt—the gun carriage, the armed forces marching in precise step, the colorful regalia, the pikemen with their spears, the vast crowds watching in silence, the pomp and ceremony that spoke of centuries of tradition and the vast power of an erstwhile empire. But the striking fact was that for all that, the grandeur could not alter the reality that the most that the assembled magnates—those in the procession, the presidents and prime ministers in the Abbey—could offer was a funeral, a coffin, a corpse, and the decomposition of the body as it rots in the ground. Human power, splendor, and greatness meet their match in death. "The paths of glory lead but to the grave."[11] Then as the carriage stopped at the doors of Westminster Abbey, the coffin was lowered, and as the procession reached the threshold, the sound of the choir wafted through, intoning the lines from "The Order for

11. Thomas Gray, "Elegy Written in a Country Churchyard" (1751), in *The Penguin Dictionary of Quotations*, ed. J. M. Cohen and M. J. Cohen (Penguin, 1960), 177.

the Burial of the Dead," from *The Book of Common Prayer*: "I am the resurrection and the life, saith the Lord. He that believeth in me, though he were dead, yet shall he live: and whosoever liveth and believeth in me shall never die."[12]

Following this climactic account in John 11, Jesus announces in the upper room that he will send the Holy Spirit, one of the Trinity, the Spirit of life, whom the unbelieving world cannot receive. The Spirit will unite believers to him, to share in the communion of the life of God the Trinity. Thus, to know Jesus the Son is to receive eternal life and be granted access to the life of the Trinity, to the union and communion that the Son shares with the Father. In short, being the Son of God, he is the giver of eternal life (John 20:30–31). This is the purpose of the Gospel of John; it is the goal of the gospel, which has its center and circumference in Christ the Son.

Behind this lies the historical outworking of the covenant of grace. At each stage, amid all the detailed promises and obligations, remaining throughout the varied settings, is the central covenant promise of God, "I will be your God, you shall be my people" (Gen. 17:7–8; Jer. 11:4 with respect to the Mosaic covenant; Jer. 24:7 concerning the return from exile; Jer. 30:22; 31:33 for the new covenant; Rev. 21:3 for the consummation). God is our God in Christ and nowhere else; we are his people in Christ and nowhere else. The covenant between God and man is Christ himself, sealed in his incarnation, death, burial, resurrection, and ascension to the right hand of the Father.

Back to Cyril—no intelligent discussion of Christology can avoid him—who repeatedly argued that salvation flows from Jesus of Nazareth being identical to the eternal Son, in his taking human nature and thereby enabling us to share his relation to the Father through faith. Donald Fairbairn relates that "in Cyril's thought, the most obvious way God gives himself to humanity is by sharing his incorruption (and consequent immortality) and his holiness." In this Cyril follows Athanasius "in viewing incorruption and holiness

12. *The Book of Common Prayer and Administration of the Sacraments and Other Rites and Ceremonies of the Church According to the Use of the Church of England* (Oxford University Press, n.d.), 337, quoting John 11:25–26.

as a result of human participation in the Logos."[13] Even more, Christ grants us sonship. This stands together with Cyril's insistence that Christ is identical to the Logos, Son by nature, "since only one who is divine by nature can give God to us."[14] Foundational to this is that Christ is Son by nature, whereas we are sons by adoption; "he must be genuinely begotten from the Father, since otherwise he could not adopt us into God's family."[15] This does not mean that we share the substance of God; rather, it refers to our status and to intimate communion with himself.[16]

Fairbairn underlines that "Cyril makes clear that the one subject of Christ is the Logos, not a person constructed by the combination of two natures."[17] His understanding of grace demands it.[18] Therefore, the flesh is the Logos's own. "Not that he suffered in the nature of his deity, but that the sufferings of his flesh are ascribed to him because the flesh is not that of some other man, but is the Logos's own. . . . Therefore, since the blood is said to be God's blood, then clearly he was God, clothed with flesh."[19]

We recall that according to Cyril, everything in the Gospels must be applied to the Logos, the Son. Consequently, "one cannot divide the sayings among two subjects considered separately. . . . We must see the Logos as the one who undergoes all the actions and experiences of Christ. Thus the 'one nature' formula concerns the personal subject of Christ, the Logos; it is not a denial of the presence of different realities (deity and humanity) in Christ."[20]

John Calvin takes a similar position. The ultimate purpose of God for our salvation, as he put it, is that sooner or later we become like

13. Donald Fairbairn, *Grace and Christology in the Early Church* (Oxford University Press, 2003), 74.

14. Fairbairn, *Grace and Christology*, 77. See also 103.

15. Fairbairn, *Grace and Christology*, 79. See Appendix A for discussion of a contrary view that lacks the imprimatur of the church's confession.

16. Fairbairn, *Grace and Christology*, 83.

17. Fairbairn, *Grace and Christology*, 118.

18. Fairbairn, *Grace and Christology*, 119.

19. *PG*, 76:281, quoted in translation by Fairbairn, *Grace and Christology*, 122. The original reads: τὰ τῆς σαρκὸς αὐτοῦ πάθη εἰς αὐτὸν ἀναφέρεται διὰ τὸ μή ἀνθρώπου τινὸς ἔιναι ταύτην, ἀλλ' αὐτοῦ τοῦ Λόγου ἰδίαν σάρκα.

20. Fairbairn, *Grace and Christology*, 127.

God, "a kind of deification."[21] This does not mean that we become God's sons ontologically. There is only one Son who possesses the substance of the Godhead. Returning to Cyril, "the ontological aspect of deification, according to Cyril, consists only of our sharing God's incorruption, holiness, and life through participation in the Holy Spirit and partaking of the Eucharist."[22] This takes us beyond our human nature *as it now is*, but not to the extent of possessing the divine substance. It is by grace that we receive the communion of the Godhead because the Logos has brought his own humanity into the fellowship of the Trinity in order to share this with us. *Theosis* follows from the reality of the incarnation; the Son joined humanity to himself so that we can partake of the divine nature.[23] Cyril is reiterating what earlier Athanasius had argued, when he consistently used *metochoi* ("partakers") for our participation in the divine nature but reserved *idios* ("proper") to the Son's relation to the Father.[24]

As to the nature of this, it is rather, as Calvin wrote, "enough for us that, from the substance of his flesh Christ breathes life into our souls—indeed, pours forth his very life into us—even though Christ's flesh does not enter into us."[25] This happens because "in his humanity there also dwells fullness of life, so that whoever has partaken of his flesh and blood may at the same time enjoy participation in life."[26]

21. "Notemus ergo hunc esse Evangelii finem, ut aliquando conformes Deo reddamur; id vero est quasi deificari, ut ita loquamur." John Calvin, *Commentarii in Epistolas Canonicas,* Ioannis Calvini Opera Omnia (Librairie Droz, 2009), 328. Later, Calvin warns of "fanatics who imagine that we cross over into God's nature so that his nature absorbs ours," which he calls "madness." Rather, the apostles taught that "we shall be partakers of divine immortality and the glory of blessedness, . . . one with God so far as our capacity will allow." John Calvin, *Calvin's Commentaries: The Epistle of Paul the Apostle to the Hebrews and the First and Second Epistles of St. Peter*, trans. William B. Johnston (Eerdmans, 1963), 330. See Carl Mosser, "John Calvin and Early Reformed Theology," in Paul L. Gavrilyuk, Andrew Hofer, and Matthew Levering, eds., *The Oxford Handbook of Deification* (Oxford: Oxford University Press, 2024), 317–34.

22. Fairbairn, *Grace and Christology*, 131.

23. Letham, *Union with Christ*, 19–55.

24. Norman Russell, *The Doctrine of Deification in the Greek Patristic Tradition* (Oxford University Press, 2004), 192–97.

25. John Calvin, *Institutes*, 4.17.32.

26. Calvin, *Institutes*, 4.17.9.

Calvin provides an illustration of what this looks like:

> We can explain the source of this by a familiar example. Water is sometimes drunk from a spring, sometimes drawn, sometimes led by channels to water the fields, yet it does not flow forth from itself for so many uses, but from the very source, which by unceasing flow supplies and serves it. In like manner, the flesh of Christ is like a rich and inexhaustible fountain that pours into us the life springing forth from the Godhead into itself. Now who does not see that communion of Christ's flesh and blood is necessary for all who aspire to heavenly life?[27]

The fact that the humanity that the Son took into union is the Son's own humanity means that, while it remains forever human, it partakes of its being united to the Son and receives properties that belong to the Son. It is humanity transformed, permeated by the Holy Spirit, the Son's own Spirit. Consequently, as the Spirit enables us to feed on Christ in the sacrament, so his life flows into us. Thereby "our souls are fed by the flesh and blood of Christ in the same way that bread and wine keep and sustain physical life."[28] This is the work of the Spirit, for "serious wrong is done to the Holy Spirit unless we believe that it is through his incomprehensible power that we come to partake of Christ's flesh and blood."[29]

Thus, Paul starts Romans by asserting that the gospel concerns God's Son, Jesus Christ our Lord. What Paul writes of the work of Christ thereafter is to be seen as the work of the one who is the Lord, one of the Trinity according to the flesh (Rom. 9:5). In 1 Corinthians 15:1–3, he writes that the gospel is about the death, burial, and resurrection of Christ. Here he is geared to the Corinthians' questions about the resurrection, the body being frequently disparaged in Greek religion. It is as the Lord, one of the Trinity, that Christ experiences this as man. In 1 Corinthians 1:30, Paul insists that Christ is the source and foundation of all the blessings of salvation.

27. Calvin, *Institutes*, 4.17.9.
28. Calvin, *Institutes*, 4.17.10.
29. Calvin, *Institutes*, 4.17.33.

Christ Is Prior to His Benefits

The Westminster Confession of Faith rehearses a standard logical order of salvation as typically understood in classic Reformed theology, while the Westminster Larger Catechism, produced by the same assembly, considers the same realities in a differently nuanced way. The confession proceeds in an orderly and logical fashion from regeneration, faith and repentance, and effectual calling through justification, adoption, sanctification, and perseverance to glorification. On the other hand, without diverging from this order or presenting a rival paradigm, the catechism places the entire *ordo salutis* under the rubric of union and communion with Christ, whether in grace in this life or in glory in the life to come (WLC 65–90). In this it signals that Christ is the source of all the blessings of salvation and that all these blessings are to be found in him. Union and communion with Christ is salvation itself, and the various particular aspects of the way in which we are brought to salvation cannot be understood outside that umbrella. This is a warning against excessively analytical thinking that breaks a whole down relentlessly into ever-decreasing parts, thereby losing sight of the unifying element.

Calvin wrote, "We see that our whole salvation and all its parts are comprehended in Christ (Acts 4:12). We should therefore take care not to derive the least portion of it from anywhere else."[30] In his sermons on Ephesians, Calvin stressed that "there is but one fountain from which we draw all spiritual good, namely, our Lord Jesus Christ, nevertheless God makes the fullness of his grace which he has put in Jesus Christ to flow out, as it were, in channels, that each one of us may receive his portion, as is expedient for us."[31] Therefore, "for this reason the holy Supper has been left to us, as a reminder that it is in our Lord Jesus Christ that we must wholly seek all things pertaining to the life of our souls. For we profess that he is our food, even to satisfy us to the full."[32] He adds that "we cannot possess the

30. Calvin, *Institutes*, 2.16.19.

31. John Calvin, *Sermons on the Epistle to the Ephesians* (1562; repr., Banner of Truth, 1973), 402.

32. Calvin, *Sermons on Ephesians*, 403.

good things of our Lord Jesus Christ to take any profit from them, unless we first enjoy him."[33] The reason is that he is "the fountain of all good."[34] Earlier, in those same sermons, Calvin located the follies of Rome as arising from "no other cause than from lack of knowing our Lord Jesus Christ and the things given him by God the Father." Roman Catholics "have . . . imagined themselves to be separated from our Lord Jesus Christ, not knowing that he has become our brother in order that we might have intimate access to him."[35]

The entire order of salvation is thus grounded on what Christ has done and, behind that, who Christ is. In 1 Corinthians 1:30, Paul writes that "Christ Jesus is made to us wisdom from God, righteousness, sanctification, and redemption." Commenting on Paul's statement, Calvin remarks that "your existence (*subsistentia*) is founded on Christ. . . . He is not speaking of our creation only, but of that spiritual being (*essentia*) into which we are born again by God's grace." He continues: "He [Paul] seeks to describe . . . our mode of existence (*modus subsistendi*) in Christ. . . . He ascribes to Christ four titles which sum up all his perfection, and every benefit that we receive from him."[36] In this, Calvin asserts, "Paul does not say that [Christ] has been given to us something to add on to, or to be a buttress to righteousness, holiness, wisdom and redemption, but he ascribes to Christ alone the complete fulfilment of them all."[37]

Thus, in the Lord's Supper we feed on Christ himself, not on a doctrine, such as justification or the covenant. It is Christ's Supper; the Son is the host who invites us. It is, as Paul writes, "communion of the body/blood of the Lord" (1 Cor. 10:16). He is our God, and we are his people, only in Christ.

33. Calvin, *Sermons on Ephesians*, 403.

34. Calvin, *Sermons on Ephesians*, 220.

35. Calvin, *Sermons on Ephesians*, 113.

36. John Calvin, *Calvin's Commentaries: The First Epistle of Paul the Apostle to the Corinthians*, ed. Thomas F. Torrance and David W. Torrance, trans. John W. Fraser (Eerdmans, 1960), 45.

37. Calvin, *First Corinthians*, 46.

Creation

Before we even get to the process of redemption, we need to remind ourselves that creation itself, the whole universe, owes its origin, continued existence, and well-being to the Son. This is evident in the Scriptures, where John, Paul, and the author of Hebrews each attribute creation and providence to him (John 1:1–4; Col. 1:15–18; Heb. 1:1–3). It was recognized by the fathers. Here are two prominent instances in their writings:

- Origen (185–254) wrote that the only-begotten Son is the image of the invisible God, and so "he invisibly bestowed upon all rational creatures a participation in himself, in such a way that each one received from him a degree of participation to the extent of the loving affection by which they adhered to him."[38]
- Athanasius (295–373) famously asserted that God chose to redeem the world by the same Word through whom he had created it in the beginning. From this, he argued that creation was made in Christ, thoroughly in conformity to Paul's discussion in Colossians 1.[39]

Since the Son, together with the Father and the Holy Spirit, created the universe by his power, and continues to uphold it, and since it is designed for him, it follows that he has proprietorial rights over it. The world around us, the whole environment, belongs to the Son, together with the Father and the Holy Spirit in the unity of the indivisible Trinity. Care for the environment is no incidental matter, nor is it to be seen in purely immanent terms as the environmental movement does, but it is vital because it is Christ's own property, over which the human race has been made stewards.

This is connected to our salvation, the consummation of which coincides with the renovation and renewal of the universe. Both are to be fulfilled in Christ. This connection between creation and the complete fulfillment of the created order, ourselves centrally

38. Origen, *On First Principles*, 2.6.3, in *Origen: On First Principles: A Reader's Edition*, ed. and trans. John Behr (Oxford University Press, 2019), 104.

39. Athanasius, *On the Incarnation*, 1.4.

included, embraces within it the drama of human creation, the fall, and the redemption that Christ brings. The leading patristic and Orthodox scholar, Andrew Louth, has described this interconnection as being like two arcs, the one surrounding and encompassing the other. They are not competitive with each other but complementary and interactive under the sovereign authority of Christ.[40]

In Ephesians 1, in the same passage where Paul unfolds the panorama of redemption, Paul also highlights the exaltation of Christ to the right hand of the Father to rule all things, the whole creation, the entire universe, for the church, which is his body. Creation and redemption are inextricably linked. So too in Romans 8:23–25, the ultimate redemption includes our own bodies, but it also embraces the renovation of the cosmos, which meanwhile has been groaning as in labor pains as it waits expectantly for its liberation. Both will occur at the return of Christ and the universal transformation that will burst into sight at that point, the ultimate fulfillment of the adoption that has already occurred (1 Cor. 15:51–57). Every plant, every tree and flower, mountain and ocean, planet and star, galaxy upon galaxy—down to the smallest particle—is his.

The Trinitarian Context

Clearly, all that the Son has done and continues to do is done together with the Father and the Holy Spirit. There are a range of works that are personally those of the Son alone, such as incarnation and atonement. Since the Trinity is indivisible, however, all three work together in all of God's ways and works; these personal works of the Son are not accomplished without the appropriate participation of each. Thus, as Calvin wrote in a sermon on Ephesians 4:6, the Father dwells in us by the Holy Spirit.[41] Again, on Ephesians 3:14–19, Calvin adds, where Paul makes two synonymous prayers

40. Andrew Louth, "The Place of *Theosis* in Orthodox Theology," in *Partakers of the Divine Nature: The History and Development of Deification in the Christian Traditions*, ed. Michael J. Christensen and Jeffery A. Wittung (Fairleigh Dickinson University Press, 2007), 32–44, esp. 35–36. Thanks to Karen Magnuson for tracking down this reference.

41. Calvin, *Sermons on Ephesians*, 333.

that his readers may be "strengthened through his Spirit in the inner man" and that "Christ may dwell in your hearts through faith," that "Christ comes to us by his Word and the power of his Holy Spirit" (vv. 16–17).[42] Furthermore, preaching on Ephesians 5:25–27, Calvin remarks that "the Lord Jesus Christ washed us when he shed his blood . . . and by the Holy Spirit," and that "we do not communicate with the Lord Jesus Christ except by the grace of the Holy Spirit."[43] Here Calvin reflects the consistent teaching of Scripture, not only in the letters of Paul but across the New Testament and foreshadowed in the Old as well.[44] Underlying Calvin's discussion of the Lord's Supper is his insistence that although Christ the Son is physically absent from us, the Holy Spirit lifts us to him in his ascended and glorified state. The inseparable works of the Trinity are a foundation stone of the classic doctrine of the Trinity.

From this we can see how Paul, in Ephesians again, places the Son's mediatorial work in a Trinitarian context, one that shapes Christian worship. Addressing the fact that Christ brings unity out of disorder, Jew and Gentile becoming one in his church, he writes that "through him [Christ] we both [Jew and Gentile] have access in one Spirit to the Father" (Eph. 2:18). The unity and catholicity of the church, which has been his theme from Ephesians 2:11, is itself grounded on the indivisible union of the Trinity. Because God is indivisible, from which eternal reality all three persons work together inseparably, he brings unity in the Son, breaking down and eradicating the alienation between man and God, and between the naturally hostile forces of Jew and Gentile, so that all are one in Christ Jesus (Gal. 3:26–29). This comes through the access we are given to the Father through the Son and by the power of the Spirit, an access that has been granted through the Son's incarnation, and most pointedly his death and resurrection (Eph. 2:14, 18). By this access we are given to share in the life of the Trinity, becoming progressively conformed to the image of the Son (2 Cor. 3:18–4:6), effected by the Holy Spirit.

42. Calvin, *Sermons on Ephesians*, 291.
43. Calvin, *Sermons on Ephesians*, 579–80.
44. See Letham, *Holy Trinity*, 1–84.

The Incarnation

The incarnation is the foundation of our union with Christ. In taking human flesh, the Son has united humanity to himself so that humanity, by the power of the Holy Spirit and through faith, is taken up into communion with the Trinity, into the life of the Trinity. Calvin stressed that the incarnation is the pledge of our salvation.[45] Indeed, he adds, in commenting on Ephesians 1:23: "This is the highest honor of the church that, unless he is united to us, the Son of God reckons himself in some measure imperfect. What an encouragement it is for us to hear, that, not until he has us as one with himself, is he complete in all his parts, or does he wish to be regarded as whole!"[46]

In taking human nature to himself, the Son affirms creation, since man is its chief part. It is a pledge of our sonship and also of the continued value of the entire creation. The resurrection is our renewal and simultaneously marks the redemption of the universe, as Paul writes in Romans 8:23–25.

Along these lines, Torrance observes that "the Christian faith starts with the knowledge of God in Jesus Christ. In that knowledge we are concerned not only with the duality of God and man in one person, but with the unity of Christ's person and his act in the one work of salvation. . . . We cannot therefore think of his person apart from his atoning work, or of his atoning work in abstraction from his person."[47] As the Nicene Creed put it, he was made man "for us and our salvation."

Furthermore, he entered a world ravaged by human sin. The first-century world was seething with anger and discontent. Israel was occupied by a foreign power, suffering from severe economic

45. Calvin, *Institutes*, 2.12.2.

46. "Hic vero summus honor est Ecclesiae, quod se Filius Dei quodammodo imperfectum reputat, nisi nobis sit coniunctus. Quanta consolatio, dum audimus tunc demum suis omnibus partibus constare et integrum velle haberi, dum nos secum habet." John Calvin, *Commentarii in Pauli Epistolas ad Galatas, ad Ephesios, ad Philippenses, ad Colossenses*, ed. Helmut Feld, Ioannis Calvini Opera Omnia (Librairie Droz, 1992), 176; John Calvin, *Calvin's Commentaries: The Epistles of Paul to the Galatians, Ephesians, Philippians and Colossians*, ed. Thomas F. Torrance and David W. Torrance, trans. T. H. L. Parker (Eerdmans, 1965), 138.

47. Torrance, *Incarnation*, 37.

problems, with large numbers forced off the land by unscrupulous landowners who were often absent; note the number of parables in which Jesus refers to absentee landlords.[48]

The Son took our place by taking our nature, and in that nature he suffered, died, and was buried. He took on himself the common infirmities of the fallen human race, sin excepted: the physical pains and weaknesses, the hunger and thirst, the weariness and sorrow. The reality of the incarnation means that one of the Trinity, according to the flesh, cried as a baby, was fed, was changed, and had diarrhea.[49] This is utterly astonishing, mind-blowing. In the unity of the Father and the Holy Spirit, the eternal Son, in condescending to our low condition, allowed himself to be cared for by human parents, entrusting himself to a young girl called Mary.

Cyril draws poignant attention to the impact of the lowliness that the Son took on in his incarnation, reaching its climax at the cross:

> It is equally possible, of course, that someone will object that it is belittling and inappropriate that God the Word should cry out, or be afraid of death, that he should pray against taking the cup of suffering or be appointed to the office of priesthood. Yes, I would agree. Such things are somewhat ignoble by comparison with the transcendent divine nature and glory, but it is precisely in them that we can see the poverty that he willingly endured for us. Whenever you find the dishonour arising from his self-emptying to be a problem, wonder all the more greatly at how much the Son loves us; you say that it is something mean, but he willingly did it for your sake. He wept like a man to protect your own tears. For salvation's sake he was afraid and at times allowed his flesh to suffer as it ought to, so that he might render

48. Roger Amos, *Matthew: A Commentary* (Paul Thomas, 2023), 561–64. Amos is one of only a few commentators to relate the content of Matthew at this point to the prevailing social and economic situation in first-century Israel.

49. Recall the discussion of Aphthartodocetism in chapter 6, which heretically denied that Jesus suffered the physical ailments that beset us on the proposed grounds that he was without blemish, and Thomas Aquinas's treatment of Jesus and human infirmities (*ST*, 1a.1–3) to which we referred in chapter 8.

> us less fearful; . . . in his humanity he was called weak, so that he might put a stop to your weakness; in prayer he reached up even in supplication, so that he might declare the Father's ear to be accessible even to your prayers. He slept, so that you might learn not to sleep when tempted, but rather to reach out in prayer. . . . Why did he thus make human weakness his very own? It was so that we might believe that he really did become a man, while still remaining what he was, God.[50]

The Cross and Burial

We will devote much less attention to the atonement than some might expect and what the subject requires and deserves. The reason for this is that this is a book about the Son as such, rather than a complete account of all his work. I have written at some length elsewhere about, and I will draw attention to other writing that explores, this immense subject more fully and, in Appendix B, consider a long-running theory that raises questions that need addressing.

Two major points need to be held together about the cry of dereliction, "My God, my God, why have you forsaken me?" (Matt. 27:46).[51] One is the reality of dereliction. Jesus was alone, deserted by his friends, betrayed by Judas, shunned temporarily by Peter, derided by passers-by, mocked, and abused. Only a handful of women and the apostle John stood by him at the cross. Above all—and this is what is most pointedly involved—he was the righteous sufferer to whom the psalm ultimately referred. Refracted through

50. Cyril of Alexandria, "A Defence of the Twelve Anathemas Against Theodoret," in *St. Cyril of Alexandria: Three Christological Treatises*, trans. Daniel King, Fathers of the Church 129 (Catholic University of America Press, 2014), 121–22.

51. See Klaas Schilder, *Christ Crucified*, trans. Henry Zylstra (Eerdmans, 1944), for a profound and penetrating exposition of Christ's atoning suffering and death. Particularly noteworthy is Schilder's treatment of Christ as an *exlex*, someone who was beyond what even the full exaction of the law could inflict, placed in a condition of utter perdition to bear the full unmitigated wrath of God, he being one of the Trinity. Here we see the total identification of God with his people in that he took upon himself to bear the burden and the curse that we had deservedly earned for ourselves.

the experience of David, it is he preeminently who cried, "My God, my God, why have you forsaken me?" It appears that his experience of ongoing communion with the Father was clouded. "He who knew no sin was made sin for us," Paul wrote (2 Cor. 5:21).

"We may not know, we cannot tell, what pains he had to bear" runs the hymn,[52] and it is true that we will never know, whatever very clever analytic philosophers may claim, for we do not have to bear the sins of the world on our shoulders, even more for the fact that we ourselves are intrinsically unrighteous. This takes the sufferings of the incarnate Son far beyond the bounds of physical and mental pain, although that was indisputably part of the mix.

Second, Jesus the eternal Son was not at any point detached from the Father and the Holy Spirit in the one indivisible being of God. There was not, and there could not be, any severance of the life of the Holy Trinity. Indeed, even in the midst of his intense agony, Jesus cries, "My God, my God . . . ," "Father, forgive them," "Father, into your hands I commit my spirit" (Matt. 27:46; Luke 23:34, 46). He continued to live in the unity of the Trinity, for "through the eternal Spirit he offered himself without blemish to God [the Father]" (Heb. 9:14).

Jesus committed his spirit to the Father. This is usually understood to mean that Jesus handed over his human spirit, much as Stephen was to do when he was being martyred (Acts 7:59). Yet there is reason to consider that this may refer to the Holy Spirit, who had anointed him at the Jordan, at the outset of his public ministry. Now that this phase had come to an end, Jesus handed back the Spirit to the Father, who had sent him. The Holy Spirit, as Cyril was to say, is Christ's own Spirit. This idea lines up with Hebrews 9:14. If it is understood this way, however, it cannot be taken in an absolute sense; after all, it was the Spirit who was to raise Jesus from the dead (Rom. 8:10–11), and he himself, with the Father, would send the Spirit at Pentecost. Moreover, the Trinity is indivisible. If indeed such an interpretation is preferred—and I am not saying that it should be—it can refer only to the Spirit as given

52. Cecil Frances Alexander, "There Is a Green Hill Far Away" (1848).

for Jesus' mediatorial ministry at his baptism, signifying that that work was now accomplished. That would be compatible with Jesus' final word, "It is finished!" (John 19:30).

It is here, on the cross, that Jesus "bore our sins in his own body on the tree" (1 Peter 2:24). According to the Westminster Larger Catechism, we are united to him in grace and glory, in this instance in his death and burial. He united himself to us to the extent of enduring the wrath of God; we share with him in deliverance from death in his resurrection.[53] The Westminster Larger Catechism expresses it well in Q. 49:

> Christ humbled himself in his death, in that having been betrayed by Judas, forsaken by his disciples, scorned and rejected by the world, condemned by Pilate, and tormented by his persecutors; having also conflicted with the terrors of death, and the powers of darkness, felt and borne the weight of God's wrath, he laid down his life an offering for sin, enduring the painful, shameful, and cursed death of the cross.

Karl Barth adds, "God has not abandoned the world and man in the unlimited need of the situation, but that he willed to bear this need as his own, that he took it upon himself, and that he cries with man in this need."[54]

The need for this arose because of human sin. A millennium ago, Anselm explored this in his epoch-making book *Cur Deus homo?* In a sustained piece of reasoning, he argued that since man had violated the honor of God, he must repay what is owed and additionally make restitution for the offense to his honor. Satisfaction must be made for sin, or else punishment will follow. But, Anselm continued, no one was qualified to do so, since all had infringed the honor of God. Only one who was not a sinner could do this. In keeping with God's character, it could be fitting only if it was done by a God-man. He would be powerful enough to do it, Anselm

53. See Letham, *Work of Christ*, 126–55, 177–80.
54. Karl Barth, *CD*, IV/1:215.

maintained, while as man it would be fitting that he should do it, and given his sinlessness he would be doing it out of his own volition.[55] While couched in the language of feudalism, and colored by the penitential system, Anselm's treatise helped pave the way for a later, fuller, and more precise biblical doctrine. For his part, Barth recognized the dire situation of the human race when he wrote, "But those who are judged and rejected and condemned by God as wrong-doers are lost and condemned to perish, indeed they are already perishing."[56] He referred to "the darkness in which there is no light," "the power of his condemnation[,] . . . the fire of his wrath which consumes and destroys them. . . . The life of God can only mean death for his enemies."[57] "God would not be God . . . if there could be any escaping the sequence of sin and destruction. It means eternal perdition to have God against us. But if we will what God does not will, we do have God against us, and therefore we hurry and run and stumble and fall into eternal perdition."[58] This is the background to the atonement.[59]

> Tell me, ye who hear him groaning, was there ever grief like his?
> Friends thro' fear his cause disowning, foes insulting his distress;
> many hands were raised to wound him, none would interpose to save;
> but the deepest stroke that pierced him was the stroke that Justice gave.

55. Anselm, *Cur Deus homo?*, 1.11–2.11.
56. Barth, *CD*, IV/1:220.
57. Barth, *CD*, IV/1:221.
58. Barth, *CD*, IV/1:221.
59. Barth has some fine words on this, but his doctrine of the atonement is marred by the universalistic coloring he gave it, Christ taking the place of all people, even though Barth distanced himself from universal salvation as such. How much easier it would be for us and for every generation of Christians if this were so. Need the apostles have risked and surrendered their lives? Need the martyrs have remained resolute and faced "the tyrant's brandished steel, the lion's gory mane"? Reginald Heber, "The Son of God Goes Forth to War" (1827). Need Ignatius have traveled all the way to Rome, knowing that he had been sentenced to be eaten by wild animals?

Ye who think of sin but lightly nor suppose the evil great
here may view its nature rightly, here its guilt may estimate.
Mark the sacrifice appointed, see who bears the awful load;
'tis the Word, the Lord's Anointed, Son of Man and Son of God.[60]

"He who is in the one person the electing God and the one elect man is as the rejecting God, the God who judges sin in the flesh, in his own person the one rejected man, the Lamb who bears the sin of the world that the world should no longer have to bear it or be able to bear it, that it should be radically and totally taken away from it."[61] This is not some fiction or make-believe. Barth is correct in pressing the point that the Reformers' expression "the imputation of the alien righteousness of Jesus Christ," *on its own*, says far too little. "Rather, the alien righteousness which has been effected not in and by us but in the sacrifice of Jesus Christ does become and is always ours, so that in him we are no longer unrighteous but righteous before God."[62] We are constituted righteous (Rom. 5:19) on the basis of the righteousness of Christ received through faith, "placed in the category of righteous persons" by God because of our union with Christ.[63] He who knew no sin was made sin for us, with the result that we might become the righteousness of God in him (2 Cor. 5:21). This goes beyond even the liberating wonders of forgiveness.

In all his life and ministry, the Son acted for us, on our behalf, but especially at the cross. There he was our substitute, "bearing our sins in his body on the tree" (1 Peter 2:24). A substitute takes the place of some other person or persons. As in soccer, a player comes onto the field in place of a colleague who is taken off, so the incarnate Son took our place and so bore our sin. He also acted as a representative, such that he acted on our behalf. As a member of

60. Thomas Kelly, "Stricken, Smitten, and Afflicted" (1804; alt. 1961), in *Trinity Hymnal* (Great Commission Publications, 1990), no. 257.

61. Barth, *CD*, IV/1:237.

62. Barth, *CD*, IV/1:283.

63. John Murray, *The Epistle to the Romans* (Eerdmans, 1965), 203–6, here 205; C. E. B. Cranfield, *A Critical and Exegetical Commentary on the Epistle to the Romans* (T&T Clark, 1979), 290–91; Letham, *Work of Christ*, 262–63.

Congress or Parliament will cast a vote theoretically on behalf of his constituents, here in all of the Son's actions we are included, since his acts are performed as ours. Yet a substitute is not the same person as the one that is replaced, and neither is a representative the same as those he represents. In this case, it would appear that the innocent one is punished and the guilty goes scot-free. In contrast, the Bible very severely condemns judges who punish the innocent or acquit the guilty (Ex. 23:6–8; Deut. 27:25; Prov. 17:5, 26; 18:5; Isa. 5:23). As I have remarked elsewhere, these problems are overcome and these twin realities, substitution and representation, are cemented by the union that Christ has established with us in his incarnation and as the Spirit applies it to us. Union with Christ provides the underlying rationale, for Christ and his people are one, and the atonement is not a legal fiction but an overpowering reality.[64] Hence, Paul can write that not only did Christ take our place and act on our behalf, but since he and we are one, we died with Christ, and so we rose from the dead with and in him (Rom. 6:1f. et al.).

By his atoning death, Christ expiates our sins, effects propitiation (Rom. 3:25–26), reconciles God to us (5:8–11), and by conquering the devil (Col. 2:14–15) redeems us from the power of sin and such enslaving forces.[65]

In the face of death itself, we are bolstered by the fact that Jesus, the eternal Son, "was buried" (1 Cor. 15:4). Writing to the people of the Thessalonian church, encouraging them in the face of the death of loved ones, Paul writes that "we believe that Jesus died . . . and rose again" (1 Thess. 4:14). Jesus, the eternal Son, one of the Trinity, has experienced *human* death and *human* burial! No obstacle in our way is greater than he endured or more formidable than he conquered.

64. Letham, *Systematic Theology*, 558–61.

65. For a much fuller exposition of the various elements in the biblical doctrine of atonement, see Donald MacLeod, *Christ Crucified: Understanding the Atonement* (IVP Academic, 2014); Murray, *Redemption*; Letham, *Work of Christ*; and other salient literature, such as Leon Morris, *The Apostolic Preaching of the Cross* (Tyndale Press, 1955); James I. Packer, "What Did the Cross Achieve? The Logic of Penal Substitution," in *Collected Shorter Writings of J. I. Packer* (Paternoster, 1998), 1:85–123.

Resurrection, Ascension, and Enthronement

At the transfiguration, Peter, James, and John see Jesus' appearance changed, made dazzling white as he is engaging in conversation with two men, Moses and Elijah. This is the transfiguration of the incarnate Son, his divine glory shining through his assumed humanity (Matt. 17:1–8; Mark 9:2–10; Luke 9:28–36; John 1:14b; 2 Peter 1:16–18). This is evident by his communicating with Moses and Elijah, engaging in discussion, speaking human language. Moreover, the focus of their conversation is his imminent departure (exodus) at Jerusalem. This theme, Jesus' imminent death and resurrection, is repeated as he and the apostles descend the mountain afterward. This is the incarnate Son who is transfigured beyond anything that could be accomplished by human art or device. He appears in glory, revealing who he is, the eternal Son, one of the Trinity, according to the flesh. His later appearances to Paul and John, both of which were after his resurrection, ascension, and glorification, struck them down, knocking the life out of them. Here Peter, James, and John are overcome, although not quite to the same extent. Nevertheless, the difference in reaction is one of degree rather than kind.

Since this was the transfiguration of Jesus' incarnate state, it presages the transfiguration of all who are united to him at his parousia (1 John 3:1–2), when we will see him as he is and we will be like him. From this angle, salvation entails the Son's transforming us into the image of his glory by the Holy Spirit. This is what Paul states in 2 Corinthians when he appeals to the case of Moses, who, when he came down from Mount Sinai after meeting with Yahweh, had to cover his face, since he was reflecting the glory of God and it was too much for the people to bear. But while this experience was confined to Moses, and the glory he transmitted was temporary because it was fading away, now that the Spirit has come we are all being transformed, and this will neither be temporary nor require concealment. "We all are being transformed from one degree of glory to another, by the Spirit of the Lord" (2 Cor. 3:18).[66] This is

66. See A. M. Ramsey, *The Glory of God and the Transfiguration of Christ* (Longmans, 1949).

the ultimate goal to which we are being drawn, magnetized, by the Spirit. We will refer to this again later in the chapter.

I have discussed elsewhere the relationship between Christ's resurrection and ours.[67] When Christ rose from the dead, there was a dramatic transformation. In line with Paul's comment in Romans 1:4, he was appointed Son of God with power by the Holy Spirit and had been given plenipotentiary authority in heaven and on earth as our Mediator (Matt. 28:18). He was Son already, in eternity, and in human weakness as a descendant of David (Rom. 1:3–4), but at this point, as our Mediator he was invested with supreme authority, raised by the Spirit of the Father (8:10–11). In purely physical terms, he was able to pass through closed doors (Luke 24:36–43; John 20:19–20), and was aware of Thomas's comments one week earlier even though he was not present in the room at the time they were made (John 20:24–28). He disappeared from sight. He ascended to the right hand of the Father.

On the other hand, there was a clear continuity between his resurrection body and his earlier presence. He ate a piece of broiled fish (Luke 24:41–43). He prepared breakfast for the disciples (John 21:4–14). He engaged in ordinary conversation. He walked for several miles with a couple of his followers (Luke 24:13–32). He sat down to a meal. He was mistaken for another person, a fellow disciple or a gardener (Luke 24:13f.; John 20:14–15).

Furthermore, Christ's resurrection and ours are a single reality, separated by indefinite time. Our resurrection is effected by the same Spirit who raised Jesus from the dead (Rom. 8:10–11). Christ's resurrection body is the basis for ours, both animated by the Holy Spirit and exhibiting the same features (1 Cor. 15:35–49). I have written on this extensively elsewhere.[68]

At the ascension he moved, in Torrance's phrase, "from man's place to God's place," from one sphere of existence to another.[69]

67. Letham, *Union with Christ*, 129–39; Letham, *Work of Christ*, 211–23.

68. Letham, *Work of Christ*, 220–23; Letham, *Union with Christ*, 60–65; Letham, *Systematic Theology*, 860–65.

69. Thomas F. Torrance, *Space, Time and Resurrection* (Eerdmans, 1976), 106–58, here 127–28.

His hands were raised in benediction, signifying that that was to be the normal, one could almost say, default position for his church from now until his return.[70] He was invested with supreme authority as Mediator (Matt. 28:18–20; Eph. 1:17–23; Phil. 2:9–11). He was crowned with glory and honor (Heb. 1:4; 2:5–9). All this was the prelude to the sending of the Holy Spirit at Pentecost (John 7:37–39; 14:1–16:28), with the transforming and empowering effect on the church.[71]

Consequently, when he revealed himself later to Saul of Tarsus and to John, they were scarcely able to bear the sight of his glory and splendor. Saul, bearing down on the disciples at Damascus, ready to consign them to prison or worse, was struck down to the ground, temporarily blinded by the blazing light that had appeared. From that moment, he was a changed man. Confronted by the Son of God, he engaged in conversation, obeyed his voice, spent time in seclusion, and emerged as the great apostle of the Gentiles (Acts 9:3–22; 26:9–19).

For his part, John in isolation, possibly in a penal colony, was met by the glorified Son and simply fell at his feet as though he were dead. Fearful, Christ reassured him, iterating the fact that he is the risen one, who conquered death because he is life itself, the Alpha and the Omega and everything in between,[72] having the destiny of the church and the world firmly and irremovably in his hands (Rev. 1:9–18). As Lord of life, of the universe he created and the people and entities within it, he is the center and heart of the salvation that he came to enact.

The Son, the Sacraments, and Salvation

For the reasons mentioned above, we are not going to enter into lengthy and complex analyses of the *ordo salutis*, for which one

70. Robert Letham, *The Message of the Person of Christ: The Word Made Flesh* (Inter-Varsity Press, 2013), 193–207; Torrance, *Space, Time and Resurrection*, 117–18.

71. See Robert Letham, *The Holy Spirit* (P&R Publishing, 2023), 137–95.

72. The expressions "Alpha and Omega" and "the first and the last" are merisms, which, in referring to the first and last elements of a sequence, intend to include all the intervening elements as well.

can refer to a host of authorities. The message is that each element is fulfilled in the Son, is administered by the Son, and ultimately consists in the Son himself. As we saw earlier, the gospel of God concerns his Son, Jesus Christ our Lord, both in his time of weakness on earth when, having become man, he lived as one of us in the low conditions of a fallen world, and also in his glory, power, and authority after his resurrection and ascension.

Therefore, as the glorified Mediator, the Son who now and forever is both God and man, whose humanity shines in glorious splendor under the direction of the Holy Spirit, he is the center and focus of the saving process we experience in the time between his ascension and his return.

He calls us to himself. As when on earth he called to the dead Lazarus, "Come forth!" (John 11:43), who then emerged from the tomb wrapped in graveclothes, so he calls us powerfully and effectually through the means he has appointed, the Word preached (5:24–28). He does this in union with the Spirit, who grants us the life that Jesus promised the Samaritan woman (4:13–14), for the glorified Christ, the eternal Son, is the resurrection and the life. In so doing, he—with the Spirit and the Father—enables us to believe and trust him, ceasing reliance on our own achievements and worth.

He unites us to himself by the Spirit through his Word proclaimed by human agents. He becomes our covenant head, the leader and perfecter of the church, the team that he has destined from before the foundation of the world for salvation, to be his partner in the unfettered work of the eons to come. Through faith, we are cleared of the accumulated guilt of all the sins we have committed and are invested with his own righteousness, given the status of sons acquitted, justified, vindicated, declared to be his brothers.[73]

He by the Holy Spirit progressively conforms us to his own image. Whereas we were renegades, "miserable offenders" in the words of the 1662 *Book of Common Prayer of the Church of England*, we are on a trajectory to be "like him" when he returns, when we

73. The term "sons" is preferable, viewed inclusively, at this point to "sons and daughters," since it denotes the reality that we share, by adoption, the same relation to the Father as does the Son.

"shall see him as he is" (1 John 3:1–2), completely conformed to his glorious identity.

All these aspects of the achievement and progress of salvation, as the Westminster Assembly defined them, are to be seen as "union and communion with [Christ] in grace and glory" (WLC 65–90). As Paul wrote in Ephesians 1:3–14, the whole panorama of salvation is "in Christ."

The sacraments of the new covenant—baptism and the Lord's Supper—are concurrent with the time between the ascension and the parousia. Among many other things, they signal both absence and presence. Christ is physically and personally absent during this time in the sense that the regular interactions that took place between him and his followers as recorded in the Gospels cannot now occur. He is also present, however, since the Spirit brings us into union with him. We are united to Christ in baptism. We feed on him in the Eucharist, the Lord's Supper.

The sacraments lead us to Christ. They do not draw us away from him, since they are all about him. The Lord's Supper is the supper *of the Lord*; it belongs to him, it refers to him, it is communion with him. Baptism is baptism *into Christ*.

The Son unites us to himself in baptism by the Holy Spirit. Of course, faith is essential, whether the faith of the one baptized or the faith of the household to which the one baptized belongs. Both are present in the New Testament. The dominant one, given the missionary situation, is the faith of the person who is baptized, given that most came from a Gentile background. On the other hand, whole households were baptized, often on the basis of the household head's profession of faith (Acts 16:31–33; cf. James 5:13–15), since corporate solidarity was the name of the game, as it is in most societies throughout history.

Paul makes clear the connection between baptism and Christ, particularly his death and resurrection (Rom. 6:1ff.). He connects it to the washing away of sins (Acts 22:16; 1 Cor. 6:9–11), which can come about only through Christ. Putting it another way, Christ unites us to himself in his sufferings and glory; Christ washes away our sins, in union with both the Father and the Spirit.

In his commentary on Ephesians, Calvin remarks that in the Lord's Supper, Christ "offers his body to be enjoyed by us, to nourish us to eternal life." Calvin adds that "in a sense he pours himself into us [and] . . . by the power of his Spirit he engrafts us into his body, so that from him we derive life." This, he confesses, is "a great mystery. . . . No language can do it justice."[74] In his preaching on Ephesians, Calvin states that by the power of the Holy Spirit, Christ makes the substance of his body and blood flow down to us.[75] This is reflected in the classic Reformed confessions.[76] The Westminster Confession of Faith states that faithful receivers "receive, and feed upon, Christ" (WCF 29.7).

Behind this is the fact that the flesh and blood of Christ are life-giving because of his having assumed human nature into union with his eternal person. The Son, one of the Trinity, took human nature into union and consequently in the resurrection he invested that nature with the qualities of being able to transmit life, so that Paul wrote that the *risen* Christ has become "life-giving Spirit" (1 Cor. 15:45). Mark Garcia argues that "Christ, salvation, and sacrament thus belong together in the sixteenth-century mind."[77] They belonged together in the fifth-century mind too, the world of Cyril. They belong together on the pages of Scripture. We pray that the twenty-first-century mind, such as it is in its fragmented state, may agree.

Salvation consists in the Son's uniting us to himself by the Holy Spirit and thus presenting us to the Father in the unity of the indivisible Trinity to share the relation he has to the Father, while simultaneously renovating the entire cosmos. This was well expressed by Maximus the Confessor in *Ambiguum 7*.[78] He wrote

74. Commenting on Ephesians 5:30–32, Calvin, *In Pauli Epistolas*, 272–74; Calvin, *Epistles of Paul*, 208–10.

75. Calvin, *Sermons on Ephesians*, 360, 403–4.

76. Someone might object and mention Huldrych Zwingli as an equal representative of the Reformed tradition. But no major Reformed confession adopts the position that has, questionably, been attributed to Zwingli. Moreover, the conclusions that Cyril drew in his eleventh anathema in his *Third Letter to Nestorius* should be borne in mind. See chapters 4 and 6.

77. Mark Garcia, *Life in Christ: Union with Christ and Twofold Grace in Calvin's Theology* (Paternoster, 2008), 149.

78. *PG*, 91:1092b–1093a.

that man is the mediator and unifier of created beings but failed in his mission. Hence, in the incarnation Christ began to unify man, restoring him to God with a view to the reunification of the whole of creation.[79] As we noted earlier, Louth has posited two arcs, embracing the soteriological and cosmic dimensions of redemption —or, in Maximus's terms, "deification," which is another word for "glorification."

Incarnation, Atonement, and Deification

The Proximate Reason for the Incarnation Was the Atonement

The incarnation was for the purpose of atonement. There could be no atonement without incarnation. Christ Jesus came into the world to save sinners (1 Tim. 1:15). This was the only solution to human sin compatible with the nature of God (Rom. 3:21–26); the prime question there was the justice of God, "that he might be just" as well as the justifier of the one who has faith in Christ. Redemption required the satisfaction of God's law, of his own justice and righteousness. Given the underlying issues—human sin, the just wrath of God, the need for perfect obedience by the substitute and representative—no other way was "fitting" (Heb. 2:10) than that the Son should become man, live in perfect filial obedience to the Father, and render sacrifice on the cross.

The shadow of the cross hangs over the entirety of the Gospels —indeed, over the whole of Scripture. Hebrews sums it up (Heb. 2:10–18). There the author demonstrates that the Son took flesh and blood precisely that "through death he might destroy the one who has the power of death, that is, the devil, and deliver all those who through fear of death were subject to lifelong slavery" (vv. 14–15). This accounts for the sufferings attendant upon this plan.

Death and resurrection is a prominent and recurring subtext throughout the Old Testament and comes to full expression in the New. It is crucial to Paul, but of the biblical writers he was by no means alone. For us, this is the most pressing existential reality that

79. See Jean-Claude Larchet, *La Divinisation de l'Homme Selon Saint Maxime le Confesseur* (Les éditions du Cerf, 1996), 109–11; Andrew Louth, *Maximus the Confessor* (Routledge, 1996), 63–77.

we and the world currently face—to come to terms with the claims of Christ that are crystallized at the cross and the empty tomb. For individual persons, eternity hangs on this—hence the urgency of gospel proclamation as exhibited in Acts.

Thus, justification is grounded in the obedience of Christ—active in his lifelong fulfillment of the requirements of God's law, and passive in his suffering the consequences of sin for those he represented and took into union. A lamb without blemish was required under the Mosaic code, foreshadowing the offering of the Son, the Lamb of God. Bloodshedding was necessary, a death offered. We receive Christ by faith, like a hand held out to receive a gift, and thus are united to him and receive his righteousness imputed to us as members of the team of which he is the captain and head. Atonement and justification are inseparably connected; Christ the Son is the ground of both.

The Reason for the Atonement Was Deification

The word "deification" (*theosis*) may sound jarring to Protestant ears.[80] It is the umbrella concept for the view of salvation in the Greek and Russian churches and those allied with them. It was the synonym for "salvation" in the Greek church in the early centuries, at the time and in the place where the foundation stones of Christian doctrine articulated by the church were laid. In the Latin church, the term "glorification" is used, with a subtle difference. Glory is what is of the essence of God, splendor too great for us to take in at this present time (Acts 9:3–9; 1 John 3:1–2; Rev. 1:10–18). Yet there is no independent quality floating around to be called "glory" or viewed in some way independently of God. Hence "deification," I'd

80. But see Carl Mosser, "John Calvin and Early Reformed Theology," in Paul L. Gavrilyuk, Andrew Hofer, and Matthew Levering, eds., *The Oxford Handbook of Deification* (Oxford: Oxford University Press, 2024), 317–34, who provides evidence that this was familiar to classic Reformed theology. He concludes, after considering the writings of Zwingli, Oecolampadius, Bucer, and Calvin, "Since the nineteenth century, the works of Albrecht Ritschl, Adolf von Harnack, and others have convinced generations of scholars that a truly Protestant theology—whether Lutheran or Reformed—is inimical to deification. Careful examination of the primary sources of the Reformed tradition tells a very different story."

suggest, has benefits because it tells us right away that conformity to the image of God, ultimately to the glory of God, is what is in view. Moreover, while "glorification" is generally adopted for the final ultimate stage of our transformation, "deification" has historically been seen as a process already begun—"the men of grace have found glory begun below," in Isaac Watts's words[81]—which will reach its fullest extent at the parousia, when "we shall be like him, for we shall see him as he is" (1 John 3:2). This is the ultimate purpose of God. The atonement is not an end in itself. It is the beginning of the end—or, putting it another way, it is the end of the beginning. The overall plan of God is that we, his church, be totally conformed to him, reflecting his glory on a finite level, sharing the relation to the Father that the Son has, in the union of the Holy Spirit—in his case a natural relation, in ours one by adoption. As Calvin wrote, "nothing more outstanding can be imagined," for "the goal of the gospel is to make us sooner or later like God; indeed it is, so to speak, a kind of deification (*quasi deificari*)."[82] Moreover, it reaches beyond even that to include the entire cosmos, which will be released from its present bondage to enjoy the full liberty of the creation as God eternally intended and planned it.

Thus Christ, upon his resurrection, ascension, and enthronement, was made head over all things for the church (Eph. 1:21–23), and given plenipotential authority over the entire creation (Matt. 28:18). This is a transformation beyond our wildest dreams.[83] We will share in the administration of the new cosmos. Hebrews 2 reflects on this. Humanity was placed in authority over the original creation, as Psalm 2 reflects (Heb. 2:5–9). Sadly, we failed to act in accordance with our place; Adam sinned, and the race came under judgment. At present, we do not see the creation in the form intended for it. The evidence is all around us and well known. But we see Jesus, seated at the right hand of the Father, and we recognize that the process has begun, definitively established in the cross and

81. Isaac Watts, "Come, We That Love the Lord" (1707).

82. Calvin, *In Epistolas Canonicas*, 327–28; Calvin, *Commentaries on Hebrews and 1&2 Peter*, 330, on 2 Peter 1:4.

83. That is, assuming that we all have wild dreams.

resurrection, and will reach its magnificent moment of liberation at the appointed time.

Meanwhile, united to Christ in his death and resurrection, we have received the Spirit of life to put to death the deeds of the body and so live, enabling us to follow in his steps all the way. "And we all, with unveiled face, beholding the glory of the Lord, are being transformed into the same image, from one degree of glory to another. For this is from the Lord who is the Spirit" (2 Cor. 3:18).

The Ultimate Reason for the Incarnation Is Deification and Cosmic Renewal

Therefore, we can say that while the proximate reason for the incarnation was the atonement, which lies at the heart of the whole biblical revelation and is pressing for us here and now, the ultimate reason is the new heavens and new earth, the eternal state of dynamic growth. This is revealed as being the ultimate purpose of God (Rom. 8:18–25, 29; Eph. 1:16–23; Phil. 3:10–16, 20–21; Rev. 7:13–17). It is a far cry from the words of "Once in Royal David's City," which says of the redeemed that "all in white shall wait around." In order to grasp this, it will help to compare the curse on creation, in terms of the ground and those who work it (Gen. 3:15–19) and its eventual deliverance (Rom. 8:23–25).

Rome was not built in a day. There are stages to pass through on the way to this destined goal. First and foremost was the atonement for sin as a prelude to its eventual complete eradication.

For us to enter the eschatological kingdom, it was necessary for two distinct but inseparably related things to occur: that atonement be made for sin (1) for us to be freed from guilt, and (2) to change our condition (Heb. 12:14 et al.), to be freed from the power of sin and to be transformed into the image of Christ.

The Bible makes clear the interaction between human sin and redemption, as it bears on the state of the universe—note the contrast between Genesis 3:15–19, where sin disrupts the environment, with Romans 8:23–25, where the redemption of humanity is concurrent with the redemption of the universe. God's Son, Jesus Christ our Lord, effects this. At the start of the chapter, we noted Paul's introduction to Romans, where he wrote that God's Son, Jesus Christ the Lord, *is* the gospel. He is the eternal Son of the Father, one of the Trinity, who lives as man, and so lives in union with us and we with him.

"Paul, . . . set apart to the gospel of God . . . concerning his Son, . . . Jesus Christ our Lord" (Rom. 1:1–4). "I am under obligation [to the gospel]" (v. 14). "I am eager to preach the gospel" (v. 15). "I am not ashamed of the gospel, for it is the power of God unto salvation for everyone who believes" (v. 16), for it concerns God's Son, Jesus Christ our Lord.

Maranatha (1 Cor. 16:22).

Thou art the everlasting Word, the Father's only Son
God manifestly seen and heard, and heaven's beloved One.
Worthy, O Lamb of God, art thou,
that every knee to thee should bow,
that every knee to thee should bow.

In thee most perfectly expressed the Father's glories shine,
Of the full deity possessed, eternally divine.
Worthy, etc.

True image of the infinite, whose essence is concealed;
brightness of uncreated light; the heart of God revealed.
Worthy, etc.

But the high myst'ries of thy name an angel's grasp transcend;
the Father only—glorious claim!—the Son can comprehend.
Worthy, etc.

Throughout the universe of bliss, the centre thou and sun;
th'eternal theme of praise is this, to heav'n's beloved One.
Worthy, etc.[84]

84. Josiah Conder (1789–1855), "Thou Art the Everlasting Word" (n.d.); tune: SUPREMACY.

Appendix A
Classic Christology and Adoption

In both this and the second appendix, I will reflect on proposals that have been around for some years that, while not new in the sense of being hot off the press, have significant implications for our view of the person and work of Christ. In both cases, I intend to highlight aspects that arouse major concerns of which we should be aware.

In his outstanding book on adoption,[1] David Garner introduces a distinctive idea on Christology, one that has gained some traction in biblical-theological circles. He argues that we are adopted as sons in union with Christ, which of course is straightforward both biblically and theologically. In order for this to happen, however, Garner contends, it was necessary that Christ first be adopted himself. Believers cannot receive the adoption as sons unless Christ was first adopted for them. He writes, "Christ brings *no* privilege of eschatological sonship (adoption) to believers if *he himself* has not attained to eschatological sonship (adoption) himself."[2] He concludes:

> To the point, there is no adoption of believers in Christ Jesus without the adoption of Christ Jesus. To insist otherwise forces a soteriological abstraction in which believers would acquire salvation in some way other than by the Son. That Paul does not use the term *adoption* for the resurrection of Christ simply cannot then lead to the simplistic and errant conclusion that Christ was never

1. David B. Garner, *Sons in the Son: The Riches and Reach of Adoption in Christ* (P&R Publishing, 2016).

2. Garner, *Sons in the Son*, 194 (italics original).

> adopted. To the contrary, Paul's method of theological reciprocity between Christology and soteriology mandates the adoption of the Lord Jesus. Since the believers' resurrection is adoption (Rom. 8:23), so, too, Christ's resurrection was his adoption (1:4).[3]

I was alerted to this book when I heard two reliable preachers recommend it from the pulpit, stating that Christ was adopted as Son.

Before we progress, it is significant to note that Garner states what has become almost commonplace among Reformed writers, that very little has been written on adoption, nothing of real significance, and that it is greatly neglected. This evidences more the limitations of the reading of the majority of modern Reformed theologians. Among other things, they have either been ignorant of or ignored the massive amount of reflection in the Greek and Russian churches on deification, which includes and embraces the whole transformative aspect of redemption. Thus, for Athanasius, "deification is a work of the Son in conjunction with the Spirit. Adoption is synonymous with deification."[4] The same applies to Cyril.[5] So too, later with Maximus, adoption is an integral element in deification.[6] Moreover, in terms of the Western church, Joel Beeke, in listing twelve hundred pages of Puritan writing on adoption, describes this perceived neglect of adoption as a "caricature."[7] It demonstrates the isolation of much

3. Garner, *Sons in the Son*, 281–82.

4. Norman Russell, *The Doctrine of Deification in the Greek Patristic Tradition* (Oxford University Press, 2004), 175. See also 183–85. "Deification," in Athanasius and the Greek tradition, denotes the entire process of redemptive transformation —regeneration, adoption, sanctification, and glorification from the Western perspective—viewed as a whole rather than analyzed into component parts.

5. Russell, *Deification*, 191–93.

6. Maximus, *Ad Thalassium*, 64, in *On the Cosmic Mystery of Jesus Christ: Selected Writings from St. Maximus the Confessor*, trans. Paul M. Blowers and Robert Louis Wilken (St. Vladimir's Seminary Press, 2003), 149–50; Russell, *Deification*, 267f.; and the essays by Jean-Claude Larchet and Thomas Cattoi, especially pages 354–55 and 430–32, respectively, in Pauline Allen and Bronwen Neil, eds., *The Oxford Handbook of Maximus the Confessor* (Oxford University Press, 2015).

7. Joel R. Beeke, *Heirs with Christ: The Puritans on Adoption* (Reformation Heritage Books, 2008), 1–14, quoted in Ian Campbell MacLeod, "'My Father and Your Father': The Nature and Privilege of Sonship" (PhD diss., Puritan Reformed Theological Seminary, 2024), 1.

biblical scholarship from the history of discussion, in keeping with the remorseless growth of specialisms.

In terms of Garner's argument, first he presents a basic premise, "Redemption required the eternal Son of God to become the incarnate Son of God."[8] He then talks of "the messianic Son" whose sonship "attained its culmination at his resurrection."[9] It was necessary for this to happen in order for both Jewish and Gentile believers to receive adoption as sons, which was not the case before.[10] This was "only proleptically and partially experienced by believers whose lives preceded Christ's life and work."[11] Everything changed for those who were believers up to that point in history, since now that the messianic Son had attained adoption, so also could they.[12] We might ask whether this applied to justification as well—did Abraham and David, not to mention countless others, receive only a provisional justification? If adoption hung in suspense, it follows that justification would also. But Paul is emphatic that this was not the case; his argument in Romans for justification by faith rests on the justification of Abraham and David (Rom. 4:1–12).

This claim flows from Garner's own particular biblical-theological commitment, not that that should demand the conclusions he reaches. Eschatology is paramount. Indeed, he says, "Only with reliance on the hermeneutically and theologically determinative function of the last days in biblical revelation, and the organic harmony of the eschatological *already* but *not yet*, will we properly grasp Paul's understanding of Christ's work."[13]

The adoption of believers depends entirely on the incarnate Son's successful attainment of sonship, Garner continues. Filial heart change on the part of believers "stems from the efficacy of Christ's *successful* sonship."[14] Is this not a contradiction in terms?

8. Garner, *Sons in the Son*, 92.
9. Garner, *Sons in the Son*, 93.
10. Garner, *Sons in the Son*, 94.
11. Garner, *Sons in the Son*, 96.
12. Garner, *Sons in the Son*, 95.
13. Garner, *Sons in the Son*, 96.
14. Garner, *Sons in the Son*, 98 (italics mine).

Christ is the Son of the Father from eternity. He had no sonship to attain successfully. Indeed, can sonship be attained? Is it not either natural or, on the other hand, bestowed legally by some form of favor or grace? It seems to posit two Sons, Christ the eternal Son and, in addition, a successfully attained sonship. Moreover, in adoptive sonship a person is not a son before the act of adoption. It would seem that before the resurrection, according to Garner, Christ was the natural Son but was not yet the adopted Son. Further, it is *persons* that are adopted. Give the duality above, it would seem that a conclusion that there are two persons would be difficult to evade.

Garner focuses on Paul. Obviously, Paul is a major figure bestriding the New Testament. But Garner has only five brief tangential references, in the text, to the Gospel of John and only three to the Petrine correspondence. The dualism between before-and-after Jesus, Old and New, is matched by a dualism within the New Testament between Paul and the insignificant others.

This more or less exclusive concentration on Paul is surprising, and more than a little disturbing, since in his Gospel John has a pervasive focus on Jesus as the Son in relation to the Father, so much so that citation is superfluous. His whole Gospel is out to establish that Jesus is the Son of God (John 20:30–31). Jesus refers to his relation to the Father in eternity, in his present life and ministry, and in the future. It is the eternal Son, the Word who has now become flesh and is living as man, but continues to be the same Word, who lives, teaches, suffers, dies, is raised from the dead, and ascends. We noted that in chapter 3, in our consideration of John 1:1–18. There is certainly dramatic transformation; after his resurrection, he passes through closed doors; he disappears. He lives as man, suffers, obeys the Father, offers himself up on the cross, and then, as Paul wrote, is invested, as Mediator and Savior, with power (Rom. 1:4; 1 Cor. 15:45; cf. Matt. 28:18–20). But it is as the eternal Son, the Word, that he lives and acts. He is in unbroken continuity with his preexistent life. He was and is the only-begotten Son. We saw in chapters 4 through 7 that this was the central theme of Cyril and the ecumenical councils. In order to grasp the issues involved here, it will be best to have read those chapters.

The book starts with extensive analysis of the single word *huiothesia*—in Paul—and proceeds without reference to Cyril, to other primary sources, or to the post-Chalcedonian developments. While a biblical theologian may not regard Cyril, directly and indirectly the main architect of the final Christological settlement, as a primary source, nevertheless he, those who followed him, and the ecumenical councils that endorsed his theology represent the distillation of the biblical and Christological understanding of the historic church. Can a viable Christology be grounded on the almost total neglect of the discussion in its most crucial period of its crystallization? Garner states that he assumes it; what is assumed, however, is the development to Chalcedon only, and that without focused examination. It reminds us of our comments at the start of chapter 6 on the almost total neglect of post-Chalcedon in the West. Garner explains it by space limitations.[15] Certainly, Garner allows that "Chalcedonian-Nicene orthodoxy grounds a proper understanding of Christ's divine and *human* sonship,"[16] although even this statement suggests two subjects, a breach of that orthodoxy. While he includes an excellent rebuttal of James Dunn's adoptionist Christology, nevertheless he warns that "it will be ill-advised to retrench into Nicene categories in a manner that wholly obscures some of the functional Christological perspectives that Dunn and others highlight."[17]

The result is that "the preincarnate Son became the incarnate Son, and then at his resurrection *was adopted* as Son of God in power, all so that we might become the sons of God by grace though him. This, contrary to contemporary bottom-up adoptionists *and* to many who seek to uphold historic orthodoxy, is the Pauline gospel."[18] However, to the contrary the witness of the New Testament, affirmed

15. Garner, *Sons in the Son*, 173. In the article cited later, his reply to critics, Garner does refer to Cyril, but from a work that antedated the Nestorian controversy. His mature Christology is found in his later work written some years after the controversy had been settled. *Quod unus sit Christus*, *PG*, 75:1253–1361.

16. Garner, *Sons in the Son*, 194 (italics original). See also 173–82.

17. Garner, *Sons in the Son*, 182.

18. Garner, *Sons in the Son*, 183 (italics original).

by the historic conciliar decisions, is to the personal identity of Jesus of Nazareth with the eternal Son of the Father and his postresurrection state. The gospel concerns "God's Son, Jesus Christ our Lord," both in incarnate lowliness, "having become from the seed of David according to the flesh," and in risen power, "appointed as Son of God with power" (Rom. 1:3–4), both states referring to the Son whom the Father sent (John 1:1–4, 14–18; Rom. 8:3; Gal. 4:4; Heb. 1:1–4; 10:5–10). It was as God's eternal Son that he lived and suffered in the flesh, and as God's eternal Son that he rose from the dead and ascended to the Father.[19] There is certainly development in his experience according to his assumed human nature, without which there could be no salvation, and the resurrection sees him invested with plenipotentiary authority as our Mediator. Nonetheless, this does not require adoption, which entails that the one adopted as a son was not a son beforehand.

Garner views Donald MacLeod's objections, where he has recourse to classic Christology, as exhibiting a "static" sonship.[20] This is puzzling, since John states that "in him [the Word] was life" (John 1:4). The Trinity is an infinite plenitude of life, hardly "static." Garner's language reminds us of the cry of progressive theology in the seventies of the last century, the voice of Christological revisionism, advocating process and change, rejecting anything "static." Indeed, Garner writes of Jesus' "growing sonly identity,"[21] "Christ's unprecedented sonship attainment,"[22] "his newfound filial status."[23] Eventually, Christ's sonship "changed forever" at the resurrection.[24] "To qualify as Redeemer, he had to *become* the Son par excellence."[25] According to Garner, MacLeod missed all this. So, we add, did the entire church for nearly two millennia. And, so he argues, if we don't accede to his suggestions,

19. See John Murray, *The Epistle to the Romans* (Eerdmans, 1965), 5–12.
20. Garner, *Sons in the Son*, 184.
21. Garner, *Sons in the Son*, 185.
22. Garner, *Sons in the Son*, 187.
23. Garner, *Sons in the Son*, 187.
24. Garner, *Sons in the Son*, 187.
25. Garner, *Sons in the Son*, 187 (italics original).

we will get everything wrong. He opposes "static eternal sonship."[26] Garner is emphatic: "Christ brings *no* privilege of eschatological sonship (adoption) to believers if *he himself* has not attained to eschatological sonship (adoption) himself."[27] These are not casual, throwaway comments; they are integral to his case. His assertion of change in Christ's sonship—unprecedented change—threatens the immutability of God.

We must assert that Christ does not *become* a son by adoption. It is we who become sons by adoption, since we were not sons before. By any reasonable understanding of adoption, the one adopted is not a son before the act of adoption. As T. F. Torrance has written on a number of occasions, taken from one of his teachers, A. E. Taylor, "a thing is what it is and no other."[28] Later, we will cite Cyril, who took a diametrically opposed position to Garner.

Garner is emphatic: "A failure to understand the Father's adoption of the Redeemer will render misunderstanding of the Father's adoption of the redeemed. Such a consequence is simply unavoidable."[29] The Savior has a "historically attained sonship";[30] "the Son of God enters a personally, historically, cosmically, and therefore soteriologically different stage of sonship. In short, Christ's resurrection *is* his adoption."[31] As a direct result, "he remains forever now the *adopted* Son of God."[32] Throughout, Garner reinforces his argument with an imperialist claim that any who disagree are thereby deprived of the ability to understand the work of Christ properly.

Garner distinguishes his proposal from the early heresy of adoptionism. This was the claim that Jesus Christ was merely a man who, at the resurrection, was raised to the status of God's Son. Garner holds to the eternal deity of the Son as one of the Trinity. He is not an adoptionist. But he makes a distinction between the natural or

26. Garner, *Sons in the Son*, 194–95.

27. Garner, *Sons in the Son*, 194.

28. Original to Bishop Butler, so I have been informed.

29. Garner, *Sons in the Son*, 195.

30. Garner, *Sons in the Son*, 195.

31. Garner, *Sons in the Son*, 196.

32. Garner, *Sons in the Son*, 196 (italics original).

eternal Son on the one hand and the incarnate Son on the other. Jesus of Nazareth *attained* his sonship by his obedient life. At his resurrection he was made Son of God par excellence (was he not that already?). Christ's "fulfillment of the covenant demands made him the Father's exclusively suitable choice for adopted Son. Thus, the eternal Son became the incarnate Son."[33] A choice? Appears to require alternatives? Garner refers to "the filial progress of the Son."[34] "Without the improvement of the Son unto eschatological-adoptive sonship, his life lacks soteric efficacy."[35] Improvement implies that something had been lacking in Christ.

Garner adds this addendum: "To insist that *huiothesia* [sonship] is soteriological and not Christological predicates that the believer receives a benefit from Christ not attained by him."[36] But if our adoption depends on Christ himself being adopted, how does Garner escape the conclusion that for the redeemed to be regenerated, Christ must have been regenerated first himself? When and how was Christ regenerated? We are justified through faith, which includes the remission of sins; when was Christ thus justified? When were his sins remitted? When was he effectually called? Garner's case implies that no one before him got *huiothesia* right, or adoption right. Because of adoption's vital place in salvation, it suggests that few, if any, got the gospel right. Even allowing for the possibility of misunderstanding, these are astonishing claims.

Perseverance enters the picture here, for "filial identity is for Christ Jesus contingent on filial fidelity; only at the end of his tenure is he declared Son of God in power."[37] So his sonship on earth in his incarnate state was provisional, contingent on his continued obedience. When he persevered—or succeeded—he had attained that sonship.[38] Do we thus attain our sonship by perseverance? Besides,

33. Garner, *Sons in the Son*, 198.
34. Garner, *Sons in the Son*, 203.
35. Garner, *Sons in the Son*, 203.
36. Garner, *Sons in the Son*, 203.
37. Garner, *Sons in the Son*, 205.
38. Contra John Calvin, *Institutes*, 2.17.6, who opposed the claim that Christ earned anything for himself.

how could the eternal Son's sonship be in suspense? Garner can contemplate these claims only by erasing the Gospel of John from his book. Jesus was not in the process of attaining sonship; he was the Son already and had been the Son from eternity. As the author of Hebrews puts it, "although he was Son, he learned obedience through the things that he suffered" (Heb. 5:8). He learned obedience; he did so as Son, according to his humanity, and did not attain a sonship that he did not already have.

Garner has been accused of Nestorianism. He has refuted such attacks and has asserted his commitment to the Definition of Chalcedon.[39] We agree that he is neither an adoptionist nor a Nestorian. As Quentin Skinner has written, "no agent can be said to have meant or achieved something which they could never be brought to accept as a correct description of what they had meant or achieved."[40] Indeed, Garner expresses his whole-hearted commitment to the ecumenical creeds and the Westminster Standards.

It is clearly possible to construe Garner's construction in a Nestorian manner. It occupies different territory from the cumulative witness of the Christian church, seen not merely in Chalcedon, which as we noted earlier had its own ambiguities, but especially in the developments that led to the second and third councils of Constantinople. There, we recall, the weight of the church's confession is on the unity of Christ, the unbreakable continuity between Jesus of Nazareth and the eternal Son—one of the Trinity—and on the single subject of all biblical references to Jesus. Jesus is the eternal Son; that is his personal identity. It was his identity while on earth. It was his identity on the cross. It was, and is, a unitive Christology. Cyril, in *Quod unus sit Christus*, which we noted was a late work, written some years after the Nestorian crisis had been settled and so reflects his mature thought, wrote that "the one assumed in this inseparable union has become the personal property of the one

39. Richard B. Gaffin Jr. and David B. Garner, "The Divine *and* Adopted Son of God: A Response to Joshua Maurer and Ty Keiser," *Them* 47, no. 1 (April 2022): 144–55.

40. Quentin Skinner, "Meaning and Understanding in the History of Ideas," in *Visions of Politics*, vol. 1, *Regarding Method* (Cambridge University Press, 2002), 77.

assuming, and while Jesus is God, the one and only true Son of God, the Word of God the Father, born of God before all ages and times, nonetheless the same one . . . has been born of a woman according to the flesh, for the form of a slave belongs to no other, but was his very own,"[41] so that "we say there is one Son . . . even when he is considered as having assumed flesh," for "he has made the human element his own."[42] Writing of the Nestorian idea that the Son needed sanctification—which could also be applied to adoption—Cyril wrote that "since the Logos is God, and holy by nature, has no need of sanctification [adoption], then it only remains to attribute this sanctification to the man assumed by the Word in a conjunction,"[43] as Nestorius had done. The link with Nestorianism is clear. As Torrance stressed in relation to Paul's statement about God's Son, the content of the gospel, in Romans 1:3–4, "to speak of Jesus Christ as Son of God means, in the same breath, speech about the Father and the Holy Spirit. No doctrine of the person of Jesus Christ in his divine and human being is possible, except in that eternal mystery and in that trinitarian context."[44] It was Nestorius who so stressed the difference of the two natures that it appeared to his opponents that he had posited the idea of two Sons. It was the Nestorians and others in their penumbra who apportioned statements in the Gospels now to the divine nature and then to the human nature and, in so doing, received the anathema of the undivided church. See chapters 4 to 6.

On the basis of Garner's theory, Jesus Christ, during his earthly ministry, would be simultaneously the eternal Son, one of the Trinity, and not yet the adopted Son. Even if, as Garner intends it, the not-yet-adopted Son is simply the eternal Son according to his assumed human nature, or according to his messianic office, there are still two Sons, one actual, one potential and provisional; "the preincarnate

41. John A. McGuckin, *St. Cyril of Alexandria: On the Unity of Christ* (St. Vladimir's Seminary Press, 1995), 75; *PG*, 75:1288.

42. McGuckin, *Unity of Christ*, 77; *PG*, 75:1289.

43. McGuckin, *Unity of Christ*, 99; *PG*, 75:1317b.

44. Thomas F. Torrance, *Incarnation: The Person and Life of Christ* (Paternoster, 2008), 164.

Son became the incarnate Son, and then at his resurrection *was adopted as* Son of God in power."[45] Postresurrection, he is the eternal Son and the adopted Son par excellence—again, two Sons.[46]

Let us reflect finally on the crucial Christological debate, which occupied us from chapter 4 to chapter 7. Donald Fairbairn points out that Cyril drew a sharp contrast between Christ's sonship and ours. He writes:

> Cyril often repeats that our divine sonship does not obscure the Creator-creature distinction, and the primary way he does this is by insisting on the difference between Christ's sonship and that of believers. We receive sonship by adoption and grace from the outside, but Christ is son by nature and in truth.

Again,

> he draws a very sharp line between Christ, the true Son, and Christians, who are sons by adoption, by being formed to his likeness through grace. Furthermore, Cyril argues that our adopted sonship depends on Christ's natural sonship. He must be genuinely begotten from the Father, since otherwise he could not adopt us into God's family.[47]

Fairbairn cites many interpreters who have noticed this in Cyril. Then Fairbairn quotes Cyril himself:

> The concept of sonship means this when applied to one who is so naturally, but the matter is otherwise with those who are sons by

45. Garner, *Sons in the Son*, 183 (italics original).

46. Garner, *Sons in the Son*, 190. For a thorough and penetrating critique of Garner's claim, especially from a biblical angle, see MacLeod, "My Father and Your Father," 149–69, 216–18. The starting point of MacLeod's dissertation is the somewhat similar controversy between Robert Candlish and T. J. Crawford in Scotland in the 1860s. See also equally critical remarks by Tim J. R. Trumper, Review of *Sons in the Son*, by David Garner, *JETS* 62, no. 1 (2019), 204–9.

47. Donald Fairbairn, *Grace and Christology in the Early Church* (Oxford University Press, 2003), 79.

> adoption (κατὰ θέσιν). For since Christ is not a son in this manner, he is therefore truly (ἀληθῶς) a son, so that on account of this he might be distinguished from us, who are sons by adoption. For there would be sonship neither by adoption nor likeness to God if he did not remain the true Son, to whose sonship our likeness is called and formed by a certain skill and grace.[48]

This is present too in Cyril's commentary on John, from before the Nestorian controversy, where he states on John 1:9 that "the Son will remain unchangeably in the condition in which he is, but we, adopted into sonship and gods by grace, shall not be ignorant of what we are." In the same place, he adds:

> Therefore we mount up unto dignity above our nature for Christ's sake, and we too shall be sons of God, not like Him in exactitude, but by grace in imitation of Him. For He is Very Son, existing from the Father; we adopted by His Kindness, through grace receiving "I have said, Ye are gods and all of you are children of the Most High." For the created and subject nature is called to what is above nature by the mere nod and will of the Father: but the Son and God and Lord will not possess this being God and Son, by the will of God the Father, nor in that He wills it only, but beaming forth of the Very Essence of the Father, He receives to Himself by Nature what is Its own Good. And again He is clearly seen to be Very Son, proved by comparison with ourselves. For since that which is by nature has another mode of being from that which is by adoption, and that which is in truth from that which is by imitation, and we are called sons "of God by adoption and

48. The translation is in Fairbairn, *Grace and Christology*, 79, from Cyril, *Thesaurus*, 32; *PG*, 75:525b. The original reads: "Καὶ πῶς οὐ πάσης ἔξω κείσονται φρενὸς ἀγαθῆς οἱ τολμῶντες ποίημα λέγειν τὸν Υἱὸν τοῦ Θεοῦ; Εἰ γὰρ ἀληθῶς Υἱός ἐστι, πῶς ἂν εἴη γενητὸς, ὁ ἐκ τῆς πατρώας προελθὼν οὐσίας; Τοῦτο γὰρ σημαίνει τὸ τῆς υἱότητος ὄνομα, φυσικῶς κατά τινος τεταγμένον. Ἕτερον δὲ τὸ σχῆμα τῶν κατὰ θέσιν υἱῶν. Ἐπειδὴ οὐκ ἐν τούτῳ Χριστός, ἀληθῶς ἄρα Υἱός ἐστιν, ὡς διὰ τοῦτο τοῖς κατὰ θέσιν ἡμῖν ἀντιδιαστέλλεσθαι · οὐκ ἂν γὰρ εἴη τὸ κατὰ θέσιν καὶ ὁμοίωσιν, μὴ προυποκειμένου πρότερον τοῦ ἀληθοῦς, πρὸς ὅ καὶ μορφοῦται τὸ εἰς ὁμοίωσιν αὐτοῦ διά τινος τέχνης καὶ χάριτος καλούμενον."

> imitation: hence He is Son by Nature and in truth, to Whom we made sons too are compared, gaining the good by grace instead of by natural endowments."[49]

Garner, directly contrary to Cyril, expressly states in an article defending his position that "adoption, then, does not serve to *differentiate* believers from Christ. . . . His adoption is our adoption."[50] He attempts to co-opt Cyril in his defense, using a citation from Cyril's *Scholia on the Incarnation*.[51] The citation merely refers to the conditions that the Son took on in taking human nature into union as his own, which is obviously not in contention here.[52] A second citation is a reference to a book by R. B. Jamieson, in which the author cites the fragment of Cyril's Hebrews commentary on a number of occasions.[53] Cyril's Christology simply does not allow Jamieson and Garner's claim. It is true that he refers to Christ's being adopted. Yet this is something very different. Cyril argues throughout that in the incarnation, from the very start, the Son granted to his assumed humanity all he has as God, including his natural sonship. He refers once or twice in the Hebrews fragment to this as "adoption," but it is adoption into the Son's *natural* sonship. By virtue of the hypostatic union, since this took place in his *person*, even in his humanity Christ is the natural Son of God, and that is the ground on which we are adopted, adopted into the *natural* Son to share his identical relation to the Father.[54] This is an outflow of the Greek view of salvation as deification; Western readers are

49. Cyril of Alexandria, *The Commentary on St. John*, trans. Philip Pusey, vol. 1, Library of Fathers of the Holy Catholic Church 43 (Oxford: James Parker, 1874), 104–5.

50. Gaffin and Garner, "Divine *and* Adopted Son of God," 154.

51. Gaffin and Garner, "Divine *and* Adopted Son of God," 151–52.

52. The passage is from a section of a Latin translation of the mainly lost Greek original. For a modern translation, see John A. McGuckin, *Saint Cyril of Alexandria and the Christological Controversy: Its History, Theology, and Texts* (St. Vladimir's Seminary Press, 2004), 294–335, here 298.

53. R. B. Jamieson, *The Paradox of Sonship: Christology in the Epistle to the Hebrews* (IVP Academic, 2021), cites Cyril on a number of occasions in which he appears to endorse Garner's argument, which is somewhat similar.

54. I am grateful to Donald Fairbairn for this observation. See also Fairbairn, *Grace and Christology*, 100.

dominated by forensic and juridical ideas that obscure this (for them) unfamiliar terrain.

Ryan McGraw, in a review of Garner's book, points out that "the primary reason why most Christians (Reformed or otherwise) have argued that Christ is the natural Son of God while we are his adopted sons is due to the unity of Christ's person. Contrary to Garner's contention, Christ does not need to bear adoption on our behalf any more than he needs to experience the new birth in our place in order for us to be born again. Authors such as John Owen argued that Christ's incarnation was an inexact parallel to and ground for our regeneration. In like manner, the unity of Christ's person seems to demand that we are adopted sons because we are united to Christ as the natural Son."[55]

Trevor Burke, in another review, remarks that "if it was so important for Jesus to undergo adoption in order that believers might be adopted, why does Garner not freely and openly describe Christ as an 'adopted Son' elsewhere in the book (or in the title)? This is the only chapter where Christ is described in this way. Moreover, by describing Christ in adoptive terms Garner runs the risk of demoting Jesus' eternal and incarnational filial status as Son of God." In that review, Burke also states that "Paul never uses the term or concept of 'adoption' of Christ but reserves it only and exclusively for Christians and the Israelites (Gal. 4:5; Eph. 1:5; Rom. 8:15, 23; 9:4). Rom. 1:3–4 is not about the adoption of Jesus but about his accession to the throne as he is appointed 'son-of-God-in-power.'"[56] As MacLeod observes, "far from making the sonship rest on the resurrection, the New Testament characteristically makes the resurrection rest on the sonship."[57] We may add that the crucial verb in Romans 1:4, ὁρίζω, means "to delimit," "define," "declare," or, most frequently, "appoint." It *never* means "to adopt," as is

55. Ryan McGraw, Review of *Sons in the Son*, by David B. Garner, *Ordained Servant Online*, February 2017.

56. Trevor J. Burke, Review of *Sons in the Son: The Riches and Reach of Adoption in Christ*, by David B. Garner, *JRT* 11, no. 3 (2017): 347–48, doi: 10.1163/15697312-01103011. See Trumper, Review of *Sons in the Son*, 204–9.

57. Donald MacLeod, *The Person of Christ* (Inter-Varsity Press, 1998), 91.

evident in Bauer, Arndt & Gingrich, Louw & Nida, and Liddell & Scott. Words have meanings. The implication derived by Garner is conjured out of thin air.

Central to Cyril's Christology was that the Son took into union a complete human nature, body and soul, in such a way that it became and was *his own* human nature. Thus, human characteristics, together with divine, are predicated of the Son. So his human growth, his full range of human experiences, and his ongoing obedience are all undertaken by one of the Trinity, according to the flesh. All that Jesus did while on earth and all that he does after his resurrection are done by the Son, the eternal Son of the Father. Thus, on the cross we have an engagement of all three persons of the Trinity for our salvation, with the work terminating on the Son. It is not a case of a major stage on the way to attaining sonship par excellence but an exhaustive identification of the eternal Son of the Father with us in our deepest predicament. There is no intervening entity between the eternal Son and us. It is not the human nature of the Son that was on the cross; it was the eternal Son himself with and in his assumed humanity. Who hung dying on the tree? It was one of the Trinity who suffered and died according to the flesh, not a probationer. It was the eternal Son who offered himself through the eternal Spirit without blemish to the Father.

Garner's proposal does not make sense. Sonship comes either naturally or by a gift, which is adoption. It cannot be attained or earned, nor is it a status or condition that can grow or be improved, as Garner writes. Either you are a son or you are not. We were not sons; now by grace we are. Worse than that, however, it is dangerous. If our sonship is patterned on Christ's as Garner presents it, it is for us something we attain, a status or condition that can grow or be improved. That is, at best, semi-Pelagian. We do not and cannot earn or attain adoption. All is of grace.

Yet there is something more. It is good that Garner holds to the eternal sonship and deity of Christ. It is good that he wants to maintain this in the midst of his thesis. It is good that he opposes Nestorianism. Yet it seems to me to be inescapable that according to his argument, the eternal Son who became incarnate is simultaneously the adopted Son-in-waiting, waiting until he has successfully attained that position. How can it be avoided that Jesus of Nazareth is personally twofold? Before the resurrection, he is the eternal Son and yet he is not, for if adoption lies in the future, you are not a son now. In contrast, the church has confessed that the eternal Son has taken human nature into personal union such that it can, appropriately, be confessed that there is "one incarnate nature of God the Word," *one person* who has, after the union, his own human nature. Thus, as stated in the Definition of Chalcedon, he is "*one and the same* Christ, *Son*, Lord, Only-begotten, recognized in two natures, without confusion, without change, without division, without separation; . . . *one and the same Son and only-begotten God, the Word, Lord Jesus Christ*."

Much the same applies after the resurrection, under Garner's line of thinking. Adoption concerns *persons*. It is *persons* who are adopted. For Garner, the eternal Son, one with the Father and the Spirit from and in eternity, is also the adopted Son, who has attained that status successfully. This is confusion and division.

Garner frequently refers to Geerhardus Vos and is clearly influenced by him. It would have been well to pay attention to Vos when he discussed this question. He wrote:

> Our Lord's eternal sonship qualifies Him for filling the office of Messiah. This office is such, and implies such a relation of close affiliation with God, such an acting as the absolute representative of God, such a profound communion of life and purpose with God, that only a Son in the highest sense can adequately fill the office. Thus the office calls for a Son. But the reverse is also true; the sonship calls for a peculiarly high office of Messiahship. If the high office seeks a high person, the high Person likewise requires that the office shall be made commensurable with his character and dignity. This results in imparting to the Messiahship a filial character, and so renders the name Son of God appropriate in a Messianic sense. From this it will be seen that the Messianic sonship is not really something separated from the eternal sonship. Jesus is not Son in two senses that have nothing to do with

> each other. The Messianic sonship is simply the eternal Sonship carried into a definite historical situation.[58]

The argument that Christ is the adopted Son is without warrant and has disturbing ramifications. It has no precedent in classic Christology; indeed, it goes right against the grain of the unitive Christology that became, and is, the benchmark for the church. The proposal highlights the danger of biblical theology running amok, unaccountable without reference to the historic creeds or responsible exegesis. It reinforces our observation at the start of chapter 6 on the neglect of the post-Chalcedonian discussions. The words of Thomas Aquinas, on whether Christ can be called the adopted Son of God, are an appropriate note on which to close:

> *I answer that,* Sonship belongs properly to the hypostasis or person, not to the nature; whence in the First Part (Q. 32, A. 3) we have stated that Filiation is a personal property. Now in Christ there is no other than the uncreated person or hypostasis, to whom it belongs by nature to be the Son. But it has been said above (A. 1 and 2) that the sonship of adoption is a participated likeness of natural sonship: nor can a thing be said to participate in what it has essentially. Therefore Christ, who is the natural Son of God, can nowise be called an adopted Son. But according to those who suppose two persons or two hypostases or two supposita in Christ, no reason prevents Christ being called the adopted Son of God.[59]

In short, Aquinas allows that the only way that the claim that Christ is an adopted Son makes sense is in the context of Nestorianism.

We encourage Garner to reconsider his thesis.

58. Geerhardus Vos, *The Self-Disclosure of Jesus: The Modern Debate About the Messianic Consciousness,* ed. Johannes G. Vos (1926; repr., Presbyterian and Reformed, 1953), 190. I thank Sherman Isbell for making me aware of this reference.

59. Thomas Aquinas, *ST,* III.23.4 *sed contra.* The entire section should be read.

Appendix B
A New Approach to an Old Error

David Moffitt, in his significant treatise on the resurrection in the Letter to the Hebrews,[1] has produced an important restatement of the claim that the atoning work of Christ took place not on the cross but in his presentation of his blood in heaven after his resurrection. While some time has elapsed since it was published, its significance for our understanding of what Christ achieved "for us and for our salvation" (Definition of Chalcedon) is of such concern that it warrants an assessment. The prime thrust of Moffitt's book is the question of the apparent absence of explicit reference to the resurrection of Jesus in Hebrews. The overwhelming consensus of scholars has been that exaltation eclipses resurrection; based on the ritual of the Day of Atonement, the high priest offered blood sacrifice and then entered the Holy of Holies. Hence Jesus, having offered himself on the cross as a sacrifice for sin, entered the presence of God following his ascension, "having passed through the heavens," from which he will reappear to consummate our salvation. On the contrary, Moffitt concludes that, far from being absent, the resurrection is right at the center. Indeed, it constitutes the brunt of the atonement. Rather than the death of Jesus, the resurrection is where the atonement is to be located. The high priest entered the Holy of Holies to offer the blood of the sacrifice, and it is there that atonement was enacted.

1. David M. Moffitt, *Atonement and the Logic of Resurrection in the Epistle to the Hebrews* (Brill, 2011).

This idea is not new. It was first advanced by Peter Abelard and then more forcefully in the seventeenth century by the Socinians,[2] and revived in the nineteenth century by Charles Gore, B. F. Westcott, and others,[3] after which it has secured widespread support. It was refuted by many scholars, including notably Alan Stibbs, Leon Morris, Wilfrid Stott, and P. E. Hughes.[4] Despite this, it is widely popular today. Moffitt presents a new slant to the claim.

Moffitt is correct that Hebrews 13:20 explicitly affirms the resurrection.[5] Additionally, according to F. F. Bruce, it is implied in Hebrews 2:15.[6] In support, Moffitt points to William Lane, who argues that Hebrews 6:2 concerns the general resurrection and that the phrase "an indestructible life" in Hebrews 7:16 is an objective event.[7] Indeed, Moffitt contends that the entire argument in Hebrews is based on Christ's resurrection: the contrast of Jesus as High Priest forever with the Aaronic priests who, by death, were prevented from continuing in office, together with the quotations of Psalm 110:4, entails his conquest of death. Moffitt concludes: "I have argued that the correlated issues of Jesus' relationship to angels, elevation to the status of high priest, and divine invitation to sit at God's right hand as the royal Son make sense on the assumption that Jesus ascended

2. See the list of names, such as Abelard, Faustus Socinus, Crellius, Biddle, and the Racovian Catechism, in John Owen, *Vindiciae Evangelicae,* in *The Works of John Owen,* ed. William H. Goold, 16 vols. (Banner of Truth, 1965–68), 12:401–11.

3. B. F. Westcott, *The Epistle to the Hebrews: The Greek Text with Notes and Essays* (London: Macmillan, 1889), 293ff.; B. F. Westcott, *The Epistles of St. John: The Greek Text with Notes and Essays* (Cambridge and London: Macmillan, 1886), 34f.; Charles Gore, *The Body of Christ* (John Murray, 1901), 252–53.

4. Leon Morris, *The Apostolic Preaching of the Cross* (Tyndale Press, 1955), 114–17, 124–28; Wilfrid Stott, "The Conception of 'Offering' in the Epistle to the Hebrews," *NTS* 9 (1962): 65–67; A. M. Stibbs, *The Meaning of the Word "Blood" in Scripture* (Tyndale Press, 1948); Philip Edgcumbe Hughes, *A Commentary on the Epistle to the Hebrews* (Eerdmans, 1977), 335–49. It is not to be confused with the Roman Catholic doctrine of the representation of the sacrifice of Christ on the cross. Rome does not deny that the death of Christ was the locus of sacrifice.

5. Moffitt, *Atonement in Hebrews,* 5–6; see also Hughes, *Hebrews,* 589–90; F. F. Bruce, *Commentary on the Epistle to the Hebrews: The English Text with Introduction, Exposition and Notes* (Marshall, Morgan & Scott, 1964), 411.

6. Bruce, *Hebrews,* 50–51; Hughes, *Hebrews,* 114–15.

7. Moffitt, *Atonement in Hebrews,* 7.

into heaven with his resurrected body. . . . The author's argument depends upon the resurrection of Jesus's human body."[8] This, of course, is correct. While Christ's overt trajectory in Hebrews is from the cross to the presence of God in heaven, with reference to the ascension, the resurrection is assumed throughout.

In a similar vein to Westcott, Moffitt argues that Hebrews always refers to Jesus' presentation of his sacrifice and blood offering as taking place in heaven. Jesus' obedient death on the cross is compared to the offering of the high priest in Leviticus, where the offering of the blood is equated with the presentation of life to God. As the sacrificial blood in Leviticus was offered *after* the sacrificial animal had been slaughtered, this occurred after the death, in Jesus' resurrection and enthronement. The crucial point, Moffitt thinks, is the indestructible life that Jesus came to possess after the crucifixion. He brings human life into God's presence and offers it as his sacrifice.[9] While the various elements of Jesus' trajectory are, of course, all realities, the question surrounds the location of the sacrifice.

As I mentioned, this is a repristinization of Westcott's theory and that of the Socinians. Moffitt ignores Stibbs and Morris, with only a cursory reference to Wilfrid Stott, each of whom established that the regular meaning of "blood" in such a context is to life laid down in death. Moreover, he skates over the author's repeated use for the sacrifice of *hapax* or *ephapax* (an event, once for all, neither repeated nor prolonged), in contrast to the terms used for "heaven," which entail an ongoing, continuous state. Indeed, Moffitt's idea of atonement is in stark contrast to how the author of Hebrews presents it, leaving aside other New Testament writers. Moffitt mentions that in his view, "Jesus's immortal, resurrection life is the sacrifice—that is, the object that Jesus offers to God—that he offered to effect atonement."[10] This entails an ongoing and continuous state, which by virtue and implication of that fact is definitely not offered once for all. In contrast, the efficacy, according to Hebrews, resides with the once-for-all offering, which can refer only to the cross.

8. Moffitt, *Atonement in Hebrews*, 215.
9. Moffitt, *Atonement in Hebrews*, 217–18.
10. Moffitt, *Atonement in Hebrews*, 219.

Moffitt argues that Jesus' offering is presented not on earth but in heaven. He mentions that the law forbade Jesus from serving as a priest on earth (Heb. 8:4).[11] This is a misapplication of the argument of Hebrews. The law restricted the Old Testament priesthood to the tribe of Levi, whereas Jesus was a member of the tribe of Judah. It is obvious that he could not be a Levitical priest. Yet that did not preclude him from being a priest as such, for the author establishes that he is a priest according to a different order, the order of Melchizedek. Moffitt proceeds to contend that the Levitical priests present their offerings to God in an earthly sanctuary, whereas "Jesus, by way of contrast, presents his offering to God in the structure located in heaven—the true tabernacle upon which the earthly one is patterned," made even clearer in Hebrews 9:12, which, Moffitt notes, is "not of this creation."[12] The primary contrast here in Hebrews 9, however, is rooted in the disparity between the blood of goats and bulls on the one hand and Christ's immeasurably superior shed blood on the other, on the shedding of blood rather than its later presentation. So much is underlined a few sentences afterward when the author comments that "without the shedding of blood there is no forgiveness of sins" (v. 22). The obtaining of eternal redemption precedes the entry into the true tabernacle, heaven.[13] Back in verse 12, the meaning of the expression "by means of his own blood" depends on *heuramenos*, the perfect participle. Moffitt translates it "resulting in his obtaining eternal redemption," redemption effected later than Jesus' death, entailing that the shedding of blood on the cross was by itself insufficient to

11. Moffitt, *Atonement in Hebrews*, 220.

12. Moffitt, *Atonement in Hebrews*, 221.

13. See the extended excursus in Hughes, *Hebrews*, 35–49. Hughes traces the history of the idea, together with the variety of forms it has taken, before providing an extensive critique and counter. Moffitt (referring to Stanley E. Porter, *Verbal Aspect in the Greek New Testament* [Peter Lang, 1989], 379–85) acknowledges that an adverbial participle preceding the verb it modifies often implies antecedent action, but Porter suggests that the participle refers to either concurrent or subsequent action when, as here, it follows the main verb. Here, Moffitt argues, concurrent action is unlikely because motion is present, so that subsequent action fits the context well. Moffitt, *Atonement in Hebrews*, 223. I suggest, however, that this does *not* fit the wider context to which we refer.

make atonement.[14] Thus, according to Moffitt, Jesus went through the heavenly structure and entered the Most Holy Place by means of his own blood and, *once there*, obtained eternal redemption by presenting his blood before the presence of God.[15] By Moffitt's reckoning, Jesus would have been best advised to have cried on the cross, "It is not yet finished" or "It is basically finished, but there is one last step to make before we can say that definitively."

Moffitt writes, "Jesus is doing in heaven what the high priests do annually on earth." This statement is based on the comparison between the earthly high priests, in a tabernacle made with hands, and Jesus, who entered heaven itself, a tabernacle not made with hands.[16] It appears that Moffitt considers that since the earthly high priest offered his sacrifice repeatedly, so Jesus' sacrifice is presented in an ongoing manner. This is directly contrary to the author's contrast between the earthly high priests, who are standing, still going about their sacrificial business, which the author considers futile, and Jesus, who has sat down, his work completed once for all. Jesus is *not* now doing what the earthly high priests did annually.

On blood offering and sacrifice in Leviticus, Moffitt claims that many recent studies point out that the efficacy of the blood rituals lies not in the death of the animal but in the application of its blood, "that is, its life (Lev. 17:11) which is the offering."[17] He writes of "the biblical text's lack of interest in the slaughter and death of the animal being offered" compared with its extensive instructions on the proper procedure after the death, on where and how the blood is to be applied.[18] This does not follow. As someone has observed, the details of death would need no explanation because they would be common knowledge in the ancient world, even today among livestock farmers. The priests would know exactly how to slaughter the animals. Moreover, the manipulation of the blood entails the blood's having been shed, which is the crucial point.

14. Moffitt, *Atonement in Hebrews*, 222.
15. Moffitt, *Atonement in Hebrews*, 223–24.
16. Moffitt, *Atonement in Hebrews*, 226.
17. Moffitt, *Atonement in Hebrews*, 257.
18. Moffitt, *Atonement in Hebrews*, 258.

Moffitt argues that even in the Yom Kippur rituals, "in and of itself, the death or slaughter of the victim, while necessary to procure the blood / life that is offered, has no particular atoning significance. Thus, it is generally the ritual manipulation of the blood that results in the redemption and purgation both of those things to which that blood is applied, and for those people on whose behalf it is offered." For atonement, blood must be brought into God's presence, he says, and come into contact with those appurtenances of the tabernacle in need of ritual purification for atonement to be made. Consequently, "if there is any focal point of Yom Kippur, it is the manipulation and presentation of the blood." Contrary to many other exegetes of Hebrews, Moffitt argues that there are not two great moments (the slaughter of the sacrifice and the presentation of the blood), since, citing Christian A. Eberhart, "the moment of slaughter . . . has no particular significance."[19] A point missed by Moffitt is that the life offered in sacrifice is life *that has been laid down in death*, as indeed Moffitt himself understands Hebrews to teach.

To follow Moffitt on his own terms, one would have to abstract Hebrews from the Pauline and Petrine letters and the rest of the New Testament. The theology of Hebrews in general shows remarkable similarities with that of Paul, which is a strong argument in support of the traditional church interpretation of the atonement. Moffitt's argument seems overly analytical, treating death, burial, resurrection, ascension, and session separately—akin to his considering Hebrews separately from the rest of the New Testament.

He concludes that "insofar as one can isolate the center of the author's understanding of atonement, it is not ultimately Jesus's death that is his sacrifice, but his life. Jesus's living presence in heaven, predicated on the resurrection and ascension of his human body, was the sacrifice he offered to God in the heavenly Holy of Holies."[20] Jesus' death was preparation for his atoning offering, according to Hebrews. It was also a paradigm for righteous suffering.[21] In short, it was a moral example, according to Moffitt.

19. Moffitt, *Atonement in Hebrews*, 271–72.
20. Moffitt, *Atonement in Hebrews*, 284.
21. Moffitt, *Atonement in Hebrews*, 285.

Moffitt continues by affirming that the author of Hebrews was thinking of Jesus' death not "as mundane slaughter" but as "part of a larger sacrificial act." The sacrificial death is not the point at which atonement was made, since "the presentation of the blood is the means of atonement."[22] For Moffitt, "[the author] locates Jesus's death at the front end of a process that culminates in the atoning moment," since "without the slaughter . . . there is no blood to manipulate and thus no atonement." A more subtle account is required. Between the death and the offering of the sacrifice is the resurrection.[23] This is in stark conflict with Peter's comment that Christ bore our sins in his body on the tree (1 Peter 2:24), with John's eyewitness report of Jesus' cry "It is finished!" and his threefold use of the verb τελειόω (John 19:28–30), and with Paul's identification of the death of the Son as the hinge of justification and reconciliation (Rom. 5:8–11). This is a problem of the post-Enlightenment methodology that isolates one biblical document from another, one author from another, treating Scripture as essentially a human composition and overlooking its nature as the Word of God with a unity that transcends the parts. We saw this in Appendix A with its restricted focus on Paul, and we see it here. I suggest that Moffitt's argument that the atonement occurs in an ongoing manner in heaven negates its decisive once-for-all nature completed on the cross, as it is presented throughout the New Testament.

22. Moffitt, *Atonement in Hebrews*, 292.
23. Moffitt, *Atonement in Hebrews*, 293.

Glossary

accidents. Characteristics of an **entity** that may be present but are not intrinsic to what it is, merely adventitious. A male human **being** is a man, but the fact that he may be a father, a husband, or a schoolteacher is not necessary to who he is, since not all men are fathers, husbands, or schoolteachers.

adoptionism. An early heresy relating to the **person** of Christ that claimed that Jesus was merely human and was elevated to divine status at his ascension.

anhypostasia*.** The dogma that the human **nature** of Christ has no personal existence of its own, apart from the union into which it was assumed in the incarnation. This means that the Son of God did not take a human **being** into union (which would entail two separate personal **entities**) but assumed a human nature. Also termed *anhypostatos*. See ***enhypostasia.

anthropological. Relating to a focus on humanity.

anthropomorphic. Relating to language referring to God but expressed in human terms.

antinomies. Two or more equally valid realities that, while appearing to be contradictory, are both, or all, true and find resolution in the wider context of the mind and purposes of God.

Aphthartodocetism. The belief that since Jesus was without blemish or spot, he could not suffer. This would be an effective denial of the genuineness of his humanity, which, being contingent and finite, was inherently liable to constraint by external forces.

Apollinaris of Laodicea. A fourth-century bishop who taught that the eternal **Logos** took the place of the human soul in the incarnate Christ. His teaching was condemned at Constantinople I (A.D. 381) because it entailed a less than fully human Christ, threatening the gospel, since if Christ had not been fully human, he would not have been able to save us.

appropriations. Works of the triune God ascribed to particular **persons**. Since God is one, all three persons act together in all of God's works. Yet each work is particularly attributable (appropriated) to one person. Only the Son became incarnate; only the Holy Spirit came at Pentecost. This does not deny that the other two persons were also involved in these acts.

Arians. Those who held the same or similar views as Arius (c. 276–337), who taught that the Son was a creature who came into being at some point, and was the agent through whom the world was made, but was neither coeternal with the Father nor of the same **being**.

attributes. Particular characteristics of God, such as holiness, sovereignty, justice, goodness, mercy, and love. See ***communicatio idiomatum; extra Calvinisticum;*** **nature of God.**

begetting (eternal). See **generation.**

being. Something that *is*, an existent. See **accidents;** ***anhypostasia;*** **Arians; emanation; entity; essence;** ***homoiousios; homoousios; hypostasis;*** **modalism; nature of God; ontological;** ***ousia;*** **participation;** ***perichoresis;*** **social Trinitarianism; subordinationism; subsistence; substance.**

Christocentric. Centered in Christ.

Christology. Teaching relating to the **person** of Christ. See **Christology from above/from below; nature; properties; unitive Christology.**

Christology from above/from below. A claim that emerged in the last century that the church fathers based their **Christology** on a prior commitment to the deity of Christ. In contrast, it was argued that Christology should proceed from below, from the historical record and from the human Jesus.

communicatio idiomatum **(communication of idioms).** The idea that **attributes** of deity and humanity are equally predicable of the **person** of Christ. Thus, it can be said of him that he wept and died, as well as his being the Creator of all things. As Paul wrote, Christ according to the flesh is God over all (Rom. 9:5).

consubstantiality. The dogma that the Son and the Holy Spirit are of the same **substance** as the Father. This means that all three **persons** are fully God, and the whole God.

creation *ex nihilo*. The teaching, based on biblical revelation, that God created the entire universe, there being no preexisting materials. Consequently, he brought into existence all **entities** other than himself.

deification. According to the **Eastern church**, the goal of salvation, which is to be made God. The Holy Spirit effects deification in us. It involves no blurring of the Creator-creature distinction, but rather focuses on the union and communion that we are given by God in which, as Peter says, we are made partakers of the divine **nature** (2 Peter 1:4). See **participation.**

deism. The claim that while God created the universe, he has no ongoing involvement with it but leaves it to operate under its own laws.

Docetism. The early heresy that Christ's humanity was apparent and not real. The term is a derivative of the Greek verb *dokein*, "to seem" or "appear." This view is heretical because if Christ were not fully man, we could not be saved, since only a perfect, sinless man can atone for the sins of man.

dualism. A positing of two separate realms that can have the effect of dividing an **entity**. See **Manichaeism; phenomenal.**

Dyophysitism. The doctrine that the incarnate Son has two **natures**.

Dyotheletism. The doctrine that there are two wills in the incarnate Christ. This supposes that will is a **property** of the **natures** of Christ (divine and human) rather than the **person**. It in no way entails that these wills are in conflict.

Eastern church. The Greek- or Syriac-speaking church, with later additions of other ethnicities, including the Russian. See **deification; monarchy; processions; relations; Western church.**

economic Trinity. The Trinity as revealed in creation and salvation, acting in our world, in human history. See **immanent Trinity.**

emanation. The idea, prevalent in gnosticism, that **beings** flowed out of a higher being as from a source. See **gnostic.**

energies. God's powers at work in the creation. According to Gregory Palamas, the **essence** of God is unknowable. We have to do with God's energies.

enhypostasia. The dogma promulgated at the Second Council of Constantinople (A.D. 553) that the eternal Son is the **person** of the incarnate Christ, a human **nature** conceived by the Holy Spirit in the womb of the virgin Mary being taken into union. Behind this lies the biblical teaching that man is made in the image of God and thus ontologically compatible with God on a creaturely level. Thus, the Son of God provides the personhood for the assumed human nature. Also termed *enhypostatos*. See ***anhypostasia*; ontological.**

entity. Being or reality, or "who." Thus, Jesus Christ is one entity. See **accidents; *enhypostasia*; creation *ex nihilo*; dualism; quiddity; theandric.**

eschatological. Relating to the last things, from the Greek word *eschatos* ("last").

essence (of God). What God *is*, his **being** (from *esse*, "to be"). See **energies; nature of God; social Trinitarianism; subsistence.**

eternal generation. See **generation.**

Eutychianism. The idea stressed by Eutyches that the unity of Christ's **person** was such that his humanity was swamped by his deity. This threatened salvation, for if Christ were not fully human, we could not be saved. Eutyches was condemned as a heretic at the Council of Chalcedon (A.D. 451). See **Nestorianism.**

extra Calvinisticum. The belief of the Reformed church, in agreement with the catholic tradition, that the Son exists beyond the bounds of the human **nature** assumed into union in the incarnation. The term was coined by the Lutherans, who claimed that the assumed humanity received the divine **attributes**, including omnipresence, by virtue of the **hypostatic union**.

generation (eternal). The unique **property** of the Son in relation to the Father. Since God is eternal, the **relations** between the Father and the Son are eternal. This is not to be understood on the basis of human generation or begetting, since God is spiritual. It is beyond our capacity to understand. See **missions; order; processions.**

gnomic will. The human will as it makes choices based on desire after a process of deliberation.

gnostic. An adherent of one of various systems of belief of syncretistic religious or philosophical natures during the time of the early church that were generally pantheistic or panentheistic, viewing the universe as an **emanation** from a supreme monad, and tending to regard the material as inferior. See **panentheism; pantheism.**

homoiousios. Greek for "of similar or like **being**." The term was used by many who were afraid that the Creed of Nicaea identified the Father and the Son. Many of these *homoiousians* gave their support to the settlement of the Trinitarian controversy in A.D. 381. See ***homoousios.***

homoousios. Greek for "of the same **being**," meaning that the Son and the Holy Spirit are of the same identical being as the Father. See ***homoiousios.***

hypostasis. Greek for "something with a concrete existence." In terms of the Trinity, it came to mean **person**. Thus, by the end of the fourth-century controversy, it referred to what is distinct in God, the way in which he is three, while ***ousia*** was reserved for the one **being** of God. See **hypostatic union; missions;** ***perichoresis; prosopon;*** **subsistence.**

hypostatic union. The union formed in the incarnation by the ***hypostasis*** of the Son in assuming a human **nature** into union. See ***extra Calvinisticum.***

immanent Trinity. The Trinity in itself, or the three **persons** as they relate to one another without regard to creation. See **economic Trinity.**

impassable. Incapable of suffering, of being constrained in any way by external forces. From the verb *patior* (*passus, -a, -um*), "to suffer."

in concreto. Relating to a concrete existent rather than an abstraction.

kenōsis. Christ's self-abasement in the incarnation. The term is derived from Philippians 2:7, where Paul writes of Christ's having "emptied himself" (*ekenosen*).

Logos/Word. The term that John uses for the Son in eternity (John 1:1–14). It denotes, *inter alia,* that he is one with, and is the exact expression of, the Father. See **Apollinaris of Laodicea; unitive Christology.**

Manichaeism. An extreme form of **ontological dualism**, holding that there are two coequal realities, good and evil.

Maximus. The most significant theologian of the seventh century. Maximus the Confessor (A.D. 580–662) was instrumental in opposing the Monothelites, who held that Christ had only one will. Maximus suffered mutilation for his stand for the truth. See **Monotheletism.**

mia physis. Literally "one **nature**." While this sounds heretical, Cyril and many Monophysites used ***physis*** for **person**. See **Monophysitism.**

Miaphysites. See **Monophysitism.**

missions. The particular **relations** of the three Trinitarian ***hypostases*** in terms of the work of God outside himself, in creation, providence, and grace. In these the Father sends the Son, while the Father and the Son (according to the **Western church**) send the Spirit. These relations are never reversed. They reflect the internal relations in the Trinity, whereby the Father begets the Son, while the Father (and the Son, according to the Western church) spirates the Spirit. See **generation; processions.**

modalism. The blurring or erasing of the real, eternal, and irreducible distinctions between the three **persons** of the Trinity. This danger can arise when the unity of God, or the identity in **being** of the three, is overstressed at the expense of the personal distinctions. It can also surface when there is a pervasive stress on salvation history, so as to eliminate any reference to eternal realities. When that is so, God's revelation in human history as the Father, the Son, and the Holy Spirit is no longer held to reveal who he is eternally in himself. See **Sabellius.**

monarchy. Sole rule, the rule of one. It refers to the unity of God, his oneness (cf. Deut. 6:4). In the **Eastern church**, it was common to base the monarchy in the Father. See **subordinationism.**

monistic. Relating to the reduction of reality to one principle.

Monophysitism. The belief that stressed "the one incarnate **nature** of God the Word," in so doing threatening the integrity of Christ's human nature. Many Monophysites preferred the term *Miaphysites*. See ***mia physis.***

Monotheletism. The idea, rejected by the church, that in the incarnate Christ there was only one will due to the will being predicated of the **person**. The reason for its rejection was that the church regarded will as a predicate of **nature**, thus yielding two natures. If there was only one will, the human nature of Christ would be threatened. See **Maximus.**

nature. Creation, or an existent, or the particular type of existent. In relation to God, *nature* is used to explain what God is like. In **Christology**, it is used for deity and human nature. See ***anhypostasia*; deification; Dyophysitism; Dyotheletism; *enhypostasia*; *extra Calvinisticum*; hypostatic union; *mia physis*; Monophysitism; Monotheletism; nature of God; Nestorianism; participation; *physis*; properties; quiddity; Theopaschism; unitive Christology.**

nature of God. What God is *like* (love, just, holy, omnipotent, et al.). These particular aspects of his **nature** are termed **attributes**. In the fourth century, *nature of God* was sometimes used as a synonym for God's **essence** or **being**. The attributes are identical with God's being, since God cannot be divided into parts. See **simplicity.**

Nestorianism. A heresy propounded by Nestorius and his followers. Concerned to stress the reality of Christ's humanity, Nestorius undermined the unity of his **person**. From his focus on the two **natures** of Christ, it appeared that deity and humanity were separate, in conjunction but not in union. Nestorius was condemned as a heretic at the Council of Ephesus (A.D. 431). See **Eutychianism; *theotokos.***

ontological. Relating to **being**, that which is. See **Manichaeism; supposit.**

order (*taxis*). The irreversible order disclosed by the **relations** among the three **persons**. In eternity, the Father begets the Son and with the Son (according to the **Western church**) spirates the Holy Spirit. In human history, the Father sent the Son, while both the Father and the Son sent the Spirit. See **generation.**

ordo salutis. The "order of salvation," or the way by which we are brought to salvation by the Holy Spirit and kept there. It encompasses effectual calling, regeneration, faith and repentance, justification, adoption, sanctification, perseverance, and glorification, all of which are received in union with Christ.

Origenists. Persons influenced by Origen (185–254) or his interpreters.

ousia. **Being** (that which is). Since there is only one God, he is only one *ousia.* The word refers to the one being of God. Before the Trinitarian crisis of the fourth century was resolved, however, this word had a range of meanings, and so there was much confusion. See ***hypostasis.***

panentheism. The idea that God and the creation are mutually interdependent, God's being in the creation and the creation in God. See **gnostic; pantheism.**

pantheism. The idea that the creation is divine, that God and the creation are identical. See **gnostic; panentheism.**

participation. The notion that believers, united to Christ, participate in the divine **nature** (2 Peter 1:4), since they are indwelt by the Spirit. This does not mean that the Creator-creature distinction is blurred or eclipsed, but expresses the unbreakable closeness of this union. Athanasius, for one, distinguished Christ, who is *proper* to the Father's **being,** since he is one in being with him from eternity, with our being *participants* in the divine nature. Cf. **deification.**

perichoresis. The mutual indwelling of the three **persons** of the Trinity in the one **being** of God. In **social Trinitarianism**, the word is used in a very different way, to claim that the three ***hypostases*** are like three human persons engaged in a dance around one another, a development hinting at **tritheism**.

persons. The Father, the Son, and the Holy Spirit. There has been much debate about whether *person* is an appropriate or adequate term for the three, in view of its modern usage, which entails separate individuals. But none of the proposed alternatives has succeeded in establishing itself, for those alternatives invariably yield a less-than-personal view of God. See **adoptionism; appropriations; Christology; *communicatio idiomatum*; consubstantiality; Dyotheletism; *enhypostasia*; Eutychianism;**

hypostasis; **immanent Trinity**; *mia physis*; **modalism; Monotheletism; Nestorianism; order**; *perichoresis*; **properties**; *prosopon*; **quiddity; relations; social Trinitarianism; supposit**; *theotokos*; **tritheism.**

phenomenal. Relating to the dualist idea of Immanuel Kant that true scientific knowledge is confined to the world that we can experience through the senses, the phenomenal. Consequently, religious and ethical claims are confined to the noumenal realm, beyond objective scientific knowledge. See **dualism.**

physis. Greek for **nature**. See ***mia physis.***

procession (eternal). The eternal **relation** of the Holy Spirit to the Father (and to the Son, in the view of the **Western church**). See **processions.**

processions. The eternal begetting of the Son and eternal **procession** of the Holy Spirit. These are matched by the **missions**, the historical sendings of the Son and the Spirit. The **Eastern church** considers it an error to call the Father's begetting of the Son a *procession*. For the East, this is a typically **Western church** confusion of the Father and the Son. See **generation.**

properties. Paternity, filiation, active spiration, passive spiration, innascibility. These are, in each case, characteristics possessed by one of the Trinitarian **persons** only in connection with the **relations** that each has. Thus, *paternity* and *innascibility* are the properties of the Father, *filiation* of the Son, *active spiration* of the Father (and the Son, according to the **Western church**), *passive spiration* of the Spirit. In **Christology**, *properties* is most commonly used for the distinctive characteristics of the **natures** of Christ. See **Dyotheletism; generation.**

prosopon. Greek for "face." The term was used in the ancient world as an attempt to describe human **beings**, with the connotation of a mask worn by an actor. As Trinitarian and Christological doctrine developed, ***hypostasis*** came into use to refer to the human **person**, and *prosopon* fell by the wayside.

quiddity. "What" a thing is, its **nature**, as opposed to "who" a **person** is. Thus, God is one quiddity, whereas the incarnate Son is two quiddities but one "who." See **entity.**

relations. The relationship in the indivisible Trinity among the Father and the Son, the Son and the Father, the Father / the Son and the Holy Spirit, and the Holy Spirit and the Father / the Son. *Relations* is the correct term because *relationships* can convey a loose unity rather than indivisible union. These are considered differently in the **Eastern church** than in the **Western church**. The relations among the three **persons** differ. The Father begets the Son and spirates the Spirit—he neither is begotten nor proceeds; the Son is begotten and (according to the West) shares with the Father in the spiration or sending of the Spirit, and does not proceed; the Spirit proceeds from the Father and (or through) the Son, but neither begets nor is begotten. These relations are irreversible. They are relations of relative opposition. See **generation; missions; order; procession; properties.**

Sabellius. A third-century heretic, who taught that the Father, the Son, and the Holy Spirit were merely three ways in which the one God revealed himself. See **modalism.**

simplicity. God's state of being one and indivisible. He cannot be divided into parts. See **nature of God; subsistence.**

social Trinitarianism. An understanding of the Trinity that sees the three **persons** as a community, interacting with one another. Its basic premise is the priority of the three persons over the one **being** (**essence**). See ***perichoresis*.**

soteriology. The doctrine of salvation (from the Greek *sōtēr*, "savior").

subordinationism. A teaching that the Son and the Holy Spirit are of lesser **being** or status than the Father. See **monarchy.**

subsistence. The manner by which the three ***hypostases*** are related to the one simple divine **essence**. This is not a real distinction (that is, a distinction between a thing and a thing), or else there would be a quarternity, not a Trinity. Nor is the distinction merely formal, or it would be purely in our own minds. Rather, it is modal, between a thing (the indivisible **being** of God) and the manner in which the thing is. Thus, while the three *hypostases* are distinct in real terms (the Father is not the Son, etc.), each is identical with the one indivisible divine being, the three subsisting in the one divine essence. See **simplicity.**

substance. (1) What a thing is in itself. (2) What God is, the one identical **being** of the Father, the Son, and the Holy Spirit. See **consubstantiality.**

supposit. An **ontological** reality—in this case, **person**.

theandric. Relating to an **entity**'s being composed of both divine and human elements.

theologoumenon. A theological opinion, expressed by an individual theologian or group of theologians, that currently lacks dogmatic backing by the church.

Theopaschism. The idea that God the Son suffers *in the flesh,* in terms of the Son's human **nature**.

theotokos **("God-bearer").** A reference not so much to Mary as to the child she bore, who was the Son of God. It denotes Jesus' deity and, since Mary is his mother, his humanity. This term Nestorius and his followers rejected, preferring *Christotokos* ("Christ-bearer"). In so doing, they jeopardized the unity of Christ's **person**. See **Nestorianism.**

the three chapters. The works of Theodoret of Cyrrhus, Theodore of Mopsuestia, and Ibas of Edessa that were anathematized at Constantinople II (A.D. 553).

tritheism. The belief that there are three Gods. An exaggerated stress on the three **persons** can, it is claimed, lead to a belief that there are three Gods, not one. See ***perichoresis.***

unitive Christology. A **Christology** that maintains that the single subject of the incarnate Son, Jesus of Nazareth, is "the same" as the eternal Son of the Father. As such, the Son / Word / **Logos** is the single subject of all his actions, acting at all times in accordance with his **natures**.

Western church. The Latin-speaking church, centered in Rome, and its later descendants, which includes Protestants. See **Eastern church; missions; order; procession; processions; properties; relations.**

Word. See **Logos.**

Bibliography

"οὐ γὰρ ἐνεργεῖ ποτε φύσις οὐχ ὑφεστῶσα προσωπικῶς." In *Doctrina Patrum de incarnatione Verbi: Ein Griechishes Florilegium aus der Wende des 7. und 8. Jahrhunderts*, edited by Basileos Phanourgakis and Evangelos Chrysos. Aschendorff, 1981.

Aelurus, Timothy. *Contre Chalcedoine*. Edited and translated by F. Nau. *PO*, 13.2.228–29.

Alberigo, J. *Conciliorum oecumenicorum decreta*. Herder, 1962.

Allen, Pauline, and Bronwen Neil, eds. *The Oxford Handbook of Maximus the Confessor*. Oxford University Press, 2015.

Althaus, Paul. *The Theology of Martin Luther*. Translated by Robert C. Schultz. Fortress Press, 1966.

Ambrose. *De Fide*.

Amos, Roger. *Matthew: A Commentary*. Paul Thomas, 2023.

Anselm. *Cur Deus homo?*

———. *De fide trinitatis et de incarnatione Verbi*.

———. "On the Incarnation of the Word." In *Anselm of Canterbury: The Major Works*, edited by Brian Davies and G. R. Evans. Oxford University Press, 1998.

Aquinas, Thomas. *Commentary on the Gospel of John Chapters 9–21*. Translated by Fabian R. Larcher. Aquinas Institute for the Study of Sacred Doctrine, 2013.

———. *Commentary on the Gospel of St. John*. Magi Books, 1980.

———. *Summa contra Gentiles*.

———. *Summa theologiae*.

Athanasius. *Against the Arians*.

———. *Letters to Serapion on the Holy Spirit*.

———. *Of Synods*.

———. *On the Incarnation*.

———. *Orations Against the Arians*.

———. *To the Antiochenes*.

Atkinson, James. *Martin Luther and the Birth of Protestantism*. 1968. Reprint, John Knox Press, 1982.

Augustine. *City of God*.

———. *Confessions*.

———. *De Genesi ad littera liber imperfectus*.

———. *De Genesi ad litteram*.

———. *De praedestinatione sanctorum*.

———. *De trinitate*.

———. *Enchiridion*.

———. *Letter 11 to Nebridius*.

———. *Letter 169 to Evodius*.

———. *On the Gospel of John*.

———. *The Works of Saint Augustine: A Translation for the 21st Century: The Trinity*. Edited by John E. Rotelle. Translated by Edmund Hill. New City Press, 1991.

Ayres, Lewis. *Augustine and the Trinity*. Cambridge University Press, 2010.

———. *Nicaea and Its Legacy: An Approach to Fourth-Century Trinitarian Theology*. Oxford University Press, 2004.

Baillie, D. M. *God Was in Christ: An Essay on Incarnation and Atonement*. Charles Scribner's Sons, 1948.

Barr, James. *The Semantics of Biblical Language*. Reprint, SCM, 1983.

Barrett, C. K. *The Gospel According to St John: An Introduction with Commentary and Notes on the Greek Text*. 2nd ed. SPCK, 1978.

Barth, Karl. *Church Dogmatics*. Edited by Thomas F. Torrance. Translated by Geoffrey W. Bromiley. 14 vols. T&T Clark, 1956–77.

Basil of Caesarea. *The Hexaemeron*.

———. *On the Holy Spirit*.

Bathrellos, Demetrios. *The Byzantine Christ: Person, Nature, and Will in the Christology of Saint Maximus the Confessor*. Oxford University Press, 2004.

Baugh, S. M. *Ephesians*. Lexham Academic, 2016.

Bavinck, Herman. *Reformed Dogmatics*. Edited by John Bolt. Translated by John Vriend. 4 vols. Baker Academic, 2003–8.

Beeke, Joel R. *Heirs with Christ: The Puritans on Adoption*. Reformation Heritage Books, 2008.

Beeley, Christopher A. *Gregory of Nazianzus on the Trinity and the Knowledge of God: In Your Light Shall We See Light*. Oxford University Press, 2008.

———. *The Unity of Christ: Continuity and Conflict in Patristic Tradition*. Yale University Press, 2012.

Bellarmine, Robert. "Secunda Controversia Generalis de Christo." In *Disputationum de Controversiis Christianae Fidei Adversus Haereticos*. Rome, 1832.

Beveridge, Henry, ed. *Selected Works of John Calvin*. Vol. 2, *Tracts and Letters, Part 2*. 1849. Reprint, Baker, 1983.

Beza, Theodore. *Ad Acta Colloquii Montisbelgardensis Responsionis*. 3rd ed. Geneva: Ioannes le Preux, 1589.

Blowers, Paul M. *Maximus the Confessor: Jesus Christ and the Transfiguration of the World*. Oxford University Press, 2016.

Blowers, Paul M., and Robert Louis Wilken, trans. *On the Cosmic Mystery of Jesus Christ: Selected Writings from St. Maximus the Confessor*. St. Vladimir's Seminary Press, 2003.

Bobrinskoy, Boris. *The Mystery of the Trinity: Trinitarian Experience and Vision in the Biblical and Patristic Tradition*. Translated by Anthony P. Gythiel. St. Vladimir's Seminary Press, 1999.

The Book of Common Prayer and Administration of the Sacraments and Other Rites and Ceremonies of the Church According to the Use of the Church of England. Oxford University Press, n.d.

Bowsher, Clive. *Life in the Son: Exploring Participation and Union with Christ in John's Gospel and Letters*. Apollos, 2023.

Brand, Thomas. *Intimately Forsaken: A Trinitarian Christology of the Cross*. Palgrave Macmillan, 2024.

Bray, Gerald. *The Doctrine of God*. Inter-Varsity Press, 1993.

Brenz, Johannes. *De Personali Unione Duarum Naturarum in Christo, et Ascensu Christi*. Tubingae: Ulrici Morhardi, 1561.

Bromiley, Geoffrey W. *An Introduction to the Theology of Karl Barth*. Eerdmans, 1979.

———, ed. *Zwingli and Bullinger*. Westminster Press, 1953.

Brown, Raymond E. *The Virginal Conception and Bodily Resurrection of Jesus*. Paulist Press, 1973.

Bruce, A. B. *The Humiliation of Christ*. T&T Clark, 1905.

Bruce, F. F. *Commentary on the Epistle to the Hebrews: The English Text with Introduction, Exposition and Notes*. Marshall, Morgan & Scott, 1964.

Bucur, Bogdan G. "Foreordained from Eternity: The Mystery of the Incarnation According to Some Early Christian and Byzantine Writers." *Dumbarton Oaks Papers* 62 (2008): 199–215.

Bulgakov, Sergius. *The Wisdom of God: A Brief Summary of Sophiology*. Williams and Norgate, 1937.

Bullinger, Heinrich. *De Testamento seu Foedere Dei Unico & Aeterno Brevis Expositio*. Zürich, 1534.

Burke, Trevor J. Review of *Sons in the Son: The Riches and Reach of Adoption in Christ*, by David B. Garner. *JRT* 11, no. 3 (2017): 347–48. doi: 10.1163/15697312-01103011.

Cabasilas, Nicholas. *Life in Christ*. Translated by Margaret I. Lisney. Janus, 1995.

Calvin, John. *Calvini Opera (Opera Quae Supersunt Omnia)*. Edited by Guilelmus Baum, Eduardus Cunitz, and Eduardus Reuss. 59 vols. *Corpus Reformatorum* 29–87. Brunswick, 1863–1900.

———. *Calvin's Commentaries: The Acts of the Apostles 1–13*. Translated by John W. Fraser. Eerdmans, 1965.

———. *Calvin's Commentaries: The Epistle of Paul the Apostle to the Hebrews and the First and Second Epistles of St. Peter*. Translated by William B. Johnston. Eerdmans, 1963.

———. *Calvin's Commentaries: The Epistles of Paul to the Galatians, Ephesians, Philippians and Colossians*. Edited by Thomas F. Torrance and David W. Torrance. Translated by T. H. L. Parker. Eerdmans, 1965.

———. *Calvin's Commentaries: The First Epistle of Paul the Apostle to the Corinthians*. Edited by Thomas F. Torrance and David W. Torrance. Translated by John W. Fraser. Eerdmans, 1960.

———. *Calvin's Commentaries: The Gospel According to St. John 1–10*. Translated by T. H. L. Parker. Eerdmans, 1961.

———. *Calvin's Commentaries: The Gospel According to St. John 11–21 and the First Epistle of John*. Edited by Thomas F. Torrance and David W. Torrance. Translated by T. H. L. Parker. Eerdmans, 1959.

———. *Calvin's Commentaries: The Second Epistle of Paul to the Corinthians and the Epistles to Timothy, Titus, and Philemon*. Edited by David W. Torrance and Thomas F. Torrance. Translated by T. A. Smail. Eerdmans, 1964.

———. *Commentarii in Epistolas Canonicas*. Ioannis Calvini Opera Omnia. Librairie Droz, 2009.

———. *Commentarii in Pauli Epistolas ad Galatas, ad Ephesios, ad Philippenses, ad Colossenses*. Edited by Helmut Feld. Ioannis Calvini Opera Omnia. Librairie Droz, 1992.

———. *In Pauli Apostolas*.

———. *Institutes of the Christian Religion*. Edited by John T. McNeill. Translated by Ford Lewis Battles. Westminster Press, 1960.

———. *Ioannis Calvini: Opera Exegetica: Volumen XII/1 Commentariorum in Acta Apostolorum Liber Primum*. Edited by Helmut Feld. Droz, 2001.

———. *Ioannis Calvini Opera Omnia*. Droz, 1992–.

———. *Ioannis Calvini Opera Selecta*. Edited by Peter Barth and Wilhelm Niesel. 5 vols. Kaiser, 1926–52.

———. *Sermons on the Epistle to the Ephesians*. 1562. Reprint, Banner of Truth, 1973.

———. *Short Treatise on the Holy Supper of Our Lord and Only Saviour Jesus Christ*. In *Calvin: Theological Treatises*, edited by J. K. S. Reid. Westminster Press, 1954.

Campbell, Iain D. "Re-Visiting the Covenant of Redemption." In *The People's Theologian: Writings in Honour of Donald MacLeod*, edited by Iain D. Campbell and Malcolm Maclean. Mentor, 2011.

Carson, D. A. *The Gospel According to St John*. Inter-Varsity Press, 1991.

———. "John 5:26: *Crux Interpretum* for Eternal Generation." In *Retrieving Eternal Generation*, edited by Fred Sanders and Scott R. Swain. Zondervan, 2017.

Cassidy, James J. *God's Time for Us: Barth's Reconciliation of Eternity and Time in Jesus Christ*. Lexham Press, 2016.

Chemnitz, Martin. *De Duabus Naturis in Christo: De Hypostatica Earum Unione: De Communicatione Idiomatum, et de Aliis Questionibus*. Ramba, 1578.

———. *The Two Natures in Christ*. Translated by J. A. O. Preus. 1578. Reprint, Concordia, 1971.

Clark, John C., and Marcus Peter Johnson. *The Incarnation of God: The Mystery of the Gospel as the Foundation of Evangelical Theology*. Crossway, 2015.

Clayton, Paul B. *The Christology of Theodoret of Cyrus: Antiochene Christology from the Council of Ephesus (431) to the Council of Chalcedon (431)*. Oxford University Press, 2007.

Coakley, Sarah. "What Does Chalcedon Solve and What Does It Not? Some Reflections on the Status and Meaning of the Chalcedonian Definition." In *The Incarnation*, edited by Stephen T. Davis, Daniel Kendall, and Gerald O'Collins. Oxford University Press, 2002.

Constas, Maximos, ed. and trans. *On Difficulties in the Church Fathers: The Ambigua: Maximos the Confessor*. Vol. 1. Dumbarton Oaks Medieval Library. Harvard University Press, 2014.

———, trans. *St. Maximos the Confessor: On Difficulties in Sacred Scripture: The Responses to Thalassios*. Catholic University of America Press, 2018.

Craig, William Lane. "The Incarnation." In *Philosophical Foundations for a Christian Worldview*, by J. P. Moreland and William Lane Craig. InterVarsity Press, 2003.

Cranfield, C. E. B. *A Critical and Exegetical Commentary on the Epistle to the Romans*. T&T Clark, 1979.

Crisp, Oliver D. *Divinity and Humanity: The Incarnation Reconsidered*. Current Issues in Theology. Cambridge University Press, 2007.

———. *God Incarnate: Explorations in Christology*. T&T Clark, 2009.

———. "On Barth's Denial of Universalism." *Them* 29, no. 1 (September 2003): 18–29.

———. "Some Desiderata for Models of the Hypostatic Union." In *Christology, Ancient and Modern: Explorations in Constructive Dogmatics*, edited by Oliver D. Crisp and Fred Sanders. Zondervan, 2013.

Cross, Richard. *Communicatio Idiomatum: Reformation Christological Debates*. Oxford University Press, 2019.

Cullmann, Oscar. *The Christology of the New Testament*. SCM, 1959.

———. "The Reply of Professor Cullmann to Roman Catholic Critics." *SJT* 15, no. 1 (1962): 36–43.

Cyril of Alexandria. *The Commentary on St. John*. Translated by Philip Pusey. Vol. 1. Library of Fathers of the Holy Catholic Church 43. Oxford: James Parker, 1874.

———. "A Defence of the Twelve Anathemas Against Theodoret." In *St. Cyril of Alexandria: Three Christological Treatises*, translated by Daniel King. Fathers of the Church 129. Catholic University of America Press, 2014.

———. *Dialogue on the Most Holy Trinity*.

———. *Epistola ad Succensum*. In *Cyril of Alexandria: Select Letters*, edited and translated by Lionel R. Wickham. Oxford Early Christian Texts. Oxford University Press, 1983.

———. *On the Unity of Christ*. Translated by John Anthony McGuckin. St. Vladimir's Seminary Press, 1995.

———. *Quod unus sit Christus*.

———. *Thesaurus*.

Daley, Brian E., ed. *Leontius of Byzantium: Complete Works*. Oxford University Press, 2017.

Davies, Brian. *Thomas Aquinas's* Summa contra Gentiles*: A Guide and a Commentary*. Oxford University Press, 2016.

———. *Thomas Aquinas's* Summa theologiae*: A Guide and Commentary*. Oxford University Press, 2014.

Davies, Brian, and G. R. Evans, eds. *Anselm of Canterbury: The Major Works*. Oxford University Press, 1998.

Davies, W. D. *A Critical and Exegetical Commentary on the Gospel According to Saint Matthew*. T&T Clark, 1988.

Davis, Leo Donald. *The First Seven Ecumenical Councils (325–787)*. Liturgical Press, 1990.

de Margerie, Bertrand. *The Christian Trinity in History*. Translated by Edmund J. Fortman. Studies in Historical Theology 1. St. Bede's Publications, 1982.

DeWeese, Garrett J. "One Person, Two Natures: Two Metaphysical Models of the Incarnation." In *Jesus in Trinitarian Perspective: An Introductory Christology*, edited by Fred Sanders and Klaus Issler. B&H Academic, 2007.

Didymus the Blind. *On the Holy Spirit*.

Dorner, I. A. *History of the Development of the Doctrine of the Person of Christ*. Translated by D. W. Simon. Vol. 3. Edinburgh: T&T Clark, 1861.

———. "System of Christian Doctrine." In *God and Incarnation in Mid-Nineteenth Century German Theology*, edited and translated by Claude Welch. Library of Protestant Thought. Oxford University Press, 1965.

———. *A System of Christian Doctrine*. Translated by Alfred Cave and J. S. Banks. Vol. 3. Edinburgh: T&T Clark, 1882.

Drake, K. J. *The Flesh of the Word: The* Extra-Calvinisticum *from Zwingli to Early Orthodoxy*. Oxford University Press, 2021.

Duby, Steven J. "Inseparable Operations and the Human Operation of Christ." *SJT* 77, no. 2 (2024): 115–25.

———. *Jesus and the God of Classical Theism: Biblical Christology in the Light of the Doctrine of God*. Baker Academic, 2022.

Eglinton, James. *Trinity and Organism: Towards a New Reading of Herman Bavinck's Organic Motif*. Bloomsbury, 2012.

Emery, Gilles. *The Trinity: An Introduction to Catholic Doctrine on the Triune God*. Catholic University of America Press, 2011.

Evans, C. Stephen, ed. *Exploring Kenotic Christology: The Self-Emptying of God*. Oxford University Press, 2006.

Fairbairn, Donald. *Grace and Christology in the Early Church*. Oxford University Press, 2003.

———. Introduction to *Fulgentius of Ruspe and the Scythian Monks: Correspondence on Christology and Grace*, translated by Rob Roy McGregor and Donald Fairbairn. Fathers of the Church 126. Catholic University of America Press, 2013.

———. "The One Person Who Is Jesus Christ: The Patristic Perspective." In *Jesus in Trinitarian Perspective: An Introductory Christology*, edited by Fred Sanders and Klaus Issler. B&H Academic, 2007.

Fenner, Dudley. *Sacra Theologia, sive Veritas Quae Secundum Pietatem*. Geneva, 1585.

Ferrara, Dennis M. "'Hypostatized in the Logos': Leontius of Byzantium, Leontius of Jerusalem and the Unfinished Business of the Council of Chalcedon." *Louvain Studies* 22 (1997): 311–27.

Fesko, J. V. *The Covenant of Redemption: Origins, Development, and Reception*. Vandenhoeck & Ruprecht, 2016.

———. *Diversity Within the Reformed Tradition: Supra- and Infralapsarianism in Calvin, Dort, and Westminster*. Reformed Academic Press, 2001.

Fitzmyer, Joseph A. *The Gospel According to Luke (I–IX)*. Anchor Bible. Doubleday, 1970.

Florovsky, Georges. "Eastern Fathers of the Fourth Century." In *The Collected Works of Father Georges Florovsky*, edited by Richard S. Haugh. Vol. 7. Büchervertriebsanstalt, 1987.

France, R. T. *The Gospel According to Matthew: An Introduction and Commentary*. Inter-Varsity Press, 1985.

Frank, G. L. C. "The Council of Constantinople II as a Model Reconciliation Council." *Theological Studies* 52 (1991): 636–50.

Gaffin, Richard B., Jr., and David B. Garner. "The Divine *and* Adopted Son of God: A Response to Joshua Maurer and Ty Kieser." *Them* 47, no. 1 (April 2022): 144–55.

Garcia, Mark. *Life in Christ: Union with Christ and Twofold Grace in Calvin's Theology*. Paternoster, 2008.

Garner, David B. *Sons in the Son: The Riches and Reach of Adoption in Christ*. P&R Publishing, 2016.

Gavrilyuk, Paul L. *The Suffering of the Impassible God: The Dialectics of Patristic Thought*. Oxford University Press, 2004.

Giles, Kevin. *The Eternal Generation of the Son: Maintaining Orthodoxy in Trinitarian Theology*. IVP Academic, 2012.

Gillespie, Patrick. *The Ark of the Covenant Opened: Or, A Treatise of the Covenant of Redemption Between God and Christ, as the Fountain of the Covenant of Grace*. London, 1677.

Gleede, Benjamin. *The Development of the Term* ἐνυπόστατος *from Origen to John of Damascus*. Brill, 2012.

Gockel, Matthias. "How to Read Karl Barth with Charity: A Critical Reply to George Hunsinger." *Modern Theology* 32, no. 2 (April 2016): 259–67.

Gondreau, Paul. *The Passions of Christ's Soul in the Theology of St. Thomas Aquinas*. Beiträge zur Geschichte der Philosophie und Theologie des Mittelalters, Neue Folge 61. Aschendorff, 2002.

Gordon, George A. *The Christ of Today*. Boston: Houghton, Mifflin and Company, 1896.

Gore, Charles. *The Body of Christ*. John Murray, 1901.

Graffin, R., and F. Nau, eds. *Patrologia Orientalis*. Paris, 1907–.

Gray, Patrick T. R. *The Defense of Chalcedon in the East (451–553)*. Brill, 1979.

———. *Leontius of Jerusalem: Against the Monophysites: Testimonies of the Saints and Aporiae*. Oxford University Press, 2006.

Gray, Thomas. "Elegy Written in a Country Churchyard" (1751). In *The Penguin Dictionary of Quotations*, edited by J. M. Cohen and M. J. Cohen. Penguin, 1960.

Green, Joel B. *The Gospel of Luke*. Eerdmans, 1997.

Gregg, Robert C. *Early Arianism—a Way of Salvation*. Fortress Press, 1981.

Gregory of Nazianzus. *Letter 101 to Cledonius*. In *St. Gregory of Nazianzus: On God and Christ: The Five Theological Orations and Two Letters to Cledonius*. Translated by Frederick Williams and Lionel Wickham. St. Vladimir's Seminary Press, 2002.

———. *Oration 25*.

———. *Oration 29*.

———. *Oration 30*.

———. *Oration 31 on the Holy Spirit*.

———. *Oration on Holy Baptism 40*.

Gregory of Nyssa. *Against Eunomius*.

———. *On "Not Three Gods."*

———. *On the Holy Spirit Against the Macedonians*.

Grillmeier, Aloys. *Christ in Christian Tradition*. Vol. 1, *From the Apostolic Age to Chalcedon (451)*. Edited by John Bowden. 2nd rev. ed. John Knox Press, 1975.

———. *Christ in Christian Tradition*. Vol. 2, *From the Council of Chalcedon (451) to Gregory the Great (590–604): Part Two: The Church of Constantinople in the Sixth Century*. Translated by Theresia Hainthaler and John Cawte. Mowbray, 1995.

Gunton, Colin E. *Yesterday & Today: A Study of Continuities in Christology*. Eerdmans, 1983.

Habets, Myk. "Putting the 'Extra' Back into Calvinism." *SJT* 62, no. 4 (2009): 441–56.

———. "A Supralapsarian Christological Interpretation of the Logos Asarkos." Unpublished manuscript, n.d. https://www.academia.edu/3615450/A_Supralapsarian_Christological_Interpretation_of_the_Logos_Asarkos.

Hall, Francis J. *The Kenotic Theory*. New York: Longmans, Green and Company, 1898.

Hanson, R. P. C. *The Search for the Christian Doctrine of God: The Arian Controversy 318–381*. T&T Clark, 1988.

Hardy, Edward Rochie, ed. *Christology of the Later Fathers*. Library of Christian Classics. Westminster Press, 1954.

Harnack, Adolf von. *History of Dogma*. Translated by James Millar. London: Williams and Norgate, 1897.

———. *What Is Christianity?* Translated by Thomas Bailey Saunders. 4th ed. Williams and Norgate, 1923.

Harris, Mark. "When Jesus Lost His Soul: Fourth-Century Christology and Modern." *SJT* 70, no. 1 (2017): 74–92.

Hawthorne, Gerald F. *The Presence and the Power: The Significance of the Holy Spirit in the Life and Ministry of Jesus*. Wipf & Stock, 2003.

Helm, Paul. *Eternal God: A Study of God Without Time*. Clarendon Press, 1988.

Hill, David. *The Gospel of Matthew*. Marshall, Morgan & Scott, 1972.

Hodge, A. A. *Outlines of Theology*. Eerdmans, 1972.

Hodge, Charles. *A Commentary on the Epistle to the Ephesians*. Banner of Truth, 1964.

———. *Systematic Theology*. Eerdmans, 1977.

Hoehner, Harold W. *Ephesians: An Exegetical Commentary*. Baker Academic, 2002.

Holmes, S. R. *The Holy Trinity: Understanding God's Life*. Paternoster, 2012.

Hoover, Roy W. "The Harpagmos Enigma: A Philological Solution." *HTR* 64, no. 1 (1971): 95–119.

Hovorun, Cyril. *Eastern Christianity in Its Texts*. T&T Clark, 2022.

———. *Will, Action and Freedom: Christological Controversies in the Sixth Century*. Brill, 2008.

Hughes, Philip Edgcumbe. *A Commentary on the Epistle to the Hebrews*. Eerdmans, 1977.

Hunsinger, George. "Election and the Trinity: Twenty-Five Theses on the Theology of Karl Barth." *Modern Theology* 24, no. 2 (2008): 179–98.

Irenaeus. *Against Heresies*.

Irons, Charles Lee. "A Lexical Defense of the Johannine 'Only-Begotten.'" In *Retrieving Eternal Generation*, edited by Fred Sanders and Scott R. Swain. Zondervan, 2017.

Irving, Alex. "A Critical Assessment of Bruce L. McCormack's Christological Proposal." *SJT* 77, no. 2 (2024): 149–62.

Irving, Edward. *The Orthodox and Catholic Doctrine of Our Lord's Human Nature*. London: Baldwin and Cradock, 1830.

Isbell, R. Sherman. *Understanding the Offer of the Gospel*. Forthcoming.

Jamieson, R. B. *The Paradox of Sonship: Christology in the Epistle to the Hebrews*. IVP Academic, 2021.

John of Damascus. *Ekdos*.

———. *On the Orthodox Faith*.

———. *On the Two Wills in Christ*.

Kannengiesser, Charles. *Arius and Athanasius: Two Alexandrian Theologians*. Variorum, 1991.

Kantouma, Vassa. *John of Damascus: New Studies in His Life and Works*. Ashgate / Variorum, 2015.

Kelly, J. N. D. *A Commentary on the Pastoral Epistles*. Adam & Charles Black, 1963.

———. *Early Christian Doctrines*. Adam & Charles Black, 1968.

———. "The Nicene Creed: A Turning Point." *SJT* 36, no. 1 (1983): 29–39.

Kenny, Anthony. *The God of the Philosophers*. Clarendon Press, 1979.

Kidd, B. J., ed. *Documents Illustrative of the Continental Reformation*. 1911. Reprint, Clarendon Press, 1967.

King, Daniel, trans. *St. Cyril of Alexandria: Three Christological Treatises*. Fathers of the Church 129. Catholic University of America Press, 2014.

Korb, Samuel. "Whole God and Whole Man: Deification as Incarnation in Maximus the Confessor." *SJT* 75, no. 4 (2022): 308–18.

Kotter, Boniface. *Die Schriften Des Johannes von Damaskos. Herausgegeben Vom Byzantischen Institut der Abtei Scheyern*. 6 vols. Walter de Gruyter, 1969–2009.

Krausmüller, Dirk. "Leontius of Jerusalem: A Theologian of the Seventh Century." *JTS* 52 (2001): 637–57.

La Cugna, Catherine Mowry. *God for Us: The Trinity and Christian Life*. Harper, 1991.

Lampe, G. W. H., ed. *A Patristic Greek Lexicon*. Clarendon Press, 1961.

Larchet, Jean-Claude. *La Divinisation de l'Homme Selon Saint Maxime le Confesseur*. Les éditions du Cerf, 1996.

Legge, Dominic. *The Trinitarian Christology of St. Thomas Aquinas*. Oxford University Press, 2017.

Letham, Robert. "Baptism in the Writings of the Reformers." *SBET* 7, no. 2 (Autumn 1989): 21–44.

———. *The Holy Spirit*. P&R Publishing, 2023.

———. *The Holy Trinity: In Scripture, History, Theology, and Worship*. Rev. and expanded ed. P&R Publishing, 2019.

———. *The Message of the Person of Christ: The Word Made Flesh*. Inter-Varsity Press, 2013.

———. Review of *The Incarnation of God: The Mystery of the Gospel as the Foundation of Evangelical Theology*, by John C. Clark and Marcus Peter Johnson. *Them* 40, no. 2 (August 2015): 334–36.

———. *Systematic Theology*. Crossway, 2019.

———. "The Trinity: The Doctrine of God and the Pulpit." In *Theology for Ministry: How Doctrine Affects Pastoral Life and Practice*, edited by William R. Edwards, John C. A. Ferguson, and Chad Van Dixhoorn. P&R Publishing, 2022.

———. "The Triune God, Incarnation, and Definite Atonement." In *From Heaven He Came and Sought Her: Definite Atonement in*

Historical, Biblical, Theological, and Pastoral Perspective, edited by David Gibson and Jonathan Gibson. Crossway, 2013.

———. *Union with Christ: In Scripture, History, and Theology*. P&R Publishing, 2011.

———. *The Westminster Assembly: Reading Its Theology in Historical Context*. P&R Publishing, 2009.

———. *The Work of Christ*. Inter-Varsity Press, 1993.

Letham, Robert, and Donald MacLeod. "Is Evangelicalism Christian?" *EQ* 67, no. 1 (January–March 1995): 3–33.

Lincoln, Andrew T. *Ephesians*. Word Biblical Commentary 42. Word Books, 1990.

Lindars, Barnabas. *The Gospel of John*. New Century Bible Commentary. Eerdmans, 1972.

Lossky, Vladimir. *The Mystical Theology of the Eastern Church*. James Clarke & Co., 1957.

Louth, Andrew. *John Damascene: Tradition and Originality in Byzantine Theology*. Oxford University Press, 2002.

———. *Maximus the Confessor*. Routledge, 1996.

———. "The Place of *Theosis* in Orthodox Theology." In *Selected Essays*. Vol. 2, *Studies in Theology*, edited by Lewis Ayres and John Behr. Oxford University Press, 2023.

Luther, Martin. *Confession Concerning Christ's Supper*. 1528. *LW*, 37:151–372.

———. "Freedom of a Christian." 1520. *LW*, 31:327–77.

———. *That These Words of Christ, "This Is My Body," Still Stand Firm Against the Fanatics*. 1527. *LW*, 37:98–124.

———. "Two Kinds of Righteousness." 1519. *LW*, 31:293–306.

Machen, J. Gresham. *The Virgin Birth of Christ*. Reprint, Baker, 1965.

Mackintosh, H. R. *The Doctrine of the Person of Jesus Christ*. T&T Clark, 1912.

MacLeod, Donald. *Christ Crucified: Understanding the Atonement*. IVP Academic, 2014.

———. *The Person of Christ*. Inter-Varsity Press, 1998.

MacLeod, Ian Campbell. "'My Father and Your Father': The Nature and Privilege of Sonship." PhD diss., Puritan Reformed Theological Seminary, 2024.

Madigan, Kevin. *The Passions of Christ in High-Medieval Thought: An Essay on Christological Development*. Oxford University Press, 2007.

Manschreck, Clyde L., trans. and ed. *Melanchthon on Christian Doctrine: Loci Communes 1555*. Baker, 1965.

Marshall, I. Howard. *A Critical and Exegetical Commentary on the Pastoral Epistles*. T&T Clark, 1999.

———. *The Gospel of Luke: A Commentary on the Greek Text*. New International Greek Testament Commentary. Paternoster Press, 1978.

Martin, Ralph P. *Carmen Christi: Philippians ii.5–11 in Recent Interpretation and in the Setting of Early Christian Worship*. Eerdmans, 1983.

———. *Philippians*. New Century Bible. Eerdmans, 1980.

Mascall, E. L. *Christ, the Christian and the Church*. Longmans, Green and Co., 1946.

Maxentius, John. *Professio brevissima Catholicae fidei*. In *CCSL*. Brepols, 1953.

Maximus. *Disputatio cum Pyrrho*.

———. *Opusculum 7*.

McCormack, Bruce L. *For Us and Our Salvation: Incarnation and Atonement in the Reformed Tradition*. Studies in Reformed Theology and History. Princeton Theological Seminary, 1993.

———. "Grace and Being: The Role of God's Gracious Election in Karl Barth's Theological Ontology." In *The Cambridge Companion to Karl Barth*, edited by John Webster. Cambridge University Press, 2000.

———. *The Humility of the Eternal Son: Reformed Kenoticism and the Repair of Chalcedon*. Cambridge University Press, 2021.

———. "Seek God Where He May Be Found: A Response to Edwin Chr. Van Driel." *SJT* 60 (2007): 62–79.

McGinnis, Andrew M. *The Son of God Beyond the Flesh: A Historical and Theological Study of the Extra-Calvinisticum*. Bloomsbury, 2014.

McGraw, Ryan. Review of *Sons in the Son*, by David B. Garner. *Ordained Servant Online*. February 2017.

McGregor, Rob Roy, and Donald Fairbairn, trans. *Fulgentius of Ruspe and the Scythian Monks: Correspondence on Christology and Grace*. Fathers of the Church 126. Catholic University of America Press, 2013.

McGuckin, John A. *St. Cyril of Alexandria and the Christological Controversy: Its History, Theology, and Texts*. St. Vladimir's Seminary Press, 2004.

———. *St. Cyril of Alexandria: On the Unity of Christ*. St. Vladimir's Seminary Press, 1995.

———. "'The Theopaschite Confession' (Text and Historical Context): A Study in the Cyrilline Re-Interpretation of Chalcedon." *JEH* 35, no. 2 (1984): 239–55.

Melanchthon, Philip. "Enarratio Epistolae Pauli ad Colossenses Praelecta" (1556). In *Operum Omnium*. Wittenberg: Zacharia Schürerio et eius sociis, 1601.

———. *Loci Communes Theologici*. 1555. Reprint, Basel: Ioannem Operinum, 1562.

Meyendorff, John. *Christ in Eastern Christian Thought*. St. Vladimir's Seminary Press, 1975.

Migne, Jacques-Paul, et al., eds. *Patrologia Cursus Completus: Series Graeca*. 162 vols. Paris, 1857–66.

———. *Patrologia Cursus Completus: Series Latina*. 217 vols. Paris, 1844–64.

Moffitt, David M. *Atonement and the Logic of Resurrection in the Epistle to the Hebrews*. Brill, 2011.

Molnar, Paul D. *Faith, Freedom, and the Spirit: The Economic Trinity in Barth, Torrance, and Contemporary Theology*. InterVarsity Press, 2015.

Moltmann, Jürgen. *The Trinity and the Kingdom: The Doctrine of God*. SCM, 1991.

Moreland, J. P., and William Lane Craig. *Philosophical Foundations for a Christian Worldview*. InterVarsity Press, 2003.

Morgan, Jonathan. "The Unity of Christ in Cyril of Alexandria's *Festal Letters*." *SJT* 77, no. 2 (2024): 163–74.

Morris, Leon. *The Apostolic Preaching of the Cross*. Tyndale Press, 1955.

———. *The Gospel According to John: The English Text with Introduction, Exposition and Notes*. Marshall, Morgan & Scott, 1971.

———. *Luke: An Introduction and Commentary*. Inter-Varsity Press, 1997.

Mother Mary and Kallistos Ware, trans. *The Festal Menaion*. St. Tikhon's Seminary Press, 1998.

Mounce, William B. *Pastoral Epistles*. Word Biblical Commentary 46. Thomas Nelson, 2000.

Muller, Richard A. "Toward the Pactum Salutis: Locating the Origins of a Concept." *MAJT* 18 (2007): 11–65.

———. "Trinity and the Son's Aseity: Formulation and Debate in Calvin and Reformed Orthodoxy." In *Understanding the Divine in Early Modern Reformed Theology*. Reformation Heritage Books, 2024.

Murray, John. *The Epistle to the Romans*. Eerdmans, 1965.

———. *Redemption Accomplished and Applied*. Banner of Truth, 1961.

Neill, Stephen. *Christian Missions*. Penguin, 1964.

Nestorius. *The Bazaar of Heracleides*. Edited by G. R. Driver and Leonard Hodgson. Clarendon Press, 1925.

Noble, Thomas A. "Paradox in Gregory Nazianzen's Doctrine of the Trinity." *StPatr* 27 (1993): 94–99.

Nolland, John. *Luke 1–9:20*. Word Biblical Commentary 35A. Word Books, 1989.

Norris, Richard A., Jr. *The Christological Controversy*. Fortress Press, 1980.

Oberman, Heiko. "The 'Extra' Dimension in the Theology of Calvin." *JEH* 21, no. 1 (1970): 43–64.

Olevian, Caspar. *De Substantia Foederis Gratuiti Inter Deum et Electos*. Geneva, 1585.

Origen. *On First Principles*. In *Origen: On First Principles: A Reader's Edition*, edited and translated by John Behr. Oxford University Press, 2019.

Owen, John. *The Works of John Owen*. Edited by William H. Goold. 16 vols. Banner of Truth, 1965–68.

Packer, James I. "What Did the Cross Achieve? The Logic of Penal Substitution." In *Collected Shorter Writings of J. I. Packer*. Paternoster, 1998.

Pannenberg, Wolfhart. *Jesus—God and Man*. Translated by Lewis L. Wilkins. Westminster Press, 1968.

———. *Systematic Theology*. Translated by Geoffrey W. Bromiley. 3 vols. Eerdmans, 1991–94.

Pelikan, Jaroslav. *The Christian Tradition: A History of the Development of Doctrine*. Vol. 1, *The Emergence of the Catholic Tradition (100–600)*. University of Chicago Press, 1971.

Percival, Henry R. *The Seven Ecumenical Councils of the Undivided Church: Their Canons and Dogmatic Decrees*. *NPNF*[2]. Reprint, T&T Clark, 1997.

Photius. *On the Mystagogy of the Holy Spirit*. Studion, 1983.

Polyander, Johannes. *Synopsis Purioris Theologiae, Disputationibus Quinquaginta Duabus Comprehensa*. Leiden: Ex Officina Elzeverianus, 1625.

Pope, Alexander. *An Essay on Man*.

Porter, Stanley E. *Verbal Aspect in the Greek New Testament*. Peter Lang, 1989.

Prestige, G. L. *Fathers and Heretics*. SPCK, 1940.

Price, Richard, trans. *The Acts of the Council of Constantinople of 553*. 2 vols. Liverpool University Press, 2009.

———. "The Council of Chalcedon (451): A Narrative." In *Chalcedon in Context: Church Councils 400–700*, edited by Richard Price and Mary Whitby. Liverpool University Press, 2011.

Radcliff, Jason R. "Thomas F. Torrance: Historian of Dogma." In *T&T Clark Handbook of Thomas F. Torrance*, edited by Paul D. Molnar and Myk Habets. T&T Clark, 2020.

Raitt, Jill. *The Colloquy of Montbéliard: Religion and Politics in the Sixteenth Century*. Oxford University Press, 1993.

Ramsey, A. M. *The Glory of God and the Transfiguration of Christ*. Longmans, 1949.

Raven, Charles E. *Apollinarianism: An Essay in the Christology of the Early Church*. Cambridge University Press, 1923.

Russell, Norman. *Cyril of Alexandria*. Routledge, 2000.

———. *The Doctrine of Deification in the Greek Patristic Tradition*. Oxford University Press, 2004.

Sanders, Fred, and Scott R. Swain, eds. *Retrieving Eternal Generation*. Zondervan, 2017.

Schaff, Philip. *The Creeds of Christendom*. Baker, 1966.

———, ed. Nicene and Post-Nicene Fathers of the Christian Church. 1st ser. Reprint, Eerdmans, 1978–79.

———, ed. *Nicene and Post-Nicene Fathers of the Christian Church.* 2nd ser. Reprint, Eerdmans, 1979.

Schilder, Klaas. *Christ Crucified.* Translated by Henry Zylstra. Eerdmans, 1944.

Schlesinger, Eugene R. "Trinity, Incarnation and Time: A Restatement of the Doctrine of God in Conversation with Robert Jenson." *SJT* 69, no. 2 (May 2016): 189–203.

Schmid, Heinrich. *The Doctrinal Theology of the Evangelical Lutheran Church.* 3rd ed. 1899. Reprint, Augsburg Press, 1961.

Schnackenburg, Rudolf. *The Gospel According to St. John.* Vol. 1, *Introduction and Commentary on Chapters 1–4.* Translated by Kevin Smyth. Burns & Oates, 1968.

Schwartz, Eduardus. *Acta conciliorum oecumenicorum.* Walter de Gruyter, 1914–40.

Sellers, R. V. *The Council of Chalcedon: A Historical and Doctrinal Survey.* SPCK, 1953.

Severus. *Ad Nephalium II.* In *Severus of Antioch,* by Pauline Allen and C. T. R. Hayward. Routledge, 2004.

———. *Letter to Oecumenius.* In *PO,* 12.2.176–77.

Shedd, William G. T. *Dogmatic Theology.* Vol. 2. 1888. Reprint, Zondervan, 1971.

Skinner, Quentin. "Meaning and Understanding in the History of Ideas." In *Visions of Politics.* Vol. 1, *Regarding Method.* Cambridge University Press, 2002.

Sorabji, Richard. *Time, Creation, and the Continuum: Theories in Antiquity and the Early Middle Ages.* Cornell University Press, 1983.

Steinberg, Michael. "Notes on the Quartets." In *The Beethoven Quartet Companion,* edited by Robert Winter and Robert Martin. University of California Press, 1994.

———. *The Symphony: A Listener's Guide.* Oxford University Press, 1995.

Stephens, W. P. *The Theology of Huldrych Zwingli.* Clarendon Press, 1986.

Stibbs, A. M. *The Meaning of the Word "Blood" in Scripture.* Tyndale Press, 1948.

Stott, Wilfrid. "The Conception of 'Offering' in the Epistle to the Hebrews." *NTS* 9 (1962): 65–67.

Studer, Basil. *Trinity and Incarnation: The Faith of the Early Church*. Edited by Andrew Louth. Translated by Matthias Westerhoff. Liturgical Press, 1993.

Sturch, Richard. *The Word and the Christ: An Essay in Analytic Christology*. Oxford University Press, 1991.

Sumner, Darren O. "The Twofold Life of the Word: Karl Barth's Critical Reception of the *Extra Calvinisticum*." *IJST* 15, no. 1 (2013): 42–57.

"The Sum of Saving Knowledge: or, A Brief Sum of Christian Doctrine." In *The Confession of Faith, the Larger and Shorter Catechisms with the Scripture Proofs at Large, Together with The Sum of Saving Knowledge*. Publications Committee of the Free Presbyterian Church of Scotland, 1970.

Taylor, John Hammond, trans. *St. Augustine: The Literal Meaning of Genesis*. Vol. 1, *Books 1–6*. Paulist Press, 1982.

Temple, William. *Christus Veritas*. Macmillan, 1939.

Tertullian. *On the Flesh of Christ*. In *The Ante-Nicene Fathers*, edited by A. Roberts and J. Donaldson. Rev. A. C. Coxe. Vol. 3. Reprint, Eerdmans, 1993.

Teske, Roland J. *Saint Augustine on Genesis Against the Manichees, and On the Literal Interpretation of Genesis: An Unfinished Book*. Fathers of the Church 84. Catholic University of America Press, 1991.

Thiselton, Anthony C. *The Holy Spirit—In Biblical Teaching, Through the Centuries, and Today*. SPCK, 2013.

Thomasius, Gottfried. "Christ's Person and Work." In *God and Incarnation in Mid-Nineteenth Century German Theology*, edited and translated by Claude Welch. Library of Protestant Thought. Oxford University Press, 1965.

Thompson, Thomas R. "Nineteenth-Century Kenotic Christology: The Waxing, Waning, and Weighing of a Quest for a Coherent Orthodoxy." In *Exploring Kenotic Christology: The Self-Emptying of God*, edited by C. Stephen Evans. Oxford University Press, 2006.

Thompson, Thomas R., and Cornelius Plantinga. "Trinity and Kenosis." In *Exploring Kenotic Christology: The Self-Emptying of God*, edited by C. Stephen Evans. Oxford University Press, 2006.

Tinker, Melvin. *Veiled in Flesh: The Incarnation—What It Means and Why It Matters*. Inter-Varsity Press, 2019.

Tollefsen, Torstein F. "Christocentric Cosmology." In *The Oxford Handbook of Maximus the Confessor*, edited by Pauline Allen and Bronwen Neil. Oxford University Press, 2015.

Torrance, Thomas F. *The Christian Doctrine of God: One Being, Three Persons*. T&T Clark, 1996.

———. *Incarnation: The Person and Life of Christ*. Paternoster, 2008.

———. *Space, Time and Resurrection*. Eerdmans, 1976.

———. "Theological Questions for Biblical Scholars." In *Reality and Evangelical Theology: The 1981 Payton Lectures*. Westminster Press, 1982.

———. *Theology in Reconstruction*. Eerdmans, 1965.

Trostyanskiy, Sergey. "The Compresence of Opposites in Christ in St. Cyril of Alexandria's *Oikonomia*." *StPatr* 90 (2017): 3–23.

Trumper, Tim J. R. Review of *Sons in the Son*, by David Garner. *JETS* 62, no. 1 (2019): 204–9.

Tseng, Shao Kai. *Trinity and Election: The Christocentric Reorientation of Karl Barth's Speculative Theology, 1936–1942*. T&T Clark, 2024.

Turretin, Francis. *Institutes of Elenctic Theology*. Edited by James T. Dennison. Vol. 1. P&R Publishing, 1992.

Twombly, Charles C. *Perichoresis and Personhood: God, Christ, and Salvation in John of Damascus*. Pickwick Publications, 2015.

Vaggione, Richard Paul. *Eunomius of Cyzicus and the Nicene Revolution*. Oxford University Press, 2000.

Vermigli, Pietro Martire [Peter Martyr]. *Dialogus de Utraque in Christo Natura*. 1575. Tiguri: C. Froschoverus, 1575.

———. *Dialogus de Utraque in Christo Natura: Illustratur & Coenae Dominicæ Negotium,Perspicuisque . . . Testimoniis Demonstratur Corpus Christi Non Esse Ubique*. Tiguri: C. Froschoverus, 1561.

———. *The Peter Martyr Library*. Vol. 2, *Dialogue on the Two Natures in Christ*. Translated and edited by John Patrick Donnelly. Sixteenth Century Essays and Studies 31. Thomas Jefferson University Press and Sixteenth Century Journal Publishers, 1995.

von Balthasar, Hans Urs. *Theo-Drama: Theological Dramatic Theory*. Translated by Graham Harrison. Vol. 4. Ignatius Press, 1994.

Vos, Geerhardus. *Reformed Dogmatics*. Lexham Press, 2014.

———. *The Self-Disclosure of Jesus: The Modern Debate About the Messianic Consciousness*. Edited by Johannes G. Vos. 1926. Reprint, Presbyterian and Reformed, 1953.

Wallace-Hadrill, D. S. *Christian Antioch: A Study of Early Christian Thought in the East*. Cambridge University Press, 1982.

Ware, Kallistos. "Christian Theology in the East, 600–1453." In *A History of Christian Doctrine*, edited by Hubert Cunliffe-Jones and Benjamin Drewery. T&T Clark, 1978.

Warfield, B. B. "The Biblical Doctrine of the Trinity." In *Biblical and Theological Studies*. Presbyterian and Reformed, 1952.

———. "Calvin's Doctrine of the Trinity." In *Calvin and Augustine*, edited by Samuel G. Craig. Presbyterian and Reformed, 1974.

Weinandy, Thomas G. "Aquinas: God IS Man: The Marvel of the Incarnation." In *Aquinas on Doctrine: A Critical Introduction*, edited by Thomas G. Weinandy, Daniel A. Keating, and John P. Yocum. T&T Clark, 2004.

———. "Cyril and the Mystery of the Incarnation." In *The Theology of St. Cyril of Alexandria: A Critical Appreciation*, edited by Thomas G. Weinandy and Daniel A. Keating. T&T Clark, 2003.

———. *Does God Suffer?* University of Notre Dame Press, 2000.

———. *The Theology of St. Cyril of Alexandria: A Critical Appreciation*. T&T Clark, 2003.

Wellum, Stephen J. *God the Son Incarnate*. Crossway, 2016.

Wesche, Kenneth Paul. "The Christology of Leontius of Jerusalem: Monophysite or Chalcedonian?" *SVTQ* 31 (1987): 65–95.

———. *On the Person of Christ: The Christology of Emperor Justinian*. St. Vladimir's Seminary Press, 1991.

Westcott, B. F. *The Epistles of St. John: The Greek Text with Notes and Essays*. Cambridge and London: Macmillan, 1886.

———. *The Epistle to the Hebrews: The Greek Text with Notes and Essays*. London: Macmillan, 1889.

Widdicombe, Peter. *The Fatherhood of God from Origen to Athanasius*. Clarendon Press, 1994.

Williams, Frederick, and Lionel Wickham, trans. *St. Gregory of Nazianzus: On God and Christ: The Five Theological Orations and Two Letters to Cledonius*. St. Vladimir's Seminary Press, 2002.

Williams, Rowan. *Arius: Heresy and Tradition*. Darton, Longman, and Todd, 1987.

Willis, Edward David. *Calvin's Catholic Christology: The Function of the So-Called Extra-Calvinisticum in Calvin's Theology*. Brill, 1966.

Wright, N. T. "*Harpagmos* and the Meaning of Philippians ii.5–11." *JTS* 37, no. 2 (1986): 321–52.

Zachhuber, Johannes. *The Rise of Christian Theology and the End of Ancient Metaphysics: Patristic Philosophy from the Cappadocian Fathers to John of Damascus*. Oxford University Press, 2020.

Zwingli, Huldrych. *Commentary on True and False Religion*. Edited by Samuel Macaulay Jackson and Clarence Nevin Heller. 1929. Reprint, Labyrinth Press, 1981.

Index of Scripture

Index of Subjects and Names

Also from P&R Publishing

This concise, practical, and devotional introduction to Reformed systematics now features study questions, memory verses, and additional resources to help readers to develop a thoroughly biblical framework for understanding and applying Christian doctrine. Revised and enhanced edition of John Frame's *Salvation Belongs to the Lord*.

"John Frame is the most creative conservative evangelical theologian of his generation, and I am delighted to recommend to another generation this excellent summary of what Christians believe. Here is the perfect combination of biblical fidelity, pedagogical utility, prose clarity, doctrinal profundity, and spiritual fecundity. Five out of five stars!"
—**Kevin J. Vanhoozer**, Research Professor of Systematic Theology, Trinity Evangelical Divinity School

"This is . . . a very practical and devotional book. . . . Read [it] to grow in wisdom; read it to cut through all the cultural noise about Christianity and get right to the heart of the Bible's message; and perhaps most importantly of all, read it to cultivate a deeper love for our extraordinary God."
—**Christopher Watkin**, Senior Lecturer in French Studies, Monash University

Also from P&R Publishing

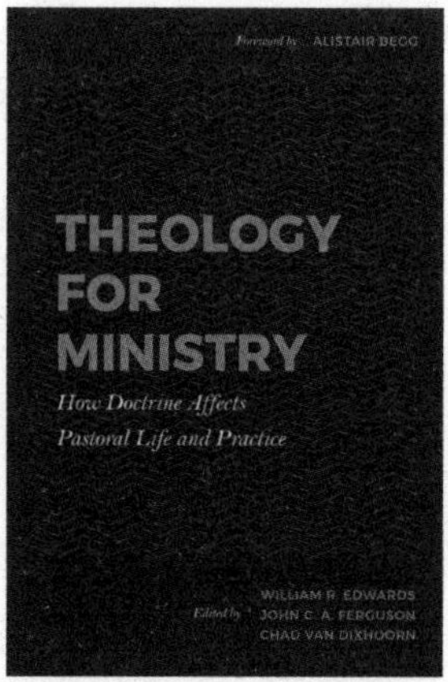

Deeply connecting theology with practice, this volume seeks to recover the rich scriptural framework for ministry that is grounded in key Christian doctrines such as the Triune God and his decrees, the person and work of Christ, and the application of all the benefits and blessings that come to us through the Spirit in our union with Christ. Contributors such as Joel Beeke, Ligon Duncan, Michael Horton, and Robert Letham write out of their experience both as pastors and theologians, providing a pattern of rich biblical-theological reflection that a vibrant ministry demands and that those engaged in ministry need in order to be sustained in their work.

"*Theology for Ministry* repays careful reading . . . as an exploration of the biblical and confessional truths that should inspire and anchor all our lives."
—**Kevin DeYoung**, Senior Pastor, Christ Covenant Church, Matthews, North Carolina

"I have learned something from every contributor in every contribution, and I think you will, too. . . . May you find here welcome encouragement from the truth of God's Word for the faithful practice of God's ministry to God's people."
—**Ligon Duncan**, Chancellor and CEO, Reformed Theological Seminary

Also from P&R Publishing

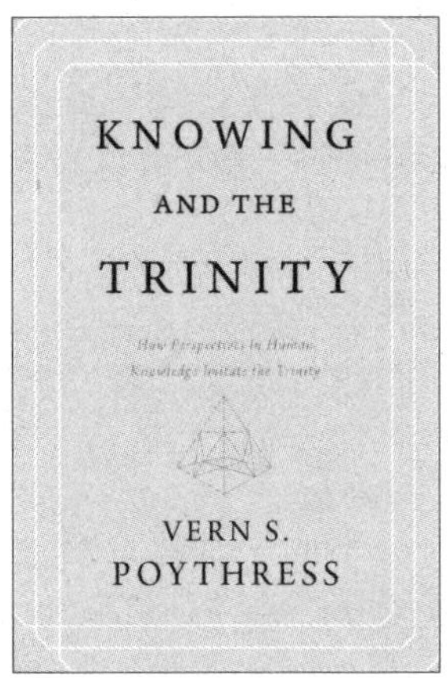

Vern Poythress is one of a growing number of theologians who have developed and used perspectival triads to further our knowledge of God. This book explores the relationship between numerous triads and God's Trinitarian character, and shows that many triads reveal analogies to the Trinity. Understanding these analogies will help readers perceive the fundamental connections between our Trinitarian God, the Bible, and our created world.

"*Knowing and the Trinity* makes no attempt to *solve* the mystery of the Trinity (as though God's triune being were a problem to himself!), nor to *dissolve* that mystery (which so endangers the pride of man's desire for autonomous reasoning, making himself the measure of all things). Rather . . . Vern Poythress allows the mystery to shine in all its glory so that in its light we see light."

—**Sinclair B. Ferguson**, Chancellor's Professor of Systematic Theology
Reformed Theological Seminary

Also from P&R Publishing

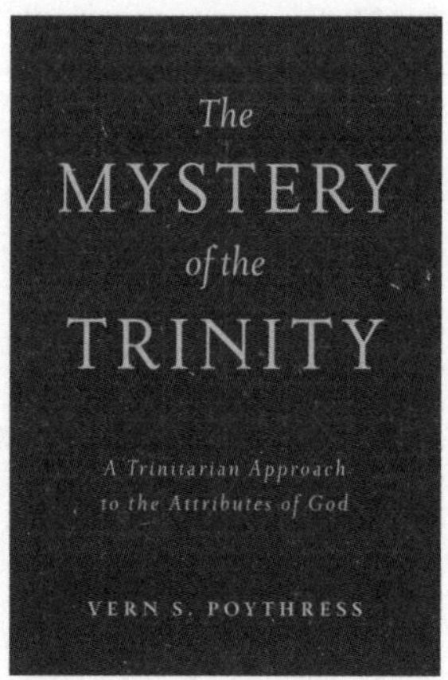

Starting with the doctrine of the Trinity, Vern Poythress addresses six challenges concerning the compatibility of God's independence with his activities in the world. The eternal activities among the persons of the Trinity offer a foundation for God's activities in the world. Alternative metaphysical frameworks for explaining God's transcendence and immanence run the danger of overriding the truths in biblical revelation.

"Dr. Poythress applies his deep knowledge of Scripture, his well-informed knowledge of historical theology, and his brilliant mind to some of the most difficult controversies in the theology of the divine attributes."
—Philip Graham Ryken

"A stimulating and fascinating book. . . . Poythress raises important questions that need addressing and offers many incisive and challenging insights."
—Robert Letham

Did you find this book helpful?
Consider writing a review online. We appreciate your feedback!

Or write to us at editorial@prpbooks.com.
We'd love to hear from you.